Fiction Writer's
workshop

THE KEY ELEMENTS OF A WRITING WORKSHOP:
clear instruction, illustrated by contemporary and classic works,
innovative exercises and methods to gauge your progress

Second Edition

JOSIP NOVAKOVICH

WRITER'S DIGEST BOOKS

Writer's Digest Books
An imprint of Penguin Random House LLC
penguinrandomhouse.com

Printed in the United States of America

ISBN 978-1-58297-536-8

Edited by Jane Friedman
Designed by Terri Woesner

Dedicated to Joseph and Jeanette

ACKNOWLEDGMENTS

Thanks to Jane Friedman for editorial advice and guidance in making the second edition.

I am especially grateful to Jack Heffron for helping me with this book. I'd also like to thank Paul Mandelbaum, Lois Rosenthal, Mikhail Iossel, Matthew Sharp, Alan Davis, Richard Duggin, John Drury, Jim Heynen, John Cussen, Barbara Seifridge, Robert Shapard, Steve Yarbrough, Manette Ansay, and my teachers at the University of Texas at Austin—Jim Magnuson, Peter LaSalle, Zulfikar Ghose.

And thank you to Sandra Cisneros, Ha Jin, Robin Hemley, and Stuart Dybek for their friendship and contribution of stories to this expanded edition.

TABLE OF contents

1   Preface

4   Introduction

Chapter 1

9   **Sources of Fiction**
Where and How to Find Material

Chapter 2

26   **Setting**
Evoking a Vivid Sense of Place and Time

Chapter 3

45   **Character**
Inventing Fictional People

Chapter 4

64   **Plot**
Strategies of Organization and Structure

Chapter 5

87 **Point of View**
Selecting the Best Viewpoint

Chapter 6

110 **Dialogue and Scene**
Handling Dramatic Action

Chapter 7

130 **Beginnings and Endings**
Options and Techniques for Opening and Closing

Chapter 8

151 **Description and Word Choice**
Choosing Effective Details, Matters of Style

Chapter 9

170 **Voice**
Finding the Narrative Voice, Creating the Voices of Characters

Chapter 10

190 **Revision**
Transforming the First Draft into Finished, Polished Fiction

Short Stories

207 "Father Sergius" by Leo Tolstoy

245 "Mademoiselle Fifi" by Guy de Maupassant

256 "My Oedipus Complex" by Frank O'Connor

266 "A Composer and His Parakeets" by Ha Jin

278 "Reply All" by Robin Hemley

286 "The Blue Hotel" by Stephen Crane

310 "The Monkey Garden" by Sandra Cisneros

314 "We Didn't" by Stuart Dybek

324 Index

330 About the Author

PREFACE

Fiction Writer's Workshop is now twelve years old, almost as old as my son. While he has grown in the meantime, and plays beautiful music on the cello, the book has remained the same, until today. This is the second edition, expanded, to make a bigger and more complete book. We have attached a mini-anthology in the back, of short and long stories, to exemplify some of the elements of the craft.

A lot can be learned from analytical reading of the works we admire, and while I presented, in the first edition of this book, many quotations from stories and novels, I didn't include entire stories. Thus, those who wanted to see examples of what I was talking about or who wanted to analyze completely on their own were driven to buy yet another book (an anthology, such as Pickering's *Fiction 100*) or more than one to study further. It is a great idea to read many books for yourself, to make reading a lifelong habit. For immediate needs, I think that the anthology in the back makes it possible to use this book as a short course, a nearly complete course, either alone or in a group. Anyhow, I don't need to preach to the choir—if you are reading this book, most likely you are a reader, and the inclusion of the anthology makes it easier to show how to read analytically.

Of course, the book is still not quite complete, and never will be. *Ars longa, vita brevis.* It would be ideal to include a few novels in the back as well, but that is definitely beyond the scope of paper affordability. I do recommend quite a few novels, from which I quote in the book, and I do suggest that your efforts and my efforts in writing always be supplemented by close reading of good fiction, short and long.

Through the past twelve years, this book has been selling very well, without much advertising, through word of mouth. It has been used in many classrooms and in even more households by people who haven't had enough time to attend a formal workshop. I have gotten many compliments on the book, and my favorite is this: I received a letter from an inmate of a Pennsylvania state penitentiary. Several inmates were using the book and writing, until the book disappeared. Someone had stolen the only copy in the high-security prison. Could I send another to them?

Strangely enough, sometimes I, too, if stuck in the middle of a story, when having doubts (*How is it done?*), resort to this book, and say to myself, wait a minute, I offered a few ideas that have worked for others. And going back to the basics—remembering to lay out some of the lazy telling in detailed scenes, to bring characters out of isolation and into contact with others; or the other way around, if the action seems hollow, to delve into a character's mind, report strange thoughts, to get into the psychology—these tidbits often (but not always) help me.

Which brings me to the debate. Are there rules in writing fiction? It's possible to err on both sides of the argument by extremism. Yes, there are many rules, such as "show, don't tell"; don't use clichés and redundancies; don't do that, and do this and that. But there are no absolute guidebooks and recipes. True, formula fiction is guided by certain rules, but even there, some invention and violation of the rule can act as a surprise and bring the writing to a higher level and intensity.

And it's fashionable to say that the only rule is that there are no rules. That sounds paradoxical and simple, yet it has been overused to the point of becoming a cliché, and can be used as an excuse for impulsive writing. Impulsive writing is worth trying out, don't get me wrong. Everything is worth trying out—writing formulaically and according to many rules, and on the other end, writing wildly. Most often, the game of writing will fall somewhere in between. And while there are no absolute rules, there are various game plans, and games have their rules. Although I offer lots of advice on how to set up point of view or chronology of events, or how to juggle telling with showing productively (that's an example where there's no absolute rule—"show, don't tell" has been discredited as an absolute; there are many exceptions, such as in Tolstoy's writing), I don't mean any of it categorically, even if I get carried away with personal conviction, and sound categorical here and there.

No matter how much technological innovation there is in writing—with hypertext and the possibility of including Web links and inserting graphics and charts—one thing remains the same: our thirst for story. Through many layers of different structures, most of us still want a story, with events, conflicts, themes, and interesting connections. It's usual to splice two stories together, to use pictures, graphs, and Web connections, to create a bazaar of possibilities, but nevertheless, somewhere in the whole structure, most of us still look for a story. An e-mail-form story appears in the anthology in the back, "Reply All" by Robin Hemley. It's possible to write a novel as a series of cell-phone texts. Nevertheless, how to use technology is beyond the scope of this book. That's another book.

This kind of book, of course, doesn't work for everybody. Creative writing programs don't work for everybody, either. Yet for many people they do. I resisted going to a writing program, and did what I could on my own, and then I realized I needed to learn more to finish my stories convincingly.

And what new insight do I have regarding the writing exercises? That it's best to approach them playfully, each as a little game, a game plan, with a few rules and lots of possibilities for violation. The exercises are not only a fine active and interactive way of reading chapters and analyzing of writing, but also a great excuse to jump into writing, to overcome writer's block, etc.

And yes, there is one rule, which I do mention in the book, along with its glorious author (you have to read the book to find out who it was who said it): *I understand you want to write? Then write!* There's hardly any other art form or sport that people profess so much desire to do as writing, yet they avoid doing it. I believe journals, exercises, and so on are a good way to overcome that contradiction, and to practice what we preach, our desire to write. Yet, if you abhor exercises, you of course don't have to do them to benefit. There's enough potential stimulus in the great passages from classic and current literature that you can see that writing can be done, that it needn't be horribly difficult, that you can do all sorts of quite specific and often simple things to achieve fantastic results.

Actually, you can use the book to scoff at what people say about writing, that it can be learned and that it can be practiced—a concept I've encountered over and over again in Russia and Croatia. Many philosophers have formulated their philosophies on the basis of disagreeing with previous philosophers, and so do many fiction writers. If you disagree with something clearly, you may formulate your way. It's quite possible that you will find many things to disagree with here, but all the better. Look for your own way.

INTRODUCTION

To be a good writer, you must have the paradoxical trait of being a gregarious loner. Marcel Proust claimed that he needed to leave his friends so he could truly be with them; while thinking and writing about his friends, he communicated with them far more thoroughly and excitingly than when he was with them at a party.

As a writer, you need a strong sense of independence, of being and thinking on your own—so go ahead, work alone. I will give you a lot of advice, but you need not take it. Especially when you disagree, you will formulate your own principles. No matter what advice I suggest in this book, which is designed to be a fiction workshop you can attend on your own, you ought to write freely. *Ought* and *free* don't seem to fit together, and that's another paradox of writing: If you can incorporate several writing principles and yet retain and even advance your independence of writing, you've got it made.

Ultimately, write any way that gives you a sense of freedom. What a teacher and a fellow workshopper might discourage as a vice might, through practice, become a virtue.

So even before you continue with this book, with its writing assignments and its advice on writing fiction, you might let yourself write absolutely anything for a couple of weeks—a hundred pages, let us say—to see if some interesting patterns emerge. That is what I did at first. I avoided advice on how to write, and I wrote several hundred pages of drafts, filled with silly puns and opinions, arbitrary plots and memories. I avoided letting anybody cramp my style. However, I think that I avoided advice and workshops a little too long; some lessons that I learned on my own, I could have learned faster from some good advice. That's why I hope that the basic principles of writing fiction outlined here, with exercises for how to implement them, will help you become a more productive fiction writer.

HOW TO USE THIS BOOK

It's simple. The chapters first give you some basics of the elements of fiction. They cover how the elements work and how you can use them in your fiction. The discussions are not meant to be definitive, but orientational.

At the end of each chapter are a dozen or more exercises, some of them calling for brief sketches, a sentence or a paragraph long, some two or three pages long. Do the exercises with an open mind. Don't dismiss them as too simple or too complicated. There are all sorts of exercises to keep you in shape in writing, just as there are scales in music. So get into shape, and stay there. When you get ready to write, or you are between writing projects, you certainly can benefit from exercises, no matter how advanced a writer you are. Keep the channels between the brain and the fingertips open—let your neurotransmitters happily leap in the direction of the page.

As you do the exercises, concentrate on the task. Don't strive for prettiness, unless that's the assignment. Strive for clarity. Communicate your thoughts and images as directly as possible. Now and then, for a change of rhythm, you may shroud things in long sentences and rich language, but in general, there's nothing more effective than a succinct, straightforward way of putting things. If you aren't direct, on the other hand, don't worry. You will have time to go back and cross out the imprecise words and put in better ones, until you are satisfied. In drawing, some people use a lot of lines to get at the expression on a person's face; some use few or only one. No matter what, give us a world. Don't rely on adjectives of aesthetic judgment, because these are abstractions. Instead of saying "ugly" or "wonderful," give us pictures to that effect. Show us what you mean, don't tell us what you want to mean.

The principle with exercises: You get out of them as much as you put in—a little more, actually. If you like an exercise, do it several times. A painter may sketch a face a dozen times, and each time is new. The French writer Raymond Queneau wrote *Exercises in Style* as ninety-nine variations of one simple event: In a bus, a man steps on another's toe. If you don't like something, still give it a try. Don't use your dislikes as obstacles. It's only too easy to find obstacles.

After each exercise, you may ask: How do I know whether I have done it correctly? In a workshop, your peers can tell you what you've missed. If you work alone, you must do it yourself. I'll simplify it for you and ask you questions to consider. Don't read these questions until you are finished with the exercise. Keep them in mind as you read over what you've done. Revise or rewrite your exercise until you get it right. There's a point at which you know that you've done your best, given the limited time you have.

So go back over what you've completed, not so much for what you've done wrong as for what you could do right, more right. Don't work on developing a self-critical—that is, self-inhibiting—consciousness; do work on developing a sense of where you can jump back in and draw one more line that'll give life to what you already have down, or where you could delete a line that may obscure our view of a good line you've drawn.

How much time should you spend on each exercise? I'd say twenty to thirty minutes should be enough. If something stimulates you, of course, keep going, up to an hour. Beyond that, if an exercise has struck a strong chord in you, I'd say you are no longer doing an exercise but are writing a story. Great. That'll be the fringe benefit to doing the exercises: You will examine many things, turn many stones, and find your treasures. Still, discipline yourself to go back to the exercises and finish them outside of your story-writing time.

If you spend five to six hours on exercises in each chapter, you could be through with this book in two months. It would be ideal to spend an hour a day, regularly, so that by the time you finish this book, you will have acquired the writing habit. This habit is the rare kind that is beneficial. It helps you sort out your impressions, memories, thoughts, and fantasies, and that should be healthy. Something in the movement of fingers on the keyboard enhances thought. I may not be particularly thoughtful as I write, but much more than if I were simply staring out the window. Some philosophers walked to think more clearly; they belonged to the peripatetic school. Walking provided them with a good flow of blood and oxygen, and with a sensation of doing, moving, going. Fingers pull your thoughts forward. Fingers are in some ways an extension of your brain, with a lot of cortex associations at their trigger. Get them going!

You don't need to wait for inspiration to write. It's easier to be inspired while writing than while not writing, so you don't need to be inspired to sit down and begin. You don't need to be "in the mood." I think you will benefit if you don't worry about moods: One, you will get in the habit of writing under any circumstances; two, since writing reflects your mental state, you will have a diversity of moods in your piece. The diversity will make your writing more interesting. You are depressed? Fine, perhaps you can portray a depressed character. Elated? Don't waste the mood on celebration. Convey it onto the page. Many pieces suffer from moodlessness; perhaps the writers are willing to work only when they are calm.

Ultimately, talk about talent, inspiration, and genius is a distraction. Sit down and do it! Whenever you lack an idea, use some of the exercises in this book—they should keep you busy.

If you think that the business of fiction is an impossible one, John Gardner ought to encourage you. In *The Art of Fiction*, he says: "Most people I've known who wanted to become writers, knowing what it meant, did become writers. About all that is required is that the would-be writer understand clearly what it is that he wants to become and what he must do to become it." In *On Becoming a Novelist*, he claims that there are more failed businesspeople than failed artists. Yet in business schools, optimism prevails.

There's a bit of a catch in John Gardner's encouragement, "knowing what it meant." What does it mean to become a writer? Primarily, determination and perseverance. This anecdote will elucidate what I mean. After graduating from a writing program in Austin, Texas, I spent a few days at the Virginia Center for the Creative Arts, where I met a distinguished Israeli novelist. Naturally, I was eager to hear his opinion of my work. I slipped him a couple of chapters from my novel in progress (by the way, that's the thing established writers dread upon meeting beginning writers). I saw him a couple of days later, and asked, "So, what do you think? Will I make it as a writer?"

He gazed at me thoughtfully and said nothing, which I found disconcerting. He finally said, "Are you sure you want to work as a writer?"

"Yes," I said.

"Then you will make it."

"So you've liked my pages."

"We aren't talking about your pages but about you."

Basically, he got the impression that I was determined. Now, what does determined mean? Does it mean writing sixteen hours a day? It's great if you can do that, but even one hour a day is enough. I heard Junot Díaz recently give a talk on the writing craft, and he said, "If you can sit on your ass an hour a day in front of the screen, you are hot shit." Anyhow, it's a long-distance sport. You are better off pacing yourself, and writing for an hour a day for ten years, than writing for sixteen hours a day for a few days and burning out. On the other hand, there are different temperaments, and enthusiastic bursts work for some, and the daily thing may work for others.

And finally, will writing change your world? If you publish a book, will you be saved from all your personal worries? I doubt it. A friend of mine, Paul Mandelbaum (who was actually my initial editor for this book, in its first edition), very much desired to publish a book when I knew him in Cincinnati. His eyes would glaze over while he was imagining his life after publishing a book. Well, I saw him in Los Angeles a couple of years ago when I was promoting my novel *April Fool's Day*, and we had dinner together. I said, "Paul, it's great to see you. In the meanwhile, you've published three books, you've realized your dream. What does it feel like to be publishing?" He thought for a few seconds, and said, "You know, it feels a lot like not publishing!"

He still had to teach part-time, and his relationship was worse; in fact, his girlfriend had just left a few months before. Paul looked glum for the rest of the evening. The moral of the story: It doesn't make sense to daydream too much about publishing—it really isn't such a great deal, and it can distract you from writing itself. Your life will remain the same—unless you enjoy writing. I have encountered writers who say, "I am happy, I am in the middle of a novel. I love writing it." In this case, to use a cliché, you can have your cake and eat it, too. Namely, the more you enjoy writing, the more likely it is that you will persevere with it, and that you will publish it. And you are a writer as long as you are writing. There's no such thing as writer as a noun. It's a verb. I am a writer at the moment since I am writing these sentences. When I get away from the table, I will be a walker.

1

SOURCES OF FICTION

Many writers say that you can find a story anywhere. The greatest source of fiction is experience. The experience need not be yours—you may observe someone else's struggle and use it for your fiction. For example, Nikolai Gogol wrote his famous story "Overcoat" from an anecdote he heard at a dinner party. A poor man had been saving up for years to buy a hunting rifle, and before he could go hunting, somebody stole it. Gogol, a better humorist than anyone else at the party, was the only one who did not laugh at this. He felt chilled and sorry for the man, and went home and wrote a story from that sorrow, about a clerk who saves for a long time to buy an overcoat. When he buys the overcoat, it gets stolen, and the man suffers, while everybody laughs and jeers at him.

Gogol transformed the original fact into fiction. Instead of a rifle, he uses a coat. Instead of dealing with hunting, he deals with office work. He had worked as a clerk, so he could bring realistic details to his story. The jeering and ridicule in the story may have been taken from the party attendees who laughed at the man whose rifle was stolen. Fiction writers can use their experiences, and the experiences of others, in their work. When transformed by the writer's imagination, even true details—like the ones that Gogol imported from his experience as a clerk—become fiction.

You do not need much for an impetus, the seed of a story. In his essay "The Art of Fiction," Henry James describes how an English woman wrote a novel about French Protestants. In Paris, as she ascended a staircase, she "passed an open door where, in the household of a *pasteur*, some of the young Protestants were seated at table round a finished meal. The glimpse made a picture; it lasted only a moment, but that moment was experience."

French novelist Claude Simon claimed that to collect materials for a novel, it's enough to take a walk around a city block. Come back, report what you saw, thought, felt, remembered, and so on, and that should do! Okay, he may be exaggerating, but his point is clear: Your experiences need not be grand to be useful as fiction material.

Simon's point affirms this principle: Write about what you know. On the other hand, some writers advise the opposite: Write about what you don't know because you will be free to imagine; knowledge will constrict you. James's method of writing from a glimpse—so that you don't know much about the people in particular, but do know about their world (James's novelist knew a lot about French Protestantism)—should give you a perfect compromise: enough knowledge, but also enough ignorance and darkness in which to guess and imagine.

Whether to write from knowledge or from a lack of it is not an either/or decision. I can't write about something that I don't know at all; and I can't write about something that I know absolutely, for what do I know? Socrates thought that the only thing he possibly knew was that he did not know anything. Last week, while leaving for school, I remembered that I had left my car keys on the counter, but they weren't there. Yet I spent an hour looking for them; I found them on the windowsill in another room. My memory was not knowledge; it was, in fact, *fiction*. Even if you write from memory, you will have enough elements of what you don't know, or aren't sure about, to avoid the constricting influence of knowledge.

I must say, however, that I have seen many people blindly follow an outline of an event in a story (they say, "But that's what happened!") even when some simple, made-up adjustment might lead to a better, more rounded story.

Your inclination may be to work not from a glimpse but from a chunk of your life, autobiographically, like Marcel Proust and Harold Brodkey, who relied on direct experience for everything—plot, details, characters. Or, your inclinations, like mine, may vary from story to story.

FICTION AND NONFICTION

How much one needs to know about what one writes varies from writer to writer and from story to story. As you write, let that be a constant assignment: Find out how much you need to know about the raw material from which you make a story. If you find out that you persevere in reconstructing events from memory as faithfully as possible, without following impulses to make up anything, or even to exaggerate and beautify or uglify details, you are a natural nonfiction writer. You might still call what you write fiction, if you like, though the term will then be the only fiction in your writing. If you can, with a straight face, tell people that what you write is fiction, you will often find yourself in a precarious position, having to explain how you made something up. I would then advise you to acknowledge that you write nonfiction, and to enjoy the apple of that tree of knowledge. There's no reason to consider fiction more glorious than nonfiction.

The reverse also can occur. You might want to become a nonfiction writer, and yet at every turn you distort things, exaggerate and embellish them, and even introduce characters, places, and events that have nothing to do with the original material. In that case, we can say you are a born fiction writer, which is much nicer than saying you are a born liar. Fiction is a lot like lying. You start from something real, but for some specific purpose (to avoid getting caught, to trick, to get money, or whatever) you change at least one key element of the account. Instead of admitting that you got a black eye in a bar when you were hitting on someone's girlfriend, you might say that you skied in Vermont and bumped into a sleeping bear's muzzle in a curve. To defend your pride, you lie and tell a story. If you habitually lie, why not get the sinful impulse out of your system through writing fiction?

How you treat your original material determines the type of writer you are. It may still be too early to classify yourself. As you do the exercises throughout the book and afterward, pay close attention to what you are doing, and you will eventually decide what you are writing: fiction or nonfiction.

On the other hand, you may do both, as do many writers, including me. Sometimes an event, or an impression, intrigues me. I don't make a decision about what I'll do with it right away. I jot down notes, write a bit here and a bit there, and I see if I get an impulse to reshape the material, rearrange, make up. If I do, I know I am writing a piece of fiction, and I encourage myself to change things even further. However, if I find that I don't transform anything, that I think about the event and write down my thoughts, I know I am writing an essay. I like essays just as much as I like stories, so I don't feel disappointed. I am happy in either case that I have something to say (essay) or something to play with (fiction).

Blending Fact and Fiction

There's always a mixture of fact and invention in writing fiction. (Are *fact* and *fict*[ion] so similar by accident? If these words were written in the old Hebrew style—without vowels—they would both be FCT, and the context would determine how you would pronounce them!)

Here's what several writers say about how they mix two kinds of FCT. My purpose in showing you this is twofold: to demonstrate that most fiction incorporates a lot of fact, and to give you models for making your own fiction.

Tobias Wolff said this about the source of his short story "Firefly": "What impelled me to write it in the first place is its emotional core—that sense, hardly unique to me, of being outside the circle of light, a feeling so pernicious that even when you are where you want to be you shy away from the joy of it and begin to fear banishment and loss."

Wolff uses his emotional experience as the core for a story that is fictional in other respects—a good way to blend fact and invention.

Joanna Scott offered this comment about her story "Concerning Mold Upon the Skin, Etc.": "I intended to refer, plainly or indirectly, to the history of medicine in each of my stories. So I went looking for fifteenth- and sixteenth-century scientists in such quirky and unreliable books as Howard Haggard's *Devils, Drugs, and Doctors*. ... Leeuwenhoek's fierce secrecy caught my attention. ... About the character of the daughter: As a fiction writer, I'm interested in the vast silences of history, and like many women, Marie floats silently in the background of her father's biography. So she became the center of the narrative, the presence that enabled me to reshape history into fiction."

Scott combines information from history books with her thematic interest, silent experiences of women, to imagine how Marie lives. History books and biographies are major sources of fiction. Once you get something intriguing from a history book, why not play with it and see where it leads you? The history need not be tremendously old—it could be close to current affairs.

Pulitzer Prize–winning author Robert Olen Butler said this about writing his story "A Good Scent From a Strange Mountain": "I finally began to hear the voice of this tale when I found an occasion—the traditional, formal leave-taking with their friends and family that the Vietnamese often make at the end of their lives—and when I found a first sentence, spoken in the voice of a man nearly one hundred years old, 'Ho Chi Minh came to me again last night, his hands covered with confectioners' sugar.' After that, it was simply a matter of letting the old man speak."

Butler relies on hearing a character's voice to carry him through writing. This ability to tune in to a person's voice and to adopt it for writing fiction works for many writers.

Robin Hemley (author of *The Last Studebaker* and *All You Can Eat*) says he works from dreams. One impression from a dream is enough to inspire a story. For example, he awoke with an image of a man digging a hole in his ex-wife's yard. He wondered why one would do something so bizarre, and in trying to answer the question, he wrote a story about a man and a woman who divorce after their baby dies, and now the man, haunted by guilt and love, digs in the yard. When I asked Hemley over the phone what other sources of fiction he used, and while he tried to describe something complex, his wife shouted, "He gets his best stories from me!" So, pay attention to dreams and spouses.

Mark Richard, author of *Fishboy*, explained that he got a whole story out of this first sentence: "At night, stray dogs come up underneath our house to lick our leaking pipes." He said, "I knew everything I needed was in that sentence. ... So I sat down one night after staring in the sand all day thinking: *At night*, etc., etc. And it all came down at once like I was just the radio."

Many writers claim that all they need is a good sentence with tension in it, and the story simply unfolds from that. I can't say that I am that lucky. Here's how I arrived at the starting points for some of my stories. Perhaps this could work similarly for you, and if not, you'll at least see where I come from when I talk about fiction.

One. My brother-in-law and his father competed in building huge homes, working so hard that they both developed heart problems. At first, I thought I would write a story about their competition, which could have made an interesting essay, but as I looked at their big granite homes, the thought that they were building their tombs crossed my mind. Out of this metaphor, I wrote a story about a man building a sophisticated tomb. For the character, I drew upon quite a few Croatian *Gastarbeiter* ("guest workers") in Germany, and came up with a composite character. Because of all kinds of superstitions in Croat villages, it was easy for me to believe in the plausibility of such a story. It's mostly made-up, but obviously, some of it is not.

I built this story from a metaphor. Rather than sprinkle the prose with metaphors, try to make your whole story a metaphor—and a prolonged metaphor, of course, makes an allegory.

Two. While living in New York City, I could not afford a computer, so I got a job where I would be able to do my writing after hours—word-processing for the Smith Barney investment bank. I worked on the fiftieth floor, and every day I mused on the sensation of suddenly feeling much heavier as the express elevator decelerated on the way down. Once, I saw a woman in advanced pregnancy wince during the deceleration, and later I wrote about a woman jumping out of an airplane and giving birth to a boy when the parachute opens. The impulse for the story came from a strong sensation.

Three. A friend once called to tell me he was in love with his psychiatrist and she forbade him to visit her. He joined a Buddhist group but could not stop thinking about her. I made up a character who desperately seeks to seduce his psychiatrist—and I pursued the conflict further, to his getting arrested and thrown into jail, and then explaining to his wife what happened. You can get ideas for stories from talking to people, especially once you hear of a clear conflict. If you pursue the conflict to its logical conclusion in your fiction, you are bound to have a developed story.

Four. A friend told me how he could not forgive his father for being a German soldier—a volunteer—during World War II, so he refused to talk to his father even when he was dying. My friend's being so adamantly principled struck me as no better than his father's participating in the siege of Stalingrad to defend Lutheranism from communism. So I wrote a story about him and his father. As I knew nothing else of the dynamic between the two, or of post-war Germany, I made up most of the details of the story, so it ended as a piece of fiction, though it began as a narrative essay.

I got the seed of this story in a conversation with a friend. What made that seed grow into fiction was my curiosity and my lack of knowledge about the two people involved. Whenever something intrigues you about the people you know, you may be better off using your fascination as the energy for a new story rather than for daydreaming and gossip. Many stories benefit from both impulses—to daydream and to gossip.

THE ORAL TRADITION

When groping through my memory, imagination, and books for something that would trigger a story, I hoped I could rely on the oral tradition, a big deal among the people of my native region. I was, in fact, so desperate to find material for stories that I used even that feeling as the material for a story. You will see what happens in my quest for fiction in these condensed excerpts from my story "The Burning Shoe":

> Nenad told me about Prince Marko, who sucked his mother's breasts for seven years, and for seven more ate nothing but honey. Marko could squeeze water out of a log dried for nine years. His horse could jump the length of nine lances and the height of three. Marko slew Musa Kesejiya, in whose breast, beneath three rib cages, were three hearts—the first working, the second dancing, and the third nesting a sleeping snake. When the snake awoke, the dead Musa leaped over the barren land.
>
> So twenty years later, remembering Nenad's telling me this, I thought that instead of going through a writing workshop in the States, I would simply listen to Nenad for a couple of days and nights and find the formula for triggering a wellspring of storytelling from our common ground. I rushed to Weeping Willow, the village in Croatia where he now lived. Where once horses ploughed the fields along a dirt road, tractors oozed green oil in puddles along a paved highway. A cracked wooden shoe hung from a pole on Nenad's house to advertise his trade, clog-making.
>
> After we shook hands and he found out what I was doing these days, sure enough, he talked so much that I couldn't squeeze in a word, except I did interrupt him: "Nenad, where did you learn how to tell tales? At the hearth, on your grandfather's knee?"

"I went to the library," he said, "read them, and told them to you right after it, while the stories were still fresh in my memory."

A myth fell apart right before my ears.

"Of course," he said, "I added a thing here and there."

"But I believed that you were an epic storyteller!"

"After every story you said, 'More!' So what could I do? I went to the library on lunch breaks."

"Still, who taught you how to tell stories? Grandmothers?"

"No. Why are you so stuck on this? It's easy to tell a story, what's the big deal? You start right here and lead the listener far away, or start far away and get us here."

"Easy to say. Do it!"

"So you are holding this beer mug. All right, start with it. A long time ago there was a beer mug, and it lived in a tavern, in an unhappy family of twenty-three beer mugs. Many a dry lip ... and off we go, see!"

"But how would you go on?"

In reply he laughed and tapped me on the shoulder so I did not know whether he could go on, or whether he was teasing me, or whether my stubborn simplicity amused him. "You want a refill?" he said.

I still insisted that he tell me a story, and I would not let him give me a ride home until he did so, just as—though it's not worthy of such an archaic comparison—Jacob held fast to the Angel of God until obtaining a blessing.

"All right, I'll tell you something like a story as we drive." He motioned me toward his Fiat clone, a Yugo, and as we opened the car doors, he said, "See that tall house? That's where my childhood home, made of baked clay, used to be. At the beginning of the war, the Germans barged in there, seized my father from the dinner table, and shot him to death against the barn.

"A couple of years later a dozen Germans walked into our yard. I hid in bed and shivered under a goose-down cover. A pair of boots stamped over the floor boards toward me, louder and louder. The cover was pulled off and a huge soldier loomed over me. An *Agkh* broke out of my throat. The German lowered his hand, I thought, to strangle me. He placed his cold palm on my forehead. Then he poured a glass of water from a bucket in the kitchen, put some white pills into the water, crushed them with a spoon, and pressed my lips with the edge of the glass against my teeth. The liquid was shudderingly bitter. I thought I would keel over and die. It was no poison, but aspirin.

"And he took a paper sack out of his leather bag and out of it a honey cake. He gave it to me. He looked sternly at my mouth as I chewed. When I finished, he handed me another, and I chewed slowly. After I swallowed the last of it, my eyes shifted toward the paper sack.

"The German raised his forefinger and shook it and said, *Nein!* He then walked out into the yard, shouted to the soldiers, and they all marched away, raising a screen of dust. Eh, my brother, you can't imagine how I felt. First he—for me it was the same German—kills my father and then gives me the sweetest cakes I've ever had—before or after."

The story goes on. Another day I visit the storyteller, he refuses to tell me stories because he's had nightmares triggered by the honey cakes and my visit. But here's another moment when he does tell a story:

Nenad's tabby jumped, grabbed the rim of his cap, and tried to pull it out of his hands. Nenad scratched the cat on the head and said, "My dear kitty."

He patted her more tenderly than I had ever seen a man his age do, and he relaxed and talked: "One night the Germans entered the village and were about to round up thirty people to kill because the partisans had killed three German soldiers. But the Germans now first axed some chickens to cook quietly on an apple orchard hill where nobody from the rest of the village could see them. There were some black cats there, and no black cats ever came to our end of the village. So when I saw a black cat running down the road with a bloody rooster's head in its mouth, I screamed, 'The Germans are coming!'

"We ran into the woods and listened to the shotguns. The Germans killed ten, but most of the people in the village were saved—by the black cat!" He picked up his tabby, which looked like a camouflaged paratrooper.

The story goes on, but the main point here for me is that what I thought was the oral tradition turned out to be bookish stuff, a dead end. However, in the story, just as I give up, the man tells me a story from his own experience. The storyteller told his story with almost traditional oral-style repetition, in a Croatian dialect, but I rewrote the story from memory, in a different rhythm, without much repetition. My retelling this makes it a tradition, that is, a transmission of stories from one generation to another, from the World War II generation to mine, the current Balkan Wars generation. The transmission is both oral and scriptoral.

Is "The Burning Shoe" fiction or nonfiction about fiction? It is both. Most materials I got directly from my experience and my conversation with a man I knew from my childhood. The cat tale and several others within the story, which I can't reproduce here for lack of space, I got elsewhere, but put them all into the mouth of the storyteller. Some details and jokes I made up, but most of the material came from my eyes and ears.

Still, the report works as a piece of fiction. The editors who published the story never asked me, "Is this true?" What concerned them was whether the piece worked as fiction. The honey cake story follows a classical bell curve (rising action, climax, resolution) of a piece of fiction, so even if it comes from the storyteller's experience (and I can't verify that) without my changing it much, that story does have the shape of fiction. So does the frame story, my quest for the oral tradition. The setting and my motives are established in the beginning—I want stories to learn how to write. The first lead turns out false—first turning point. The second lead (the story about the beer mug) also turns out to be a pipe dream—second turning point. My desire to hear a story yields one just as I am giving up, on the way out. That's climax, getting the real thing, the cake story. The story continues, with falling action, more anecdotes (the cat story), and this resolution, in the form of an epiphany:

> As I walked to the train station, the leaves in the woods—the tongues of the wind—murmured. The stones on the shoulder of the road crunched beneath my feet and told me how Jesus was tempted in the desert to make bread out of stones and instead how he later made wine out of the water. The stones retold me how the vicious armies and the good people had passed. And I thought, *If the stones can tell the stories, I can too.*

I was not thinking this as I left the storyteller for the second time, so the resolution is fictional. I made up most of the dialogue and the descriptions, such as the blue Bosnian mountains appearing as workers' shirts on the line. I changed all the names.

But the story is mostly autobiographical. Notice that in analyzing the story, I freely use *I* for *I*. I don't say, "the first-person narrator," which I would use if this were a piece of nonautobiographical fiction cast in a first-person point of view. (More on the persona business in chapter five.)

My quest for the oral tradition disabused me of mythical notions of some kind of *Odyssey* coming down to me through a peasant. I had bad luck in my quest: An old man, whom my brother, a doctor, had met on his rounds in a Slavonian village, died just several days before my coming to talk to him, and an old woman who also could tell great stories was ill when I visited her. There were several other peasants I could get in touch with, but now these peasants, some of whom were Serbs and some Croats, wouldn't say a word and wouldn't trust anybody because of the recent war. So that avenue was closed to me.

But not other things that people talk about. It's healthy to listen to how people talk and what they say, because some of the best storytellers are not writers. Communication with the audience to them is the most important experience in telling a story, and because of that, they talk rather than write. Those of us who prefer to write and are somewhat awkward speakers should certainly emulate on the page the liveliness of an original communicator, if possible. Perhaps you can hound some of these good talkers.

I believe my experience in researching and writing "The Burning Shoe" could be useful to you. You may look for your special source—where you spent your childhood, where you heard old railway workers talk, Appalachia, Harlem, wherever. By all means, do that. You may be more successful in your search for a direct source than I have been. But while you are looking for one thing, be open to recognizing another that might be just as good or even better. Looking for old folk tales, I recognized a new tale. I wish I followed this paradigm more often myself, but I'll be happy if you do.

FURTHER SOURCES OF FICTION

You can get stories from almost anywhere. William Faulkner described this quest for materials: "An artist is completely amoral in that he will rob, borrow, beg, or steal from anybody and everybody to get the work done."

Rob the Cradle

Draw on your childhood mercilessly. Leo Tolstoy was only twenty-two when he wrote the trilogy that made him a writer, *Childhood, Boyhood, Youth*. Charles Dickens based several of his long novels on his childhood.

Willa Cather wrote, "Most of the basic material a writer works with is acquired before the age of fifteen." Recently, I talked to Deborah Joy Corey (author of the novel *Losing Eddie*), who told me that she was writing her third book, still about her childhood. She was almost embarrassed about not outgrowing it, but I think she's lucky. Of course, drawing on your childhood doesn't mean that you write straight memoir; transform the material, use it to build other characters, write in the third person, if necessary, or in the first, if you like. Write the way Mark Twain wrote *The Adventures of Huckleberry Finn*, using his childhood experiences but creating a persona certainly different from himself, with a different voice. Or write autobiographical fiction. But don't neglect this primary source of fiction.

Rob the Grave

Look into the lives of your ancestors and tell their stories. Maxine Hong Kingston (author of *The Woman Warrior*) has successfully done this in her autobiographical fiction. Knowing little about how her ancestors lived in China and the United States, she filled the gaps in her knowledge through flights of imagination and through the power of the word. She described believably and poetically the agonies of her great-grandfather in building the railways. You can invoke and summon the ghosts of your ancestors, for they live on, somewhere in you. Throw words at them, your memories of them, as bait, and they might come out. At least a version of them will appear: yours. They will not be the same great-grandfathers as in "real life," for you don't know that much about their real lives—of necessity, they will come out as fictions, apparitions, illusions.

Rob From Books

Learn from the works of other writers. I don't mean that you should plagiarize, but you can write variations on themes. It's easy to imagine that there is something derivative and secondary in this method, something offensive to the concept of originality. But even the very idea of a story is something we take on as a tradition. It's just as silly to claim to be a nontraditional story writer as it is to claim that you are independent if you still live in your mother's house. So, working in a tradition is a form of gratitude to your literary ancestry. And a form of inheritance. If you stand to inherit a fortune, you may be foolish to renounce your parents and grandparents. Look at some historical precedents. Homer composed *The Odyssey* and *The Iliad* out of battle reports; Virgil patterned *The Aeneid* on Homer's work and, in a way, continued it; Dante wrote *The Inferno* based on Odysseus's trip to the underworld and on incidents from *The Aeneid*; and hundreds of works take from Dante. And James Joyce, in *Ulysses*, went back to *The Odyssey*, making the trip home a psychological experience of trying to understand how the mind works with words.

Here's another literary lineage. In *Notes From Underground*, Fyodor Dostoyevski writes, "Only if I could become an insect!" Franz Kafka takes this line and makes "The Metamorphosis" out of it: "As Gregor Samsa awoke that morning from uneasy dreams, he found himself transformed in his bed into a gigantic insect."

In reaction to Kafka's opening line, Gabriel García Márquez said: "When I read the line I thought to myself that I didn't know anyone was allowed to write things like that. If I had known, I would have started writing a long time ago." Márquez wrote his story "A Very Old Man With Enormous Wings," strewing the angel's wings with parasites and insects.

Once, while trying to finish a biblical story, I wrote a tale. I wanted to write a variation of Jacob's exile. It intrigued me that, while in love with Rachel, he mistook Leah for her at their wedding. For a while, I kept too close to the original. Then I reversed the genders: A woman cannot tell the difference between two brothers; a man usurps his brother's place in her bed. It struck me that nowadays—in our merciless age of electricity and information—this sounded highly unrealistic, so as a challenge I set the story in modern-day Salt Lake City.

Whenever you don't get your impetus to write a story from real life, look into books, for this is your medium. When something startles you in your reading, take off from there. Either try a variation on a theme, or venture ahead into something new.

EXERCISES

A general exercise: Look at the stories in the anthology in the back of this book and write a few pages as a variation on the theme of each story. In the comments on each story, I offer a few suggestions. After analyzing the stories, find some element you admire, and see whether you can apply it in your writing. Write a page in the mode of each story.

1. One page. According to Henry James, one writer wrote a novel from a glimpse of a seminary students' dinner party. Write a scene of a story from a glimpse you have had of a group of people—in a café, in a zoo, on a train, or anywhere. Sketch the characters in their setting and let them interact. Do you find that you know too little? Can you make up enough—or import from other experiences—to fill the empty canvas?

Objective: To find out if you can make much out of little. If you can, great. If you can't now, don't worry, you might be able to later. Or, you'll have to get your stories from other materials.

Check: Can you visualize these people further? Can you begin to hear at least one person speak? If not, go back and find a way of talking that might fit one of the people in the group, and carry on from there.

2. Three paragraphs. When you go out to a restaurant or a bar, jot down your observations in a notebook. In one paragraph, describe a loner's looks and behavior. In another, a couple's looks and interaction. In the third paragraph, describe how a waiter or bartender communicates with the customers. Some of these kinds of observations will come in handy to augment a scene, if not to make an entire story. (You could do a similar exercise elsewhere, jotting down your observations of people in a grocery store or at a street corner.)

Objective: To gear your observations of the world around you toward writing.

Check: Have you found something intriguing that raises questions that beg to be answered? For example, I once saw outside the Ritz Hotel in New York a woman in a fancy fur coat digging with her bare hands through a trash can for soda cans. What the hell was she doing? Was she poor but just looked rich? Was she rich and in the habit of hoarding so much that she could not let a five-cent can rest in peace? Did she throw an incriminating love letter into the garbage and then only pretend that she was doing something else in case she was followed by a private detective? See, a story easily begins to suggest itself and to offer several directions of development from one intriguing glimpse. True, I don't see something that intrigues me like this every day, but a couple of times every month is enough to write a new story every month. The main goal is to find something to wonder about, and that wonder should generate the story.

3. Two to three pages. Write down your first three memories. Can you make a story out of any of them? Try. Even if you aren't sure what you remember exactly, keep going. Imagine that you remember more than you do. Expand and rewrite in the third person, and forget it's you. This could be precious material for you. Renowned psychiatrist Alfred Adler thought that first memories reveal the psychological leitmotif of your life.

Objective: To begin to write stories that deeply matter to you.

Check: Have you been playful about this? Kids play, and even when they don't, they have a certain charming way of thinking. Have you hooked your imagination into childhood logic? If your drafts sound grave and heavily psychological, go back and lighten them up by inserting funny insights.

4. Two to three pages. Write down the first dreams you remember. Don't mention that they are dreams.

Objective: Similar to Exercise 3. Remember that in dreams you can't be held accountable for making everything plausible. Strange things happen, and not everything is explained. Don't punctuate, just drift words and images together into a dreamlike stream of consciousness. You can't remember all the details of your early dreams—or maybe you can—but don't let that deter you from writing at least two pages. If you manage to get into a primitive, dreamlike state of mind, you'll create strange connections and images. This approach could be productive for helping you develop unique moments in stories.

Check: Read what you've written. Do you have something bizarre? If not, distort things. For example, bring in wolves to create an expressionistic painting, because that's what dreams do. They express your hidden fears. And fears should mobilize you into a fight-or-flight alertness; use that energy for flights of fancy.

5. One page. Recall a physical or verbal fight, and construct it as one scene.

Objective: To see that some kinds of stories come pretty easily, as this one will. When I use this exercise in class, my students' pens keep moving even after the class is over. Struggle, war, quarrel, or any kind of conflict is an energetic source of stories.

Check: Is the writing dynamic? Are the words appropriately quick and strong? Cross out excess adjectives and adverbs and long, Latinate words; use short ones.

6. Two to three pages. Think about an incident that you avoid remembering—or can't clearly remember—and write about it. Write about a moment of terror you experienced, or about a defeat that hurts your pride. You can choose a terrible incident that, though crucial to you, you could not witness. For example, when my father was dying, I came to his bedside late, when he was probably unconscious, bloody foam on his lips. My brother witnessed all the stages of my father's death and heard his last words, yet it was I who wrote a story of the death—probably because I missed it. For years, I could not write about it, but when the event was sufficiently removed from me, it easily became a story, with hundreds of made-up details.

Objective: To help you deal with what matters. Even if you are afraid to think about something—or *especially* if you are—muster the courage to plunge right into the middle of your frightful memory. You will come up with something that matters to you, and if you evoke it clearly, it should matter to the reader, too.

Check: Don't. Keep going for a long while before you look back. This should be an uncensored outpouring. Save it, and revise months later.

7. Two to three pages. (From writer-teacher Jim Magnuson:) Write "My mother never …" at the top of a page, then complete the sentence and keep going. Read what you've written only after you are finished with the draft.

As you write, begin to fictionalize. Construct scenes. Take out sentimentality (statements like "My mother is my truest friend"), and forget the subject is your mother. Take yourself out, too.

Objective: To probe your background beyond the usual limits. No harm—it'll be fiction. If you think of what your mother does, you may not write fiction; but if you write what she doesn't do (what your mother never did) and imagine her doing it, you create an interesting match of character and action.

Check: You should find something surprising and outrageous in what you've written. If you don't, perhaps you did not loosen up enough. Try again, with a variant: "My father never …"

8. Two to three pages. Read Bible stories. Can you make variations? Can you finish the story of Cain? The story of Jacob and Esau? Joseph and Potiphar's

wife? In Midrashim—that is, the Hebrew tradition of interpreting biblical stories through filling in the gaps—one basically expands a given story. Can you do that?

Objective: To learn how to play with variations on a theme. Don't ever say, "It's been done." If it's worth doing once, it's worth doing twice.

Check: Did you run out of the story too quickly? Make people talk, eat, wash, and do a whole series of ordinary things, until they become real people to you. Linger on details. You needn't stick to the original. If the story sounds too stiff and formal, like an old translation, go back and rewrite it in simple and dynamic language. If the ancient times don't do anything for you, nor you for them, transfer the action to present-day America.

9. One to two pages. Do some historical events intrigue you? Do you keep wondering how things really happened, outside of the glory of patriotic propaganda? Can you find a figure that was only mentioned, like Marie in Joanna Scott's comments on page 12? Now, describe the historical event as seen by that briefly mentioned person, and make the person play an important role.

Objective: To use history to create fiction. After all, the history we get is reconstructed from letters, hearsay, newspapers, archaeology, and so on—sounds like writing fiction from multiple sources!

Check: Same as in Exercise 8.

10. Two pages. Give one intense emotion you've experienced—envy, fear, greed, lust—to a fictional character. Make sure the character is not you, but the emotion should be yours. Create a scene employing the fictional character and the emotion. Involve another person as an antagonist or a co-protagonist.

Objective: To get a good start—and a core—for a story.

Check: Review what you've done after you've written a couple of pages. Is the character radically different from you? Her way of talking should be different from yours, as should her way of walking, drinking, and so on. But the basic emotional conflict should be yours.

11. Two to three pages. Imagine some event that could have happened to you but did not—something that you wanted or feared. First, make up the basic outline of the event, and then incorporate true details. Put your teapot and cats into the story; they won't sue you. Your knowledge of these details will help you convince your reader of the truthfulness of the story's main event. Don't spend much time on introducing this event or on drawing conclusions. Just give the scene with your desire (or fear) acted out. Keep yourself as the main protagonist.

Objective: Desire and fear are the most productive dynamos of fiction and imagination. Around the desire (or fear) you can easily integrate the character, conflict, setting—all the basic elements of fiction easily fall into place once you have a character with a strong motive.

Check: Have you given a clear enough picture so the reader can identify with the desire? Or have you given a terrifying enough picture so the reader understands your character's fear? If not, go back and add convincing details—show the threat, the needle, the gun, the blind alley.

12. Two to three pages. As soon as you wake up tomorrow morning, jot down what you remember from your dreams. Keep a dream journal for three or four days. Then choose the one dream that puzzles you most and write a brief story—or a story sketch—out of it. Ask: How could a thing like that happen? And then make it happen, no matter how unrealistic and absurd. Use a deadpan approach. Don't worry about being caught saying something unbelievable. Make it believable by introducing real details, as in Exercise 11.

Objective: To get your stories from wherever you can. Why not get them from your freshly revealed subconscious?

Check: Are the dream's images and events beginning to make sense? Some connections, no matter how wild, should take place. If not, analyze the words to see which images recur and connect to others. Try to bring logic to the connections, some kind of cause and effect, or conflict, or desire that needs to be realized but is obstructed.

13. Write two to three pages of a story about first love. It could be yours or, if you have kids, your child's. Or, of course, it could be completely fictional. Many of these exercises based on your memories are a good basis for memoiristic nonfiction, and if you don't make any imaginative shifts and if you don't make things up, that is what they will be. I have used *Fiction Writer's Workshop* when I taught a nonfiction course, and many of these exercises were quite useful for that class. Your writing can go either way, into fiction or nonfiction. But if you are eager to write fiction more than nonfiction, deliberately make things up, give your experience to another character, or another person's experience to someone else. By the way, when I tried to write a story of my first love, I couldn't pull it off. Later, I could put in some fragments or aspects of the experience into a story about someone else, I could improvise and make things up, and the pages that I used were better that way than in the original version.

Objective: Nearly everything is worth trying out to get a story going, even love.

Check: Read the pages you have come up with. Are they interesting? If there is too much telling about your emotion, and not enough for us to see, the story might be too internal, as many stories involving a strong emotion tend to be. Being too close to the materials can make it difficult to externalize, so perhaps you could make a shift, and give the experience to someone else, someone different from yourself.

14. Three to five pages. Read the biography of a historical person, such as Mother Jones or Sitting Bull or Ludwig van Beethoven, and write a story based on one of the incidents in his or her life. Write a few pages in which you faithfully try to understand what happened. Then write a few pages of another story in the life of the same famous person, totally making it up, and not worrying about accuracy. For example, Thomas Bernhard wrote a novel, *The Loser*, in the shape of a memoir, about his studies at the Salzburg Music Conservatory with Glenn Gould. Well, Glenn Gould never studied in Salzburg. Bernhard deliberately made up the whole autobiographical novel, making it glaringly inaccurate. In this day of faithful accuracy, in which historical fiction often outdoes the history itself in amount of research and authentic detail, it is quite liberating to take that license to make up and to write something based on history for the sheer joy of making things up and creating an alternative history, a what-if history. There's a book by Anne Bernays and Pamela Painter entitled *What If?*, and "what if" is quite a useful reminder to make things up amidst the recalled facts.

Objective: To play with a story that is already there—filling in the details or taking off into a wild fancy.

Check: Which version is working better for you—the realistic one, getting into the details of the historical person's life, imagined to the best of your ability? Or the wildly fictional approach?

15. Two to three pages. Write a few pages of fan fiction. Namely, take a rock star (or some other person whom you admire), and make that person do something unexpected. For example, Jim Morrison could be visiting the SPCA to get a cat, or Roger Federer could be talking to his grandmother, trying to find out his roots (the way he plays, his roots could be ET). You could do this all with a straight face, seriously, but this kind of fiction easily lends itself to parody, so you might deliberately write a spoof of fan fiction.

Objective: Our culture, mass media, is a junkyard of pop-culture gossip. It's the materials we all have, willy-nilly. Why not use it—the world around us—for fiction? And here's your chance for revenge, if you are tired of all the fan stuff—make it as ridiculous as it is.

Check: Is it fun? And beyond the fun, do we recognize the pop characters you are writing about? If you don't mention the name of Madonna or Sharon Stone or Stephen King, will we know whom you are writing about?

2

SETTING

When and where does your story take place? Give us that place. Setting means a certain place at a certain time, a stage. You might even start your fiction by showing us the stage briefly. For example, Grand Central Station during the morning rush hour on the first day of winter in 1988. You might give us the details of the train station (the flipping of destination letters on the blackboard, slushy water on the tiles, loudspeakers crackling with Long Island nasality) and the people (the jacketed commuter crowd, a gaunt police officer with a startled dog). What startled the dog? We are ready to visualize the action now that we have the stage and something to look for on it.

PLACE FOR A PLACE

Do you need real places for your fiction? The strongest novels I can think of—*War and Peace, David Copperfield*, and others—are set in real cities or during real wars. Setting has these days fallen out of fashion at the expense of character and action. Perhaps this trend has to do with our not being a society of walkers. Big writers used to be big walkers. Almost every day, Honoré de Balzac spent hours strolling the streets of Paris; Charles Dickens, the streets of London; Fyodor Dostoyevski, the streets of St. Petersburg. Their cities speak out from them.

There is a common argument against detailed descriptions of setting: They can be outright dull. In their eagerness for excitement, readers often skip the passages that deal with establishing the setting. I certainly do—it took me years to return to Thomas Hardy's *The Return of the Native* because the first ten pages of the novel are spent mostly in describing landscape, and no matter how fine the descriptions, I suspect that even the English readers of the leisure class skipped those pages.

Many writers avoid laying out the setting because they fear boring their readers, but the lack of a vivid setting may, in turn, cause boredom. Without a strong sense of place, it's hard to achieve suspense and excitement—which depend on the reader's sensation of being right there, where the action takes place. When descriptions of places drag, the problem usually lies not in the setting, but in presenting the setting too slowly. Make your descriptions dynamic and quick; give bits of setting concurrently with characters and action. Take cues from drama: It would be a peculiar play in which all the props were displayed for half an hour before the actors walked on stage. Stage managers give you only the pieces necessary for a scene with actors already present. So as you write, though you may have sketched out all the jails, creeks, and mules, don't show them all first, before the characters. And when you show the setting, be selective, giving only a few details that evoke a place. If the chosen details are vivid, the readers will piece together the whole picture from their imaginations. Leave them that pleasure.

I've mentioned vividness (a result of using setting correctly) as a necessity for excitement. Fiction, in many ways, is similar to painting. Henry James certainly thought so. In "The Art of Fiction," he writes: "The analogy between the art of the painter and the art of the novelist is, so far as I am able to see, complete. Their inspiration is the same, their process (allowing for the different quality of the vehicle) is the same, their success is the same. They may learn from each other, they may explain and sustain each other." Medieval paintings had no landscape for background, and the characters they portrayed expressed little emotion—no laughter. By the end of the Middle Ages, exuberant life appeared in the foreground, and landscapes and cityscapes in the background. Coincidence? I don't think so. So, give your characters—children of your imagination—a lot of rich ground to move on, to play out their drama. A child with sand on a beach has a chance to be more active and creative than a child without sand.

These days, many writers—certainly not all—withdraw their gazes from city architecture and country life, and as they do, their fictional worlds diminish. The exterior and the interior go together. A destitute vision of what's around us can't result in a wealth of inner substance. Writing that deals only with ego—Did my father abuse me?—to my mind attains the humorless bleakness of a medieval painting, in which only the questions of sin (abuse) and pardon (recovery) matter. A character, let's say a sculptor, is interesting by virtue of what he does to the stones around him. If we never see the sculptor tackle the stones and other materials, his being a sculptor is merely an abstract trait. Whatever happens psychologically can be expressed in the environment: Mark Twain's humor in *Huckleberry Finn* would not work without the Mississippi setting.

Of the journalist's six questions—who, what, when, where, how, and why (a good piece of fiction strives to substantiate as much as a good piece of journalism does)—setting answers two—where and when—and therefore is extremely important.

Real or Imagined Setting

Before beginning to write a piece of fiction, decide whether you want to use a real place for your setting, or an imagined one. The advantage of anchoring your writing in a real place—entirely or partially—is that you will be rooted, you will draw new inspiration (and some old ghosts) out of the houses and streets. Each town, street, house has its own history; if you walk around a street, talk to its residents, read about it in old newspapers, you might unearth all kinds of interesting facts that will compete to enter your fiction. In portraying a place accurately, don't fear a lawsuit, which could happen only if the locations give unmistakable leads to real people. So, import your characters from other places and mask them so that not even their fathers would recognize them, or better yet, make them up.

Notice how proud people are if their town has been used as a setting for a movie. The same is true of a successful book that uses an authentic setting. However, if you fear lawyers, you can always change the name and the looks of the town and its streets, and lie in a disclaimer on the front page that any resemblance to real places is purely accidental. I think, though, that if you have a talent for lying, you are better off transforming the places you know in your fiction than making such disclaimers.

SETTING AS THE GROUNDWORK OF FICTION

For me, setting has been the primary source of fiction. Once I left Croatia, I began to set most of my stories there. That caught me by surprise because I had been terribly eager to get to the States. My stories gained resonance from my knowledge of Croatian towns far more than from American settings, which took time to reach my imagination. People ask me if my work is autobiographical. "No, it's topographical," I say, and though people stare at me blankly, I do mean it. I write about places.

The importance of the setting could be expressed in this formula: Setting = Character = Plot. Out of a place, a character is formed; out of a character's motives, plot may follow. This may sound like a psychological theory that the milieu is everything, that a character is a product of her environment. On the other hand, to disregard the importance of setting and to rely on a character's innate nature may sound too much like determinism. If the genes or something else in a character take care of everything, why bother playing out the drama in the environment and on a novelistic stage? Without places and actions influencing the character, you can't have much link between events. For a novelist, the theory favoring environmental importance can usually function better than the theory disregarding its importance.

A compromise, giving weight to both nature and nurture, works best. This approach could be expressed as Setting + Character = Plot. Out of a character's relationship with the setting, or out of the character's conflict with the setting, you get the plot (or at least a part of the plot, or a dynamic backdrop for your plot). The character, of course, has some independent inner core, some traits that can't be explained merely by environmental influences.

Let me illustrate this formula in practice. In my story "Rust," a setting and character in conflict with each other generate the plot:

> If you walk through the green and chirpy tranquility of the park around the castle at Nizograd, Yugoslavia, past the Roman Baths, you will come upon this monument: two dark, bronze partisans stuck on a pedestal uncomfortably high, back to back, one perpetually about to throw a hand grenade, another shoving his rifle into the air and shouting a metallic silence, his shirt ripped open. Their noses are sharp, lips thin, cheekbones high, hands large and knotty. ... The monument was done by Marko Kovachevich, a sculptor educated at the Moscow Art Academy, who was a Communist before the war and one of the first partisans.

The sculptor's work, as a part of the place, introduces to us the man and, later, his home completes the picture:

> His house was a grand sight—the redness of its bricks cried against the forest in the background. Its massiveness cast a long shadow over the backyard, prostrate and vanishing in the darkness of the woods. What was in the shadow attracted even more attention, so much so that the bright house would sink into a shadow of your mind, while the darkened objects in the backyard would begin to glow—planks of wood with bent nails sticking out, bike chains, rusty train wheels, tin cans, cats, buckets, winding telephones, a greater disarray than Berlin on May 2, 1945. The backyard seemed to be a witness to the collapse of an empire. Marko seemed entrenched in a war of sorts, with chaos gaining the upper hand.

By casting the shadows of World War II in a story set in the seventies, I build the plot. Marko, as a World War II guerrilla fighter, continues his fight, now against his former comrades, against the town, and against himself, because he does not know how to live in peace. Instead of working as a sculptor, he makes tombstones, to bury communists. Just as his iron strength rusts, and he collapses, without ever conforming (since he got stuck in the past), so does Yugoslavia collapse, for the second time (since she got stuck in the World War II mentality, which gutted any kind of progress). The setting is as much a character as Marko is. I wrote this story in the eighties—before Yugoslavia collapsed. I don't mean that there was anything prophetic in the story. The setting gave me nearly everything—the seed for a grand character and for the intuition about Yugoslavia's doom.

Even if the setting and the character together do not give you the plot, your story should appear as though the formula worked so that the place, the people, and the action are integrated. If you import a plot from a newspaper (or wherever) and apply it to places and people you know, you must transform the places and the people so that the plot—what happens—would be completely believable. Your characters should have sufficient motives to act the way they do, and these motives should be tied to the environment. To give a simple example, don't organize a water polo game on a baseball field; or if you insist, you must first make a swimming pool in that field. But it's simpler to find a swimming pool elsewhere.

SETTING AS ANTAGONIST

In a wide range of stories—Westerns, journey stories, nature adventure stories, detective stories, war stories, prison stories, Gothic romance, and most successful nongenre stories—setting provides the groundwork for the action. For example, Guy de Maupassant set many of his stories in the aftermath of the Franco-Prussian War. In his story "Ball of Fat," he describes Rouen before the arrival of the Prussian troops:

> A profound calm, a frightful, silent expectancy had spread over the city. Many of the heavy citizens, emasculated by commerce, anxiously awaited the conquerors, trembling lest their roasting spits or kitchen knives be considered arms. ... Shops were closed, the streets dumb.

When the Prussians come:

> A strange, intolerable atmosphere like a penetrating odor, the odor of invasion ... filled the dwellings and the public places, changed the taste of the food.

Since a character can be shown better in defeat than in victory, de Maupassant uses the setting to unmask people. A prostitute is brave and generous—she shares her last food with a group of rich travelers and lets herself be raped by a Prussian officer in order to set the travelers free. When it becomes their turn to share their food, they refuse, despising her on "moral" grounds.

The Man-Against-Nature story (in which a character struggles, usually for survival, against a natural element) depends entirely on setting. (See further discussion of this kind of story in chapter four.) For example, in "To Build a Fire" by Jack London, a man encounters a powerful antagonist, the cold, while he hikes in the Yukon territory in the middle of winter:

> As he turned to go on, he spat speculatively. There was a sharp explosive crackle that startled him. He spat again. And again, in the air, before it could fall to the snow, the spittle crackled. He knew that at fifty below spittle crackled on the snow, but this spittle had crackled in the air. Undoubtedly it was colder than fifty below.

London describes how creeks freeze through to the bottom, except for springs under the snow, which "hid pools of water":

> Sometimes a skin of ice half an inch thick covered them, and in turn was covered by snow. ... There were alternate layers of water and ice skin, so that when one broke through he kept on breaking through for a while ... wetting himself to the waist.

In subzero temperatures, being wet means freezing to death, unless you build a fire. The man falls into a spring and builds a fire, but a wind buries it in snow, and he freezes to death. After reading this story, you will remember the crackling of spittle in the cold much better than the man. (This detail, by the way, turns out to be false—I've spat in windchill of minus eighty in North Dakota, and nothing crackled. But for me, London's description still crackles.) The setting is the main character of the story, as grand and unforgiving as God in the book of Genesis.

Setting can sometimes generate the plot directly. For example, Nikolai Gogol based his novel *Dead Souls* on nineteenth-century rural Russia, where a population census was conducted once every five years. If the last census was in 1830, and a serf died in 1831, the serf's death would be registered in 1835. Gogol's plot: A schemer travels around the country buying up dead serfs—relieving the landowners of the tax on them—to appear rich so he can mortgage his fictitious property and raise cash to buy real property. The schemer relies on the distance between the villages so that he won't get caught as a swindler.

The setting need not be exotic, nor do you need it only if you write a long story or a novel. Even a short piece of fiction benefits from a strong sense of place. Jim Heynen, author of the story collection *The One-Room Schoolhouse*, sets his stories on an Iowa farm. I suppose if you don't live in Iowa, the setting may strike you as exotic, but if you do, it will not. The same applies to any place. Heynen's trust in the place created a genre: Midwestern farm tale. Here's an excerpt from one, "Dead Possum":

> The boy whose job was to check the level of the big cattle drinking tank found a dead possum floating in it. ... The dead possum had a big red apple wedged in its wide-open mouth. It looked like somebody with a big mouth who had been bobbing for apples.
>
> The boy wanted to yell for the others to come see, but knew they wouldn't believe him or, even if they did, wouldn't be in the mood. One of them would probably say something like, A dead possum with an apple in its mouth? Why don't you ask him to share?
>
> Isn't this something? he said to the cows. Isn't this something?
>
> Some nodded, then stepped past him to drink.

Heynen does not even have a distinct character here, just "the boys," which gives us more of a setting of boyhood than a single boy as a character. The place—populated with animals, vegetables, and farm boys—makes the story. Heynen gives the place—no more than necessary—as the story moves along. This way, there's no risk that the reader will say, "When does this description end? I hope soon."

He offers two viewpoints taken by the boys. Some treat the dead possum as quite familiar—and one boy treats it as something truly extraordinary. The group of boys, feeling jaded, familiarize even strange things, but the boy who checks the water level defamiliarizes them, finds something exotic in the potentially drab place on a dreary day. As a writer, you should attain the skill for defamiliarizing your immediate surroundings, like the boy.

Every place is exotic to those who are far away from it. Write about the places exotic to you—but it's cheaper (no airfare), and usually more effective, to find the exotic in the familiar. The trick is to treasure your impressions of the places you know well. When you neglect a place, you impoverish yourself.

Heynen is right to give us a young boy as the bearer of the freshest vision. I took my eight-month-old son to the zoo to see the elephants. He found a bee circling around us far more intriguing than a dancing elephant. Instead of noticing gibbons leaping in trees, he noticed fish in the water. It struck me that his perspective had a tremendous advantage over mine: He saw the world, while I saw the zoo.

By noticing with a fresh eye the fall of a common apple, Newton revolutionized science. He did not need a pineapple.

But you need not limit yourself to the places you know. If you write science fiction, you do not run away from the obligation to give us a setting. Without creating a thorough setting—imaginary science and technology, fashion, architecture, cuisine, drugs—you don't make a good science fiction story. So devise ideas and images that will be unfamiliar to the reader, but make them appear familiar.

And for historical fiction, you can't have experienced every place and time. So you research to make sure that your characters in 1920 don't watch television, and that your characters in Philadelphia of 1840 have the option to ride trains or at least listen to the whistles.

SETTING FOR SPECIAL EFFECTS

Many stories spring out of strong settings—even those that don't *use* setting. In movies, music and landscape shots often appear as a backdrop for the action, especially to augment suspense or romance, and sometimes simply to dazzle you. The quality of photography—the selection of details, the angles of light and shadow—engage you most. In writing, you can achieve similar effects with words describing landscapes and cityscapes. So consider the following auxiliary uses of setting.

Setting as Quality of Vision

In a dialogue scene, delicate imagery and metaphors may seem unnatural to your reader, so break away from the drama occasionally to give bits of the stage—the clanking of spoons on china. Here's your chance to show your skill and speed, to build your reader's confidence in your narrative vision. If your words render a setting keenly, the reader might be inclined to accept the psychological insights implied in the action and dialogue. With sharply observed bits of the world, you convince. A touch of extraordinary landscaping here and there may be enough to draw us into the story and to keep us in it.

In *The Easter Parade*, Richard Yates grabs our attention in a printing-room scene by engaging our perception:

> Workmen hurried everywhere, all wearing crisp little squared-off
> hats made of intricately folded newspaper.
> "Why do they wear those paper hats, Daddy?" Emily asked.
> "Well, they'd probably tell you it's to keep the ink out of their hair,
> but I think they just wear 'em to look jaunty."
> "What does jaunty mean?"

Shortly after the dialogue, Yates gives this description:

> They watched the curved, freshly cast metal page plates slide in on conveyor rollers to be clamped into place on the cylinders; then after a ringing of bells they watched the presses roll. The steel floor shuddered under their feet, which tickled, and the noise was so overwhelming that they couldn't talk; they could only look at each other and smile, and Emily covered her ears with her hands. White streaks of newsprint ran in every direction through the machines, and finished newspapers came riding out in neat, overlapped abundance.

There's a lot of dialogue before and after this moment; the narrative pause effectively grounds the scene. Yates makes us feel that we are there in the pressroom, with the ringing bells, shuddering floor, tickling feet. Although the novel is not about the newspaper business, but about two girls growing up unhappily, this scene establishes a strong backdrop. The daughters are impressed by their father, and they are ready to believe anything he tells them. Reading scenes like this, I believe, too, for I am there—I see. I see the father's workplace. If I didn't, his working for a newspaper would not mean much.

Here's an example of the quality of vision in Michael Ondaatje's novel *The English Patient*. In the scene, a Bedouin healer treats a wounded man:

> He crouched by the burned man. He made a skin cup with the soles of his feet and leaned back to pluck, without even looking, certain bottles. With the uncorking of each tiny bottle the perfumes fell out. There was an odour of the sea. The smell of rust. Indigo. Ink. Rivermud arrowwood formaldehyde paraffin ether. The tide of airs chaotic. There were screams of camels in the distance as they picked up the scents. He began to rub green-black paste onto the rib cage.

Ondaatje engages your senses. "The smell of rust": You smell and see. "Screams of camels": You hear and see. "He began to rub green-black paste onto the rib cage": You see and feel. The texture of the sensations is so rich that you experience the scene before you can doubt it. This healer's handling his tools in his desert creates and sustains a scene—with substantiated characters in a setting. By substantiated, I mean that you see the healer at work with his substances. Ondaatje does not merely tell, he shows.

Mood and Atmosphere

You can set the tone of a scene with your handling of the setting. This is especially important in horror stories, romance, and other "mood" genres.

Here's a mood-setter from a Gothic classic, Emily Brontë's *Wuthering Heights*:

> One may guess the power of the north wind, blowing over the edge,
> by the excessive slant of a few stunted firs at the end of the house; and
> by a range of gaunt thorns all stretching their limbs one way, as if
> craving alms of the sun. ... The narrow windows are deeply set in the
> wall, and the corners defended with large jutting stones.

The narrator completes the image of the house's exterior with this description:

> A quantity of grotesque carving lavished over the front, and especially
> about the principal door, above which, among a wilderness of crum-
> bling griffins, and shameless little boys, I detected the date "1500."

Then she gives us the interior:

> Above the chimney were sundry villainous old guns, and a couple of
> horse-pistols, and, by way of ornament, three gaudily painted canis-
> ters disposed along its ledge. The floor was smooth, white stone: the
> chairs, high-backed, primitive structures, painted green: one or two
> heavy black ones lurking in the shade. In an arch, under the dresser,
> reposed a huge, liver-colored bitch pointer surrounded by a swarm of
> squealing puppies; and other dogs haunted other recesses.

The barren landscape—with stunted trees, thorns, and lack of sunshine—creates a threatening mood. The interior of the old house, with its darkness, intensifies the sensation of threat. The smooth white stone adds coldness. Although
the mere mention of all these details would create a threatening enough mood,
the narrator does not stop there. She slants the verbs to distort the picture, to
make it spooky. Chairs lurk in the shade. Dogs haunt recesses. Even the adjectives are slanted: villainous guns. She could have described pretty much the
same thing with different verbs—chairs repose in the shade, dogs roam in the
recesses—and she would have relaxed the mood. She guides us with verbs, adjectives, and adverbs toward a single mood.

However, you don't always need to use a long description to be effective. For
example, German writer Günter Grass, in his novel *Dog Years*, gives us a startling detail to establish a surreal atmosphere:

> ... where the dike burst in '55 near Kokotzko, not far from the Men-
> nonite cemetery—weeks later the coffins were still hanging in the
> trees—but he, on foot ...

This is the middle of a half-page-long sentence, and the humble placement of
the image of coffins hanging in trees only sharpens its effect, to augment the

theme of postwar Germany, where war deaths hover in the air. Grass does not need to point with slanted verbs and modifiers at this grotesque image. It does its own work—but isn't subtle, since it is a loud image.

Grass's technique is not superior to Brontë's technique. They achieve different effects. Brontë's narrator, passionately involved in the story, explicitly works on the mood, which anticipates disaster. Grass's narrator, ironically detached, works his way out of a catastrophe, without needing to embellish it. Both methods are effective. When you choose a narrator emotionally involved in a drama, you might choose Brontë's method; when you want distance, choose Grass's cooler, more matter-of-fact method.

Foreshadowing

You can use setting to steer the reader's expectations. Mood is a big part of foreshadowing. In the preceding example, Brontë foreshadows something frightening. The mention of villainous guns raises the suspicion that someone will be murdered. Darkness, griffins, and haunting dogs forecast something on the verge of the supernatural. Later, she delivers on most of her promises.

In Stephen Crane's "The Blue Hotel," a Swede believes that Nebraska is the Wild West and that he will be killed there. He provokes a fight, wins it, goes to another bar to brag about it, and there he is killed. As we follow him, we encounter these images:

> In front of the saloon an indomitable red light was burning, and the
> snowflakes were made blood-colour as they flew through the cir-
> cumscribed territory of the lamp's shining.

The snowy night and the red flakes obviously foreshadow the bloodshed. In your writing, you may strive for a bit more subtlety, but it's probably best to be somewhat obvious. If your foreshadowing is too subtle, there won't be any shadows to see.

Setting as Alpha and Omega

In a screenplay, before every take you must indicate whether you are inside or outside, and what the time of day is. As a fiction writer, you may find these establishing shots tiresome, but you are not exempt from the obligation to establish where you are and at what time of day the drama takes place. Of course, now and then it becomes boring to say, "in the evening." So you may try twilights, dusks, noons, teatimes, and some other times, but eventually, even these will run dry. So be it. You still need to write, "in the morning," just as in dialogue you must rely on one simple word, *said*. If you don't tell when your action takes place, it might appear to happen in some generic time, or always, as a repeated action. Unless you want that effect, indicate the days and nights.

For an example of how to open a piece of fiction with a setting and orient us as to the time the action takes place, take a look at Dickens's brief opening of *Our Mutual Friend*:

> In these times of ours, though concerning the exact year there is no need to be precise, a boat of dirty and disreputable appearance, with two figures in it, floated on the Thames between Southwark Bridge, which is of iron, and London Bridge, which is of stone, as an autumn evening was closing in.

The beginning draws us into a scene. We have a stage. At first we do not see the characters and the boat clearly, but enough is established for us to begin seeing and wondering.

In introducing the setting, it's important that you orient us, make it clear where we should be imaginatively. Here's how Guy de Maupassant opens "Mademoiselle Fifi." He places us in an interior, with a vantage point toward the exterior:

> The Major Graf von Farlsberg was reading ... with his booted feet on the beautiful marble fireplace, where his spurs had made two holes, which grew deeper every day, during the three months that he had been in the chateau of Urville.
>
> A cup of coffee was steaming on a round marquetry table, stained with liqueurs, charred by cigars, and hacked by the penknife of the victorious officer. ... After throwing three or four enormous pieces of green wood onto the fire—for these gentlemen were gradually cutting down the park in order to keep themselves warm—he went to the window. The rain was descending in torrents, a regular Normandy rain, which ... formed a kind of wall with oblique stripes.

Although de Maupassant does not tell us directly that it's daytime, he makes it clear: He tells us several paragraphs later that the cup of coffee is Major's sixth cup that morning, and that the officer looked over the flooded park (which he could not see at night).

Both of these openings set up moods and expectations—first, for some murky action; second, for whimsical deeds to kill the boredom of a rainy day.

You can also close a story with the impressions of a place, which, in cinematic terminology, can create a perfect fade-out. This is how James Joyce closes his story "The Dead" after the main character realizes that without having passionately lived, he will fade away and die:

A few light taps upon the pane made him turn to the window. It had begun to snow again. He watched sleepily the flakes, silver and dark, falling obliquely against the lamplight. Yes, the newspapers were right: Snow was general all over Ireland. It was falling on every part of the dark central plain, on the treeless hills, falling softly upon the Bogg of Allen and, farther westward, softly falling into the dark mutinous Shannon waves. It was falling, too, upon every part of the lonely churchyard on the hill where Michael Furey lay buried. It lay thickly drifted on the crooked crosses and headstones, on the spears of the little gate, on the barren thorns. His soul swooned slowly as he heard the snow falling faintly through the universe and faintly falling, like the descent of their last end, upon all the living and the dead.

What's more to say after this? If the story ended with a philosophical statement, the impact would be smaller. Because Joyce ends the tale in this way, you'll carry the images for days after you've read the story.

Setting as a Character Portrait

It's hard to describe a person's face in a fresh and telling way. After all, in how many ways can you describe eyes and a nose, if you don't rely on metaphors? Not many. However, by describing a person through how he arranges his surroundings, you have quite a few options.

In *Dead Souls*, Nikolai Gogol uses objects in a living room to portray a character:

A lemon completely dried up, and no larger than a broken walnut-wood knob from an arm-chair; a wine glass covered with a letter, and containing some sort of liquid and three flies; ... a toothpick, which was quite yellow, and with which the owner had probably cleansed his teeth prior to the arrival of the French in Moscow. ... From the middle of the ceiling hung a chandelier enveloped in a linen bag, to which the accumulated dust gave the aspect of a silkworm's cocoon with the worm in it. ... It would have been impossible to affirm that a living being inhabited the apartment, had not an ancient, threadbare nightcap, which lay upon the table, borne witness to the fact.

The setting of the room gives us the character, a hoarder. This portrayal is augmented by other details:

For all of his domestic servants ... Pliushkin had but a single pair of boots, which was always to be found in the vestibule. Anyone who was summoned into the master's presence generally ran across the yard barefooted; but on entering the vestibule he pulled on the boots, and, thus arrayed, made his appearance in the room. ... If anyone had glanced out of the window in the autumn, and especially when the first morning frosts were setting in, he could have seen all the house-serfs taking such leaps as are hardly made on the stage by the most accomplished dancers.

How's that for describing a stingy character? Certainly better than a pile of adjectives. To adhere to the principle show, don't tell, characterize people by what's around them.

EXERCISES

1. First (two pages), describe the town you grew up in—the streets, shops, schools, churches, rivers, bridges, rails. Don't mention your emotions; don't be sentimental.

Then (half a page), indicate a place in the above sketch where something happened. Map out the event with special attention to the physical details of the setting. It need not be a big event—your shattering a window or seeing a teacher you had a crush on kiss a cop will do. Naguib Mahfouz, the Egyptian Nobel prize winner, wrote a novel, *Midaq Alley*, describing life on a little street in Cairo.

Objective: To remind you of your treasures. If you have a strong sense of place, it'll be easy for you to write a lot. Let the bricks speak.

Check: Have you described the childhood places vividly? Do you mention enough details to construct a visual impression? Do you engage other senses, not only sight? Read your descriptions slowly. Are you there? If you haven't mentioned enough real details, perhaps you aren't there. Try it again, until you mention the concrete objects you see. You can revise the exercise, deleting and inserting words, until you feel that you've brought us into your town.

2. Two pages. Make a one-page list of all the objects you remember from your childhood home. Don't use any particular order or many adjectives. Don't censor yourself—something seemingly unimportant may evoke strong impressions.

Read your list and circle the objects that evoke the strongest feelings and memories of events. What are these events? Do you see a story lurking there? Now write one page and describe one of these events. Rely on topography. Where exactly did it happen? What objects were involved?

Objective: To let your home begin to write stories for you. Memory is your best source of settings.

Check: Same as Exercise 1. Now go over the details and cross out the ones that don't evoke strong impressions. It's good to bring out many details and then select the ones that work best; select a few, condense. Your reader will appreciate this economy.

Make sure that you haven't used sentimental vocabulary. It's fine to be sentimental, but mentioning the sentiments won't give them to the reader. Connecting the details with the events might. For instance: "I walk down the yellow marble stairs where my grandfather slid one winter and broke his hip. That was the last step he took; he died shortly after the injury. In the space beneath the staircase I find my old dog's house, with his shaggy hairs caught in the rough edges of the wood planks, although the dog is long gone." If you don't dwell on the emotional significance of the grandfather and the dog, but move on, you avoid sentimentality. If the grandfather is important, you can show that in a scene, an interaction with the man so we can experience him and your loss of him. We won't miss an abstraction about the man.

3. Two pages. Describe with care the most ordinary items you can think of. Look at them as though they were strange and unusual. Conversely, describe extraordinary things—meteors, rockets, and so on—in familiar language as just another stone or a piece of rolled sheet metal.

Objective: To learn how to control your distance from the objects you describe. If you are too close, you may not see the shape; if you are too far away, you may not see the details. Get into the habit of shifting the focus away from what would be your automatic focus, and you will see items in a fresh way. Practice the art of creating surprising details. Skip something obviously important and use something apparently unimportant.

Check: Do the ordinary objects sound fascinating? Do the extraordinary objects sound ordinary but interesting? If not, go back, and in the first half of the exercise give us the details that amaze, and in the second, details that make us take a good look. Everything you observe with interest should sound interesting.

4. Three one-page descriptions. Describe three places you have been. Don't worry about pretty words; mention the important and some unimportant details you remember.

Objective: Sooner or later, you'll need these places in your stories. It's good to have them handy, so you don't have to make up everything at once. You need a hospital? Pull it out of your files. You do it anyway—your brain has the files, and as a writer, you'll facilitate your job if you let your papers or your computer share them. Externalize your materials. Of course, when fitting these descriptions into a piece of fiction, you'll need to tailor them for desired effects—mood, atmosphere, foreshadowing—so you'll need to pick and choose your details.

Check: Have you been specific enough? Instead of a bird, let it be a pigeon; instead of a tree, a cedar. Have you externalized enough? Instead of a place being enjoyable (which is your internal reaction to it), mention, for example, the murmur of champagne.

5. Two pages. Describe places where you have worked—a hospital ward, a law firm, an army barracks, a fish cannery, a restaurant, an oil rig, and so on. Describe how the people handle their tools and machines. If you are at a loss, take a look at Richard Yates's example on pages 33–34, and try to describe a workplace, similarly engaging our senses.

Objective: To concentrate on the details and energy of a workplace. Workplaces make perfect story setups because they make it easy for you to integrate the place and the character. People shape the place, the places shape the people. Remember the importance of linking place and character for plot development (or for a plot backdrop).

Check: Would we know we were in a chocolate factory—or wherever you choose—without your telling us? If you stated, "This is a chocolate factory," delete the sentence, and see whether the place still is clear. It should be, if you've let us feel, hear, smell, and taste the work. If you haven't, go back and mention the sounds, smells, sights, and feel of the place.

6. One page. Describe a train ride—the rhythm of the rails clicking, the sound booming back from a close wall, the sensation of motion when a parallel train moves and yours doesn't, the sticky beer stains on the floor, the smell of new towns, and so on. (Or, if you prefer, describe a different kind of ride—on a boat or in a car, for example.)

Objective: To show the experience of travel. Journey is one of the basic story forms. Maybe you carry a story that the setting of travel will give birth to. Try it. (For example, a friend of mine wrote a dozen postcards from Germany to the States, and when she got back was surprised that nobody got them. She had mistaken a clean German garbage bin for a mailbox.)

Check: Have you shown us the train? Go back over the description and delete adjectives—beautiful, menacing—that tell us what you'd like to show us. Have you described the corridors, signs (in what languages?), lights?

7. One page. Describe the setting of a Man-Against-Nature story. Use a mountain you've climbed, or a river you've rafted, or a sea you've sailed. Describe the flora, fauna, weather, but not yourself (become subjective later). Give us what you saw, as precisely and objectively as you can. Show the nature, the danger.

Objective: To learn how to landscape dramatically, truthfully.

Check: Did we get a sense of danger from your description? Delete adjectives (like *terrifying*) and change metaphors into realistic pictures. (Instead of "Each wave was a dragon frothing at the mouth," let it be something like "The tall wave crests burst into foam above us.") If, after the psychological projection—emotional adjectives and metaphors—are taken out of the picture, we still get the sense of terror, you've done a great job. Later—if you choose to go on with the story—you can switch into metaphoric and hallucinatory vision of the terror.

8. One page. Write a story opening set indoors, and include the occupants of the rooms. What time of day is it? What's the weather like? (For an example, read the excerpt from "Mademoiselle Fifi" on page 37.) Then write the last page for the same story. Close with an impression given by the environment, which should correspond to the mood you want the story to express.

Objective: To learn how to visualize a stage for a story. Once you are mentally in the place, you'll be able to envision the action and move forward. The same is true with ending the action.

Check: Can we see what you are talking about? I don't mean every eyelash in the onion soup and every cigarette stub on the bathroom tile floor—you don't need to count lashes and stubs, but do mention them.

9. Two pages. Write one page preceding the death of a car salesman from his point of view. Describe street traffic, weather, pedestrians, or birds in such a way that we begin to feel the gloom and resignation of the man about to die.

Then write one page preceding the birth of a daughter, using the same street as above, to create a sensation of hope, anxiety, and joy from the perspective of the car salesman.

Set up the mood for both events through the choice of details. Don't be too obvious about what you are doing, but don't be too subtle, either. (But if this inhibits you, make a parody of foreshadowing—be either too obvious or too subtle!)

Objective: To realize the expressive potential of objects and places.

Check: Do your images accumulate to create an atmosphere of gloom and resignation in the first half of the exercise, and of anticipation in the second? Do you achieve a gradual increase in intensity? If not, reorder the images to create the progression.

10. One page. Describe a setting for a horror story. You might pattern it after Emily Brontë's example on page 35. Use the same lack of narrative distance as she does—let your narrator show us an ominous atmosphere through choice details, and let her tell us about it also, through slanted verbs and adjectives, just as Brontë does. The balance should be in favor of the details. (If horror does not appeal to you, try to achieve another mood.)

Objective: To practice using setting for a strong mood, using all your means, showing and telling.

Check: Did you evoke the mood? Although it's all right if some of your imagery turns out to be stock horror stuff (howling winds), make sure that at least some of your images are original, new things that you haven't seen before. (For example, Brontë uses this fresh, memorable image: "range of gaunt thorns all stretching their limbs one way, as if craving alms of the sun.")

11. Two pages. Recall your favorite bridge—surely you have one. Describe it in one page from the perspective of a woman who has received a letter offering her a great job.

Then, in one more page, describe the same bridge from the perspective of the same woman, who has just found out that her boyfriend committed suicide. In both instances, don't mention emotions, plans, regrets. Leave the expression of the emotions to your selection of details—the bridge's stones, the vegetation on the river banks, the water, the river traffic.

Objective: Same as in Exercise 9. Work like an expressionist painter. Don't worry about being realistic and precise with detail. Paint in broad strokes—slant and twist—to make the commotion of the soul looking at the bridge as visible as the bridge itself.

Check: If, in the first part, you express cheer, do you give us a flock of swallows fluttering over cherry trees on the banks of the river? In the second part, do you show a grimace on an ancient face with blank stones for eyes? Or something similar?

12. One page. Make a character visible through her surroundings. If she loves plants and cats and hates people, her house might assume certain traits. Sketch the house, listing the sights, smells, sounds. (See pages 38–39 for how Gogol does it.)

Objective: To learn the power of setting as a means for character portraits. Bits of environment are your tubes of paint.

Check: Read the sketch. Do you give us precise details? Rather than "The place smelled stuffy," do you show the stuffiness? Rather than showing "plants," list the names of plants.

13. Two to three pages. Analyze Sandra Cisneros's story "The Monkey Garden," beginning on page 310. The story is like an exercise to describe a garden with flowers, smells, worms, and discarded objects, and to put children into this garden of Eden. Now recall a remarkable garden you have experienced, and play with it—maybe you've had a story you could tell us, something you did or something that happened to you in the garden, or you could make one up. Or both. A garden is a very visual place, but it is also olfactory. Describe this garden first for a charming childhood story, a loss of innocence. Then for a murder story. Then for a love story. Will the same garden assume different hues, shades, smells, sounds, depending on the genre you choose? Might that be too predictable? How about switching around, using the garden drawn for a horror story to serve as a setting for a love story, and the garden drawn for the love story as a setting for horror story? I think diffusing

the genre expectations, rather than playing along with them, might give you a bit of freshness in your approach.

Objective: To let the chemistry of a setting help you in assembling the moments of a story, which could take off by association from the details.

Check: Have you managed to invoke our senses, particularly engaging our ears and nostrils and skin? If nothing is happening yet to trigger story-making, put a few people in the garden, or work from memory, putting yourself and whomever you remember in the garden into the scenes.

14. One page. Go into a church or temple or mosque or ashram; wander into a place of worship that is not pertaining to your religion, and describe precisely what you see. Try to do it as respectfully as possible.

Objective: Understanding what other people believe, when you don't believe the same thing, is a precious writerly skill. These days, it may be the essential human skill, to be able to get along respectfully, with genuine interest in other cultures, not merely tolerance (not that this can be taught in an exercise). Assuming a respectful attitude toward every culture could expand your ground for writing stories.

Check: If you crossed out the words that directly indicate where you are (such as *mosque* or *Catholic cathedral*), would your reader know where you are?

3

CHARACTER

Most people read fiction not so much for plot as for company. In a good piece of fiction, you can meet someone and get to know her in-depth, or you can meet yourself, in disguise, and imaginatively live out and understand your passions. The writer William Sloan thinks it boils down to this: "Tell me about me. I want to be more alive. Give me me."

If character matters so much to the reader, it matters even more to the writer. Once you create convincing characters, everything else should easily follow. F. Scott Fitzgerald said, "Character is plot, plot is character." But, as fiction writer and teacher Peter LaSalle has noted, out of character, plot easily grows, but out of plot, a character does not necessarily follow. To show what makes a character, you must come to a crucial choice that almost breaks and then makes the character. The make-or-break decision gives you plot. Think of Saul on the way to Damascus: While persecuting Christians, he is blinded by a vision; after that, he changes and becomes St. Paul, the greatest proselyte. Something stays the same, however; he is equally zealous, before and after. No matter what you think of the story of Paul's conversion, keep it in mind as a paradigm for making a character.

Of course, not all characters undergo a crucial change. With some characters, their unchangeability and constancy makes a story. In "Rust," my story about the sculptor turned tombstone-maker, everything (the country, family, town) changes, except the character. Even his body collapses, but his spirit stays bellicose and steadfast. Here he is, at work:

> He refused to answer any more of my questions. His hands—with thick cracked skin and purple nails from hammer misses—picked up a hammer. Veins twisted around his stringy tendons so that his tendons looked like the emblem for medicine. He hit the broadened head of the chisel, bluish steel cutting into gray stone, dust flying up in a sneezing cloud. With his gray hair and blue stubbly cheeks he blended into the grain of the stone—a stone with a pair

of horned eyebrows. Chiseling into the stone, he wrestled with time, to mark and catch it. But time evaded him like a canny boxer. Letting him cut into rocks, the bones of the earth, Time would let him exhaust himself.

Seven years later I saw him. His face was sunken. His body had grown weaker. Time had chiseled into his face so steadily that you could tell how many years had passed just by looking at the grooves cutting across his forehead. But the stubbornness in his eyes had grown stronger. They were larger, and although ringed with milky-gray cataracts, glaringly fierce.

Whether or not there's a change in you, character is not the part of you that conforms, but that sticks out. So a caricaturist seeks out oddities in a face; big jaws, slanted foreheads, strong creases. The part of the character that does not conform builds a conflict, and the conflict makes the story. Find something conflicting in a character, some trait sticking out of the plane, creating dimension and complexity. Make the conflict all-consuming, so that your character fights for life. Stanley Elkin, author of *The Dick Gibson Show*, emphasized the need for struggle this way: "I would never write about someone who is not at the end of his rope."

Think of the basic character conflicts in successful stories. "The Necklace" by Guy de Maupassant: Mme. Loisel, unreconciled to her lower-class standing, strives to appear upper class, at all costs. Out of that internal conflict ensues the tragedy of her working most of her adult life to pay for a fake necklace.

"The Girls in Their Summer Dresses" by Irwin Shaw: Though married and in love with his wife, a young man is still attracted to other women.

In Henry James's "The Beast in the Jungle": John Marcher waits for some extraordinary passion to take hold of him; he dreams of it so much that he does not notice he is in love with May Bertram, who is at his side all along. Only when she dies, of neglect, does he realize it.

In "The Blue Hotel" by Stephen Crane: The Swede, visiting a small town in rural Nebraska, imagines that he is in the Wild West and consequently sets himself against a bar of ordinary people whom he imagines as gamblers and murderers.

In all these stories, characters suffer from a conflicting flaw. Aristotle called these character flaws *hamartia*—usually interpreted as "tragic flaw" (most often hubris or arrogance) when we talk about tragedies. Sometimes, however, a flaw may not lead to disaster, but to a struggle with a subsequent enlightenment. (St. Paul's zeal, for example, leads him to an epiphany.)

A flaw could result also from an excessive virtue. Look at the opening of *Michael Kohlhaas* by the early-nineteenth-century German writer Heinrich von Kleist:

Michael Kohlhaas ... owned a farm on which he quietly earned a living by his trade; his children were brought up in the fear of God to be industrious and honest; there was not one of his neighbors who had not benefited from his goodness and fair-mindedness—the world would have had every reason to bless his memory, if he had not carried one virtue to excess. But his sense of justice turned him into a robber and a murderer.

Since his horses were abused at a border crossing between two principalities, and he could not get a just compensation in courts, Kohlhaas takes justice into his hands and burns down the castle where the horses suffered. In addition, he burns the city of Dresden, which protected the offenders. His sense of justice provokes a war. His uncompromising virtue may amount to vice—certainly it's a flaw, the plot-generating flaw.

ROUND AND FLAT CHARACTERS

Most of the characters in the above examples could be called round characters because they have three dimensions, like a ball. These characters are complex, possessing conflicting traits. Mme. Loisel is both frivolous and responsible. The Swede is paranoid yet insightful. John Marcher is sensitive yet callous. In writing, you must not oversimplify—that is, create flat characters. (It's all right to have flat characters as part of a setting, but not as part of an interactive community, the cast of your story.)

Flat characters have few traits, all of them predictable, none creating genuine conflicts. Flat characters often boil down to stereotypes: fat, doughnut-eating cop; forgetful professor; lecherous truck driver; jovial fatso; shifty-eyed thief; anorexic model. Using these prefab characters can give your prose a semblance of humor and quickness, but your story featuring them will have about as much chance of winning a contest as a prefab apartment in an architectural competition. Even more damaging is that you will sound like a bigot. As a writer, you ought to aspire toward understanding the variety of human experience, and bigotry simply means shutting out and insulting a segment of the population (and their experiences) by reducing them to flat types.

But can you have a character without types? What would literature be without gamblers and misers? The solution, I believe, is simple: Draw portraits of misers, but not as misers—as people who happen to be miserly. And if, while you draw misers as people, you feel that you fail to make characters but do make people, all the better. Ernest Hemingway said, "When writing a novel, a writer should create living people; people, not characters. A character is a caricature." So, give us people. ("Give me me.") Let the miser in me come to life—and blush—reading your story.

SOURCES OF CHARACTERS

Where do you find fictional people?

Ideal Method

You can completely make them up, using psychology textbooks, astrology charts, mythology, the Bible, or, simply, your imagination. This is the ideal method—ideal in the sense that you work from a purely intellectual creation, an idea about a character whom you have not observed and who is not you. Although, by using this method, you don't draw from people you know to make your characters, you must speak of real passions, and each character must appear like a real person. "Real person" is a bit of a contradiction in terms because *persona*, the Latin root for person, means "mask." We usually take a mask to be the unreal, phony part of a person. But wearing a mask at a carnival can help you live out your true passions that otherwise, due to social pressures, you would keep in check. Fiction is a carnival. So give us real passions with good masks, and everybody will be fair game! Make up character masks, release dramatic conflicts beneath them, and you will create startling people, such as those you would like, or fear, to meet.

Autobiographical Method

The mother of all character-creation methods—though not necessarily the one you should use most—is the autobiographical method, for it is through your own experience that you grasp what it is to be a person. Because of this, you are bound, at least to some extent, to project yourself into the fictional characters you render by any other method. Many writers project themselves into all the characters they portray. This is, metaphorically speaking, the fission approach: An atom may be split into several parts, during which an enormous amount of energy is released. Fyodor Dostoyevski split his personality into many fictional ones, all of them as temperamental as he. Mel Brooks, the comedy writer and movie director, thinks this is the primary way to write: "Every human being has hundreds of separate people living under his skin. The talent of a writer is his ability to give them their separate names, identities, personalities, and have them relate to other characters living with him."

Biographical Method

In the biographical method, you use people you have observed (or researched) as the starting points for your fictional characters. This seems to be the most popular method. Despite legal limitations on the biographical method, don't shut down this basic source of fictional characters. Hemingway said that if he explained the process of turning a real-life character into a fictional one, it would be a handbook for libel lawyers. The notion that writers work this way will keep some people quiet around you lest you broadcast their secrets. For a long while, it irritated me that my older brother would not believe that I was becoming a writer; and now that he does, he irritates me even more because he does not tell me anything about himself. To find out about him, I talk to our middle brother, and as soon as my older brother finds out that that's how it works, he probably won't talk to him, either.

Most fictional characters are directly, or at least indirectly, drawn from life. E.M. Forster, author of *A Passage to India*, said: "We all like to pretend we don't use real people, but one does actually. I used some of my family. ... This puts me among the large body of authors who are not really novelists, and who have to get on as best they can." (By the way, most novelists are not really novelists, and they must get on as best they can. Nobody is born with this stuff, and hardly anybody becomes quite secure in the craft. I think that's comforting: Novelists are regular people, like you and me.)

Using the biographical method, writers often compose their characters from the traits of several people. To express it with another term from nuclear physics, this is the fusion approach: You fuse character traits the way you fuse atoms. Lillian Hellman, author of *Pentimento*, supports this view of making fictional characters: "I don't think you start with a person. I think you start with parts of many people. Drama has to do with conflict in people, with denials." She looks for conflicts in real people and gives these conflicts to her fictional characters, whose traits she gets from other people.

Mixed Method

The fourth way to create fictional characters is the mixed method. Writers frequently combine the biographical and the ideal methods since there's a limit to relying on direct knowledge of characters. In part, this stems from our inability to know people in depth. W. Somerset Maugham, author of *Of Human Bondage*, said: "People are hard to know. It is a slow business to induce them to tell you the particular thing about themselves that can be of use to you." Unless you are a psychiatrist or a priest, you probably will not find out the deep problems of the people around you. That does not mean you can't use some aspects of the people you know. But soon, you must fill in the gaps, and let's hope that then you will create a character independent from the real-life model. You may use ideas and imagination, or it may happen spontaneously, as it apparently did to Graham Greene, author of *The Human Factor*, who said: "One gets started and then, suddenly, one cannot remember what toothpaste they use. ... The moment comes when a character does or says something you hadn't thought about. At that moment he's alive and you leave it to him." If your character begins to do something different from what the real-life precedent would do, encourage this change, and forget about the real-life model. Soon, you should have someone answering to the necessities of your plot and conflicts, not to the memory of the person you started with.

The ideal to strive for is a character who will come to life seemingly on his own. It will no longer be the person from life outside the novel that served as a starting point, but a fictional person, who not only is there to be written about, but who, in an optimal case, writes for you. Erskine Caldwell expressed this blessed autonomy of fictional characters: "I have no influence over them. I'm only an observer, recording. The story is always being told by the characters themselves."

Not all writers give their characters autonomy and allow them to dictate what to write down. John Cheever said: "The legend that characters run away from their authors—taking up drugs, having sex operations, and becoming president—implies that the writer is a fool with no knowledge or mastery of his craft. This is absurd." Of course, Cheever believed in his method and distrusted the methods of other authors. I think it's silly when a writer assumes that his method is the method for all writers. However, it is good to learn what approaches exist, to try them all, and to see which work best for you.

But one principle about constructing characters can be stated unequivocally. Whether your characters attain autonomy or not, whether they come from you or from Greek myths, the more you get to know them, the better you will work with them. To work with a character, you might need to sketch it in several ways. You could start with this questionnaire (or make one up for yourself): Name? Age? Place of birth? Residence? Occupation? Appearance? Dress? Strengths? Weaknesses? Obsessions? Ambition? Work habits? Hobbies? Illness? Family? Parents? Kids? Siblings? Friends? Pets? Politics? Tics? Diet? Drugs? Favorite kinds of coffee, cigarettes, alcohol? Erotic history? Favorite books, movies, music? Desires? Fears? Most traumatic event? Most wonderful experience? The major struggle, past and present?

If you give quick, spontaneous answers, you might surprise yourself with the character that emerges. Don't worry if this works like a Rorschach blot, if it reveals something about you. You might do it in a silly way, have fun, and still get an idea for a character. And you might do it quite thoughtfully, in relation to your plot, if you've chosen one. (Let's say your plot involves a son who gambles away his patrimony, until he becomes a father, and then works so hard to leave his son with a patrimony that he can't spend any time with him, and his son disowns him. You must devise character traits that would make this plausible.) If you don't have a plot yet, some of the answers to these questions—particularly the last one, the character's major struggle—might give you ideas.

Once you know almost enough—you hardly ever know enough—about the character, test her out. Portray her.

PORTRAYING A CHARACTER

The way you present a character is at least as important as where you get the character. Fleshing out your characters in various ways may take up most of the story. So if you learn how to make your characters act on a stage, in your setting, you'll certainly be able to write stories. In this section, you'll find a variety of ways to portray a character.

Summary

You can tell us outright what your fictional characters are like and what they do. If you answered the questionnaire at the end of the previous section, you have a rough character summary. Link the character traits that strike you as the most important ones, and you'll have a complete character summary. Here's a classic summary from *Don Quixote* by Miguel de Cervantes:

> This gentleman, in the times when he had nothing to do—as was the case for most of the year—gave himself up to the reading of books of knight errantry; which he loved and enjoyed so much that he almost entirely forgot his hunting, and even the care of his estate.
>
> He so buried himself in his books that he spent the nights reading from twilight till daybreak and the days from dawn till dark; and so from little sleep and much reading, his brain dried up and he lost his wits.

Cervantes goes on with the summary for several pages, but I think this excerpt gives you an idea of how summary works. We find out Don Quixote's work and leisure habits, hobbies and passions, and the consequences of pursuing these—his obsession with books results in his illness, madness.

The advantage of this method is its simplicity and readability: The writer quickly focuses on the main character's conflict and supplies the background we need to know. You clearly set up expectations for what follows if you use this method in or near the beginning of your story. Unless you botch the summary, your reader will easily understand what the main character traits and conflicts are about.

The disadvantage to this method is that you are bound to tell, rather than show, what your character is like—this method makes it hard to see and hear the character. While the summary goes on, no dramatic action, no dialogue, takes place. We are waiting. Still, the character summary is often worth risking; after you orient

the reader clearly and quickly, you will not need to stall the dramatic action (in order to supply the background) once it begins to take place.

Here's another example of how summary works, from *The Sun Also Rises* by Ernest Hemingway. See how quickly we learn the character's main concerns:

> Robert Cohn was once middleweight boxing champion of Princeton. Do not think that I am very much impressed by that as a boxing title, but it meant a lot to Cohn. He cared nothing for boxing, in fact he disliked it, but he learned it painfully and thoroughly to counteract the feeling of inferiority and shyness he had felt on being treated as a Jew at Princeton. There was a certain inner comfort in knowing he could knock down anybody who was snooty to him, although, being very shy and a thoroughly nice boy, he never fought except in the gym.

This is the opening of the novel. There's no scene for us to visualize, but we receive the basic outline of the character's psychology and motivation. Later, we'll hear the character speak, see him act, but for now, we have some guiding ideas about him (and the novel), which will help us understand what follows.

If this approach strikes you as too much "telling," try to show all the information in a dramatic scene, and you'll realize that you'll need at least several pages to do it. Since the action Hemingway is concerned with is not in the past but in the dramatic present (which will follow), to go back into the past dramatically would dissipate the novel's focus. The summary gives us the relevant aspects of the past, so we can stick with the dramatic present. While it's not the most graceful method, it's certainly useful.

Repeated Action or Habit

This is the most common notion of character—the expectation of how a person will behave in a given situation, based on the observation that she has behaved like that many times, that she has the habit. This may be an effective way of describing a person when you don't have the time to go into the scenes to show us how she behaves. Here's an example from "Where Are You Going, Where Have You Been?" by Joyce Carol Oates:

> She was fifteen and she had a quick, nervous giggling habit of craning her neck to glance into mirrors or checking other people's faces to make sure her own was all right.

Now we know that in many situations the girl behaves this way. It would take an awful lot of time to show this habit dramatically. If the sole point of the scenes were to show her habit, the scenes would be a strain on the reader. Describing it in a summary will save you time. That's the advantage. The disadvantage is that doing this will delay your entry into your main dramatic scenes, where the story takes place.

Self-Portrait

The writer may let the character introduce himself to us. Again, this usually will be a summary of the basic concerns, at least in the beginning. Notice that a self-portrait can be achieved indirectly, as Hemingway's narrator does in the example of character summary from *The Sun Also Rises*. The narrator says, "Do not think that I am very much impressed by that as a boxing title, but it meant a lot to Cohn." In this sentence, we notice a certain sense of superiority, perhaps arrogance, on the part of the narrator. When he characterizes Robert Cohn as "very shy and a thoroughly nice boy," we hear the narrator's voice. Who would speak of a twenty-year-old as a "thoroughly nice boy"? We begin to make inferences about the narrator. The narrator's summary gives us an explicit portrait of Robert Cohn and an implied and indirect self-portrait. Good economy.

Here's a direct self-portrait by the narrator of *Notes From Underground* by Fyodor Dostoyevski:

> I am a sick man. ... I am a spiteful man. I am an ugly man. I believe my liver is diseased. However, I know nothing at all about my disease, and do not know for certain what ails me. I don't consult a doctor for it, and never have, though I have a respect for medicine and doctors. Besides, I am extremely superstitious, sufficiently so to respect medicine, anyway (I am well-educated enough not to be superstitious, but I am superstitious). No, I refuse to consult a doctor from spite. ... My liver is bad, well—let it get worse!

Here, the advantage over the third-person summary is that the way sentences are put together, the way of thought, is our picture of the character just as much as the content of the thoughts. The Underground Man thinks in paradoxes, spitefully, in intentional self-contradictions. He certainly prepares us for the humorous and self-destructive acts to follow, so the disadvantages of this method—that it is not dramatic and that it does not create pictures—are not significant.

Appearance

Image is not everything, but it does account for a lot. Through how a person looks, you may try to infer what the person is like; but appearances may be deceptive. Still, to suggest the person's character, you may select and interpret details, to guide the reader's expectations.

George Eliot uses this approach in the following paragraph from *Middlemarch*:

> Miss Brooke had that kind of beauty which seems to be thrown into relief by poor dress. Her hand and wrist were so finely formed that she

could wear sleeves not less bare of style than those in which the blessed Virgin appeared to Italian painters; and her profile as well as her stature and bearing seemed to gain the more dignity from her plain garments, which by the side of provincial fashion gave her the impressiveness of a fine quotation from the Bible—or from one of our elder poets—in a paragraph of today's newspaper.

Eliot draws a portrait of a Victorian lady who drives the modesty of her dress to such an extreme that we are alerted by it. Immediately after this, Eliot gives us an inkling of how to interpret the appearance: "She was usually spoken of as being remarkably clever, but with the addition that her sister Celia had more common sense." Miss Brooke is so ascetic that she creates problems for herself; she imprisons herself in a sterile marriage to a priestly scholar. Her appearance points in the direction of the key conflict of the novel.

Eliot's description works like a painting, in which the surface details suggest character and mood. Sometimes the appearance of a character can indeed attain the quality of a good drawing, a cameo, as in the following example from "Patriotism" by the Japanese writer Yukio Mishima:

> For the beauty of the bride in her white over-robe no comparisons were adequate. In the eyes, round beneath soft brows, the slender, finely shaped nose, and in the full lips, there was both sensuousness and refinement. One hand, emerging shyly from a sleeve of the over-robe, held a fan, and the tips of the fingers, clustering delicately, were like the bud of a moonflower.

Notice how in the two above examples, the authors draw the hands more successfully than the faces. While hands are often more difficult than faces to render in paintings, in writing it's the reverse, because writing can capture motion and activity better than painting can. Hands can do more than faces can—unless we are mimes, and even with mimes, hands are at least as active as faces. In describing faces, it's easy to resort to smiles and frowns, and difficult to strike a fresh image. With hands, you can play with a large array of possibilities.

You can characterize someone even by his feet or his walk, as Thomas Hardy does in *The Mayor of Casterbridge*:

> His measured, springless walk was the walk of the skilled countryman as distinct from the desultory shamble of the general labourer; while in the turn and plant of each foot there was, further, a dogged and cynical indifference personal to himself.

No matter how you describe a character's appearance, your reader must be able to see it. If you rely on an adjective and give us little besides, you will probably fail to make us visualize anything. In his novel *The Citadel*, British author A.J. Cronin makes this mistake and gives us an example of what not to do:

> Late one October afternoon in the year 1921, a shabby young man gazed with fixed intensity through the window of a third-class compartment in the almost empty train labouring up the Penowell valley from Swansea.

This is the opening line from the novel. It accomplishes a lot in terms of setting, but the adjective *shabby* adds nothing. Judging from our being in a third-class compartment, we would get the notion of shabbiness anyhow, and "shabby" does not in any way give us the look of the man. *The Citadel* is an excellent novel, and it's good to see that not everything needs to be perfect for a novel to succeed. If you don't want to describe appearance, perhaps you can get away with it—but then don't pretend that you are depicting. Scratch out the shabby.

Scene

In a scene, you set your character in motion. Especially if she's speaking, you can show us the character in action, without needing to summarize and generalize, although you may supplement the scene with a summary.

Christopher Isherwood, in "Sally Bowles," draws a character portrait in a scene with dialogue:

> "Am I terribly late, Fritz darling?"
>
> "Only half of an hour, I suppose," Fritz drawled beaming with proprietary pleasure. "May I introduce Mr. Isherwood—Miss Bowles? Mr. Isherwood is commonly known as Chris."
>
> "I'm not," I said. "Fritz is about the only person who's ever called me Chris in my life."
>
> Sally laughed. She was dressed in black silk, with a small cape over her shoulders and a little cap like a pageboy's stuck jauntily on one side of her head:
>
> "Do you mind if I use your telephone, sweet?"
>
> "Sure. Go right ahead." Fritz caught my eye. "Come into the other room, Chris."
>
> "For heaven's sake, don't leave me alone with this man!" she exclaimed. "Or he'll seduce me down the telephone. He's most terribly passionate."
>
> As she dialed the number, I noticed that her fingernails were painted emerald green, a colour unfortunately chosen, for it called attention to

her hands, which were much stained by cigarette-smoking and as dirty
as a little girl's.

Here, we meet the character through her voice, appearance, and action, as though
in a theater, and certainly, she is theatrical. She says, "He's most terribly passionate."
This string of three adjectives is a kind of sophisticated excess that achieves a theatrical sound, as though we were listening to an ironic actor. Isherwood guides us to
interpret the details, to see the little girl behind the sophisticated guise. The hands
are as dirty as a little girl's. Emerald green for fingernail paint seems gaudy and
excessive; in her attempt to appear sophisticated, she fails, but achieves a charm,
especially through her flirtatious talk: "He'll seduce me down the telephone."

The advantage of introducing a character in a scene is that we hear the character's voice and diction, and we see the person. So when the narrator analyzes
this character, he does not do it abstractly, but in conjunction with what we have
seen and experienced. The scene combines appearance, action, and dialogue; it's a
highly versatile approach. The drawback is that you can't supply the background
easily without stalling the scene.

Sometimes you can introduce a character through action, so we begin to see
her without needing much dialogue, as does Bobbie Ann Mason in "Shiloh":

> Leroy Moffitt's wife, Norma Jean, is working on her pectorals. She
> lifts three-pound dumbbells to warm up, then progresses to a twenty-
> pound barbell. Standing with her legs apart, she reminds Leroy of Won-
> der Woman.
>
> "I'd give anything if I could just get these muscles to where they're real
> hard," says Norma Jean. "Feel this arm. It's not as hard as the other one."

The advantage of this method is that the reader is immediately with you, visualizing, experiencing a scene. You can show and suggest what you could have told
us about—such as that Norma Jean is a fitness nut, a bodybuilder, a self-obsessed
person. The scene implies all this information without such a blatant interpretation, so it's less judgmental than a summary to this effect would be. (This is most
lifelike. We watch how people behave, we never see abstract qualities such as self-
obsession—we merely see the signs, symptoms, which we interpret.) The author
leaves the opportunity of judgment to the reader. Whenever you can, show character traits acted out in scenes. If you are interested in directly judging your characters, of course, rely on summaries and interpretations. (Judgment does have its
virtues—it's abstract, possibly philosophical.)

The disadvantage to the scenic characterization method is that it's awkward to
construct scenes that are outside of the main time frame of the story, unless you do
flashbacks and memories. There's a limit to how many flashbacks you can handle

without destroying the flow of the story. And there's a limit to how many things you can show, anyhow. Thus, although scenes are probably the most attractive method of characterization, you probably need to resort to summaries of relevant character deeds and inclinations outside of the story's time frame.

Combining Techniques

Most developed character descriptions combine two or more approaches. During the course of a novel, we see a character in the ways the author chooses for us. That, too, is lifelike—you hardly ever experience all the aspects of a friend right away. It takes time—different situations, communications, perceptions, and thoughts.

In Flannery O'Connor's "The Artificial Nigger," we see three approaches—habit, summary, and appearance:

> The alarm on the clock did not work but he was not dependent on any mechanical means to awaken him. Sixty years had not dulled his responses; his physical reactions, like his moral ones, were guided by his will and strong character, and these could be seen plainly in his features. He had a long tube-like face with a long rounded open jaw and a long depressed nose. His eyes were alert but quiet, and in the miraculous moonlight they had a look of composure and of ancient wisdom as if they belonged to one of the great guides of men.

"Strong character" is an abstract summary. "A long tube-like face" is a caricature, appearance. "He was not dependent on any mechanical means to awaken him" is a habit summary. These traits give us a quick synopsis of this man, which lead us into a scene, where we observe him in action:

> Mr. Head went to the stove and brought the meat to the table in the skillet. "It's no hurry," he said. "You'll get there soon enough and it's no guarantee you'll like it when you do neither."

Now we hear him talk. Later we'll see him talk and act at greater length, each time getting to know him better. O'Connor's approach is incremental.

Here's a portrait of a paranoid schizophrenic, drawn by summary of habits, appearance, and psychology. In "Ward VI," Anton Chekhov portrays the character so gently that he undermines our trust in the diagnosis of madness; later in the story, we begin to perceive Russian psychiatry as mad, so that the character is quite justified in feeling persecuted:

> Ivan Dmitrich Gromov ... is always in a state of agitation and excitement, always under the strain of some vague undefined expectation. The slightest rustle in the entry or shout in the yard is enough to make

him raise his head and listen: are they coming for him? Is it him they are looking for?

I like his broad pale face with its high cheekbones. ... His grimaces are queer and morbid, but the fine lines drawn on his face by deep and genuine suffering denote sensibility and culture, and there is a warm lucid gleam in his eyes. I like the man himself, always courteous, obliging, and extremely considerate in his treatment of everyone except Nikita. When anyone drops a button or a spoon, he leaps from his bed and picks it up.

I think this is an excellent pattern, combining not only summary and scene, but also sympathy. Chekhov treats a type, a paranoid schizophrenic, with enough sympathy that the type no longer threatens to reduce the human qualities and complexities of Ivan's character. Ivan has become a person for us.

Gustave Flaubert portrays the title character from *Madame Bovary* in a succession of different approaches. Each time we meet her, we see a different aspect of her, in a new light, and in a new approach:

[Brief silent scene:] She made no comment. But as she sewed she pricked her fingers and then put them into her mouth to suck them.

[Silent scene, habit, appearance:] As the room was chilly, she shivered a little while eating. This caused her full lips to part slightly. She had a habit of biting them when she wasn't talking.

[Psychological summary:] Accustomed to the calm life, she turned away from it toward excitement. She loved the sea only for its storms, and greenery only when it was scattered among ruins. She needed to derive immediate gratification from things and rejected as useless everything that did not supply this satisfaction. Her temperament was more sentimental than artistic. She sought emotions and not landscapes.

And later, Flaubert stages Madame Bovary, just as Isherwood does with Sally Bowles.

I recommend this pattern of multiple approaches particularly for your main characters in a novel. If your character is complex enough, you might try all the approaches you can think of to understand who you are creating. Your reader will probably get involved, too, trying to understand with you. The trick is to be genuinely curious about the people populating your fiction.

EXERCISES

1. One page. Describe a remarkable person you admire—a teacher, minister, carpenter, doctor. What makes the person unique? Avoid sentimental state-

ments (e.g., "I know Mother will always be there for me"). Can you make us see her? Hear her?

Objective: To create heroes from people you admire. Admiration for others is a writer's best friend (unlike self-admiration). As you admire a person, you naturally select traits and details that present the person in a heroic light. So you already know how to make heroes! With this capability, you are ready to become a fiction writer.

Check: Have you given us the person? If not, go back and show us your character struggling with a problem.

2. One page. Look in a mirror and describe who you see. If you have a scar, tell us briefly how you got it. If your nose is broken, recall how it happened. If you're wearing lipstick, tell us how you selected the color. Don't get carried away and begin to tell us stories—not yet. Come back to your face, mention other details, and describe them objectively.

Objective: To learn how to use bits of appearance as triggers for storytelling. Beginnings of stories are etched into many faces. The word character stems from the Greek word for "a chiseled cut, an etching, a groove."

Check: Did you give us enough detail that we could begin to draw your portrait? We don't need to complete it on the page—let it be open enough for imagination to play—but we do need to have something we can visualize.

3. One page. Describe somebody's character by the shape, posture, and gait of his body. Don't describe his head, and don't tell us that the character is lazy or happy. Show these traits through body language.

Objective: To learn how to look at evidence of character in the whole body, not just the face. The body expresses the mind. Take a look at Hardy's example on page 54. See how he builds meaning out of the man's walk. Perhaps he pushes the meaning his way—he knows what he wants us to see in the walk. Similarly, in Flaubert's example on page 58, Madame Bovary's sucking her fingers is obviously sensual. Don't be afraid to do likewise. Namely, be slightly subjective; interpret for us what we see—show us, even tell us, what psychology the body expresses.

Check: Do we see enough of the body's shape and motion? For example, if you're describing a nervous patient in a hospital, did you mention his feet wrapped around a chair's leg like the emblem of medicine?

4. Four half-page exercises. Describe somebody's hands so that we get the idea that she is (1) nervous, (2) artistic, (3) rich (or poor), and (4) ill. Describe your hands at work. Review the examples from *Middlemarch*, "Patriotism," and "Rust" in this chapter.

Objective: To broaden the range of physical details you use when describing characters. Since what you can accomplish by describing noses and eyes may be too much strain on these organs, it's good to let the whole body do the work of developing the character. Just think of the skills you have in your fingers. Pay attention to appearance and motion.

Check: Are the hands expressing impulses? Can we see all you say? Rather than saying that the hands are nervous (graceful, sensual, determined, and so on—adjectives that can rarely be visualized), do you give us a picture of a forefinger digging its bitten nail into the side of the thumb? (It's all right to say that hands are nervous, but show it, too.)

5. Eight half-page exercises. Draw—in words—portraits of four striking people. First, look into various faces to see whether any geometric shape, likeness of an animal, or other dominant trait emerges as an abstraction of the face. You can do this anywhere—on a train, in a bank line, in a bar—but don't blame me if you get a black eye in the process. Choose the most telling lines. Is there one dominant word—*le mot juste*—that could bring the lines together? Try to achieve the efficiency of a caricature artist who draws a likeness of Leonid Brezhnev by sketching his overgrown eyebrows in several strokes, and Mick Jagger by outlining his big lips.

Then portray four people by summarizing their behavior succinctly.

Objective: To learn how to select the most telling details, and how to compress behavior into a succinct summary.

Check: Have you singled out one trait in each sketch? (For example, if you've seen Senator Bob Dole on television, you've probably noticed how much he blinks—according to my study, at least fifty times per minute, on average. So you could caricature him as a blinker.) If you have five or six traits, cross out all but one.

6. Two to three pages. Create a character without relying on anybody you have known or seen. You might consult an astrological chart. (For example: The sun in Aries is supposed to be egocentric, impulsive, solitary. Make the rising sun be in Capricorn—ambitious, exhibitionistic, methodical. Do you see any conflict arising from combining the two signs?) Place this person in a social context, let's say a cocktail party, and have him exchange several lines with the hostess. Let Sally Bowles from Isherwood's example on page 55 be the hostess.

Objective: To learn how to work from an idea, rather than from a real-life precedent, in making up a character.

Check: Have we gotten a sense of what this person is like? If not, insert a telling detail—such as in Exercise 5—and then place your fictional person in a social context with dialogue (like Sally Bowles).

7. Two to three pages. Write a comic scene in which a virtuous person struggles with one secret passion and resists the temptation. For example, make a kleptomaniac minister steal a pocket watch from a needy and sick parishioner—and then return it during the prayer for her.

Objective: To learn how to go straight for the conflict as the core of a fictional character.

Check: Did you create an engaging scene? You might go back and concentrate on the minister's hands and words.

8. Two to three pages. Is there something in your past you are ashamed of? Make up a character different from you and let him deal with the conflict at the root of your shame. No doubt, you'll have a lot of energy behind this exercise; it should be easy to write, as long as you forget that you are the starting point. Dostoyevski's *Notes From Underground* is a classic story done using this technique.

After you are finished, think of something in your past you are proud of. Make this a starting point for a character different from you, and write two to three more pages describing this character's triumph.

Objective: To learn how to create characters who are different from yourself, using the fission method.

Check: Is your character alive? If not, let him move, speak, act. And let's see what he looks like. Besides giving us the general traits of the person, make the person concrete for us. Concentrate on several minute details—for instance, two red hairs sticking out of a mole, a quivering nostril, the sound of a snapping jaw, the smell of Dove soap.

9. Two pages. "Man is his desire," said Aristotle. Make a character desire something, and make the desire his driving force. Then, through a scene or a summary, create reasons why he can't have what he wants, ever. Let him try to get it at all costs anyway.

Objective: To draw a character around a flaw—an overwhelming desire—because that's the recipe for plot. Show the character persevering beyond reasonable limits.

Check: Have we gotten the sensation of desire? Make the object of desire desirable in our eyes—make us see from the character's perspective.

10. Two pages. To paraphrase Aristotle, "Man is his fear." Make a character fear something, and arrange her life as an elaborate defense mechanism. You might show the house the character lives in, the clothes she wears, the car she drives, the animals she keeps, all centered around this leitmotif. For an example on how to use setting to portray character, go back to the previous chapter and look at Gogol's miser.

Objective: To learn how to select details around a psychological theme.

Check: Did you give enough details around the character to exhibit her fright? If she's scared of bullets, let her wear a bulletproof vest in the middle of a heat wave.

11. Four half pages. Present the character from Exercise 1 in four ways, half a page each. First, make a summary of what the character is like; then show him through his looks, through a speech in a scene, and through combining several methods.

Objective: To learn how to present the same person in different ways, because that's what you might need to do in a story.

Check: Does the character appear consistent in each description? Review on page 58 how Flaubert shows Madame Bovary as sense-oriented in each example.

12. One page. Portray a personality type, giving us the person with all her complexities. Use a mixed approach—a summary, a habit portrayal, and a brief scene.

Objective: To learn how to make a round character where it's easy to slip into stereotyping. Don't feel superior to your characters—if you despise them, your reader will be tempted to do likewise with your prose. "Nothing human is alien to me," said Terentius, an ancient thinker. Whatever human beings do comes from something that you share with them—so try to step into the character's role imaginatively. Experience with the characters to understand them.

Check: Have you sympathized with your fictional character? Look at how Chekhov describes Ivan Gromov, the paranoid schizophrenic, earlier in this chapter. Chekhov's narrator even says, "I like him." If in your exercise you ridicule a type, or in any way sound aloof, rewrite it, using "I like him," and showing what you find likeable in the person.

13. One page. Base a character on the strength of refusal. How strongly a person resists a temptation is one common way of defining character; it's limited, but it can work in a piece of fiction. See how vigorously Father Sergius struggles to resist temptation (in the story beginning on page 207 of the book). Make the struggle difficult and not fixed. In the end, just as we believe that Father Sergius has won, he succumbs to temptation. But he continues to struggle—it's not over. You could combine this with a "We Didn't" kind of imaginative stimulus (this story begins on page 314). For example, in the case of an alcoholic, you could say, *he didn't* (or *I didn't*): He didn't drink scotch that evening. He didn't drink beer during the football night. He didn't finish the glass of red wine at the party, or at any rate, it was not a full glass. He at least didn't get drunk. He didn't finish the six-pack.

Objective: To create scenes with a strong struggle—not only external but also internal. A struggle that is merely external, not engaging a person's psychology, is often hollow. And a struggle that is purely internal, without any test in actual scenes, is pretty abstract. Resisting a temptation presents a dual motivation: to do it and not to do it. Some stories don't even have a single motivating force in a character, and this is a chance to luxuriate in an excess of motivation, which should give you enough dynamic force for the story.

Check: Have you presented us with both the outer action and temptation (descriptions of the object of desire), and the inner struggle (presented through thoughts and arguments, pro and con)?

4

PLOT

Plot is the plan—the design—of your story. Or, to put it less architecturally and more organically: Plot is the nervous system of your story. In the same way that nerves connect your brain and muscles so you can move and live, plot interconnects and moves the elements of your story.

Of the journalist's six questions, plot answers as many as three: what, how, and why. Plot is the key event of your story and the logic between the event and the supporting events, which serve to illuminate it. Plot establishes the causes and the consequences. Here is an example of a basic plot, taken from "The Death of Ivan Ilych" by Leo Tolstoy: "Ivan Ilych's life had been most simple and most ordinary and therefore most terrible." The connection between the daily routine and terror—ultimately, death—organizes the story.

To establish this connection, Tolstoy relies on a traditional philosophy based on causes and effects. A plotted story usually depends on the connection between causes and effects (or at least on a correlation among events) and on basic values to be treasured, such as life and love. Fyodor Dostoyevski could not have written his novel *Crime and Punishment* if his premise had been that human life is worthless, because what difference would it have made if Raskolnikov killed an old woman and got punished? Along these lines, playwright Harold Hayes said: "The essence of drama is that man cannot walk away from the consequences of his deeds."

Some modern and postmodern writers—accepting Werner Karl Heisenberg's principle of uncertainty and doubting the theories of causality and of the linearity of time—have been incapable (or unwilling) to think up plots. Many writers work around plots—doing "experimental" fiction—because, supposedly, in our nuclear society it's not easy to find coherent logic in the events around us. However, the premise of meaninglessness should not warrant experiments, since the idea of experiment is based on the logic of cause and effect (or at least, of correlation between phenomena), trial and error, and learning from these meaningfully. Why experiment otherwise? So we need not look to philosophy to defend us against our basic obligation to organize our fiction coherently. Sure, it would be nice to say that philosophers have dispensed with the dubious notions of causality and meaning; hence, we can simply pile words on the page randomly, and that'll be high art. This might be an enjoyable way to write, but not to read. Since writing is an act of communicating—or at least a simulation of communication—we do need to make our words and events link coherently.

Plot clearly depends on basic values. What do your characters treasure most? Put it at stake. Let them fight for it. Let them fight for life, love, money, jobs. If your characters care about nothing, the actions around them might become random. Without passion, forget about plot. Even Albert Camus's *The Stranger*—in which a man is sentenced to death not so much because he committed murder as because he did not cry at his mother's funeral—would not work if it did not rely on a framework of expected passion, against which the character's indifference draws meaning.

I am not saying that you must believe in meanings of life and in moral values, but your characters, at least some of them, must. Fiction is like a medieval passion play. If you take away the prospect of crucifixion, the passion, then the play is gone. And passion is why most people read novels. Could romance survive without it? How about horror? Crime? Murder mystery? No murder mystery will work without a motive, the motive usually being some kind of passion.

To summarize (at the risk of oversimplifying): Plot depends on passions—on how characters struggle to fulfill them.

ORIGINS AND TYPES OF PLOT

Since we need not wait for the new experiments and findings in literature to write well-plotted stories, let's look into the tradition of plot. The concept of plot comes to us from Aristotle's analysis of drama, particularly tragedy: "The perfect plot ... must have a single, and not (as some tell us) a double issue; the change in the hero's fortunes must be not from misery to happiness, but on the contrary from happiness to misery; and the cause of it must lie not in any depravity, but in some great error on his part; the man himself being either such as we have described, or better, not worse, than that."

So much for happy endings! Much serious fiction involves tragedy. Leo Tolstoy's *Anna Karenina* opens with "All happy families are alike, but each unhappy family is unhappy in its own way," and ends with Anna's suicide. Why should one write such depressing stuff? I think it's the nature of thought to deal with problems, with something amiss that can be—and may not be—straightened out and solved. If there are no problems, there is no thought. A mathematician without problems is idle, and so is a writer. Since most plots evolve largely from the main character's motivation, it's most efficient to place the problem in the main character, to give her the error that she must struggle to solve.

From Aristotle's idea of a person's flaw being the most efficient agent of plot (see chapter three), you see how tightly character and plot are intertwined. A person's flaw brings about problems and conflicts. Anna Karenina's falling in love outside her tedious marriage as an uncontrollable error brings her in conflict with her husband, her children, and herself—enough problems ensue to fill seven hundred pages. Working from character is perhaps the most prevalent way of evolving a plot, as it is for Norman Mailer, who said: "Generally, I don't even have a plot. What happens is that my characters engage in an action, and out of that action little bits of plot sometimes adhere to the narrative." Mailer gives his characters problems. Without a character flaw, the character can hardly be rounded and interesting, in the sense that there's nothing to worry about and solve when we deal with him. A perfect character is a dead equation, as far as fiction is concerned.

Of course, having serious problems does not mean that all will end unhappily. If the outcome were so predictable, suspense would be lost. We need not share Aristotle's Balkan predilection for tragedy. Happy endings after a serious (or a silly) struggle are possible but certainly should not be the rule—especially not in the realistic novels that span a lifetime. Life ends in death; so unhappy endings are a natural tendency in much realistic fiction. (In most fiction written from fantastic, religious, and stoical premises, there's not much tendency toward unhappy endings.)

But realistic fiction that deals with families (rather than only individuals) may naturally tend toward a happy ending. Life may end in the death of one person, but it goes on in the birth of many. So perhaps the most comprehensive paradigm of true-to-life plot could be that of Jacob and his family. When he dies, he dies happily, because eleven sturdy sons with grandsons are at his side.

How you solve your character's problems and errors, of course, should conform to no formula, except, I'd say, don't make it predictable. Make the struggle genuine and fair, with equal chances for failure and success. Although your worldview (and your characters' worldviews) will largely shape the tenor of your fiction, do respect this necessary principle of the uncertainty of outcome.

Character-Conflict Plots

There are several basic plots that are based on character conflict. The conflict most often takes place between a protagonist (the character we sympathize with and root for) and an antagonist (the protagonist's opponent). These are the plots:

Man Against Man (we should perhaps say Person Against Person, but it would sound odd, since this old list is famous in this shape)

Man Against Self

Man Against Nature

Man Against Society

Man Against Machine

Man Against God

God Against Everybody

Most fiction falls into these categories of "against"—that is, they are based on conflict. There are exceptions—for example, Ivan Turgenev's *Sketches From a Hunter's Album*, but the "sketches" can be seen as essays on hunting in the country. Even so, they are Man Against Nature (at least the hunted grouse would probably think so). If this seems depressing, try putting "for" in place of "against," and you will see that by implication there still will be an against. Man for Man could take place in the midst of a war, in which case Man would be against Society, the foreign and perhaps even the domestic army. Man for Nature might turn out to be Man Against Machine and Man Against Corporate Society.

You don't need much to make up a plot. Work from a conflict. The conflict suggests escalation of struggle into a climax—so follow the potential for a story that the conflict suggests. Once you know what happens in your story, you can organize the rest. If you have a clear conflict between two (or preferably three or more) characters, everything else will follow—even the beginning! You introduce the fight—and to make it intelligible, you introduce the fighters and the ring. Conflict may take the shape of a quarrel, a fight, or a war—depending on the magnitude of action and reaction. A quarrel that precipitates a divorce may be more important to the protagonists than the Vietnam War taking place at the same time.

Most strong conflicts—from the protagonists' point of view—resemble war. War is a useful metaphor for analyzing action in a story. In a war, there usually is a contested territory—the Golan Heights, Nagorno-Karabakh, Sarajevo Airport. If you can manage to clearly define the contested territory in a story, you will have a powerful focus, out of which the story may flow with surprising ease. For example, conservative parents may battle their liberal and impoverished daughter, who wants an abortion. Clearly, the battle is localized on the uterus of the young woman, and to write the story, we must put the family together and let them fight. In terms of the simple chart of Man Against Man, this plot would become Woman Against Society, Woman Against Woman (Daughter Against Mother), and in the long run, perhaps at the crisis point, it would boil down to Self Against Self, if the woman gets to choose. No matter what other forms a conflict assumes, in most fiction the conflict will entail Self Against Self, since the motivation that moves the struggle is usually internal, a part of the character's psyche.

Lest you think that plots are a grim business, I'd like to point out that the word origin for protagonist and antagonist comes from the Greek *agonia*, meaning "competitive play." So no matter what agony of plot you go through, it's just a game.

Nonconfrontational Plots

Slice of Life
If you still don't like any kind of *agonia*, no matter how playful, there are ways of writing nonconfrontational plots. One model is the ultrarealist (and sometimes surrealist) slice of life. Your plot is governed by the details and chores of a day—or an hour—of a character's life. You show what it's like to wake up in the character's apartment, walk down a street outside it, visit a bakery, drive to work, and chat with colleagues. All that traditionally is the periphery of the story—the realistic details—becomes the center of the story; and the various confrontations and conflicts become the periphery. "Yeah, sure, I am going to jail in a month, but that's just a vague idea of something in the future, which at the moment recedes in the steam of coffee." If you understand your world like this, that the details around you are more important than the events, this may be the type of plot—antiplot, really—for you to play with. In a story like this, scrupulous attention to setting is an absolute must.

Revelation or Epiphany
Another model for a nonconfrontational story centers around revelation or epiphany. The story comes to a moment in which the protagonist has a personal insight. James Joyce used this theological concept for his stories. Consider, for example, the ending of his story "The Dead" (see chapter two). After learning that his wife has loved someone more deeply than he has loved anybody, and while staring into the falling snow, Gabriel experiences an epiphany about his mortality. (There are confrontations in the story, but they pale once the epiphany takes place.) All the story's events accumulate toward this moment, literally, like snow, through which he now sees himself as though for the first time. (In the old paradigm of conflicts, the story sets out to be Man Against Woman, but the man realizes that the conflict is deeper than that, and for a

moment the drama centers around Self Against Self, until he realizes that even this does not suffice. The epiphany about mortality transcends conflicts.)

Revelation could take place within a struggle, but revelation may be more important than the struggle. Here's a moment of such a revelation from Mary Gaitskill's "The Girl on the Plane." A man and a woman talk. The woman confesses her alcoholism. He's attracted to her and thinks he will reveal nothing about himself, will be casual. But this is what happens:

> "And about that relationship," he went on. "That wasn't your loss. It was his." He had meant these words to sound light and playfully gallant, but they had the awful intensity of a maudlin personal confession. He reached out to gently pat her hand to reassure her that he wasn't a nut, but instead he grabbed it and held it. "If you want to talk about mistakes—shit, I raped somebody. Somebody I liked."
>
> Their gazes met in a conflagration of reaction. She was so close he could smell her sweating, but at the speed of light she was falling away, deep into herself where he couldn't follow.

The man had participated in a gang rape, and though he saw himself as an onlooker rather than a participant, this revelation emerges and startles him. It also shuts down the communication with the woman next to him. It could be seen as a Man Against Woman story, or a Man Against Self—there are elements of both—but mostly it's a story of epiphany, of revelation about oneself. The man has met himself, his past, in a new way.

Epiphany should not be confused with a trick ending. For example, if you write a story in which a young woman looks forward to getting together with a man, giving this the appearance of a date, and then, in the last line of the story, it turns out that the man is her dad—and that's the whole point—you are not making an epiphany. The main character knew it all along, and the writer chose to hide this information to surprise us later. Now, this may be charming, but it's cheap. The character must come upon some genuine discovery.

Journey

Journey, as a form of nonconfrontational plot, may combine well with epiphany. For example, Dante's *Divine Comedy* is set up as a series of journeys that lead to insights about heaven, purgatory, and hell. And a current example: Diane Johnson, in "Great Barrier Reef," sets a man and a woman, who think they may be in love, on a journey to the reef off the coast of Australia. The woman sulks throughout the journey, resentful that she is not enjoying herself, that she is stuck in a group of fat and aging Australians. When she arrives at the reef, she undergoes something close to a vision:

He was as dazzled as if we had walked on stars, and, indeed, the sun shining on the tentacles, wet petals, filling the spongy holes, made things sparkle like a strange underfoot galaxy. He appeared as a long, sandy-haired, handsome stranger, separate, unknowable. I, losing myself once more in the patterns and colors, thought of nothing, was myself as formless and uncaring as the coral, all my unruly, bad-natured passions leaching harmlessly into the sea, leaving a warm sensation of blankness and ease. ... For me, the equivalent of J.'s happiness was this sense of being cured of a poisoned spirit.

Seeing the man as distant, she realizes that they will never marry, but at the same time, the beauty of the setting calms her and gives her something that's much more essential to her than marriage—a sense of herself as a part of nature rather than apart from nature. Afterward, she behaves spontaneously and has fun.

Johnson, who took the same trip as her protagonist, said about the story: "It seems to me that the Great Barrier Reef was a good metaphor for the condition of every traveler, barred from understanding the mind and customs of other peoples and places by the ideas and emotions she brings with her."

Journey gives you a natural motion for your story, for your plot. Setting here may be even more essential than the characters, and it certainly gives you chances to paint and reveal something verging on the transcendental, as you expand the psychological limits beyond the personal.

Creation

One of the oldest types of story, the story of creation, need not be confrontational. In forming a sculpture or composing a symphony or inventing a light bulb, nothing needs to be an enemy. That's not to say there is no challenge, but it's the challenge of knowledge and skill, not of defeating someone, except one's own lack of faith.

Combination Plots

Many stories combine elements of nonconfrontational and confrontational plot. The situational story or story of predicament almost always does—in Franz Kafka's "The Metamorphosis," for example: "As Gregor Samsa awoke one morning from uneasy dreams he found himself transformed in his bed into a gigantic insect." Something strange has happened; this is not primarily a struggle of Man Against Himself or Society, though it may become that later on. The story evolves mostly as a puzzle. Aristotle said, "Wonder is the beginning of philosophy." He could have equally well said, "Wonder is the beginning of story." How do you reconcile this, a man in an insect's body? Clearly you must straighten out something here, and the stranger the predicament, the more you must do. You must give us realistic details, to begin with, so we'll accept the strangeness. The difference between how things are and how they ought to be gives you the potential, the voltage, for the energy of your story.

Here's another predicament, from Peter Taylor's "The Old Forest":

> I was already formally engaged, as we used to say, to the girl I was going to marry. But still I sometimes went out on the town with girls of a different sort. And during the very week before the date set for the wedding, in December, I was in an automobile accident at a time when one of those girls was with me. It was a calamitous thing to have happen—not the accident itself, which caused no serious injury to anyone, but the accident plus the presence of that girl.

When you read this, you wonder how this guy got into the soup he's in, and even more, how he'll get out of it. Out of this predicament, Taylor raises many questions—the story becomes a sty of Southern morals and manners. The straightening out of the initial distortion drives the story forward. Eventually some conflicts are established, but at first what's important is the wonder; and in the end, the insights and epiphanies matter more than the conflicts.

TIME SEQUENCE AND PLOT

For structuring and plotting a piece of fiction, timing is one of the most important elements. Fiction, like music, is a temporal art. How the time passes during the reading of the novel shapes the fictional experience. A symphony classically opens with an allegro, a fast movement. An andante or adagio, a slow movement (usually lyrical and thoughtful), follows, before two fast movements of varying speeds. Likewise, from the start, a piece of fiction should move quickly, and when it decelerates, it should become lyrical and thoughtful, as do many novels in quiet moments. A slow movement without lyricism and thought is untenable, as is a quick movement without an orchestrated rush of action. Vary your narrative speed, especially in long pieces. As you reach the climax, you can linger on details (and render a confrontational dialogue, if the plot warrants it)—that is, develop scenes and achieve the dramatic slow-motion effect, amid the otherwise quickly paced evolution of drama. Each story may follow its own pattern of fast and slow movements; I don't want to push any bell curves of excitement, but your story does need to reach a crescendo sooner or later. (Development of climax scenes is covered further in chapter six.)

How your story is organized depends on the sequence of events. In most cases, it's best to handle time sequences in the simplest way possible. The clearest way to deal with time is to follow an action from beginning to end. Many eighteenth- and nineteenth-century biographical novels open with the birth of a character and end in his death, and many contemporary biographical novels cover a good chunk of a character's life. (Short stories rarely can cover so much time successfully—a development taking place from a couple of minutes to a year or two seems to be the usual span of the short story.) Likewise, you can start a story with the beginning of a conflict and end with its resolution. Since this structure is often too slow, writers frequently jump into the middle of the story's conflict and work forward from there, occasionally supplying—as briefly and unobtrusively as possible—the necessary background information, without stalling the forward movement of time. (Which means, if you need to go back in time, it's usually best to summarize a past action and move on, rather than to dramatize the past action as a developed flashback and get stuck in the past for pages.)

However, you might open at the end of an action (to show the reader what the purpose of the narrative will be), and then trace the beginnings of the event in your second chapter. This is how "The Death of Ivan Ilych" works. We are introduced to the dead man in the first chapter. In the following chapters, we start with his family background, his youth, and trace his biography efficiently, toward his mishap and disease and dying. Other than the lead, the story evolves in a linear fashion, from A to Y—from the earliest event up to the death, which precedes the wake (Z). We could delineate the chronology as Z, A-Y. The Z in the beginning gives us a reason to find out the rest. This is realistic—if you've been to funerals, you immediately recognize this as a paradigm of a death story. How did he die? When? What kind of man was he?

Murder mysteries, too, have justifiably nonlinear time sequences. We start with the discovery of a body—for example, a corpse in a phone booth in a lobby of a Wall Street law firm. As the investigation moves forward, timewise, with the new events, we also move backward, timewise, learning about the dead character's life and getting clues as to who the murderer is. We reconstruct the events leading to the murder from A to Y (Z is the premise for the investigation).

Much good fiction, however, attains the quality of "one thing led to another, and before you knew it.... " This seeming inevitability, one thing leading to another, can be best attained in a clean time sequence. The thing that leads to another should precede that other. This is basic for achieving urgency and suspense. Suspense depends on the question "What will happen next?" There are exceptions, of course, such as finding out a surprising fact about the past, but this revelation works best within a steady stream of investigation moving forward.

Setting events in a straightforward time sequence may appear old-fashioned, but it can be a sophisticated discipline. When you don't want to commit yourself to knowing causes and consequences, you might still establish correlations between events—temporal and spatial sequences of what happens in your story—as though you were conducting a scientific study; without stating that A causes B, it's enough to establish that A correlates with B. For example, instead of saying that the sun causes warmth in a stone, we can say: "The sun shone on a stone, and then the stone became warm," as British philosopher David Hume said. Here, the two events—the sun shining and the stone becoming warm—are put into a temporal, rather than a causal, sequence. This method of making clear temporal relations lets the reader draw inferences and conclusions for herself. Whenever you can, out of consideration for your reader, use clean time sequences; they are easiest to follow and they speak for themselves.

HOW TO GENERATE PLOTS

The solutions for generating plots will partly overlap with what we covered in previous chapters. The primary generators of plots are character and setting—but sometimes a strange situation can give you that initial impetus. Learn from Franz Kafka's "The Metamorphosis" and Peter Taylor's "The Old Forest" (see pages 70–71) about how to create plots from predicaments. Make up a strange situation and ask, "Why and how is it possible?"

If the idea of plot still intimidates you, and if you don't come up with plots before beginning to write your novel, don't be nervous. You can still write novels. In a *Paris Review* interview, Nelson Algren said, "I've always figured the only way I could finish a book and get a plot was just to keep making it longer and longer until something happens ... you know, until it finds its own plot ... because you can't outline and then fit the thing into it. I suppose it's a slow way of working."

You are lucky if you can spontaneously outline plots, but if you can't, get them somewhere. Steal them. Shakespeare stole them from Plutarch's *Lives*. Dostoyevski plundered newspapers.

You can find plots anywhere. Here's an example: I got a plot from a Baptist tract, in which self-abuse was likened to a hawk who flies high, gradually loses altitude, and crashes. When you find the body, you see a weasel's canines lodged in the hawk's breast. Instead of losing altitude, a boy who practices self-abuse loses good posture and grows blind. To make this fable feasible, I imagined myself as a boy with a pet hawk. After I read a book about hawks, the story—that is, the related details—came out easily. Trying to imagine how a hawk limited to an attic would feel, I chose freedom as the central theme of the story. I think that theme helped me bring the basic plot outline to life, because then I could generate and organize details to express the theme. Here's an example from the story:

> Yahbo flew the length of the attic and smashed into the glass window. He fell to the floor, stood up, flew back to the opposite end of the attic, vanishing in darkness under red roof tiles; and, in a couple of minutes, he flew again, pointing his body straight to pass through the space between wood laths. He crashed down again, to the sandy floor. Slowly he stood up and hopped to the window ledge, flapping his wings, scraping them against the raw bricks of the wall. Bewildered, he stood precariously on the ledge, his beak open and uttering no sound. A white film drew over his eyes and slowly peeled back into his head, his hazel eyes widening and glowing with wrath. Perhaps he could not understand what kind of air it was which did not let you out but showed you the wonders of your emerald homeland. He faced east like a Muslim facing toward Mecca, or like a Jew toward Jerusalem; for him the glass was an invisible wall of wailing.

The idea of freedom gave me the basic motivation. The hawk wants to fly home. But he has an obstacle. I made the boy's experience the same: frustrated longing for freedom. With the theme and the motivation, I brought many details together in a unified story.

You can create a plot by using a trick. Art Corriveau used an interesting trick to write his story "With Mirrors." At night he transfers odd fragments written during the day into a shoebox. One night these fragments led to a story: "I decided to draft a story from the first three slips of paper I pulled from the box. Slip number one: 'Montreal is a weird place; write a story set there.' Slip number two was from last summer in Boston: 'What's up with the blond guy outside Park Plaza? Nods whenever you pass by. Is he a hustler or just friendly?' Slip number three: 'Write about a room in a magician's house where you disappear when you walk into it.'"

He says the story was easy to write from this setup. The story opens as follows:

> When Zastrow says he can't pay me this time but he'll teach me a few tricks instead, I tell him sorry but I left the farm too many years ago. I tell him he'd better try one of the boys a little farther up the block.

Note that his first card gives setting (actually, only mentions it); second, character; third, bits of setting, character, and plot. We have a question here: "What does this character want?" To answer it, Corriveau unleashes a magician, whom he makes gay, so that the basic motivating force of the story—want—could propel the action. The magician wants sex but can offer magic rather than money; the blond hustler wants money, and would prefer to be with women, but can't get out of his economic bondage; he "disappears" in the magician's room.

Some people use this trick of cards quite systematically. They keep one pile of cards with brief character sketches, another with brief setting sketches, and a third with brief action sketches. They draw a card from each pile, put them together, and see if a story begins to suggest itself—then they repeat this process until the cards seem right. Thus you make connections among different possibilities for setting, character, and action. How you connect these elements will make your plot. That's how imagination works: You create many permutations and select the most effective ones. This card method, even if you don't employ it physically, could liberate your imagination. Use the method's logic. Make many random connections until you can make sense of one of them. In this way, you avoid the most obvious connection—the right person at the right place at the right time doing the right thing. Many plots work best with at least one "wrong" element: the right person at the right place at the wrong time. And you can make permutations even out of this, making a "wrong" choice in any of the four places. This "wrong" might turn out to be right for the energy of your story as you try to fit it in.

Another way to find plots is to parody existing ones. Your plot becomes a variation on a theme, a completely legitimate way to compose music and certainly to write stories. For an example of a Western parody, here's a segment from Stephen Crane's "The Bride Comes to Yellow Sky":

> Potter was about to raise a finger to point the first appearance of the new home when, as they circled the corner, they came face to face with a man in a maroon-colored shirt who was feverishly pushing cartridges into a large revolver. Upon the instant the man dropped this revolver to the ground, and, like lightning, whipped another from its holster. The second weapon was aimed at the bridegroom's chest. ...
>
> The two men faced each other at a distance of three paces. He of the revolver smiled with a new and quiet ferocity. "Tried to sneak up on me," he said. "Tried to sneak up on me! ... The time has come for me to settle with you, and I'm goin' to do it my own way and loaf

along with no interferin'. So if you don't want a gun bent on you, just mind what I tell you."

Potter looked at his enemy. "I ain't got a gun on me, Scratchy," he said. "Honest, I ain't. ... You know I fight when it comes to fighting, Scratchy Wilson, but I ain't got a gun on me. You'll have to do all the shootin' yourself."

His enemy's face went livid. He stepped forward and lashed his weapon to and fro before Potter's chest. "Don't you tell me you ain't got no gun on you, you whelp. Don't tell me no lie like that. There ain't a man in Texas ever seen you without no gun. Don't take me for no kid." His eyes blazed with light, and his throat worked like a pump.

"I ain't takin' you for no kid," answered Potter. His heels had not moved an inch backward. "I'm takin' you for a—fool. I tell you I ain't got a gun, and I ain't. If you're goin' to shoot me up, you better begin now. You'll never get a chance like this again."

So much enforced reasoning had told on Wilson's rage. He was calmer. "If you ain't got a gun, why ain't you got a gun?" he sneered, "Been to Sunday-school?"

"I ain't got a gun because I've just come from San Anton' with my wife. I'm married," said Potter.

"Married!" said Scratchy, not at all comprehending.

"Yes, married. I'm married," said Potter distinctly.

"Married?" said Scratchy. Seemingly for the first time he saw the drooping drowning woman at the other man's side. "No!" he said. He was like a creature allowed a glimpse of another world. He moved a pace backward, and his arm with the revolver dropped to his side.

Crane clearly parodies the conventions of Westerns—the sheriff and his antagonist, tough talk, gun drawing, and so on. Though the story is comic, Crane manages to make it serious, too, by introducing a complication. The sheriff has gotten married. You can parody any type of genre story, and throw in a new element. While you have fun playing with the genre, poking a bit of fun at it, you might still make it a serious story, as Crane does. The marriage "deconstructs" the stereotypical Western situation. Stripped of the predictable model, Scratchy is at a loss, out of genre, and you can sympathize with him.

Almost anything is worth trying out in constructing a plot. A friend of mine is writing a series of stories based on television commercials. Some things will work, others won't. Experiment. Sketch many preliminary drafts for your fiction, and use the ones that promise to work. Only a few ideas need to work to keep you busy for a year or longer. One way of testing whether an idea for a story (or a novel) will work is to begin with a big moment—a crisis scene—and decide whether or not your characters can carry on a good fight and an engaging conversation.

PLOT AS GUIDE FOR THE FINAL DRAFT

For some writers, the notion of plot is more important in revising a story than in drafting it. Plot demands that all the parts of your story are coherent in relation to the main event. This is the Chekhov's-gun principle: If you display a gun in the first act, you'd better use it before the curtain falls. (Of course, sometimes you may use a gun for atmospheric purposes, such as when you portray a police station or a Western town. But if you continually display a gun, it must figure in a key event; otherwise, it will count as a loose end—and loose ends do not advance the action.)

So go through your story and make sure that whatever objects you display prominently serve their purpose. Let these objects appear again, to connect the earlier scene with the later ones, or use your guns in an action. The same holds true for characters: If you introduce one in the beginning, presumably she'll reappear later and play a role. You may use characters as a part of the setting and for no other purpose, especially in travel stories, but that can lead to a loose structure. Novels have more room for such luxurious usage of objects and characters, but even there it's healthy to put your players to the best use.

NOVEL PLOT VS. SHORT-STORY PLOT

There's no strict border between the short story and the novel, though it's safe to say that a manuscript longer than two hundred double-spaced pages is a novel. A manuscript shorter than fifty pages is a short story. Whatever falls in between could be called a novella, although many people prefer to call a manuscript between fifty and a hundred pages a novelette.

Novel comes from Italian for "the news." *Novella*, "little news." *Novelette*, "tiny news." I think it's useful to keep in mind the etymology of these words. When you write a novel, inform us, tell us as though reporting the news. Offer big news, with many complexities, witnesses, participants. For a novelette, perhaps gossip is a good enough model.

Story comes from the Greek word for "history" (*historia*), meaning both "story" and "investigation," and later from French *histoire*, "an account of an event." These words might remind us that a short story is best told as an event thoroughly investigated and accounted for. The short story invites concentration on a singular event and its background; a novel disperses attention to a series of events, in the way, for example, that war reporting does, when it searches for an overarching coherence. (There are many exceptions, so it's not crucial that you follow this plan.)

The magnitude and number of events can determine the length, and therefore the category, of your story. A short story can be constructed around a moment of revelation, around a singular event, around one character. For novels we usually need several events and several characters, and frequently several turning points and revelations.

Still, there is no simple rule here. Some short stories have plots that could be used in novels. Thomas Mann wrote the short story "Felix Krull"—which outlined the life of a man—and then made a novel out of it. This is a biographical plot—it follows a good part of a man's life starting from childhood. That Mann chose to span a long time helped him to make a long piece of writing. On the other hand, James Joyce's long novel *Ulysses* simulates a man's perceptions during a single day. Joyce stretches the story through his investigation of how the mind works—he covers free associations, daydreams, memories; all the minor actions of a day take on the proportion of significant events.

The idea of writing a novel may be terrifying and inhibiting. It was for me. So I tricked myself into believing that I was writing short stories rather than a novel. I made each chapter of the novel into a short story. I linked the short stories through setting and characters and overarching events. Once I had enough for half the novel, I no longer feared the size of the form. In fact, I used the notion of the novel to liberate me from another anxiety. In a short story, most elements must connect—you mustn't have obvious loose ends. In a novel, you need not worry about this as much. Ideally, you should connect the narrative elements, but since nobody can remember all the details, flaws in their interconnectedness will not be held against you. (And when you make connections in a novel, you'll get credit for the endurance of your own attention span.) So, once I accepted that I was writing a novel, I could allow my chapters loose ends and plan to connect them several hundred pages later (accumulating perhaps a tension of expectations regarding whether the connections would take place). If I forgot to connect everything, the reader would probably forget to worry about it, too, as long as I made most of the connections. I did not need to write perfect endings (the hardest part of the short story) in the sense that everything would fit neatly. Not having to worry about perfect coherence—because there's hardly ever such a thing—made writing the novel easier for me than writing short stories. Of course, you still must integrate a great many details. I guess what makes it easier in the novel is that you have more time and more opportunities to do so.

Still, many short story writers ask, "How do you make a narrative that long?" "Well," I ask, "how do children grow? They eat many slices of bread." A novel routinely eats many slices of life to fatten up and grow longer, but more important, to make us as readers get to know the characters, settings, and plots, as well as the unsummarizable aspect of plots—the intricacies of perceptions and motivations.

PLOT VS. PLOT OUTLINE

I have used the word *plot* in the broad sense, to mean a story plan. But some writers think that plot cannot be separated from the story and still be plot. To use the example of the nervous system, with which we began this chapter, you can't have nerves functioning outside the body. Notice how Vladimir Nabokov plays with the notion of separateness of plot in *Laughter in the Dark*:

> Once upon a time there lived in Berlin, Germany, a man called Abinus. He was rich, respectable, happy; one day he abandoned his wife for the sake of a youthful mistress; he loved; was not loved; and his life ended as disaster.
>
> This is the whole of the story and we might have left it at that had there not been profit and pleasure in the telling.

Nabokov uses a gambit opening: He shows us the plot right away, giving up suspense that might come from one aspect of plot, that is, from the uncertainty as to what will happen. Yet, the novel is as suspenseful as a thriller. Perhaps Nabokov wanted to show that the plot is not the driving force of a story. In this summary of the novel, however, Nabokov does not give us the full plot. We have one explanation: The man left his wife because of a young mistress. As I read I knew what would happen, and why it would, but I did not know how—and the drama took place mostly in the how, in the details of seduction and deception, which Nabokov handles with marvelous descriptive skill. Nor did I know fully why the man would leave his wife for a younger mistress. Many men fall in love with a younger mistress yet do not leave their wives. To give all the psychological motivation, which causes action, you must show the man's way of thinking, feeling, perceiving—through details. And exploring the motivation takes much more than a paragraph, probably most of the novel. Plot and story are not two separate entities. Nabokov shows that plot cannot be properly summarized and still be plot; it becomes a plot outline.

I used to find myself in this predicament: I have a plot, I write it down, and then I say, "So what?" The story has not come to life; I failed to generate the details, the scenes. I thought too much in terms of plot outline rather than in terms of character and place and event. Sometimes students ask me, "What do you think of this story?" And they proceed to tell me a plot outline. I tell them I'd be able to say what I thought only after I read the plot outline developed in a drafted story. The plot outline is like a game plan in basketball or football. It can look good on a chart, but once the ball flies, it does not suffice. You must have the players. If a player trips, other players may have to come up with a new plan. The plan is not sacred; it shifts, depending on the position of the players on the field and on the flight of the ball in the wind.

Although plot outline is not the same as plot, it's good to have a guide as you go through all the story details. Image-making is a forest in which you can easily get lost unless you have a map and compass—an outline. Some people don't work from outlines, yet they conceive plots because they have interconnected their characters, places, and events.

If you don't write from an outline, once you have finished a story, you still should be able to see its outline, the way after a touchdown it's easy to draw a chart of what happened in the play. Something must happen, and in the end, we must know why it has happened. Plot is partly what you discover in the writing of a story, not what you insert. You raise questions and seek answers, connect your sentences into paragraphs, paragraphs into chapters, chapters into novels. This thread of investigation may be a thin one, but you must have it to give yourself and your reader something to look for.

Keep in mind that though you may write happily without a plot, the reader may not enjoy reading a plotless story.

EXERCISES

1. Two to three pages. Outline a story from the example on pages 67–68 of the parents who don't want their pregnant teenage daughter to have an abortion. Briefly sketch the daughter first, then her parents. Out of the conflict, brainstorm several possibilities, and select three possible outcomes. For example, this conflict could become a Woman Against Society plot, Woman Against Woman (mother), or Woman Against Self. If you continue to write the story, you will, of course, narrow the selection to one outcome, but it still may contain the three lines of conflict.

Objective: To practice exploring the possibilities of a conflict. From one basic conflict, you can derive several plots. Recognize your best possible plot from the sketches.

Check: Did you let the plot work as cause and effect? Characters and their conflicting desires are the cause. Have you found the right effects? Do your outcomes follow smoothly and reasonably from the characters in the conflict?

2. No more than three pages. Imagine a strange situation that begs to be explained. Instead of explaining it, plot a story about it. For example, an investment banker—before making a deal that would earn him two million dollars in

commissions—cancels his engagement to a supermodel, joins a Benedictine monastery, and takes a vow of poverty, chastity, and obedience. The story would investigate why the banker made this decision.

Objective: To learn how to work from wonder. Make your stories puzzles, more for yourself than for your reader. This will make you ask the most relevant questions related to the plot: Why? How?

Check: Have you offered a plausible solution to the puzzle? Have you given your protagonist sufficient motivation for his actions? "He just felt like doing it!" won't do, since it does not offer a genuine explanation. Let's first learn how to write a coherently plotted story; arbitrariness is easy—no need to learn how to do it. But to make connections among different events, so they work like logical arguments, requires thought and trial and error.

3. Three pages. "Ivan Ilych's life had been most simple and most ordinary and therefore most terrible." Using this summary statement from Tolstoy's "The Death of Ivan Ilych" as a model, but using a different character, in an American town, write the crisis point of the story, a scene in which your character discovers that he's ill.

Objective: To learn how to make connections between one part of a story and another—somebody's lifestyle and its consequences.

Check: In Tolstoy's story, because Ilych leads an empty life, he pays attention to surface details too much. He fusses around the house so much, making sure the furniture looks perfect, that he trips and injures his kidneys—it turns out, fatally. Does your scene have a similar connection between the lifestyle and illness so that the illness is not a pure accident but a consequence?

4. Two to three pages. Write a parody of a Western story climax, preferably a duel. Take a look at what Stephen Crane does in "The Bride Comes to Yellow Sky." Recall the plot of a Western story or movie and parody it. Exaggerate and make fun of the elements.

Objective: To practice writing parodies. When we write, sometimes we subconsciously imitate and parody the forms of stories we are familiar with. There's nothing wrong with that, but for a change, do it consciously. This way, you gain distance and an overview of what the genre is about. And this also can become a conscious technique for irony. Some of the best literature has been written this way. Cervantes wrote *Don Quixote* as a parody of chivalric lore.

Check: Did you include enough elements of a traditional Western? Have you added an untraditional element, as Crane does with the wedding?

5. Two to three pages. Recall the plot of the last romance novel you read. (If you don't read romances, use a murder mystery.) Outline it. Is the plot novelistic?

How many important events occur, how many characters are involved, how much time elapses? Could the novel be reduced to a short story? Try to write the climax of the story, parodying the original, and introducing an untraditional element.

Objective: Same as in Exercise 4.

Check: Similar to Exercise 4. Make sure you've used enough traditional elements of the genre.

6. Three pages. Plot three variations of a realistic short story, one page each, starting with a character's conflict in a setting. From the same conflict, think up three different resolutions. In each case, make an honest effort to create a good story outline.

Objective: To learn how to express what happens in a story succinctly and simply. Something must happen in the story, and it must be clear. If you start with a character, make the character want something that makes sense given the setting. Frustrate the desire, and see where you can go from there to satisfy it. For example, Nikolai Gogol's "Overcoat" opens with a clerk's wanting a warm coat because a St. Petersburg winter is approaching and his old coat is falling apart. The character's desires work with the setting.

Check: Have you set up the conflict clearly? Do we know why your character wants whatever he wants, and does this make sense in the setting you've chosen? Is it clear what results could evolve from this conflict? Now read what you've done and choose the best outline. (Could you write a full story from this? Try when you have enough time, outside of this course.)

7. Four pages. Outline the plots of two of your favorite novels and two of your favorite short stories, centered around the traditional scheme of conflicts (Woman Against Woman, Woman Against Society, and so on).

Objective: To learn how to summarize the plots of the stories you write, or are about to write. Learning how to summarize the plots of novels you've read may make this easier. You may change the summary once you're into the story, but it's certainly good to have some kind of plan.

Check: In each story summary, did you explain why the main event happens? For each novel summary, did you have at least three major characters and three major events? (Some novels have fewer than three characters, but these are exceptions.) What are the main conflicts in the novels?

8. Three pages. Write a journey story that climaxes in a life-altering insight. Recall a journey you've taken and use yourself as your fictional persona. Make the story autobiographical and topographical. If you haven't experienced a big realization on a journey, don't worry—take any important insight you've had elsewhere and make it come to you at the end of the journey.

Objective: To experience the journey-story form. Paint with your words, and make the sights correspond to thoughts.

Check: As you read, did you get a feeling you were traveling? Make sure you haven't simply relied on unexpressed memory and its associations so that it would be you alone who would get that feeling. Have you communicated it to us by engaging our senses and thoughts? When the big insight comes, does the landscape change from ordinary to extraordinary? See how Diane Johnson, in "Great Barrier Reef," makes stars out of starfish.

9. Look up the character and setting sketches you did in the previous chapters. Summarize the best sketches and write them down on blank index cards. Summarize the plot outlines from above. Mix the cards the way Art Corriveau did, until you find a workable combination. Be playful. You need not know the whole action in advance.

Objective: To learn how to enhance your imagination. Imagination is simply the ability to make strange connections seem plausible.

Check: Have you integrated the action with the characters into the locales? In your scene, do we see bits of the setting and characters? Do we get a feel for what the people are like?

10. Three to four pages. Continue this story (from "An Occurrence at Owl Creek Bridge" by Ambrose Bierce):

> A man stood upon a railroad bridge in northern Alabama,
> looking down into the swift water twenty feet below. The
> man's hands were behind his back, the wrists bound with a
> cord. A rope closely encircled his neck. It was attached to
> a stout cross-timber above his neck.

Tell us how and why the man got into this predicament, and where, if anywhere, he goes from here.

Objective: To work from a strange situation. Learn how to jump into the story right at its crisis moment and work from there—forward, backward, whichever way you see fit to explain what's going on.

Check: Does your story make sense? Have you convinced us that a real man—with realistic thoughts, feelings, perceptions—is there?

11. Three pages. Steal this plot from Herodotus's *The Histories*: Croesus, the king of Lydia, thought that he was the most fortunate man on earth. He heard that a powerful kingdom, Persia, was expanding from the East, under its ambitious king, Cyrus. Croesus asked an oracle whether he should advance his forces against Persia and got an answer that if he did so, he would destroy a powerful

empire. So he attacked. But it was his empire he thus destroyed. Here's a scene immediately after the defeat:

> Cyrus chained Croesus and placed him with fourteen Lydian boys on a great pyre. ... Croesus remembered with what divine truth Solon had declared that no man could be called happy until he was dead. Till then Croesus had not uttered a sound; but when he remembered, he sighed bitterly and three times, in anguish of spirit, pronounced Solon's name.
>
> Cyrus heard the name and told his interpreters to ask who Solon was. ... Croesus related how Solon the Athenian once came to Sardis, and made light of the splendour which he saw there, and how everything he said had proved true, and not only for him but for all men and especially for those who imagined themselves fortunate. ...
>
> While Croesus was speaking, the fire had been lit and was already burning round the edges. ... The story touched Cyrus. He himself was a mortal man and was burning alive another who had once been as prosperous as he.

Now, write this story in more detail. You might go back in time and construct a one-page scene in which Solon laughs at Croesus's wealth, and Croesus is tempted to punish Solon. Then, write a page in which something terrible happens to Croesus after Solon's departure. (In Herodotus's story, Croesus adopts an exiled nobleman, and the nobleman kills Croesus's son by accident in a hunt.) Next, write a page that would immediately follow the text above. Don't worry if your details aren't quite authentic for ancient Asia Minor. (If you like the story and want to adopt it, you might research in history books to make sure that your details are authentic.) Make Croesus and Solon communicate in simple English. Plunge into the story imaginatively. (Don't be discouraged if the writing turns out to be slow and difficult. It often does!)

If you don't like Herodotus's story, find some incident in a history book that intrigues you, and begin a three-page story from that.

Objective: To learn how to borrow plots. Having a plot (plot outline) may not be enough. Give life to the story by bringing in your interpretations, themes, and insights into people's motivations. Learn how to project your imagination into a different place and time and make it come to life.

Check: Do your pages sound like excerpts from a story? I mean, have you gone beyond the summary, so that you bring us into the story with details and dialogue? Have you lingered on motions, descriptions, thoughts? If you answer most of these questions with a no, go back and rewrite according to the criteria I've given you.

12. Three pages. Modernize the plot you used in the previous exercise. Instead of two kings, have two investment bankers—or two military officers, one American, the other Vietnamese—go through something similar.

Objective: To learn not only how to steal but how to transplant and transform plots so they suit you. Adopt them, make outlandish plots land in your culture. For example, Jane Smiley adapted the plot of *King Lear* for *A Thousand Acres*, a novel set on an Iowa farm.

Check: Same as in Exercise 11.

13. Four pages. Take a character, a place, and a time, and write three one-page plot outlines of potential stories. In the first case, place the right person at the right place at the wrong time. In the second, the right person at the right time at the wrong place. In the third, the right time, right place, wrong person. In the end, choose the outline that promises to become the best story, and write one page, plunging into the main action in detail (even with dialogue, perhaps, if you construct a scene that warrants it), testing whether there's life in this for your imagination.

Objective: To learn how to make outline permutations out of several basic elements for a story, and to put the best story outline into practice to see whether it will work.

Check: In your outlines, do you have clear conflicts? Are they realistic? Can you make them plausible?

14. Three to four pages. Can you plot a murder mystery? Choose the murderer, the victim, and the motive for the murder. Outline first how the murder happened, and then how the investigation will proceed and who'll conduct it. Let the investigator have her motives—not simply solving the mystery. Then parallel these two plots. Open with finding the body. Keep the investigation going forward, following some wrong clues and some right ones, until the resolution occurs.

Objective: To outline a piece of fiction with a dual time motion—one current, another past—until the two meet.

Check: Does your plot make sense? Is it plausible? If not, how could you make it plausible? Different motives?

15. Two to three pages. Take "We Didn't" by Stuart Dybek as a paradigm. Start with something that a character wants but can't quite get—for example, fame. Just imagine a writer who publishes a story, and is almost well known, and then he publishes a novel, and thinks he is well known, except nobody recognizes his name on the plane, on the bus, and in the street.

Objective: To stimulate your imagination with the alternatives to the factual events. Sometimes it's easier to think of what didn't happen.

Check: Are you visualizing in detail the events that didn't happen, and in the meanwhile telling us something that did, constructing an event? You can see how sensory the details are in "We Didn't." The details help you visualize and get into the scenes; they are the chemistry and alchemy of imagination.

16. Three to five pages. One of the most frequently asked questions relating to the plot is "What is the story about?" The theme of the story is essential. So work from a theme. We could have had a whole chapter on the issue of theme. However, there's a danger in thinking too much about what the story is about, as we might begin to interpret the story before it's even there. Theme is a useful concept, however, to clarify a story lacking clarity. While most stories spring out of character and event—something happened, and let me tell you how—some spring out of a theme. The assignment for this exercise is to write a story starting with a theme. You can look in the back and read "Father Sergius," which has a clear theme: struggle with temptation, with lust. Or "The Blue Hotel"—fear of strangers. There are, of course, other issues in these stories, but it's easy to find the dominant theme. So find a theme and write a few pages creating scenes centered around the theme. For example, greed, that very American emotion. Well, the whole world suffers from it, but the American MBA programs have sanctified it.

Objective: To test whether this method might work for you to generate fiction.

Check: Read your pages. Is the theme there? Is it clear what the scenes are about? If the story turns out to be about something else, but it's energetic and it interests you, what the heck—that could be great, too; you are generating fiction. Sometimes an overt theme reveals another theme, anyhow, in a different layer.

5

POINT OF VIEW

Where does the story come from? Who is telling it? To answer these questions, writers use the point of view (POV)—the vantage point(s) from which the story is observed. News stories are filled with *he said, she said, according to,* and other indicators of information sources. Fiction is hardly under less obligation, even though the sources are invented. The fictional source of information corresponds to the POV.

FIRST-PERSON POV

The most natural POV is the first-person singular, since all stories and trials originate with someone, an "I," witnessing what happens. All other POVs spring from this mother of all POVs.

Here is an example of the first-person POV from "Sister Imelda" by Irish writer Edna O'Brien:

> I had met Sister Imelda outside of class a few times and I felt that
> there was an attachment between us. Once it was in the grounds,
> when she did a reckless thing. She broke off a chrysanthemum and
> offered it to me to smell.

The telling of a story usually occurs after the events; in the above example it comes years later. Although the "I" character was a schoolchild, the narrative first person is not, and therefore tells the story in an adult's language. We must distinguish between the author and the narrator (between Edna O'Brien and the first-person adult narrator), and between the narrator (the adult looking back) and the character (the child).

The first-person character and the first-person narrator can appear to be one and the same, as in Mark Twain's *Huckleberry Finn*:

> Miss Watson she took me in the closet and prayed, but nothing
> come of it. She told me to pray every day, and whatever I asked for

I would get it. But it warn't so. I tried it. Once I got a-fish-line, but no hooks.

Huck Finn the narrator sounds the same as Huck Finn the boy, and the novel sounds like something spoken. Mark Twain invented the child's voice as his narrative means of perception for his fiction. But Mark Twain is not Huck Finn. The first-person POV in fiction does not represent the author. The first person is a persona; *persona*, as discussed in chapter two, means "mask." This POV should be different from you; he should be free to have his own religion, politics, aesthetics, that may, but need not, coincide with yours. You as the author should not be blamed for what your persona does. If your persona is a serial killer, nobody should assume that you are a serial killer. If your fictional "I" performs acts of kindness surpassing Mother Teresa's, this will not qualify you for the Nobel Peace Prize. E.L. Doctorow said that "a novelist is a person who can live in other people's skins." Writing in the first person helps you identify and empathize with characters who are very different from you.

This does not mean that you can't write about your essential concerns. On the contrary, now that you have a persona, a mask, you can bring out your demons and angels. As we discussed earlier, fiction is a carnival; behind your mask you can express yourself much more freely.

When the first-person protagonist is really you and the events in the story are taken directly from your experience, you are probably writing an essay, or autobiographical fiction (which sounds like—and to some extent is—a contradiction in terms). Of course, you can cross the boundary between fiction and nonfiction. There are no German shepherds and barbed wires, no Berlin Wall, between the two branches of writing. The Berlin Wall has collapsed in many ways. But make sure that this collapsed wall expands your world, rather than shrinks it.

The first-person narrator can tell a story with herself as a central character, or she can be one of the minor characters. Or she can tell somebody else's story, barely mentioning herself except to show where the information comes from. Some literati argue, however, that the carrier of the first-person POV must always be a central character. Ostensibly we may follow and observe somebody else, but it's the story carrier's epiphanies and insights that matter to us most because we have identified with her vision. This may not always be true, but if your first-person POV carrier is an observer of somebody else's action, your reader will ask, "And what about this guy watching all this? Isn't he responsible, too?" Gear your narrative, then, to answer these questions, no matter how subtly.

First-Person Multiple POV

In this variation of the traditional, first-person approach, you use several first-person narrators and alternate among them, usually beginning a new chapter with each change of narrator. This strategy offers a diversity of voices, viewpoints, and ways of thinking. It allows you to convey just as much as through an omniscient narrator, without the arrogance of the omniscient sound and with the advantage of diverse voices.

Since the same event means different things to different participants and observers, the event can be presented richly, without an artificial extrapolation of what actually happened. Let the reader jump to conclusions and form an objective picture. William Faulkner explained his reasons for using this narrative strategy in *The Sound and the Fury*:

> I tried to tell it again, the same story through the eyes of another brother. That was still not it. I told it for the third time through the eyes of the third brother. That was still not it. I tried to gather the pieces together and fill in the gaps by making myself the spokesman. It was still not complete. ... I never could tell it right, though I tried hard and would like to try again, though I'd probably fail again.

For short pieces, too, first-person multiple POV may be a fine way to write, especially in a story centered around a sharp conflict. Still, since a short story must establish a focus quickly and maintain the focus, jumping POVs might disrupt its flow.

Epistolary Fiction

Letters are almost always written in the first person. Many novels—especially in the nineteenth century, such as Johann Wolfgang von Goethe's *The Sorrows of Young Werther*—have been epistolary, or written in the form of correspondence. We as readers become voyeurs prying into these personal revelations.

The advantage of writing letters is that you can visualize a correspondent and aim your voice at him as your audience. This might be a good model for any POV. Rather than writing for posterity and a national audience, find one trustworthy ear to talk to. John Steinbeck, author of *The Grapes of Wrath*, said: "Your audience is one single reader. I have found that sometimes it helps to pick out one person—a real person you know, or an imagined person—and write to that one."

Akin to epistolary fiction, the diary form also uses the first-person POV. The narrator writes to come to grips with an event and perhaps to keep it preserved for memory. The advantage here is that you may get rid of all self-consciousness and establish a frank voice.

Nowadays, fewer people write personal letters, so the epistolary novel is not a frequently used form. But a similar means-of-communication form has sprung up, the phone novel, which has the appearance of a telephone conversation transcript—Nicholson Baker's *Vox* and parts of Evelyn Waugh's *A Handful of Dust* use this approach. This is an objective—or theatrical—POV, since we as readers get the experience of being an audience, listening to conversations.

First-Person Narrator's Reliability

Philosophically, the first-person POV is the least problematic: The narrator has seen something, and now tells us about it.

However, when the source of information is singular, there are no checks for the truth of what's said. We can wonder if the reporter is telling the truth. (Of course, in fiction, nothing is reliable, but we strive to appear reliable.) We find the simplest paradigm of the unreliable narrator in the sour-grapes fable: The speaker says that he did not want the grapes anyway, they were too green, when it's clear that he wanted but could not get them.

Here's an example of a self-conscious unreliable narrator, from Fyodor Dostoyevski's *Notes From Underground*:

> I was lying when I said just now that I was a spiteful official. I was lying out of spite. I was simply amusing myself with the petitioners and with the officer, and in reality I never could become spiteful. I was conscious every moment in myself of many, very many elements absolutely opposite to that.

What can you believe here? Reconstructing the true motives beneath the surface presented by the narrator is a part of the pleasure of reading an unreliable narrator. The narrative becomes a study of a split personality, a hypocrite, or a liar. Since quite a few people fall into these categories—we probably all do, at least now and then—this narrative strategy is often the perfect choice for a story.

Pros and Cons for First-Person POV

The first-person POV offers advantages and disadvantages that you should be aware of before using it in your fiction. The advantages include the following:

1. It's technically the least ambiguous. The reader always knows who is seeing and interpreting the narrative action. No artificial objective knowledge is assumed. If the first person makes faulty inferences, the reader will accept them as part of the narrator's unreliability.

2. In our era, subjectivity—even in the sciences—seems to be the prevalent mode, so we need an option for telling a story subjectively, and first-person POV certainly gives you that option.

3. In first person, you can choose a voice most freely. While third-person narrative basically restricts you to standard English, in the first person you may use slang, bad grammar, and everyday language to arrive at an authentic narrative voice.

4. First person offers smooth access to a character's thoughts. You don't have to worry about awkward switches in pronouns, like "He opened the door and thought, *I better thaw the chicken.*"

Here are the disadvantages to the first-person POV for you to consider:

1. We can't take an outside look at our carrier of POV, unless we place a mirror somewhere, and mirrors have been overused in fiction. Avoid them unless you find no other solution. (Compensate for the inability to look directly at your character by reporting her thoughts about her appearance.)

2. From the first-person POV, faithful reproductions of diverse dialogues may be implausible. Your first person may appear to be a theatrical genius with an amazing ear. On the other hand, to render almost every dialogue in one or two voices may be monotonous. Generally, it's better to err toward the interesting side—good reproduction of dialogue.

3. That an "I" tells the story implies that the "I" is still alive. Thus, one source of possible suspense—whether the character will survive—vanishes in the first-person POV.

4. It's hard to create a compelling new voice for each story. Many productive short story writers find it easier to write in the third person because they don't have to invent voices so frequently. Once you create a strong voice, you might want to stick with it for a series of short stories or a short novel.

THIRD-PERSON POV

In third-person POV, the writer uses *he*, *she*, or *they* rather than the first-person *I*. After choosing third person, the writer must then select which type of third-person strategy best fits the piece of fiction.

Third-Person Omniscient POV

In this POV, which is used infrequently in contemporary writing, the narrator knows everything about all the characters, places, and events involved. Since not everything can be presented simultaneously, the author jumps from inside one head to inside another. We observe from many angles. The "camera" is conveniently set wherever the action is, so coverage of the story is akin to television coverage of a basketball game.

In the example below, from *Middlemarch*, which is mostly in third-person omniscient POV, George Eliot frequently makes comments in the first person, taking a panoramic view of the narrative, sweeping through history, philosophy, and individual minds:

> At present I have to make the new settler Lydgate better known to anyone interested in him than he could possibly be even to those who had seen the most of him since his arrival in Middlemarch.
>
> Lydgate's spots of commonness lay in the complexion of his prejudices, which, in spite of noble intention and sympathy, were half of them such as are found in ordinary men of the world: that distinction of mind which belonged to his intellectual ardour did not penetrate his feeling and judgement about furniture or women or the desirability of its being known (without his telling) that he was better born than other country surgeons.

As you can see, the narrator seems to knows everything. She can tell us more about a settler than anybody, including himself. She tells us about human nature; she makes no bones about this being an artificial narrative. She intrudes on the exposition of the narrative, saying what she plans to do with it. Intrude may not be the right word, though, in the omniscient narrative, since the reader is invited to share the omniscience and is given the credit of being constantly aware of the novel's artificiality.

Here's a contemporary omniscient narrative, from *Einstein's Dreams* by Alan Lightman:

> At some time in the past, scientists discovered that time flows more slowly the farther from the center of earth. ... Once the phenomenon was known, a few people, anxious to stay young, moved to the mountains. ... People most eager to live longest have built their houses on the highest stilts. Indeed, some houses rise half a mile high on their spindly wooden legs. Height has become status. When a person from his kitchen window must look up to see a neighbor, he believes the neighbor will not become stiff in the joints as soon as he, will not lose his hair until later, will not wrinkle until later, will not lose the urge for romance as early. ... Some boast that they have lived their whole lives high up, that they were born in the highest house on the highest

mountain peak and have never descended. They celebrate their youth in the mirrors and walk naked on their balconies.

The narrative here does not enter into specific people's heads. The narrative voice knows everything—science, customs—but the author does not ostensibly jump in to tell you about his stance. Jumping into the minds of two or more people and showing their thoughts is the standard feature of most omniscient writing. Here's an example from "August 2002: Night Meeting" by Ray Bradbury:

> "Good lord, what a dream that was," sighed Tomas, his hands on the wheel, thinking of the rockets, the women, the raw whiskey, the Virginia reels, the party.
>
> How strange a vision was that, thought the Martian, rushing on, thinking of the festival, the canals, the boats, the women with golden eyes, and the songs.

Properly speaking, most omniscient narratives have the nature of a series of third-person limited omniscient POVs, with occasional essayistic explanations of what the world is like in the interim.

Third-Person Limited POV

This POV—with its variants—is the most common one used nowadays. There are at least three kinds of third-person limited POVs:

Third-Person Subjective POV

This POV resembles the first-person POV except usually it's done in standard English rather than in the character's voice. For example, "As Judy watched monkeys jump on trees, she thought about getting into shape and remembered that her mother wanted to buy her a ski cap." Here, we have access to a person's thoughts and feelings, just as we do in first person.

Third-Person Objective POV

We observe what our "she" is doing without entering her head, and we don't attribute the observation to another character. You don't reveal the viewer—the way you don't see the person holding a camcorder. "As she faced the monkey cage, she rubbed ChapStick over her thin lips."

Third-Person Limited Omniscient POV

This is a contradiction in terms. If the POV is limited, it can't be omniscient. However, since this term is so widely used, we could use it, too, though I prefer to call this a third-person limited flexible POV. The two names for this POV are interchangeable. Both are in currency. This POV combines the objective and the subjective approaches: "As Judy watched monkeys jump on trees, she rubbed ChapStick over her thin lips and remembered that her mother wanted to buy her a ski cap." We can see Judy and learn what she thinks. (For possibilities of irony in this approach—the author knowing more than the character—read Gustave Flaubert's paragraph about Bovary's gambling at the end of this chapter.) Although a narrator is not revealed, there must be an incognito narrator. It's difficult to distinguish between the third-person POV narrator and the author. You may assume that most readers will interpret whatever the hidden third-person narrator says to be the author's viewpoint.

Here's an example of a third-person subjective POV from Doris Lessing's "The Habit of Loving":

> But he would not go to the hospital. So the doctor said he must have day and night nurses. This he submitted to until the cheerful friendliness of the nurses saddened him beyond bearing, and he asked the doctor to ring up his wife. She promised to find him someone who would not wear a uniform and make jokes.

And later, from the same story, after the man marries a freelance nurse:

> "But you are nothing but a child," he said fondly. He could not decipher what lay behind the black, full stare of her sad eyes as she looked at him now; she was sitting cross-legged in her black glossy trousers before the fire, like a small doll. But a spring of alarm had been touched in him and he didn't dare say any more.

From an objective distance, the narrative jumps into the main character's head, and from there we observe how other characters look and behave, and decipher how they feel, without entering their heads. We are limited to one person's knowledge.

Despite some initial distance toward the character, this POV resembles the first-person POV: We follow the thoughts of one person and see from that person's POV. Lessing's approach is mostly subjective—our vantage point does not step out of the main character's head for us to be able to observe him. Later in the narrative, when she needs to describe the man, she brings up a mirror so she doesn't have to leave his vantage point.

Conventionally, in the third-person limited perspective, the author should not intrude by having the narrator step in and tell something about himself or offer some universal truth. This authorial intrusion is more irksome here than in the omniscient narrative, because the additional jump here will be from the limited to the omniscient POV.

Because it offers the leeway to say whatever the author pleases, the third-person omniscient is the most flexible, and in a way, the most forgiving POV. So it's surprising that it's not in fashion. Perhaps since we have good reasons to be skeptical about nearly everything, the omniscient voice may sound too dogmatic. Yet, because of the freedom to point out that the narrative is an artifice, third-person omniscient could sound less dogmatic than the third-person flexible.

Third-Person Multiple POV

This sounds like omniscient POV, and the difference may be subtle, but it's best to see it as a series of third-person limited POVs minus authorial intrusions. Czech writer Milan Kundera alternates two POVs from chapter to chapter in "Let the Old Dead Make Room for the Young Dead":

> [Chapter I] He was returning home along the street of a small Czech town, where he had been living for several years. He was reconciled to his not too exciting life.

> [II] She knew the path to her husband's grave from memory, and yet today she felt all at once as if she were in this cemetery for the first time.

> [III] Not long ago he had turned thirty-five, and exactly at that time he had noticed that the hair on the top of his head was thinning very visibly.

The narrative follows the protagonists' POVs—we know what they think and what they see—so it's an alternation of two third-person subjective POVs.

Objective POV

Sometimes this perspective is blurred under the third-person objective POV, but we should distinguish an objective POV, which does not focus on one person, from the limited objective POV. Another name for this is the theatrical POV. We observe the action of two or more protagonists, favoring none of them with an exclusive focus, as though in a play. The author does not comment on anything, does not enter people's heads, but merely presents to us the drama as objectively as possible. Ideally, no hidden third or first person lurks anywhere. Of course, there are limits to objectivity; some people consider everything subjective. No doubt, the author will taint the narrative, but as long as she does it with subtlety, the scene will appear objective. Ernest Hemingway's "Hills Like White Elephants" is one of the most popular examples of this narrative stance:

The warm wind blew the bead curtain against the table.

"The beer's nice and cool," the man said.

"It's lovely," the girl said.

"It's really an awfully simple operation, jig," the man said. "It's not really an operation at all."

The narrative offers a recording of a conversation in which a couple is probably discussing an abortion. The reader is allowed to be the judge of what's going on but, of course, must work harder than usual to infer the meaning of the narrative.

UNUSUAL POVs

Occasionally, you may get tired of using the basic first- and third-person POVs. After much use, the first may sound too individualistic, and the third too distant and objectifying. Or you may feel stuck in a routine. For a fresh angle of vision, or for a special effect, you may resort to less frequently used POVs. The names for POVs come from the personal pronouns, so besides the ones we covered, there are "we" (first-person plural POV), "you" (second-person singular POV—and also plural in the sense of "y'all"), and various permutations of these and of the ones we've already covered. After excursions to the less frequently used POVs, you'll probably want to return to the prevalent first and third person, which will become fresh again.

Second-Person POV

The author makes believe that he is talking to someone, describing what the person addressed is doing. But the "you" is not the reader, though sometimes it's hard to get rid of the impression that the author is addressing you directly. Here's an example of this POV, from "Main Street Morning" by Natalie M. Patesch, a contemporary American short story writer:

> Your knees are weak as you lean against the freshly painted red, white, and blue fire hydrant. Your impulse is to run toward them, crying out, me too! me too! You can now taste your own long denial; you want to run and tell her all about your thirty-one years without her and have her cry out with absolving certainty: Oh what a beautiful daughter you are!

I find it a little confining to be told what I am doing and what I am thinking and what I am to do, as though I were following a recipe. If I get rid of that impression, the "you" can be quite engaging. Since the plea of this POV is for immediate attention, most often it is told in the present tense. The present brings us into the time of action, suspends any knowledge of the future, and you as the reader are invited to identify directly with the character. This POV can sound too insistent, as if the writer is grasping for the reader's attention. It can also sound journalistic, since much travel reporting is done in second person.

First and Second Combined

You can combine the second-person POV with the first, as does Margaret Atwood in "Hair Jewellery":

> Between my fits of sleep I thought about you, rehearsing our future, which I knew would be brief. Of course we would sleep together, though this topic had not yet been discussed. In those days, as you recall, it had to be discussed first, and so far we had not progressed beyond a few furtive outdoor gropings and one moment when, under a full moon on one of those deserted brick streets, you had put your hand on my throat.

Here, the first- and second-person POV are combined to an excellent effect. This is the type of POV combination, or address of me to you, frequently found in love poetry, and Atwood's story is a love story of sorts, so the story benefits from the tradition. Yet, strangely enough, this POV combination is rare.

First and Third Combined

You can also combine first- and third-person POVs, as does Russell Banks in "Sarah Cole: A Type of Love Story":

> I felt warmed by her presence and was flirtatious and bold, a little pushy, even.
> Picture this. The man, tanned, limber ... enters the apartment behind the woman.

This combination of POVs helps to develop the theme—a narcissistic man's affair with a homely woman. The narcissist switches the narrative into the third person to take a look at himself, the way a person might like to see himself on a screen; he also deals with his cruelty in the affair like that, projecting himself into another person, to understand his guilt. You could use first- and third-person combined POV for other kinds of characters, especially for those with a personality dichotomy, where you want to look at a character from different angles.

Third-Person Plural Observer POV

Here, the perceptions of an event do not come from the angle of the central character, but from a group of characters who watch the protagonist, as in "Mother" by Italian fiction writer Natalia Ginzburg:

> One day when they were out for a walk with Don Vigiliani and with other boys from the youth club, on the way back they saw their mother in a suburban cafe. She was sitting inside the cafe; they saw her through the window, and a man was sitting with her. Their mother had laid her tartan scarf on the table.

"They saw her through the window." We see the mother from the standpoint of the boys.

For the theme of the story, a mother's adultery, this is an effective angle. Her children's observation keeps her imprisoned in the role of motherhood, from which she tries to escape by becoming a lover. The story is secondarily about the boys, too, and our observation of their elusive mother through their eyes creates an effective narrative distance—appropriate because the boys are about to become orphans.

First-Person Collective Observer POV

This POV is ideal for small-town narratives, where an individual lives under communal scrutiny. This is how William Faulkner uses it in "A Rose for Emily," after an incident in which Miss Emily claims that her dead father is alive:

> We did not say she was crazy then. We believed she had to do that. We remembered all the young men her father had driven away, and we knew that with nothing left, she would have to cling to that which had robbed her, as people will.
>
> She was sick for a long time. When we saw her again, her hair was cut short, making her look like a girl, with a vague resemblance to those angles in colored church windows—sort of tragic and serene.

The reader follows the motions and the acts of one person through a group's viewpoint; somebody in the group, as the narrator, speaks for the group, never drawing attention to his identity, as though he does not have any, other than belonging to the group. Faulkner never individualizes the "we" observing Miss Emily, so he keeps the narrative distance between "us" and "her." This first-person plural POV fits the theme of a woman living under the oppressive communal gaze. If you set your stories in a small community—schools, towns, churches, families—and you focus on a secretive individual in conflict with the community, try this POV.

Stream of Consciousness

This technique evolved from cognitive theories about consciousness. In *Principles of Psychology*, philosopher William James, in striving to describe the thought process, coined the phrase "stream of consciousness."

Here's a segment of a stream of consciousness from *Ulysses* by James Joyce, written as a direct interior monologue. Note that for the sake of approximating the mental verbal flux, Joyce omits punctuation, since in our thoughts we probably don't punctuate. Joyce presents the stream of consciousness as Molly Bloom's thoughts, not as a piece written for an audience:

> Father Corrigan he touched me father and what harm if he did where and I said on the canal bank like a fool but whereabouts on your person my child on the leg behind high up was it yes rather high up was it where you sit down yes O Lord couldnt he say bottom right out and have done with it what has that got to do with it and did you whatever way he put it I forget no father and I always think of the real father what did he want to know for when I already confessed it to God he had a nice fat hand the palm moist always I wouldn't mind feeling it neither would he Id say by the bullneck in his horsecollar I wonder did he know me in the box I could see his face he couldnt see mine of course he never turn or let on still his eyes were red when his father died theyre lost for a woman of course must be terrible when a man cries let alone them Id like to be embraced by one in his vestments and the smell of incense off him like the pope besides theres no danger with a priest if youre married.

Molly recalls a confession and a confessed sexual encounter with a boy, daydreams about the priest, and thinks about euphemisms and about men crying. The thoughts may seem random, but at the same time, they have a narrative coherence. We find out what and how Molly thinks, what she did, what she'd like to do. Joyce communicates a rich texture of Molly's experience in this rush of consciousness. This technique is basically the first-person POV, a direct interior monologue. To follow the principle "show, don't tell," you directly show thoughts. Most often, we simply summarize thoughts without showing them, but in crucial moments of your narrative, you may want to show them.

You can resort to the stream of consciousness whenever you want to bring the reader intimately into a character's experience, so this is potentially an excellent way to characterize. The technique is well suited for moments of indecision, waiting, pondering, and quiet contemplation, as well as for moments of violent crisis (such as being wounded or shocked). Stream of consciousness may have slow-motion effect if you use it amid action. Naturally, if you overuse this method you will not increase but, rather, decrease suspense, since stream of consciousness tends to meander into the future, past, and present, without a sharp focus.

The major drawback of stream of consciousness is that it's cumbersome to read in large chunks. While writing it is often fun, it usually isn't fun to read. Be considerate to your reader, and edit your streams of consciousness so that there's always something interesting going on, in terms of language, images, and thoughts. Use the stream of consciousness in small doses, in fairly brief passages (perhaps no more than a page at a time) to enhance rather than kill your narrative tension.

SHIFTING POVs

Switches in POV irritate some readers and certainly most editors unless you establish the pattern early as the form of the narrative. So, if for no other reason than the practical one of getting published, most writers must respect the conventions of POV. Beginning writers often write pages from the perspective of one person and then suddenly, mid-sentence, they might switch like this: "While he bit his nails and thought that she did not understand him, she brushed her hair and thought that he needed therapy." In one sentence we enter two heads. If the narrative is not otherwise omniscient in form, this switch jars us. If the POV switches throughout, it still should not shift within the same sentence. Conventionally, when you switch from the thoughts of one person to the thoughts of another, you start a new paragraph or, more often, a new chapter. Otherwise, your narrative will be jumpy.

Consistency is one guideline. If you plan to use multiple POVs, make this clear as early as possible. After chapter (or paragraph) one, in which your POV focuses on Jim, open chapter (or paragraph) two with Julie's POV. Then you can shift back and forth with each new chapter (or paragraph), if necessary. You have prepared the reader for these shifts.

Sometimes POV shifts can be effective. This is what E.M. Forster said about switching POVs—from omniscient to limited and to objective:

> A novelist can shift his viewpoint if it comes off, and it came off with
> Dickens and Tolstoy. Indeed this power to expand and contract
> perceptions (of which the shifting viewpoint is a symptom), this right

to intermittent knowledge: —I find it one of the great advantages of the novel-form, and it has a parallel in our perception of life. We are stupider at some times than others; we can enter into people's minds occasionally but not always, because our own minds get tired; and this intermittence lends in the long run variety and colour to the experiences we receive.

Switching POVs can establish the source of knowledge that we discussed in the beginning of the chapter. So, for example, we can derive information about an event initially in the first person. After the story has been assembled from several witnesses, and enough inferences have been made to cover even what has not been told by the witnesses, the event may be described without reference to the sources; things can assume an objective third-person perspective—and a composite report can be written about the motives of everybody involved.

Gustave Flaubert employs this strategy in *Madame Bovary*. He starts in the first-person plural (or collective):

> We were in class when the headmaster came in, followed by a new boy, not wearing the school uniform, and a school servant carrying a large desk.

After Bovary and his background have been introduced, the first-person observers drop out, and Flaubert gives us information, confident that we will have the impression that it has been gathered from witnesses, such as we had in the beginning. So after the first chapter, until the last, when the first-person plural POV reappears, the novel is narrated in a variety of third-person POVs, depending on what the novel needs to cover. For a while, we follow Mr. Bovary. Sometimes we get his thoughts, other times we observe and analyze him:

> To shut himself up every evening in the dirty public room, to push about on marble tables the small sheepbones with black dots, seemed to him a fine proof of his freedom, which raised him in his own esteem.

Notice the duality of perception of Bovary's action. We learn that he derives a sense of freedom from playing dice. At the same time, the distant and hidden carrier of the third-person POV gives us an ironic angle on that freedom with the phrase "push about ... small sheepbones with black dots." The dice are reduced to their banality, something Bovary does not see, and thus we are invited to see Bovary as bovine and banal. In many other chapters, the narrative focuses on Madame Bovary. In some passages, the narrative gives us the setting, the town of Yonville, with its history as a given knowledge. The novel employs many strategies. It would be too simple to say that it's written in the omniscient POV, although in sections it is. In other parts, it's written in a succession of different third-person flexible POVs, with authorial interpretations. I won't call it intrusion because the interpretations are done gracefully enough not to stall the narrative.

Unusual Shifts of POV

If you carefully read even some of the best fiction, you will find unusual switches. For example, in the much-praised objective POV used by Hemingway in "Hills Like White Elephants," from which we read a brief section earlier, these two sentences occur:

> The shadow of a cloud moved across the field of grain and she saw the river through the trees.
>
> He looked up the tracks but could not see the train.

You can see that someone is looking, from the outside. But to report what someone is seeing means you are in the person's head. How do we know that she saw the river? Perhaps she looked at the trees without seeing the river. In the second sentence, how do we know that he could not see the train? These brief POV shifts may be inadvert, but perhaps Hemingway intentionally switched from objectivity to subjectivity, for one reason or another—maybe to make a disclaimer of objectivity. Who knows? Maybe we need an omniscient critic to explain this to us.

If you switch POVs, be in control, and don't apologize or try too hard to cover your tracks because that will either intrude on the narrative or slow it down. Simply do it in a regular enough fashion. Propel the reader into the new angle.

Here's an example of doing it gracefully, from Leo Tolstoy's "The Death of Ivan Ilych." The POV shifts from one character's thoughts to his appearance, from subjective to objective:

> Peter Ivanovich, like everyone else on such occasions, entered feeling uncertain what he would have to do. All he knew was that at such times it is always safe to cross oneself. But he was not quite sure whether one should make obeisances while doing so. He therefore adopted a middle course. On entering the room he began crossing himself and made a slight movement resembling a bow.

Tolstoy takes us from the character's thoughts to the appearance of his action—"a slight movement resembling a bow"—economically, with the help of one word, *resembling*. This is a good model, particularly in the third-person limited. After Ivanovich spends some time observing Ivan Ilych's corpse and musing on Ilych's life in the first chapter, the second chapter opens with the history of Ilych's life. The transition takes place in a sharp way: The second chapter opens with Ilych as the subject. A new chapter as a new beginning opens up the possibility of starting from another angle. First, Ilych's history is objective, in the form of summaries, but in later chapters, the narrative focuses on Ilych's feelings, becoming quite subjective. The subject—the experience of dying—justifies the method of contracting the focus from the outside in.

Virtual Shift of POV

There's a way of getting into other people's thoughts without jumping POVs. Here's an example from Anton Chekhov's "Lady With the Dog." The story is told from a man's POV throughout, but at a crisis point, the narrative POV seemingly switches to the woman:

> She glanced at him and turned pale, then glanced again with horror, unable to believe her eyes, and tightly gripped her fan and the lorgnette in her hands, evidently struggling with herself not to faint.

Note that once we have the woman's perspective, Chekhov lets us know that we are not actually in her head, that we have reconstructed what must be going on in her mind. One word does the trick of distancing the POV: *evidently*. "Unable to believe her eyes" may be inferred from observation; or at any rate, our third-person POV, still with the man, could infer this. So in third-person limited, if you seemingly switch, indicate that we haven't actually switched POV but have observed deeply.

EXERCISES

1. Two pages. First, in one page, describe an event—stealing a fake gold ring in a department store—in the first-person POV. Use the language that would come most naturally to the character you choose, preferably slang.

Then write another page, describing the same event from the POV of the sales clerk, in the first person.

Objective: First, to gain experience constructing a primary, protagonist first-person POV. Then, to experience constructing an observer/minor participant POV.

Check: In the first example, have you given us thoughts, feelings, and perceptions of the thief, using *I* as in "I was sure that I could slip the ring onto my pinkie"? Does she know that the ring is fake? She shouldn't—why would she bother otherwise?

In the second example, have you used *I* as in "I could tell that this clown was about to make the move. She was out of breath and her cigarette-stained fingers shook"? The clerk should know, of course, that the ring is fake, and perhaps he should be ironic about the thief because he knows something she doesn't.

2. Two pages. Describe in one page the event in Exercise 1 in the third-person subjective POV, focusing on the thief. Since this will be similar in the scope of knowledge and angle of vision to the first part of Exercise 1, you might simply rewrite what you've done there, now in the third person. In addition to changing pronouns, change the diction to standard English.

Then write another page, describing the same event in the third-person limited flexible POV, focusing on the thief. Write both an outside description (how the action looks) and, at a different point, an inward one (what the character thinks and how she perceives the sales clerk).

Objective: To gain experience writing in the third-person subjective POV, with its concentration on the experience of the protagonist; and then to try out the third-person limited omniscient—or flexible—with its freedom to present the protagonist from whatever angle suits you.

Check: For the first part, can what you described be seen from your thief's angle? For the second part, do you have a dual perception, typical of a flexible stance? For example, have you indicated that the gold ring is fake but that the thief does not know it?

3. Three paragraphs. Describe an event on a battlefront, in which a soldier accidently—or not so accidently—kills his brother in friendly fire. Describe this from the omniscient POV. Open with a paragraph about the history of the war, perhaps musing on the nature of wars. Second paragraph: Describe the actions and thoughts of the friendly-fire soldier—up to pulling the trigger. Third paragraph: Describe the actions and thoughts of the soldier right before and during being shot at. As he gasps a final breath, give him an insight into the afterlife.

Since you are free to cover the field from any vantage point, external and internal, strive for an orderly succession of angles of vision.

Objective: To experience the multiple nature of the omniscient POV.

Check: Make sure that you have not shifted from one character's thoughts to another's in midsentence. Have you described how these soldiers look, what they think and feel, and what dying is like? Even though subjective insights about death are inaccessible to the living, make one up, playfully, if need be.

4. Three pages. Event: A male doctor examining a woman patient may be sexually harassing her. She cuts his ear with a scalpel. A nurse watches and does not rush to help the doctor. Describe the event three times, in the third-person subjective POV, using all the characters present.

Objective: To practice writing different interpretations of the same event, depending on the POV. Try to make the event appear different in each.

Check: Does the event appear radically different from each character's experience? If not, go back and write at least two different interpretations. The nurse and the patient could have a similar interpretation, for example, but the doctor, a different one.

5. Two to three pages. Construct an unreliable narrator. (You could do this in the form of a letter, as part of an epistolary story, or in a diary entry, as part of a diary story.) You might use the ring thief from Exercise 1 or the friendly-fire soldier from Exercise 3. Let the thief retell the incident, not only denying that she'd stolen the ring, but telling us why she had never even been interested in rings—how, in fact, she had always despised them. But let her tone contradict her statements.

Objective: To learn how to write in the unreliable first-person POV.

Check: Have you managed to portray the narrator's betraying the real meaning of her statement? For example, before or after saying that she despised rings, has she gotten carried away, describing the ring lyrically, showing her desire for it?

6. Two pages. First, write a one-page description of an important event from your childhood from a child's first-person POV. Use a child's language. Then write another page, in adult language, describing the same event from the perspective of an adult looking back.

For the first part, Huck Finn could be your model; for the second, Edna O'Brien's "Sister Imelda" (see page 87). Don't worry if this turns out to be more nonfiction than fiction.

Objective: To learn how to cover a single event from different angles of language and vision.

Check: Did you use poor grammar in the first part? Maybe you should. Is the perspective adequately naive?

In the second part, do you have a dual perception of what happened? For example, the adult narrator could recollect the childhood naiveté without using childhood language (though some for flavor might not hurt) and at the same time comment in adult language about how naive it was.

Do the different POVs offer you different insights and observations?

7. Two pages. Write an autobiographical story—perhaps the one from Exercise 6—so that it doesn't sound autobiographical. Cast it in the third-person limited POV and use a character different from you. In the end, after you change characters, make up new details and lines of dialogue, and exaggerate the drama. The actual event from which you started should be simply a scaffold for building your story.

Objective: If you write from experience, the first person will only strengthen the nonfictional origin of your story. The third-person POV should help you distance yourself from the event psychologically. Now that you are looking at it from far away, why be bound by what actually happened? You are free to look for story possibilities in the initial situation.

Check: Has something other than the pronouns and diction changed? Namely, have you fictionalized the event? If not, go back and change the town in which this took place, create a different set of parents, and make the character's desires and fears quite different from yours.

8. Two pages. Using first-person POV, write about a fantastic event and make it believable. For example, write about the Great Flood from the standpoint of one of Noah's daughters. Don't use fancy, biblical language, but familiar, simple English. Make sure to avoid anachronisms, such as a reference to Oprah or some other pop culture icon.

Objective: To familiarize a distant event and a distant person by using the first-person POV in an informal way.

Check: Examine your vocabulary to make sure you haven't used anachronisms. For example, in this sentence, within the context of the Great Flood, there would be several inappropriate expressions (italicized): "*Wow*, when the doves flew out, it was *postcard-pretty* out there, just like *Daytona Beach* during *spring break*." And for believability, do you have mosquito bites (or something similar)? With all that water around, it would make sense.

9. One page. Write about a scene of misunderstanding in a love story, using the combined first- and second-person POV. If you like, write this in the form of a letter. (See the excerpt from "Hair Jewellery" by Margaret Atwood on page 97).

Objective: To practice this POV strategy. For a love story, this is a particularly well-suited POV. So give it a try.

Check: Have you given approximately the same amount of playing time to "you" as to "me"? Balance the two.

10. Two pages. First, write a page of a story from the standpoint of a horse, in the first person. Let the horse kick a visitor, an IRS agent.

Then, on another page, describe the same incident from the standpoint of the horse's owner, a farmer.

Objective: To fail in the first instance, and get rid of the impulse to write from an animal's POV. (This is a common, and misguided, impulse in aspiring writers, perhaps because it offers an opportunity for cute and clever observations.) To succeed in the second instance. Animals' lives can be fascinating—a good subject for stories, provided we avoid anthropocentric assumptions about what they think.

Many beginners are drawn to an animal POV, and instead of the animal, they create some human in disguise, often moralizing about how bad people are to their environment. While the objectives of such writing may be noble, the execution usually isn't.

That does not mean that you can't write an animal story from a human POV, but let the human watch the animal, without jumping into the animal's head. You also can write animal stories from the third-person objective POV. But be cautious with the third-person animal subjective and the first-person animal POVs.

I don't want to be dogmatic about this, despite my never having encountered a successful animal POV story in the workshops I've taught. After all, Richard Bach successfully used an animal POV (third-person subjective) in his novella fable, *Jonathan Livingston Seagull*.

Check: In the first part of the exercise, is your horse consistent in what he knows? Does he know what tractors are but not know other vocabulary, such as *barn*, *rifle*, *telescope*? Either make your horse know all this vocabulary and don't worry about it, or reduce it to a minimum. Good luck!

In the second part, if you've described the horse's thoughts and feelings, have you modified them with phrases such as *seemed to wonder* and *evidently felt* to indicate that these statements are inferences, not shifts of POV?

11. Three to five pages. Write about a disagreement you had with somebody, from her POV, in the first person, in her voice. Don't make her an unreliable narrator. Take an external look at yourself, in this case in the third person, although you might want to do a first- and second-person POV combination if you prefer.

Objective: To learn how to see from other people's POVs. This exercise is good not just for writing, but for getting along in friendships, marriages, societies.

Check: Has your antagonist become the protagonist of the story? Have you found weaknesses in your position and shown them? If not, go back and reveal them.

12. Four paragraphs. First, write one paragraph from the third-person subjective POV, then switch to describing the feelings of other people, relying on *seemed*,

obviously, clearly, and other indicators that the POV has remained external. Look at Chekhov's example from "Lady With the Dog" on page 103.

Then write another paragraph. From the third-person subjective POV—describing a person's feelings—switch into the objective POV, describing the person's actions externally. Look at Tolstoy's example from "The Death of Ivan Ilych" on page 102.

Then write two more paragraphs. End one paragraph with the thoughts of one person in the third-person subjective POV. Start a new paragraph, with the third-person objective POV focused on another person.

Objective: To practice switching POVs smoothly.

Check: For the first paragraphs, have you started with the thoughts of the POV person, then switched to an objective outside look? For a switch, do you use *seemed to* and similar indicators for the thoughts of the observed person?

13. Three pages. Mark has been hired to burn down buildings. After burning down the fifth building, he's caught. Now give us his story. For the first page, start from the POV of the arsonist's ex-roommate, Eric, in the first person, giving Mark's character portrait. Eric tells us what Mark was like and how he assembled Mark's story—from letters, message machines, police, firefighters, and Mark's brother-in-law. Then switch for the second page to third-person objective, dropping Eric from the narrative and focusing on Mark setting his first fire at a liquor store. For page three (the climax), use the third-person subjective POV, describing Mark's fear of being caught as he runs away from his fifth building, a rent-controlled apartment complex. No need for transitions between these pages. New page, new chapter, new POV.

Objective: To create shifts that would account for the source of the knowledge of the story. Though these days it's not necessary to trace the assembling of the story from definite sources of information, it's still healthy to keep in mind how information is gathered, and what could be known, and what may be made up. For example, it might seem illogical that, starting from Eric's POV, we could find out exactly how Mark felt and what he thought; but if it's clear that Eric imagines and reconstructs the story, the way a historian reconstructs a culture from archaeological finds, the story will become acceptable, and perhaps the shifting POV will make the narrative more—rather than less—convincing.

You need not write your first novel like this, but don't get stiff in the joints before you make such shifts. Be sure that you know how to make POV transitions, even if you don't need them in a particular story.

Check: Proofread to make sure that you have stuck with Eric's subjective POV in the first page (*I thought, I felt, I wondered* and so on); with Mark's limited objective in the second page (e.g., "His back hunched, dressed in a black business suit, Mark tiptoed among aluminum garbage cans"); and for the last page, that you bring us into Mark's way of seeing (e.g., "Mark was sure that this was not a dog's shadow").

14. Two to four pages. Write a story in a combination of a plural "we" and singular "I" and "you." You can see this kind of POV at work in "We Didn't" by Stuart Dybek in this back of this book. The story starts with "we," and the first paragraph is told from that POV. The second is in the first-person singular, "I." A few paragraphs later, we have a "you" POV. The POV doesn't actually shift—part of the "we" is "I," and another is "you," so it's simply the first-person plural parsed into its components. The second-person POV element here has a sensation of revisiting the event to explain further what "you" may not have known about what was going on—there's a bit of revelation here.

Objective: To write a few engaging pages in this inclusive POV. The narrator is engaged with the listener (or reader), "you," who acts as both the audience and the participant in the events of the story, and the narrator, "I," acts as a speaker and a participant.

Check: Is it working for you? If the characters are too abstract, rewrite and add a strong voice to it, in the first person, and put in the people you know, whom you could address, to bring it all closer to your imagination.

6

DIALOGUE AND SCENE

A scene (the term taken from drama) is continuous action set in one place. Actors move on a stage, talk, fight, make love. But unlike in theater, in fiction you don't have to supply all the furniture, paint, heat. You supply a bit of background, and the reader constructs more out of it. As we've seen in the chapter on setting, it's enough that you list the details that compose a setting. From your concrete nouns, your reader will visualize the setting.

To construct a good scene, you must be able to describe the setting, evoke characters, and clearly present their actions. These elements already have been covered in previous chapters. However, before we can discuss how to write scenes, we must consider one more key element: dialogue.

DIALOGUE

Writing dialogue probably is the most essential skill you need. Since most big scenes, and many minor ones, rely on dialogue, you must be able to write it well. Writing dialogue should be easy for most of us. It astonishes me how many people believe they are no good at writing dialogue (even the people who are good at it)—yet they spend hours per day talking and listening to others talk. In fact, the narrative aspects of writing fiction should be more difficult, because how much time do we spend listening to narratives? Not much.

Many writers, however, claim that dialogue is the easiest aspect of writing fiction. For example, James Jones, author of *From Here to Eternity*, said, "Dialogue is almost too easy. For me. So much so that it makes me suspicious of it, so I have to be careful with it. ... There are many important issues and points of subtlety about people, about human behavior, that I want to make in writing, and it's easy to evade these—or do them superficially, do them halfway—by simply writing good dialogue."

Two points regarding this quote. First: Dialogue does not accomplish everything, so don't despair if you don't trust yours. Some writers—Gabriel García Márquez, for example—depend much more on narrative than on dialogue and yet write great fiction. Just as you can avoid narrative, you can avoid dialogue, though in either case, you handicap yourself. However, it's possible to write well with a handicap, just as it's possible to play a sport with one. For example, Ivan Lendl won the European junior tennis championship without a competent backhand. He ran around the balls on his left and hit them with his forehand, or chopped them on the backhand. You can avoid dialogue, summarize, describe, and have a chopped line here and there, but why handicap yourself? It was only after Lendl developed a tremendous backhand that he won a U.S. Open.

On the other hand, even with good dialogue, you will need some narrative to stage your scenes and to connect them to other parts of the story. Dialogue alone rarely constitutes a scene. Look at the example from Donald Barthelme's story "Basil From Her Garden," in the section "Forms of Dialogue" (page 115). That's not a scene. You may turn it into one, with an imaginative effort, but you have no props to go by right away—no stage clues. We need to see the characters and their stage. So don't expect that all you need is great dialogue, and forget about description, setting, and the rest that we have talked about so far.

The second point regarding Jones's quote: Dialogue is easy. It's what you've been doing almost every day, most of your life.

Dialogue as Conversation

Dialogue is basically conversation. Your characters talk to each other. They should sound like real people. This could mean that all you need to do is transcribe people's conversation. Unfortunately, it's not that simple—or rather, fortunately, it's not that complicated to write dialogue. Real conversation may sound like this:

> "Er, Jim, have you heard the latest thing, on, what's his name, you know, er, I mean the guy who's so much like in the news—"
>
> "This coffee sucks. Well, I've been too busy lately, all the job applications and all—"
>
> "Shit, he's a pop singer, oh jeez, why can't I remember his name, like, he's like real famous, I mean, er, you know?"
>
> "Uh huh."
>
> Pause. A cough. "He's hiding, you know who I mean, er, he's got an—damn it!—"
>
> "Sure, it's easy for those guys, they're all millionaires. Well, where's the waitress?"
>
> "Uh huh."

Even in a direct transcription resembling this one, you can't indicate where both characters speak at the same time, where vowels drag, consonants double, and so on. Moreover, in real speech, you get a person's melody of voice, see his body language, and so you might suffer all the hesitations and indirectness and irrelevancies much better than when you read the transcript in print. You can't reproduce real speech. You can approximate it now and then, but your dialogue should be quicker and more direct than real speech.

"Dialogue should convey a sense of spontaneity but eliminate the repetitiveness of real talk," said Elizabeth Bowen. It may be effective to use *or something*s, *I mean*s, and *sort of*s for the sense of realism and spontaneity, especially where hesitations simulate not only the sound of real speech, but psychologically indicative moments. But use these fillers sparingly.

Moreover, your character needn't talk unless there's a point to be conveyed. Eudora Welty said that "only the significant passages of their [characters'] talk should be recorded, in high relief against the narrative." So make your talk matter, and find the right balance between realism and economy of speech.

To make realistic dialogue, create a distinct voice for every character. By his diction (word choice) you reveal a character's region, class, education, and style of thinking (logical, impulsive, spiteful, etc.).

Give each character a voice with a distinctive level of diction. Let some speak in fragments, others in complete sentences; some in slang, some in professional jargon, others in standard English; some with fashionable and others with idiosyncratic vocabulary—of course, all within the reasonable limits of what kind of story you write. Where do you get people's voices? Listen. Remember. If you need to, record. Some people are fortunate because they remember sounds rather than images. The sound more than compensates for the lack of image. Frank O'Connor, for example, said, "I just notice a feeling from people. I notice particularly the cadence of their voices, the sort of phrases they'll use, and that's what I'm all the time trying to hear in my head, how people word things—because everybody speaks an entirely different language. ... I cannot pass a story as finished ... unless I know how everybody in it spoke, which, as I say, can go quite well with the fact that I couldn't tell you in the least what they looked like. If I use the right phrase and the reader hears the phrase in his head, he sees the individual."

If you are primarily a visual person, you may rely on vivid images with great success, but you still need the sounds. Get them any way you can. Record people, study their talk, study dialogue and dialects.

Dialect

When using dialect, don't alter your spelling radically. To evoke a drawl, don't triple vowels. Don't skip consonants. Here and there, you might alter a word or two, but don't overdo it, because most readers resent having to slow down. Create a dialect through unique word choices and syntax. For example, in this scene from Bernard Malamud's *The Assistant*, the words—*insurinks* for insurance, and *macher*, a jack-of-all-trades—gives us a flavor of Yiddish and helps to evoke a New York immigrant ghetto:

> "I make a living." The macher spoke soundlessly. "I make fires."
> Morris drew back.
> The macher waited with downcast eyes. "We are poor people,"
> he murmured.
> "What do you want from me?"
> "We are poor people," the macher said, apologetically. "God loves the
> poor people but he helps the rich. The insurinks companies are rich."

Also, the macher's fondness of proverbs—"God loves the poor people but he helps the rich"—gives us a sense of the person speaking.

To be safe, use the dialects you are familiar with, but don't fear them. I must admit that since I did not grow up speaking English, and since my visuals are stronger than my sounds, I feared dialects for years. But I realized that Faulkner and Steinbeck hadn't used any region's dialect exactly. They made their own variations of dialects. Every person, in a way, speaks his or her own dialect. So after you study a regional dialect for a while, you could make your own variation of it. I lived in Nebraska for three years, and instead of writing about the people there, I wrote about animals. When the writer Rick Bass asked me, "So why don't you write about Nebraskans?" I said that, as a stranger, I couldn't do their dialect. "Come on," he said. "Who knows how people in Lynch, Nebraska, talk? Make up your own Lynch dialect. Who's gonna question you?" He was right. I don't have to use every Nebraskan's deviation from the standard English to feel that I have rendered Nebraskan farmers. On the other hand, just using a couple of regional words won't do the job. *Y'all* and *reckon* aren't enough to make a Southerner. If you need a Southerner, find a few elements of the dialect's grammar, syntax, and word choice (other than clichés such as *reckon* and *y'all*) that evoke the sound of Southern speech.

When you write in dialect, here and there you may change the spelling of a word to create a realistic sound, as does Norman Mailer in the following scene from *The Naked and the Dead*:

> Ridges laid down his shovel and looked at him. His face was patient
> but there was some concern in it. "What you trying to do, Stanley?"
> he asked.
> "You don't like it?" Stanley sneered.
> "No, Sir, Ah don't."
> Stanley grinned slowly. "You know what you can do."

... "Aah, fug it," he said, turning away.

Ah for a Southern way of saying *I* works, Now that we can begin to hear the Southerner, Ridges, we don't need every word rendered in dialect—an occasional one will do. If the reader knows the dialect, she'll fill in the drawl and other Southern sounds for herself; if she doesn't, she probably won't appreciate odd spellings anyhow. So be a minimalist with regional expressions, unless you have a special reason to be ultra-realistic and to accomplish a speech reproduction.

Obscenities

What about "fug" in Mailer's dialogue? Mailer wrote this a while back, when using obscenities in fiction was unfashionable, if not illegal. I'd still say it's good to be conservative. Obscenities have been overused, so the shock value is gone, and the boredom of valuelessness has set in. Anthony Burgess said, "When I wrote my first Enderby novel, I had to make my hero say 'For cough,' since 'Fuck off' was not acceptable. With the second book the climate had changed, and Enderby was at liberty to say 'Fuck off.' I wasn't happy. It was too easy. He still said 'For cough.'" Obscenities are easy, and people resort to them when they need an easy solution. You rarely need to be overly realistic, just as you don't need to reproduce every *er*.

Child's Speech

Sometimes it's enough to reproduce a child's logic rather than the sound of a child's speech, as does Vasily Aksenov in "Little Whale, Varnisher of Reality." Although this is a translation, the child's logic makes a realistic scene—in which a child cuts in between an adulterous couple:

> She lifted her hand and put the palm of this hand to my cheek ... stroked. ...
>   Just then Whale came squirming in between us. He tugged the pretty lady by the sleeve: "Hey, take your old umbrella and don't touch Daddy. He's my Daddy, not yours."

Only a child could confuse a woman with another child competing for parental affection. And children at a certain stage are extremely possessive, so Whale's intrusion, by its realism, adds credibility to the story. There's charm in how children make odd, and yet obvious, connections.

Forms of Dialogue

Dialogue can range from straight dialogue, without any interpretation between the lines, to hardly any lines and a lot of exposition between them. In

"Basil From Her Garden," Donald Barthelme strips the dialogue for the sake of absurdity, perhaps to mimic the impersonality of a psychiatric session:

> Q: What do you do, after work, in the evenings or on weekends?
> A: Just ordinary things.
>
> Q: No special interests?
> A: I'm very interested in bow hunting. These new bows they have now, what they call a compound bow. Also, I'm a member of the Galapagos Society, we work for the environment, it's really a very effective—
>
> Q: And what else?
> A: Well, adultery. I would say that that's how I spend most of my free time. In adultery.

You can vary dialogue, using a combination of direct and indirect addresses, as I did on page 113 in reporting my conversation with Rick Bass. I put his words in direct quotations; I reported my words indirectly, using that to introduce the content of what I said. These shifts in treatment emphasize his points more than my objections.

In theater, actors can show you shades of meaning through the intonation of their voices, body language, and other means. In Barthelme's example, we have no indication of body language and setting, so the dialogue is not really a scene.

A writer need not despair at not being able to render intonations and voices perfectly, because he can, between the lines, describe action, as does Irwin Shaw in "The Girls in Their Summer Dresses":

> "Look out," Frances said, as they crossed Eighth Street. "You'll break your neck."
> Michael laughed and Frances laughed with him.
> "She's not so pretty, anyway," Frances said. "Anyway, not pretty enough to take a chance breaking your neck looking at her."
> Michael laughed again. He laughed louder this time, but not as solidly. "She wasn't a bad-looking girl. She had a nice complexion. Country-girl complexion. How did you know I was looking at her?"
> Frances cocked her head to one side and smiled at her husband under the tip-tilted brim of her hat. "Mike, darling."

Good dialogue often manages to evoke intonation, as does the last line from the above example, but there are serious limits to that, so the tone can be described, and body language can turn it into a scene.

Body Language, Character, and Dialogue

Sometimes the more important part of dialogue takes place in body language and in the exposition between the lines, as in "The Real Thing" by Doris Lessing:

> He was more on guard than he knew, although he had said to himself before arriving, Now, careful, the slightest thing sets her off. Every line of him said, "Don't come too close." He leaned back in his chair, even tilting it as she leaned forward towards him.

The dialogue here is summarized, with emphasis on its essential quality, body language.

In a scene with dialogue, the words may run contrary to the general meaning of the scene. In the following example—from "The Last of Mr. Norris" by Christopher Isherwood—a character, eager to mask his nervousness at a German border crossing, speaks about Greek archaeology quite out of context:

> He spoke so loudly that the people in the next compartment must certainly be able to hear him.
>
> "One comes, quite unexpectedly, upon the most fascinating little corners. A single column standing in the middle of a rubbish-heap ...."
>
> "Deutsche PassKontrolle. All passports, please."
>
> An official had appeared in the doorway of our compartment. His voice made Mr. Norris give a slight but visible jump. Anxious to allow him time to pull himself together, I hastily offered my own passport. As I had expected, it was barely glanced at.
>
> "I'm traveling to Berlin," said Mr. Norris, handing over his passport with a charming smile; so charming, indeed, that it seemed a little overdone.

The dialogue establishes a dramatic scene, with suspense, and at the same time it characterizes Mr. Norris—his duplicity, pomposity, timidity. In the excerpt from "Sally Bowles" by Christopher Isherwood, on page 55, the contrast between Sally's sophisticated speech and her appearance (dirty hands) portrays her more vividly and insightfully than summary could.

Good dramatic dialogue is multilayered, so that in addition to body language and direct meaning, there's another parallel meaning to what's being said. The following dialogue—from "Four Meetings" by Henry James—establishes two characters (the aloof narrator and a trickster posing as a painter), and it raises the tension of the indirect confrontation:

> "Composes well. Fine old tone. Make a nice thing." He spoke in a charmless vulgar voice.

"I see you've a great deal of eye," I replied. "Your cousin tells me you're studying art." He looked at me in the same way, without answering, and I went on with deliberate urbanity: "I suppose you're at the studio of one of those great men." Still on this he continued to fix me, and then he named one of the greatest of that day; which led me to ask him if he liked his master.

"Do you understand French?" he returned.

"Some kinds."

He kept his little eyes on me; with which he remarked: "Je suis fou de la peinture!"

"Oh, I understand that kind!" I replied.

Simplistic dialogue, which strives to accomplish only one thing, often falls flat because it is too transparent. Complex dialogue like James's creates drama; it's complex. And there's a subtext—what's not said directly.

The narrator sometimes tells us how what's said is said: "I went on with deliberate urbanity." At other times, he implies and shows indirectly. He is cynical. That could have been made explicit by adding a modifier, as in: "'Oh, I understand that kind!' I replied sardonically." This adverb would summarize the tone, but the diction accomplishes the meaning without the writer's spelling it out. "I replied" suffices. With his choice of detail, between the lines of dialogue, the narrator expresses his attitude toward the artist: "He kept his little eyes on me." "Little eyes" conveys that the narrator despises the artist and deems him cunning and petty.

Dialogue and Information

Every sentence in a piece of fiction conveys some kind of information. Dialogue brings us close to the characters and their conflicts. If you need history, philosophy, biology, or most other sorts of information, put them in the narrative part, unless your characters are historians, philosophers, and biologists. If you set a story in the Vietnam War and you need some background history, don't put it all in dialogue between two soldiers. That would sound unnatural and, moreover, would be much slower than giving the history in narrative. Don't let your characters sound like a bunch of journalists pumping people for information (unless that's what they are).

Since dialogue does convey information about people's struggles, make sure you don't give us banal and irrelevant information. Avoid realistic dialogue introductions; summarize the introductory pleasantries and move on:

After they shook hands, Jim asked Bill about the loan.

"Oh, that."

"Yes, what else? I've got kids to feed, and you're ..."

Now every line will advance rather than stall the story because we have jumped into the essential part of the conversation.

If a conversation pattern—verbal abuse, for example—occurs many times, and that's the main point, don't give us all the instances. Give us a dramatic one, when it counts, and summarize the others.

SCENE

So that we can properly discuss how to create a scene, go back to chapter one and reread the scene of the German soldier giving aspirin to the boy from "The Burning Shoe." The story describes the village before the scene, but even during it we get the wooden floors, the bucket of water in the kitchen, the down cover. These sparse elements of the setting keep us seeing the stage.

In a scene, almost all the elements we've discussed so far come together. You portray characters dynamically—characters whom you may have sketched in summary before the scene. They express themselves by what they do and how they do it, what they say and how they speak, and by what they think (if they carry the POV). In "The Burning Shoe" scene, we see that the boy, although scared, is lusty—he wants more honey cakes; the soldier, although surprisingly benevolent, is strict and practical—he says "Nein!" when he thinks he has erased the boy's bitter taste of the aspirin. The action taking place as part of the scene shows us what the characters are like. There's no need to tell it now.

In a scene you advance the plot. Whatever conflict evolves must culminate eventually in a scene, where the protagonists and the antagonists meet and clash, as the boy and the soldier do. The introductory statements lead us into the scene and raise our expectations—the Germans, since they had killed the boy's father, threaten to do more harm. So when the soldier walks into the bedroom, stamping with his boots, and pulls away the down cover, there's tension. Will he strangle the boy? The question hovering in the slowed-down action creates the tension. It's essential to slow down even quick action, if tension is going to work, and in the "The Burning Shoe" scene this is accomplished with concentration on the sensory details and thoughts (stamping, cold hands, creaking throat, bulging eyes, "I thought, to strangle me") and with outright delay. The soldier withdraws his hand and pours water into the glass and puts some substance into it. Our old question recurs—will the soldier kill the boy? Again, sensations keep us engaged and wondering—the glass pressing the lip against the teeth, the shudderingly bitter liquid, and the boy's thinking that this must be poison.

And now, at the culmination point, the surprise occurs. We find out that the bitter liquid is aspirin. The soldier gives the boy honey cakes. Not that every culminating scene must have a twist, a surprise, but you must raise expectations and delay answering them. The answer must come gradually, through sensory details (or a dialogue exchange, or both) of the action. Keep your reader guessing.

To construct a scene, you must bring a conflict to it—the characters must want or fear something that might happen during this scene. In other words, a scene must have a plot of its own, which of course must relate to the overall plot of the story. Everything that concerns the characters—who they are, how they relate to each other, how they conflict—must be fleshed out, embodied, dramatized, seen (that is, scened). You must dramatize whatever abstract plans and plot outlines you have, so that the reader will be able to play the drama in her mind.

Although the scene in fiction resembles the scene in theater, it is usually easier to do in fiction. You don't need to worry how to get a character off the stage, and you can fast-forward, summarize, tell, reveal characters' thoughts without speech and grimaces. But theater still remains a paradigm of what scenes are. A play is impossible without scenes. So is fiction, except perhaps for experimental fiction. In theater, characters act in a certain time at a certain place. This applies in fiction, too: Unless you specify the time and location of the action, your action is unrealized, abstract.

How to Prepare for the Big Scene

For a piece of fiction, you need at least one fully realized scene, taking place here and now (or there and then). The essential story is an event—what happened, who did it, to whom, where, when, how, why. You may prepare for the event without making scenes and without concretizing scenes in a time and space, but the event itself must be created on the page: continuous, like a piece of music, and spatial, like a painting. And the event must make sense—that is, all the characters, places, conflicts, and other elements must plausibly connect here.

The most dramatic moment of your story usually will combine dialogue, scene, description, and the other elements of fiction. But before this scene can take place, you often need to introduce the necessary background, characters, and conflicts, so that once the big scene—the culmination of the story—occurs, you won't need to interrupt the action and take us offstage to fill us in.

In preparation for your culminating event, you can use several minor scenes and summarize several potential scenes into a generalized one. For example,

"Every Sunday morning, she walked to the Unitarian Church. As she walked, she would spit at the hedges." "Every Sunday" dissolves the action into a blurry repetitive scene, as do *would*, *often*, and *always*. Instead of constructing many small scenes to show us that she walks every Sunday, we have simply summarized this.

Such generalized scenes do not offer sharp detail, because on different occasions, the repeated action would be somewhat different. One Sunday it would be sunny, so the woman could walk in sandals; another Sunday it could snow, so she'd walk in boots; and so on. We reduce the amount of detail when we make summary scenes of repeated action.

Of course, as usual, there are exceptions to this rule. In a summary scene, you can come close to a realized scene, with many details, as in the case below, from John Cheever's "O Youth and Beauty!":

> Then if the host had a revolver, he would be asked to produce it. Cash would take off his shoes and assume a starting crouch behind a sofa. Trace would fire the weapon out of an open window, and if you were new to the community and had not understood what the preparations were about, you would then realize that you were watching a hurdle race. Over the sofa went Cash, over the tables, over the fire screen and the woodbox. It was not exactly a race, since Cash ran it alone, but it was extraordinary to see this man of forty surmount so many obstacles so gracefully.

We can imaginatively reconstruct this action, see it acted out without a gun and with a gun, in different yet similar houses.

This type of habitual action can set up the pieces—character, setting, conflict—but it will not do as a climax. In the climax of the above story, Cash's wife kills him with a gun. There are no *if*s and *would*s there. It takes place only once. A miracle is not a usual event, and a story works like a miracle; so it must take place as a here and now, only once. If it happens many times, it's a custom, not a miracle. You can introduce and develop a conflict through non-scenic narrative—but the culminating point of your story inevitably must be laid out as a scene or several scenes.

If you don't need to mention every Sunday, don't. Get us right into a scene to show us the characters and places on one crucial Sunday, when our main event takes place. However, especially in a long piece of writing, you probably will need to compound and summarize scenes. So learn to summarize the auxiliary action and dramatize the key moments. P.G. Wodehouse advised: "I think the success of every novel—if it's a novel of action—depends on the high spots.

The thing to do is to say to yourself, 'Which are my big scenes?' and then get every drop of juice out of them."

Silent Scenes

In preparation for the big scenes, many writers use silent scenes. These are not necessarily summary scenes, but descriptions of actions.

Certainly many war, crime, horror, and erotic scenes don't need to contain dialogue. Consider the following scene from *All Quiet on the Western Front* by Erich Maria Remarque:

> Suddenly in the pursuit we reach the enemy line.
>
> We are so close on the heels of our retreating enemies that we reach it almost at the same time as they. In this way we suffer few casualties. A machine-gun barks, but is silenced with a bomb. Nevertheless, the couple of seconds has sufficed to give us five stomach wounds. With the butt of his rifle Kat smashes to pulp the face of one of the unwounded machine-gunners. We bayonet the others before they have time to get out their bombs. Then thirstily we drink the water they have for cooling the guns.

From what goes on before this scene, we know exactly where we are, and the action here is timed, gruesomely vivid (as is appropriate for a war story), and concrete, yet not tremendously detailed. Smashing a face to pulp is vivid enough to make you wince. The image of drinking water for cooling guns lets us even taste the scene. Remarque does not need to describe the metallic watery taste in aluminum cups—we probably have these sensory associations anyhow. This appeal to our taste buds makes the scene powerful, although there's no dialogue.

In *One Hundred Years of Solitude*, Gabriel García Márquez uses no dialogue in the following erotic scene:

> Jose Arcadio's companion asked them to leave them alone, and the couple lay down on the ground, close to the bed. The passion of the others woke up Jose Arcadio's fervor. On the first contact the bones of the girl seemed to become disjointed with a disorderly crunch like the sound of a box of dominoes, and her skin broke out into a pale sweat and her eyes filled with tears as her whole body exhaled a lugubrious lament and a vague smell of mud. But she bore the impact with a firmness of character and a bravery that were admirable. Jose Arcadio felt himself lifted up into the air toward a state of seraphic inspiration, where his heart burst forth with an outpouring of tender

obscenities that entered the girl through her ears and came out of her mouth translated into her language.

This scene engages our sensory imagination (hearing, touch, sight, smell, even balance), even though many things are metaphoric ("seraphic inspiration"). The lovemaking is not given to us blow by blow, but yet it is concretized enough in time—"the first contact"—and place—"on the ground, close to the bed." This scene may not be erotically thrilling—most readers probably don't get into an amorous mood reading this. But the exquisite language and imagery give you an aesthetically strong experience. In writing good erotic scenes, the beauty of the writing matters most.

Although Márquez's scene indicates some kind of talk, this scene has no dialogue. Many such scenes could be useful to show what's going on before the major conflicts escalate into big, fully realized scenes, which should usually contain dialogue.

The Big Scene

Once we know enough about the characters and their conflicts, we can enter big scenes. Here's a big scene from "The Blue Hotel" by Stephen Crane. We have seen the paranoid Swede in other chapters. He expects snowy Nebraska to be the Wild West, where everybody cheats at cards; he trembles with fear that someone will kill him, thinks he sees people cheat at cards, gets into a fist fight with an innkeeper's son, wins, and then becomes cocky and moves to another bar. And just when he celebrates his being a tough guy, this is what happens. He insists that the bartender drink with him, but the bartender refuses:

"Well," cried the Swede, "listen hard then. See those men over there? Well, they're going to drink with me, and don't you forget it. Now you watch."

"Hi!" yelled the barkeeper, "this won't do!"

"Why won't it?" demanded the Swede. He stalked over to the table, and by chance laid his hand upon the shoulder of the gambler. "How about this?" he asked wrathfully. "I asked you to drink with me."

The gambler simply twisted his head and spoke over his shoulder. "My friend, I don't know you."

"Oh, hell!" answered the Swede, "come and have a drink."

"Now, my boy," advised the gambler, kindly, "take your hand off my shoulder and go 'way and mind your own business." He was a little, slim man, and it seemed strange to hear him use this tone of heroic patronage to the burly Swede. The other men at the table said nothing.

"What! You won't drink with me, you little dude? I'll make you!" The Swede had grasped the gambler frenziedly at the throat, and was dragging him from his chair. The other men sprang up. The barkeeper dashed around the corner of his bar. There was a great tumult, and then was seen a long blade in the hand of the gambler. It shot forward, and a human body, this citadel of virtue, wisdom, power, was pierced as easily as if it had been a melon. The Swede fell with a cry of supreme astonishment.

The prominent merchants and the district attorney must have at once tumbled out of the place backward. The bartender found himself hanging limply to the arm of a chair and gazing into the eyes of a murderer.

"Henry," said the latter, as he wiped his knife on one of the towels that hung beneath the bar rail, "you tell 'em where to find me. I'll be home, waiting for 'em." Then he vanished. A moment afterward the barkeeper was in the street dinning through the storm for help and, moreover, companionship.

The corpse of the Swede, alone in the saloon, had its eyes fixed upon a dreadful legend that dwelt atop the cash-machine: "This registers the amount of your purchase."

We have nearly all the elements of storytelling here. Besides dialogue, we have action: "The Swede had grasped the gambler frenziedly at the throat, and was dragging him from his chair."

Body language: "He stalked over to the table, and by chance laid his hand upon the shoulder of the gambler."

Vivid similes and metaphors: "pierced as easily as if it had been a melon."

A steady POV: (this is told from an objective POV, from a short range) "and then was seen a long blade." We are watching this. We don't see the action from any participant's mind, and we don't know who the narrator is. This is a theatrical POV.

Most of the story comes together in the image of the lonely Swede's corpse, with its eyes fixed on the sign reading "This registers the amount of your purchase." This scene seemed inevitable throughout the story, yet in a previous seemingly climactic scene, the Swede had won; our old expectations—which have driven the story forward suspensefully—have been fulfilled after we nearly quit them. But so that this would not be a linear plot, another chapter follows. From witness accounts, it turns out that the innkeeper's son was cheating at cards. The Swede was paranoid but not wrong.

This scene, while excellent, is not perfectly graceful. Although the third-person narrative is not an omniscient one, the narrator is not quite hidden, because we get the interpretation of the scene: "human body, this citadel of virtue, wisdom, power." But by this point in the story, the reader has accepted Crane's foregrounded narrator, who carefully observes and makes interpretative forays into the narrative. This kind of authorial presence is not in fashion today, and modern readers probably find it distracting. The objective distancing from the narrative actually reveals a subjective interpretation of the story's theme.

Earlier in this chapter, I said that using adverbs with dialogue tags usually doesn't work. But in this scene, we have an exception: "'How about this?' he asked wrathfully. 'I asked you to drink with me.'" "Wrathfully" augments the tone; the anger would not be sufficiently visible without the adverb. A well-placed adverb may enhance your showing of an action.

This outline—summary scenes, minor scenes, and silent scenes leading up to the big scene—is a classical story structure, but certainly not the only one. Many stories work differently. They may open with a big scene, then supply background, then go on to other big scenes. Some stories take place as a single continuous scene. And some big scenes may not contain dialogue—for example, the aspirin scene from "The Burning Shoe" contains only one spoken word, *nein*. How you prepare for the big moments in your fiction and how you construct the big scenes depend mostly on your subject matter. Having said this, I will also say that the classical story structure—with alternation among small scenes, narrative, and big scenes with dialogue—probably is the best choice whenever your subject matter allows it. The advantage of this structure is its variety of approaches: the changes of pace (from slow to quick, with both a quick pace and slow-motion effects in the climax action) and the changes in focus (from distant to close-up). This variety increases the possibility that the reader will stay fresh from page to page.

EXERCISES

1. One page. Write a composite scene of a woman and a man living happily together—their weekend routine. Use constructions such as "Every Sunday, they would go out for brunch."

Objective: To learn how to make chronologically composite scenes. You might need these to build toward a dramatic change. There'll be a Sunday, perhaps, in which the story crisis takes place, when they won't be able to go out for brunch. There you'd switch from the usual "every" scene to the specific "once" scene.

Check: Is your scene vivid? If it isn't, it's not a scene but a narrative summary. Let the reader smell the java, taste the butter on the croissant. On the other hand, is the scene too specific? You shouldn't have time-bound sentences, such as "It's awful that the earthquake split our bedroom in half a couple of hours ago, isn't it?" This is too specific, too dramatic, too unrepeatable to characterize a usual brunch.

2. One page. Describe a lovemaking scene, without being too explicit. A good erotic scene depends more on suggestion than on complete revelation. This may be difficult to do. Avoid statements like "She was excited" and "He moaned with pleasure." Namely, steer away from clichés and summaries. Try to be fresh.

Objective: Not necessarily to arouse your reader, but instead, to dazzle him with exquisite images. Learn how to combine vivid imagery and graceful sentences.

Check: Have you engaged our senses? Make sure this is not all visual. Touch and smell. Do you have staple expressions, such as "She was swooning in ecstasy"? Delete them. Use fresher language, the way Márquez uses "seraphic inspiration" for ecstasy. And since the reader can't hear the ecstasy, offer an image that suggests it, as Márquez does with the words entering the girl's ears and coming out of her mouth translated in her own language.

3. Two to three pages. Describe a war scene, showing a horrible deed without mentioning that it is horrible.

Objective: To show rather than tell. In a scene, more than anywhere else, this is crucial. Telling is a summary. Showing is a scene. "It looked horrible" tells and does not show. Here, it's not so important that your sentences be graceful; on the contrary, construct some choppy ones to reflect the subject matter.

Check: Have you engaged our senses? If not, go back and surprise us. Let us taste something, the way Remarque lets us taste gun-cleaning water at the end of his scene. Let us feel something, like salty mud in our nostrils.

4. Two pages. Write a scene with your protagonist engaged in some kind of activity just before she is ambushed or assassinated. Let the protagonist notice and misinterpret the clues of danger; and let her hesitate with the intuition of the danger and still go into the trap. You could play with atmospheric details and the character's thoughts to achieve foreshadowing and suspense.

Now write the same scene from the perspective of the antagonists who are setting the ambush. Create the uncertainty of a hunt.

Objective: To prepare for the climax scene with foreshadowing and suspense. Excite the reader with the sensation of impending danger (with skillful choice of details and clues), and yet don't make it too obvious what will happen, so that the reader genuinely won't know in advance. It's good to keep your mind open so that, although you may drive the narrative toward an assassination, something else could happen instead. If you surprise yourself, you will surprise the reader, too.

Check: Did you insinuate what's to appear through sensations—smells, sounds, visual clues? Writing, "I had a sense of foreboding as I approached the cave" or "The dark evergreens looked ominous against the pale sky" won't do. "Foreboding" and "ominous" is what you're striving to achieve—not mention. If you strike *ominous* from the sentence, you could rewrite and improve it: "The evergreens, dark against the pale sky, appeared like a brotherhood of monks clad in black robes and sworn to silence." That would not be particularly subtle either, but at least you would not glaringly state "ominous." In fact, pointing sharply toward what's ahead may not be bad. The same sentence could be rewritten, "The dark evergreens appeared like moist knife blades poking into the pale sky." The notion of murder and a knife will be raised. The main goal is to create expectations, which need not be fulfilled neatly.

5. One page. Write a scene from the POV of a woman who comes home from work and is about to discover her boyfriend's lover.

Objective: Similar to Exercise 4, though not necessarily as suspenseful. Let the woman misinterpret—at first—the clues that somebody might be around.

Check: Did you provide enough sensory clues giving us a notion that somebody might be present in the house? Smells? Sounds? Keep them subtle.

6. Two pages. Use a tape recorder and record a dinner conversation. (If you don't have such gadgets handy, listen carefully and write quickly.) Transcribe the conversation. Then read what you have. Most likely, the transcript will be . cumbersome to read, with all the pauses, fillers, and so on. Edit it. Take out all the repetitions. Read it again. Perhaps now it's too spare. So put back a few repetitions for the natural sound, and, here and there, describe minimal actions between spoken sentences—slurping the soup, clanking the china—so the dialogue does not appear to be suspended in a vacuum. These little details will turn the dialogue into a scene. Now the conversation should read smoothly, if for no other reason than because you've read thousands of dialogues done in that vein.

Objective: To learn to distinguish between real conversation and written dialogue. In your final dialogue, keep the best parts of the actual conversation, and the best artificial props—if any—you came up with in rewriting.

Check: Since this is an exercise in revision, the check is included in the task description.

7. Two pages. Reproduce a quarrel you've had. Don't edit for diversity of insults, subtlety of word choice, dignity of the scene. Just give it to us, raw.

Objective: A quarrel is a paradigm of dynamic dialogue. Conflicting motives drive word choices. Even if there's no quarrel in your dialogue, use a conflict to propel the conversation.

Check: Is it clear what the quarrel is about? It may be about two issues, one on the surface, another beneath it, but at least let the theme of the surface quarrel be clear. If it's too confusing, it won't work. Anger, probably more than any other emotion, helps the mind simplify problems into sharp outlines.

8. Four one-page dialogue scenes. Write probing dialogue between (1) a demented psychiatrist and a client, (2) an evangelist and a philosophical homeless person, (3) a police officer and a burglar who pretends to live in the apartment from which he is stealing, and (4) a mother who's just miscarried and her four-year-old, who wants a baby sister.

Objective: To practice writing different people's dialogue. Let characters speak spontaneously, pulling you in and saying things almost on their own. Perhaps once you begin hearing a voice, the voice will write and you will merely record.

Check: Do the characters sound different from each other? They should. Do your characters talk at cross-purposes? They should. Let them evade answering questions. Sometimes a question should be countered with another question. Sometimes the answer should have nothing directly to do with the question.

9. One page. Describe body language during a conversation without reproducing any of the dialogue. Have a party of three at a table, two men and a woman. One man is in love with the woman, the woman is in love with the other man, and he's in love with himself. Describe their postures, inclinations of their bodies, hand motions, and so on—the way Doris Lessing does in "The Real Thing," on page 116.

Objective: To learn how to show bodies talking. Some ambiguity of gesture is all right. Some psychologists think that even the direction a crossed leg points with its foot indicates who the leg-crosser likes most in a circle. Of course, these social psychologists don't make it any easier to attend a party, because they expand the potential for self-consciousness, but they do make your task of writing easier. Even if they are wrong, they do what you should do in fiction: They make gestures meaningful.

Check: From the social dynamics you've given us, is it clear who's after whom? Is it clear that the second man is a narcissist? Does he constantly glance at mirrors and touch up his fragile hairdo?

10. Two pages. Now let us hear what these people from Exercise 9 talk about. Intersperse their words into the description you already have.

Objective: To learn how to mix body language and dialogue.

Check: Do all your characters sound distinct from one another? Could you tell without direct dialogue tags who's talking? Does the content of what's said reveal who's after whom? Is the narcissist boasting? Is the first man insulting him?

11. Two pages. Write a dialogue, without using *said* or any other words indicating speech. Rely on punctuation marks and all the strategies for avoiding *said* that we've discussed in this chapter.

Objective: To practice avoiding direct dialogue tags.

Check: Is it always clear who's talking? If not, go back and insert *said* and other tags, to make it clear wherever needed.

12. Two to three pages. Write a dialogue between a father and daughter. She is looking forward to a trip to Alaska, which he's promised, provided that she got all A's on her finals. However, the father has lost all his savings gambling that afternoon when she comes home with her transcript. He can't afford the trip, yet he doesn't have the heart to tell her. Meanwhile, she got a C in English but forged an A on the transcript. Let him marvel at her improvement in English and ask to see her brilliant essay on honesty; and let her keep evading his request, asking about Alaska and going about her business, packing for the trip.

Objective: To practice constructing dialogue that serves to avoid giving information, to mislead, and to forestall dreaded questions.

Check: Is there a lot of cross-purpose conversation? There should be. Are there irrelevant things said out of context? There should be, like in Christopher Isherwood's "The Last of Mr. Norris" (page 116). Is there body language to show anxiety? Defensiveness? Faked emotion? Pauses? Ignored questions?

13. Two to three pages. A very common dialogue trope, especially in a quarrel, is that one speaker interprets in his own words what has just been said by the other, giving it an additional spin that wasn't there to begin with. We do it silently anyway, trying to read beyond what has been explicitly said. It is generally a very poor technique for understanding people, because we translate their terms into ours liberally and often insultingly. For example, John says to his wife, Jane:

"We shouldn't eat white bread any more."

"You mean to say I am fat and I should diet?"

"No, not that, I've read that whole wheat gives you more energy. We wouldn't need so much coffee and we'd save money."

"Oh, you are saying I am spending too much money? By the way, whole wheat or not, it's all the same. What matters is whole grains."

"OK, that's what I mean. You're saying that I am stupid?"

"No, but if you want to diet, do your research first. And I agree, you should diet. You are fat."

Objective: Just a little dialogue etude and a reminder to skew dialogue a bit for the sake of dynamic energy.

Check: Are the listeners misinterpreting what is being said? Putting their words into other people's mouths? That's the idea.

BEGINNINGS AND ENDINGS

A good piece of fiction resembles a multi-course meal. You begin with an aperitif or an appetizer. If you can afford it, of course, you'd like a delicacy before you get down to the nitty-gritty of knife-handling and chewing.

Some story beginnings offer the burning quality of cognac; others, the salty allure of caviar; and some we prefer to skip as though waiting for fast food.

Some writers write the beginning last; others write it first. Gabriel García Márquez says he labors over his first paragraph for days, and when he has it down, the rest comes easily. Some writers need to know the end before they begin; others need to know only the characters, whom they set into motion to find their own endings and beginnings. Others, like Jerzy Kosinski, have both the ending and the beginning before they do the rest: "I always start a novel by writing its first page and its last page, which seem to survive almost intact through all the following drafts and changes." Experiment and see what works for you.

As you write, you need not despair if you don't have a brilliant beginning. Perhaps your ending will become your beginning in the final version. Maybe you will chop off both the draft ending and the beginning, and a passage from the middle of the story will emerge as the dynamic beginning. Many writers assume we have had enough beginnings and endings, and they spare us. This minimalist approach—give me just the story without the décor—is possible in short stories, but in novels, it's harder—probably impossible—to achieve.

I admire graceful beginnings and endings, so although my aesthetics in other respects might be minimalist, I see no reason why you should deprive yourself (and your readers) of their grace.

BEGINNINGS

After the cover art and the title, beginnings are your first impression, or rather, expression. The cover may be beautiful, the title sonorous, but if the first lines sound dull, the first impression will be dull. From social psychology, we know that the first impression is often the most important one, that after all kinds of other impressions settle, the last impression will probably resemble the first. Because of this notion, many writers belabor their openings, to make them stunning.

While it's important to be interesting in the first lines, beginnings must accomplish much more. To resort to a prolonged comparison: In a chess opening, you try to win—and control—the greatest amount of space with the fewest moves possible. You open and develop your pieces, place them in striking distance of the opponent's pieces, with a view to the engagement—the middle game, in which you'll maneuver toward the winning end game. You might aim to have a preponderance of pawns on one side, so once all the heavy pieces are exchanged, you advance a single pawn. A good player never aims to play a trick in the first five moves if she respects her opponent. Likewise, if you respect your reader, you don't resort to tricks in the opening, for these are short-lived. Like a sound chess opening, an opening of fiction must accomplish more urgent goals than "brilliant combinations." (Reserve those for the climactic action.) Introduce your characters, give us the place and time where the story occurs, and raise a question, complication, or crisis that we are to follow—something to intrigue us, so we want to keep reading.

Unlike bombastic journalism, which relies on opening with a bang, fiction can open less loudly. Here's an example of a bang opening by Truman Capote, in "Children on Their Birthdays": "Yesterday afternoon the six o'clock bus ran over Miss Bobbit."

Yes, this catches our interest, but what next? It'll be hard to match the intensity of the beginning in what follows. The story starts with a climax rather than working toward one; instead of looking forward, we look backward, and the whole story might be an anticlimax. (Actually, despite the drawback of bombast, Capote does manage, with considerable skill, to make a good story. But that's an expert feat, not something a beginner can expect to emulate.)

Some bangs may work effectively, provided they are timed well and delayed a bit, as this, from George Gissing's *New Grub Street*:

> As the Milvains sat down to breakfast the clock of Wattleborough
> parish church struck eight; it was two miles away, but the strokes
> were borne very distinctly on the west wind this autumn morning.
> Jasper, listening before he cracked an egg, remarked with cheerful-
> ness: "There's a man being hanged in London at this moment."

This is a skillful jab—not an outright bang in the first sentence, but in the second. The first one draws characters and an orderly setting (useful, for we need to know where and with whom we are) in lyrical strokes, so the hanging announcement startles us. It's harder to startle in the first sentence because there's nothing prior that the sentence could contrast with. Still, if the punch has been delayed, its intensity has been magnified, and the problem remains: Where do we go from here, if our hero's already hanged in the second sentence?

If you open without murdering anybody on the first page, you have less to live up to, and you still might create intrigue, as does the beginning of Heinrich von Kleist's "The Marquise of O——." Not only does this opening have the quality of a hook (not a punch)—raising a question of what to look for in the story—it also introduces a crisis and a character:

> In M——, an important town in northern Italy, the widowed Marquise of O—— a lady of unblemished reputation and the mother of several well-brought-up children, inserted the following announcement in the newspapers: that she had, without knowledge of the cause, come to find herself in a certain condition; that she would like the father of the child she was expecting to disclose his identity to her; and that she was resolved, out of consideration for her family, to marry him.

The introduction—"lady of unblemished reputation"—contrasts with what follows five lines down. The question is raised, which we will follow through most of the novella: Who's done it? Who has impregnated the lady? We are not hooked as fish but as fishermen, to stare into the stream of words to come, and to catch the guy.

True, the action must go pretty high to surpass the shock of an incognito impregnation; and von Kleist does deliver the escalation of the action—plunder, rape, and murder. We start high, slow down, and go higher. In terms of music, we could express this as allegro, adagio, allegro, vivace. The good opening facilitates this dynamic structure. Whenever you have a dramatic hook, you must live up to it.

I've quoted another brilliant opening by von Kleist, from *Michael Kohlhaas*, on pages 46–47, where the startling moment occurs at the end of the first paragraph, rather than at the beginning. The virtuous man, driving his virtue to an extreme, has become a murderer. We have motivation to find out how such a paradox could occur. And the murder is not the culmination of the story; the climax is that a peasant war will start and Dresden will burn.

Von Kleist has managed to keep up with the high expectations that his opening hook created.

Rather than opening with a dazzling hook, you might open with something more essential: character, setting, theme, and style. If the point is to invite the reader into your story, it's usually good to open with fine writing—show the reader that he can trust the narrator, that the narrator has the skill, the mischief, the humor, and the charm, to tell a good story—as Charles Dickens does in *Little Dorrit*:

> Thirty years ago, Marseilles lay burning in the sun, one day. A blazing sun upon a fierce August day was no greater rarity in southern France then, than at any other time, before or since. Everything in Marseilles, and about Marseilles, had stared at the fervid sky, and been stared at in return, until a staring habit had become universal there. Strangers were stared out of countenance by staring white houses, staring white walls, staring white streets, staring tracts of arid road, staring hills from which verdure was burnt away. The only thing to be seen not fixedly staring and glaring were the vines drooping under their load of grapes. These did occasionally wink a little, as the hot air barely moved their faint leaves.

If this opening were to show up in a fiction workshop as a student's work, I suppose most participants would jump at it and demand that the repetition of "staring" be diminished. But the repetition works stylistically—Dickens carries the staring theme the way a musician might sustain a theme, weaving it through a long passage, accruing a mood and a playful rhythm. Staring and glaring and winking—clearly, he's had fun writing. At the same time, he introduces us to the setting (Marseilles) and an important theme (scrutiny).

If you don't manage an opening that announces a theme explicitly, in a paradoxical fashion, as does von Kleist in *Michael Kohlhaas* (or Dickens, with "It was the best of times, it was the worst of times"), don't despair. Consider laying out a theme and raising an anticipation implicitly, on a metaphoric, poetic level. Here's one effective opening—from Stephen Crane's *The Red Badge of Courage*—that works through images rather than ideas:

> The cold passed reluctantly from the earth, and the retiring fogs revealed an army stretched out on the hills, resting. As the landscape changed from brown to green, the army awakened, and began to tremble with eagerness at the noise of rumors. It cast its eyes upon the roads, which were growing from long troughs of liquid mud to proper thoroughfares. A river, amber-tinted in the shadow of its banks, purled at the army's feet; and at night, when the stream had become of a sorrowful blackness, one could see across it the red, eyelike gleam of hostile camp-fires set in the low brows of distant hills.

This opening sets up expectations. The quality of images persuades us to keep reading, and the promise of finding something (rather than getting it right away) sets us fishing. The hook may not be visible, but that's fine—the worm is. Thematically, from the title, we know we will read about courage; and from the first paragraph, that we will read about fear—"tremble with eagerness." "Eye-like gleam of hostile camp-fires set in the low brows of distant hills" tells us we are listening to a skillful narrator.

And notice that the paragraph takes its time. It's not a bang opening. From my observation and informal surveys with students and friends, it seems most people read at least half the first page when browsing. This means two things to me. First, you don't need to open with a bang or a trick. Your command of the language and images will assure the reader more than a glistening image out of context. Relax, and concentrate on leading into the story most appropriately in terms of your theme.

Second, if you do have something bizarre and fantastic going on, state it by the end of that half page, or even right in the beginning. In the first several sentences, readers will accept almost anything that will work as a premise for the story. If your character is an angel or a thoughtful shoe, say so right away, while the grace of laying out the premises and promises still covers you. Of course, what follows had better be convincing.

Ways to Begin

There are many ways to begin a story. Learn and use these various methods just as a good chess player learns not to rely on only one opening. Different openings may encourage you to write in a variety of ways, which I think is important especially as you experiment, looking for your best work pattern.

Setting

Here's an example of opening with a setting, from F. Scott Fitzgerald's *Tender Is the Night*:

> On the pleasant shore of the French Riviera, about halfway between Marseilles and the Italian border, stands a large, proud, rose-colored hotel. Deferential palms cool its flushed facade, and before it stretches a short dazzling beach. Lately it has become a summer resort of notable and fashionable people ....

This sets the stage and raises our expectations—high-society members will show up here and play. "Lately" may indicate that we are going to deal the newly rich; there may be an ironic quality to the adverb. "Flushed facade" may lead into questions of shame amid glamour. The advantage of this opening is that we know where we are, and we have begun to anticipate the actors, but we don't have any definite questions yet. We are easing into the novel, which is fine, perhaps in the spirit of the theme.

Ideas

If you open with an idea, you take a risk—the piece might promise to be too intellectual, dry, essayistic. However, ideas—especially if expressed in the first person or in dialogue (or monologue)—sometimes serve multiple purposes, as in this example from Charles Dickens's *Hard Times*:

> Now, what I want is, Facts. Teach these boys and girls nothing but Facts. Facts alone are wanted in life. Plant nothing else, and root out everything else. You can only form the minds of reasoning animals upon Facts: nothing else will ever be of any service to them ....

The idea of facts being everything indirectly portrays the speaker (a principal) and the place (a boarding school). And the idea becomes a theme, nearly a leit-motif for the novel. So, far from a dry abstraction, an idea may accomplish as much as a well-chosen image.

Strong Sensations

Sensations quickly invite your reader to begin experiencing your narrative, and therefore many writers favor sense-oriented beginnings, as does Jessica Hagedorn in *Dogeaters*:

> 1956. The air-conditioned darkness of the Avenue Theater smells of flowery pomade, sugary chocolates, cigarette smoke, and sweat.

This opening may contain an overload of sensations, but it works. The reader receives a strong impression of the setting. And a part of the setting, time, we get immediately—"1956"—even before we have begun to look for a sentence. The introduction follows two questions: *when* and *where*. *When* is immediately and unobtrusively given as abstract information, and *where*, as a sensory atmosphere.

A single strong sensation gives our imaginations clear entry into the story. We don't have to start working right away, to try to sort out a complex image. William Faulkner, in "Barn Burning," focuses on a single smell: "The store in which the Justice of the Peace's court was sitting smelled of cheese." We are in the scene at once, experiencing, without having to decide on which sensation to concentrate. No need to cajole us to get there.

A Need or Motive

Nothing propels the characters and the readers as efficiently as a definite need, and the sooner the need is identified, the better. Katherine Mansfield, in "Marriage a la Mode," introduces the characters' wishes right away:

> On his way to the station William remembered with a fresh pang
> of disappointment that he was taking nothing down to the kiddies.
> Poor little chaps! It was hard lines on them. Their first words always
> were as they ran to greet him, "What have you got for me, daddy?"
> and he had nothing.

It may be equally effective to open by stating what the character does not want.

Action

Our animal eyes most quickly notice movement. Starting a story with action will catch your reader's attention. Look at how Irwin Shaw does it in "The Eighty-Yard Run":

> The pass was high and wide and he jumped for it, feeling it slap flatly
> against his hands, as he shook his hips to throw off the halfback who
> was diving at him.

Sex

Sexual images excite some people and tire others, but overall, the tactic of opening with sex has worked for many writers—it certainly does for Tama Janowitz in *Slaves of New York*:

> After I became a prostitute, I had to deal with penises of every imag-
> inable shape and size. Some large, others quite shriveled and pendu-
> lous of testicle.

This opening promises a great deal of (fictional) self-revelation; and since many people read fiction to find out about the aspects of people's lives that aren't otherwise easily observable, this is a good hook. But sometimes the use of a sexual image may sound like a desperate plea for attention. Opening with sex has the advantage of grabbing a reader's attention, and the potential disadvantage of appearing cheesy.

Symbolic Object

If in your first sentence you describe an object, whether you intend it to be a symbol or not, most readers will treat it as a symbol, and they'll probably ask, "Why do we start with this thing? What does it mean?"

The expectations created by a described object could give you an effective opener. This technique works for Jean Stafford in "A Country Love Story":

> An antique sleigh stood in the yard, snow after snow banked up against its eroded runners.

A sleigh evokes all kinds of associations—Santa Claus, freedom, travel, and the quaintness of a bygone era. And the eroded runners indicate that the bygone perhaps can't be recaptured.

The advantage of opening with a symbol is that, besides giving us thematic expectations, the object gives us something concrete to visualize and play with. The disadvantage is that this prominent position may bring an overload of the reader's expectations and interpretations to the object, so that the opening might appear overly subtle.

Character Portrait

Your opening could provide an external look at a character, such as this one from Charles D'Ambrosio's "Her Real Name":

> The girl's scalp looked as though it had been singed by fire—strands of thatchy red hair snaked away from her face, then settled against her skin, pasted there by sweat and sunscreen and the blown grit and dust of travel.

The story centers around a terminally ill girl; although we don't know yet that she's dying, we begin to see that something is amiss, and our unease will grow throughout the story, until her death.

The disadvantage of this type of opening is that it'll take a while before the action starts—we'll go through a summary with various thoughts and generalizations before a scene can begin. The main advantage is that we go straight for the character; we learn right away what the character does; we hear her voice. The advantage is probably greater than the disadvantage—for when the story's action begins, we will be prepared. We'll know the character—her main concerns and themes.

Question

Like Ivan Turgenev in *Fathers and Sons*, you can begin your narrative with a question:

> "Well, Peter, any sign of them yet?" This was the question addressed on the 20th of May, 1859, to his servant—a young and lusty fellow with whitish down on his chin and with small dim eyes—by a

gentleman of just forty years of age, in a dusty overcoat and check trousers, as he emerged hatless on the low steps of a posting-station on the X highway.

Most motivation for reading comes from questions. Reading becomes a search for answers. So asking a question is the most direct way to get the reader to work with you.

The advantage is that the question, if it's part of a dialogue, leads us immediately into a scene—we jump into the middle of the action, something is going on in the first line. However, that may prove to be a disadvantage, too, because we don't know the speaker yet, nor the place where he speaks, and supplying this background quickly after the question may appear stilted, as it does in the above example. Still, this can be an effective opening, because it's important for your reader to have questions.

Scene

A scene naturally combines action, setting, and character. Even a brief scene may do all this, as does the opener of Alexander Pushkin's "The Queen of Spades":

> Card-playing was going on in the quarters of Narumov, an officer in the Guards.

One simple sentence introduces all three elements. The advantage is that an action will be in progress as we join it; we skip preparations. We jump into the middle. Yet, unlike in an opening with a common hook, nothing extreme has happened, so the action can escalate, not decelerate.

Travel

In this type of opener, the character and the reader share the same experience: Both arrive as strangers to a place. This shared experience is an effective lead, and if it hadn't been done so many times, I'd certainly recommend it as one of the best ways to start a story. Even so, if your setting is interesting enough, this technique should be effective.

Travel as a background can set the mood, as in Reidar Jönsson's *My Life as a Dog*:

> The snowflakes had a hypnotic effect on me. I was getting more and more drowsy, but I needed to keep my eyes open. What if I missed my station and got off at the wrong one, rushed out into the white arctic tundra, totally dazed, only to be met by wolves who were ready to tear me to pieces! Now, that would be unforgivable and unworthy of a true Trapper.

This works—because we experience the narrator's thoughts and perceptions. The setting we see in travel gives us access to the character.

Character's Thoughts
Saul Bellow opens his novel *Herzog* with the main character's thoughts:

> If I am out of my mind, it's all right with me, thought Moses Herzog.

We are in the character's mind, which is where the reader probably wants to be; it makes sense to get there right away, especially in a psychological novel. The disadvantage of this method is that thoughts are abstract—we don't see anything yet. But the thought is interesting and paradoxical enough that it could make us curious; we may ask, "What kind of guy is this, who doesn't care whether he's crazy?"

Prediction
Richard Yates opens his novel *The Easter Parade* with a bit of foretelling:

> Neither of the Grimes sisters would have a happy life, and looking back
> it always seemed that the trouble began with their parents' divorce.

This evokes an ominous tone of prophecy, so that you tend to read on with a sense of foreboding, which, dramatically, can work. The downside is that this opening might reveal the end (in general terms), thus perhaps decreasing suspense.

Anecdote
Anton Chekhov opens "In the Ravine" with the following paragraph:

> The village of Ukleyevo lay in the ravine, so that only the belfry and
> the chimneys of the cotton mills could be seen from the highway and
> the railroad station. When passers-by would ask what village it was,
> they were told: "That's the one where the sexton ate up all the caviar
> at the funeral."

The entertaining anecdote lures us into the story. The humor, however, does not prepare us for the spirit of the story—a tragic one with a baby's death. But maybe the humorous mood struck in the beginning intensifies the tragedy, and perhaps caviar and funerals have symbolically to do with the death of a baby. Still, this example reminds me that some openings function to entice the reader into the story, without necessarily setting the key mood, theme, and so on. Perhaps too much can be made of all that. Most readers, after all, probably say, "Come, entertain me!"

A Final Comment on Beginnings

Obviously, you can start your novel or story in many ways, some of which we haven't mentioned. You might come up with some unique approaches, although it's not uniqueness that's most necessary in the beginning, but an orientation for the reader. To prepare your reader for your story, you must—not long after the first sentence—introduce the setting, character, and problem (or crisis), something that the rest of the piece will solve. And while you introduce these elements, make the reader begin to see, hear, experience, and get involved in your story. Entertain your reader.

How you'll accomplish all this should partly depend on the subject matter, and partly, of course, it'll be arbitrary. Many people think there's only one possible "right" opening for each story, and sometimes I agree. But often, I think, you can enter a story—a description of an event—in many ways, and several of them may work. "All roads lead to Rome," the old saying goes. You may enter the city from nine directions, and although where you enter will shape your experience of Rome, once you reach the Colosseum, all this may not matter much. You are with the lions now. (But you'd better remember where you entered if you want to leave the Colosseum and Rome.) So while it's healthy to learn how to open in many ways, it's also healthy not to get lost. Use openings for what they are: entrances to something larger than themselves. The beginning must lead somewhere. The threads you start here must continue. The beginning (besides the ending) is the least forgiving place for loose ends. Here, you commit yourself to themes, places, characters. If you can't keep the commitment, find another beginning, another door that leads in.

THE END GAME

Thomas Fuller said, "Great is the art of beginning, but greater the art is of ending." It seems many writers agree that endings give them more trouble than beginnings do. That's partly because in the ending—especially in short stories—everything needs to fit; in the beginning, we don't yet know what needs to fit, so almost everything appears acceptable.

It is particularly true that short stories must end adequately; all the strings must tie in. David Lodge says in *The Art of Fiction*: "One might say that the short story is essentially 'end-oriented,' inasmuch as one begins a short story in the expectation of soon reaching its conclusion, whereas one embarks upon a novel with no very precise idea of when one will finish it."

With novels, while it's essential to resolve the conflicts you raise, frequently the last page does not matter much—it's a kind of exit two-step jig. If the series of conflicts has resulted in many deaths and births, how one waves good-bye after all this won't matter. Some good friends of mine don't like good-byes, and after we spend days talking, we part quickly, almost in midsentence. Nothing will now change the good times and conversations we've had. I'm not saying that your novels don't need to reach a resolution, but in many cases it does not matter much how they end after the resolution—you may spend quite a few pages settling accounts and fading out.

In a novel, it is clear when the end will occur—the book ends, physically. You can't hide it, unlike in movies, in theater, in symphony.

Let's compare a long novel to Beethoven's Fifth Symphony: After the amazing music, we get a prolonged announcement of the end, and when the end finally comes every fool in the audience knows it's the end. Yes, you've given me a shattering experience, but I'll do fine without all this militaristic pomp after it. His end works as a kind of punishment, in the name of the idea of the End.

Now, having said this, I do acknowledge that we still need to end somehow. In a novel, the prolonged announcements of the end are even more absurd than in the symphony hall, because the quantity of pages under my forefinger tells me when the end comes, so there's no point in playing hide-and-seek.

Both in the novel and the short story, once you reach the resolution, exit quickly. You might make one victory circle, like a skater with a medal on her neck, to part from the readers with a graceful exhibition, but this is not necessary. Or, if your story cannot reach a resolution, exit it once this has become clear.

Types of Endings

Although there are many ways to end a piece of fiction, in all of them you may strive to achieve basically the same goal: Give us another look, or angle, or thought, on what has just taken place in your fiction, something that will put it all in perspective.

When you are about to end a piece, decide which image or thought you want your reader to carry as the last impression. I think that endings with striking sensory images are often preferable to abstract analysis. Even church services end either with bread and wine or with music, not with abstractions. In fiction, too, a taste of wine aged in centuries-old oak barrels may end the supper evocatively.

Circular Ending

I can't generalize about all endings, but in a great many pieces of writing, endings must give an answer to the questions, concerns, and images set forth in the beginning. The beginning and the ending may sometimes tie together quite neatly.

In a novel, you sometimes find the first paragraph functioning as the last. We already know the beginning of *My Life as a Dog* by Reidar Jönsson, on page 138. The same paragraph serves as the ending of the novel. It makes sense, given that the novel is a bildungsroman, the story of a boyhood of a future writer, so at the end he writes the first page of the book:

> One day I might tell somebody the truth. I know exactly how I'll begin: The snowflakes had a hypnotic effect on me. I was getting more and more drowsy, but I needed to keep my eyes open. What if I missed my station and got off at the wrong one, rushed out into the white arctic tundra, totally dazed, only to be met by wolves who were ready to tear me to pieces! Now, that would be unforgivable and unworthy of a true Trapper.

That type of circularity works in this case, but sometimes it may appear strained and artificial.

Matching vs. Nonmatching Ending

A matching ending is pretty close to a circular one; the first image, transformed, serves also as the last. The end answers the concerns of the beginning directly.

The beginning of Jean Stafford's "A Country Love Story" is quoted on page 137. Now let's read the ending:

> She knew now that no change would come, and that she would never see her lover again. Confounded utterly, like an orphan in solitary confinement, she went outdoors and got into the sleigh. The blacksmith's imperturbable cat stretched and rearranged his position, and May sat beside him with her hands locked tightly in her lap, rapidly wondering over and over again how she would live the rest of her life.

The story starts in the sleigh and now ends in it, giving it an obvious unity.

I'll give several examples of such rounded-off endings under other headings to follow, but often such endings aren't a necessity. For example, Kafka's "The Metamorphosis"—whose beginning is perhaps (almost unavoidably) the most frequently quoted, and whose ending is rarely quoted:

> They [Mr. and Mrs. Samsa] grew quieter and half unconsciously exchanged glances of complete agreement, having come to the conclusion that it would soon be time to find a good husband for her. And it

was like a confirmation of their new dreams and excellent intentions that at the end of their journey their daughter sprang to her feet first and stretched her young body.

The story does not end with the same character, Gregor. It's not in the fantastic mode any more. The end could hardly be more dissimilar from the beginning. But indirectly, it's appropriate—it presents a contrast to Gregor's agony and intensifies the sensation of his being superfluous. The world could go on quite well—actually better—without him. This ironic, apparently unmatching ending probably works better than another cockroach image could.

Surprise Ending

This is occasionally called the O. Henry ending, although Guy de Maupassant, and other writers before him, practiced it. In "The Necklace," a woman named Matilda borrows a necklace, loses it, buys a glass replica, and works as a washer woman for fifteen years to replace the lost one with a genuine diamond necklace. She gives the genuine necklace to its owner, who says:

> "You say that you bought a diamond necklace to replace mine?"
> "Yes. You did not notice it then? They were just alike."
> And she smiled with a proud and simple joy. Madame Forestier was touched and took both her hands as she replied:
> "Oh! my poor Matilda! Mine were false. They were not worth over five hundred francs!"

Trick Ending

This is not the same as the surprise ending, although it may be a surprising one, too.

If Kafka had told "The Metamorphosis" without revealing to us that Gregor Samsa was in a cockroach's body, and he saved this line for the last, it would be a trick ending, or a cheat ending. I am hard-pressed to give you any examples from literature, because a trick ending is usually enough to ensure that a piece of writing will not be regarded as literature.

Ambrose Bierce's "An Occurrence at Owl Creek Bridge" comes close to it. A man is being hanged. But after this, we get the story of the man's escape, for most of the story, until the man reaches his home:

> Ah, how beautiful she [his wife] is! He springs forward with extended arms. As he is about to clasp her he feels a stunning blow upon the back of the neck; a blinding white light blazes all about him with a sound like the shock of a cannon—then all is darkness and silence!

> Peyton Farquhar was dead; his body, with a broken neck, swung
> gently from side to side beneath the timbers of the Owl Creek bridge.

Bierce tricks most readers into believing that the man has escaped. And then, bang, we are back, continuing the opening. This all makes sense now, when you think about hallucinations, theories of a mind racing before death, and so on. He has tricked us for a worthwhile purpose. But it's not the ending that's a trick—it's the middle of the story. The ending fits the beginning perfectly. Thanks to the beginning, it works.

Summary Ending

You can summarize the outcome of the story. For example, in Guy de Maupassant's "Mademoiselle Fifi," a French prostitute can't bear to be humiliated by a Prussian officer; she stabs him to death, runs, and hides. These events are dramatically presented, but the outcome is summarized at the end:

> A short time afterward, a patriot who had no prejudices, who liked
> her because of her bold deed, and who afterward loved her for herself,
> married her, and made a lady of her.

The main dramatic event takes a couple of hours, so the rest is narrated summarily. In such cases, this strategy works better than dragging on with the story. However, the summary lends the story an air of a tale—which you may or may not want. Many movies have used this device, as a way of going outside of the frame of the event covered in the picture, without having to linger and decelerate—and therefore this device may seem too familiar. But, since it is used pretty rarely in current fiction, summary endings can be a good option. Tom Wolfe successfully uses a summary ending for *The Bonfire of the Vanities*, as does Marilynne Robinson in *Housekeeping*.

Open Ending

Many writers object to a neat ending because it seems contrary to ordinary experience, which keeps going after an event is "over," and in which the repercussions of the event are seen in new experiences. Not even the death of one person ends the experience of others, and as long as you have at least two characters in a story, you might need to account for how the survivors keep thinking, feeling, experiencing. If you agree with this outlook, you might use open endings. Exit a piece of fiction while the action is ongoing. Much is said about beginning *in medias res*, but you can also exit in the middle of things.

For an example, let's take a look at *The Fixer* by Bernard Malamud. Yakov Bok, an apolitical Jewish man, has come to Kiev from his shtetel (Jewish village) around 1914. After he's unjustly accused of murdering a Christian boy, without indictment, he spends a couple of years in solitary confinement, undergoing all kinds of extreme torture. When a bogus indictment arrives, he's escorted by Cossack soldiers to his trial, where his chances are slim. However, a revolution might take place soon (we, as readers, know that the October Revolution is near). These are the thoughts and images that end the novel, on Yakov's way to the trial, which we never reach:

> Afterwards he thought, Where there's no fight for it there's no freedom. What is it Spinoza says? If the state acts in ways that are abhorrent to human nature it's the lesser evil to destroy it. Death to the anti-Semites! Long live revolution! Long live liberty!
>
> The crowds lining both sides of the streets were dense again, packed tight between curb and housefront. There were faces at every window and people standing on rooftops along the way. Among those in the street were Jews of the Plossky District. Some, as the carriage clattered by and they glimpsed the fixer, were openly weeping, wringing their hands. One thinly bearded man clawed his face. One or two waved at Yakov. Some shouted his name.

We don't know how the trial will end. Will Yakov be sentenced to death and shot before the revolution takes place? Or will the revolutionaries free him? We are left in suspense as to the major events in the novel. However, one theme is resolved: Yakov is a changed man. He wants a revolution, while in the beginning he considered himself apolitical. So we have a character change, resulting from insights. But the major source of suspense, whether the character will be freed or executed, remains open, unresolved. As I read the story, I did not worry whether he would start considering himself political, but whether he'd survive.

Still, I think this is a successful ending; it answers some psychological questions, yet leaves off without resolving the action. I remain anxious for Yakov, and I can start imagining different endings—the author's open ending invites me to become active, to imaginatively end the novel's action.

Some endings may be completely open, without answering any of the raised questions—which indirectly could point at the unanswerability of the questions. For example, *The Fixer* could have ended in suspense without any character change. Many absolutely open endings are actually anti-endings.

Ending With an Idea and an Image

This is how Milan Kundera ends *The Book of Laughter and Forgetting*:

> Everyone was delighted with the idea, and a man with an extraordinary paunch began developing the theory that Western civilization was on its way out and we would soon be freed once and for all from the bonds of Judeo-Christian thought-statements. These were phrases Jan had heard ten, twenty, thirty, a hundred, five hundred, a thousand times before—and for the time being those few feet of the beach felt like a university auditorium. On and on the man talked. The others listened with interest, their naked genitals staring dully, sadly, listlessly at the yellow sand.

The juxtaposition of the theory about Western civilization and genitals staring at the yellow sand works as irony. For a novel of ideas that deals with a communist dictatorship, this certainly makes a cynical closing statement.

Musing About Ending

Just as there are many self-consciously drawn beginnings, there are many endings that draw attention to themselves, with musings about what it means to end. Here's Naguib Mahfouz's ending of *Midaq Alley*:

> I will be patient so long as I live, for do not all things have their end?
> Oh yes, everything comes to its nihaya.
> And the word for this in English is "end" and it is spelled: END. ...

A Final Comment on Endings

No matter what type of ending you use, you must end skillfully and gracefully, because this is the reader's last impression of your piece, which will cast light on the whole piece retroactively. That's why it's good to end with an effective image or an interesting thought.

If you are not satisfied with what a brief ending can achieve, and you still have the urge to explain something, you might write an epilogue. You might write a couple of epilogues, for that matter—the way Tolstoy does in *War and Peace* (first epilogue, sixteen chapters; second, twelve chapters—totaling over a hundred pages) with musings about history, war, and so on—if you are blessed with the reluctance to end your novel. You could also write a commentary and then decide where to put it, at the end or the beginning. Dickens playfully solves the problem of where elucidation belongs like this, in *Our Mutual Friend*, entitling his epilogue "Postscript: In Lieu of Preface."

EXERCISES

1. One paragraph. Write the opening of a Western, with an odd action involving several animals. Imitate Larry McMurtry's opening of *Lonesome Dove*:

> When Augustus came out on the porch the blue pigs were eating a rattlesnake—not a very big one. It had probably just been crawling around looking for shade when it ran into the pigs. They were having a fine tug of war with it, and its rattling days were over. The sow had it by the head, and the shoat had the tail.

But use different animals—burros, horses, roosters, hawks, cats, possum, skunk, sheep, bears, coyotes.

Objective: To lead into a setting in an active way, with something already going on; also, to entertain.

Check: Do we get a sense of place, through these animals and their background? Is your opening amusing? Pass it on to your neighbor (mother, spouse, whoever happens to be at your mercy) and see whether she smiles.

2. One paragraph. Write the opening of a romance, with the heroine meeting her lover-to-be. If you can't do this with a straight face, do it as a parody.

Objective: To play with a formulaic beginning, since most romances start this way. If you do this as a parody, the purpose is to practice the technique and have fun. When you exaggerate something, you might understand more clearly how it works.

Check: Have you portrayed the lover-to-be attractively enough? He mustn't be easy to get, nor be a slob (except in a parody), nor should he be too stereotypical (as, let's say, a handsome doctor with salt-and-pepper hair).

3. One paragraph. Write the opening of a psychological novel about a large family, set in a small town. Lead us into the town as though we were in a train (look at the *My Life as a Dog* example on page 138) or in a car.

When you finish your paragraph, choose a quotation from the Bible, the Koran, the Bhagavad Gita, or any literary work that seems to be appropriate, and use it as an epigraph.

You could, if you use a famous quote, paraphrase it, the way George Orwell does this one, in *Keep the Aspidistra Flying*: "Though I speak with the tongues of men and of angels, and have not money, I am become as sounding brass, or a tinkling cymbal. And though I have the gift of prophecy, and understand all mysteries, and all knowledge; and though I have all faith, so that I could remove mountains, and have not money, I am nothing."

Objective: To describe an experience of travel so that readers will feel they are getting to a place and are in the right mood for what follows. Also, to learn how to use quotes. If you've chosen the theme of your story, address it with a quote.

Check: Do you provide a sensation of travel? Do you engage enough senses? Do you show mesmerizing effects of stripes on the road, or falling snow, or apparently revolving fields?

For quotations, be sure they relate to your theme, at least obliquely.

4. One to three pages. Begin a story of your own for a couple of paragraphs by continuing this opening from "Love Is Not a Pie" by Amy Bloom: "In the middle of the eulogy at my mother's boring and heartbreaking funeral, I started to think about calling off the wedding."

Objective: To use somebody else's energetic first sentence to begin your story. If you see a story emerging, keep going for at least a couple of pages. Later, if you finish the story, cut the first line, or transport it before the text, as a quote.

Check: Do you get ideas for a story? Do you have a scene that keeps you imagining? If not, paraphrase the beginning as "In the middle of the eulogy at my mother's boring and heartbreaking funeral, I started to think about accepting John's proposition." Does this work better? If not, try "In the middle of the toast at my mother's boring wedding, I started to think about her impending funeral." If this does not work for you, find an opening, and play the game of variations, until you hit something that triggers thoughts and scenes.

5. Three to four pages. Open the story with its chronological end, either a wedding or a funeral. Make it a substantial scene—at least a page. Then start chapter two, at the story's chronological beginning, with where the romance started (for the wedding), or the disease occurred (for the funeral). Outline the rest of the story, and write the story's last paragraph, which should chronologically precede the beginning.

Objective: To learn how to open with the last event of the story, which will serve as the starting point and the goal toward which all your narrative will focus.

Check: Are you coming up with enough ideas about what could happen in the lives of the people involved? For example, if you chopped both the beginning and the end, would there be enough interesting material left in the middle? If so, when you finish a draft of the story, you might cut off the death or the wedding frame.

6. One page. Open a novel with the description of a birth, from the standpoint of the mother.

Objective: To practice opening a biographical novel at the chronological beginning. Especially if you are a man, imagining a story from a mother's POV, with her sensations, thoughts, and so on, will do you a lot of good. You will have to fictionalize.

Check: Give it to a mother and ask her if you've described it well. Or find several accounts of births and, although each birth is unique, make sure that yours contains similar elements.

7. Three pages. Write the last three pages of a story of a love affair. A woman breaks into her boyfriend's apartment and discovers his answering machine tapes. She listens to the messages, which cast a new light on the relationship. As she does this, a criminal breaks in, and she makes a bargain with him.

Objective: To have the past and the present clash (or meet with a new insight and development).

Check: Are the tapes interesting? (After several tape-recorded messages, she could compare what they say to what she remembers, to heighten their importance.) Is the action dramatic—with scenes staged, described, and fleshed out in dialogue?

8. One page. Write a deliberately upbeat ending of a romance, perhaps the romance from Exercise 2. But change the genders to vary the story from the usual romance formula; write from a male POV, and let the man overcome a temptation, and come back to his wife all the wiser.

If you don't like the formula or are tired of it, parody it, vent your mischief on it. However, if all your stories have unhappy endings, you could probably benefit from doing this exercise seriously. If the formula irks you, get rid of the temptation business, but end your story in an upbeat way.

Objective: To make money. I'm joking, but not entirely. To practice the varieties of religious experiences? Yes, as endings.

Check: Does your upbeat ending sound corny? It shouldn't, not in well-done formula fiction. It might help to use poetic images at the end, rather than obvious generalizations as thoughts. If you want to express thoughts, they should be interesting.

9. One to two pages. Write the beginning of a story (jumping into the complication of an action or a crisis) and the ending (coming out of a resolution), so that they reflect each other. To intensify the connection between the beginning and ending, use the same symbolic object in both. For example, Jean Stafford, in "A Country Love Story," uses the antique sleigh as the first and the last image. When we come to the sleigh at the end, we realize we have taken a journey.

Objective: To practice matching endings with beginnings, in a concrete way, concentrating on objects as symbols. You don't have to know what the symbols mean—they'll work anyway.

Check: Did your object evoke many associations for you? Jot them down, without censoring them. Then analyze how these associations relate to the events in the story. You might make use of these associations to tighten the connections among the beginning, the ending, and the rest of the story.

10. Write a story outline. Then write the first and last paragraph of the story, so that the two have hardly anything to do with each other.

Objective: To practice contrasting the ending with the beginning.

Check: Does the ending make the beginning look like an orphan? It should, to show how much we have departed from it.

11. Outline a story and write its surprise ending.

Objective: To practice using a variety of endings.

Check: Is the ending truly unexpected? Does it make sense? Could it happen, given the plot outline?

12. One to two pages. Describe a character's death, accounting in detail the thoughts and perceptions of the dying. Imagine that you are ending a long novel that involves an exhausting life.

Objective: To be able to end in a traditional way, yet with a new twist—some new description, analogy, image of what awaits all of us. Use insights from psychology and physiology to shape your description. Could you write an upbeat description of death?

Check: Is the description convincing, vivid, serious—not pompous, sentimental, and preachy?

13. Start a story with "I couldn't ..." Just imagine what you couldn't do, and a whole world might open up in imagination.

Objective: The power of negative thinking—negative dialectics. Things won't be denied in imagination, and an attempt to do so can bring them out in full force.

Check: Is your beginning engaging and vivid? Are you getting us into a scene? If not, rewrite; get us to be right in a concrete place and time.

8

DESCRIPTION AND WORD CHOICE

Description should be a basic skill, your way of showing and seeing. You need vivid detail, not only to give life to your story, but to supply proofs. The more outlandish your plot, the more you must ground it in realistic detail to provide verisimilitude, similarity to truth. Gabriel García Márquez claims that in a journalistic article one false piece of information is enough to invalidate the article, and in a piece of fiction one striking and true detail may be enough to lend credibility to the entire story. In "A Very Old Man With Enormous Wings," he describes an angel who lands on a beach. Why should we accept his fantasy? Because the details bring the celestial down to earth:

> There were only a few faded hairs left on his bald skull and very few teeth in his mouth. ... His huge buzzard wings, dirty and half-plucked, were forever entangled in the mud.

And later:

> He was lying in a corner drying his open wings in the sunlight among the fruit peels and breakfast leftovers that the early risers had thrown him. ... The back side of his wings was strewn with parasites.

How can we doubt parasites in the wings? The realistic description makes the fantasy acceptable, gives it credence. His style of writing is magical realism, and the magic does not go from heaven to earth first, but rather, from earth to heaven, from worms to angels. Especially if you are interested in writing fantasy, science fiction, or historical novels, you must learn how to select the basic, authenticating detail in order to convince the reader.

As a fiction writer, however, you run into strong resistance against descriptions. Today's readers seek quick scenes, action, and energetic dialogue. So why bother to describe, when description slows the pace of your fiction? The reader will probably leap over your poetic descriptions to get to the next drama. And how can your fiction compete with the stunning landscapes and awesome special effects of the movies? Impossible.

Perhaps. With well-chosen words, however, you have a chance to practice a real craft, to make much out of little, out of a dog-eared dictionary, alone, in an individual effort—and that is close to creation, which takes place *ex nihilo*, out of nothing. (Movies come into being out of millions of dollars, as team efforts with large staffs; movies make much—and sometimes surprisingly little—out of much.) Remember that a reader cooperates with you; the reader will day-dream, free-associate, and imagine, starting from your words. You only need to place the word correctly so it opens the internal movie houses, concert halls, restaurants, and botanical gardens in your reader's head. More may happen in the reader's than in a movie-goer's head precisely because, on the surface, words are sketchy and incomplete: The reader jumps in and completes the work, actively imagining, not passively receiving. And if you describe succinct-ly, you need not fear that you will bore the reader. So there is no reason (except financial) for you as a writer to feel worsted by movies.

HOW TO DESCRIBE

Some writers try too hard, when they want to evoke an image, by mentioning every aspect of the object they're describing. This is not necessary. It is enough to list the key aspects of an image and then rely on the power of words to evoke. You don't need to supply all the colors and nuances. Márquez merely mentions the parasites in the angel's wings, and the reader's imagination does the rest of the work. Another common mistake in descriptions is to rely on adjectives—sometimes piles of them—to create pictures. (It's all right to use adjectives sparingly, provided you mostly rely on concrete nouns to show images.)

In description, you directly show what can be seen, and indirectly, what can be inferred, such as mental states. You must show even emotion: It's easy to say outright how your characters feel, but explanations usually flatten your nar-rative. You can get away with telling how your central character, the carrier of the POV, feels, since you have access to his mind, but we need evidence for the feelings of others. How do we know that Joan is bored, that Peter is ashamed, that Thomas is skeptical? Show how they look and behave, what their hands are doing, and the reader will infer the emotion.

Be especially descriptive with powerful feelings. If you use a vocabulary of passion to describe weak feelings and exaggerate what your characters should feel, you write sentimentally. André Gide said: "Often with good sentiments we produce bad literature." Dramatize, show, demonstrate strong feelings; *men-tioning* strong feelings only cheapens them. Describing the symptoms of these feelings may evoke the impression of them for the reader, provided you don't resort to clichés, like *rivers of tears, swooning, racing of the heart*. Each strong feeling is a new sensation for the person experiencing it; so when you describe the feeling, you must create a fresh description.

Descriptions need not be long to show a great deal. For example, Charles Dickens describes a ruined and depressed person like this: "He looked like his own shadow at sunset." "Ruined and depressed" conveys information but evokes no picture; Dickens's sentence both conveys the information and paints a grim picture. A compact description that delivers convinces the reader that she need not practice speed-reading on your prose.

Descriptions are perhaps even more important for the writer than for the reader, because they keep the writer close to the scene and help him visualize, concretize, and participate in the story. It's good not to interrupt the momentum of the fictional action when describing. John Gardner claims that good writing attains the quality of an uninterrupted fictional dream. Pause to describe, and you may lose the dream. It's best to use dynamic descriptions, whenever feasible, as Flannery O'Connor does in "A Good Man Is Hard to Find":

> She stood with one hand on her thin hip and the other rattling the newspaper at his bald head.

In the action of rattling the newspaper, we find that the man has a bald head. She does not pause to give us a separate sentence on that account.

Another example from the same story:

> She set him on her knee and bounced him and told him about the things they were passing. She rolled her eyes and screwed up her mouth and stuck her leathery thin face into his smooth bland one. Occasionally he gave her a far-away smile.

The descriptions are part of the dynamic scene. This is a good technique when an action takes place and when description can be brief. However, when you must describe many details, it may be best to pause the action and concentrate on the task at hand.

In the previous chapters, we have covered some aspects of description—setting and character—but we need to cover how these two elements can work together in a description. The setting can express a character's mind; and a character's mind can shape our perception of the setting. This interaction of the setting and character often amounts to a mood. In a description, you can create a mood. The visible world helps you express a psychological state. For example, in the following passage from a story of mine, "Bread and Blood," I could have simply said that, while marching in the defeated army, the character, Ivan, was doomed to the feelings of futility and fear. But mentioning futility and fear probably would evoke no images—these words would be abstract, the reader would not be invited to participate in the story. With descriptions, I give body to the abstraction, to Ivan's mental state, and the reader can easily identify with this embodied mood:

> Past a burned-out and gutted steel mill, the decimated regiment of
> Croat Home Guards stumbled through a field of craters that bombs
> had dug. Out of the waterfilled craters rough-skinned gray frogs
> leaped as beating hearts that had deserted the bodies of warring
> men and now roamed the doomed landscape. Ivan found the sudden
> leaps of so many hearts out of the gray earth unsettling. He could not
> see any of them, until they were in the air, so that it seemed to him
> that the earth was spitting up useless hearts and swallowing them
> back into the mud.

Ivan's anxious state of mind shapes our perceptions of the environment, which become almost hallucinogenic. A happy member of a victorious army would see the frogs differently, perhaps as a cheerful rhythm of the liberated land coming to life.

At the same time, the environment shapes our experience of Ivan's mind. Since I show bomb craters and leaping frogs—something for the reader to visualize—I am free to summarize Ivan's feelings, without fear that I am telling and not showing. I am doing both, while at the same time I mirror the mind in the setting and the setting in the mind. I can now tell that Ivan found what he saw "unsettling." I can guide the reader's perception of the scene through Ivan's eyes—the frogs appear as "useless" hearts. "Useless" is a summary, an evaluation of what's shown. If you create a mood through imagery, you are free to interpret the mood, to guide it explicitly, especially if you thereby clarify a character's perception. The descriptive scene here works as an expression and clarification of Ivan's state of mind.

I think this is an essential technique in writing fiction—with a bit of expressive showing, you can advance the telling of the story. If I tried to show everything—without choosing several telling details, and without slanting the perception of the scene through metaphors and summaries—it would have taken me pages of landscaping, and the effect would have been diluted. And if I tried to tell and explain everything taking place—without showing where we were—the story would become abstract and lose its impact.

Through the details you choose, you can control the distance from which your reader watches the action. If you focus on a detail that is apparently peripheral to the action, you may create an ironic distance, the way Stephen Crane does in "The Blue Hotel" in the middle of describing a fight:

Of course the board had been overturned, and now the whole company of cards was scattered over the floor, where the boots of the men trampled the fat and painted kings and queens as they gazed with their silly eyes at the war that was waging above them.

We aren't watching the fight directly, but through the eyes of the painted kings and queens; the qualification of these eyes as "silly" imparts a sense of silliness to the fight. Instead of heeding the blows exchanged, we pay attention to the cards, putting the blows into ironic perspective. We are not consumed by the scene: We have the leisure to observe and draw parallels between the cards and the players.

Finally, a good description—besides setting mood and establishing perspective—creates an aesthetic experience for the reader. As you read, the author's skillful strokes pull you right into the action. The continuation of the fight in "The Blue Hotel" achieves a dazzling cinematic quality:

For a time the encounter in the darkness was such a perplexity of flying arms that it presented no more detail than would a swiftly revolving wheel. Occasionally, a face, as if illuminated by a flash of light, would shine out, ghastly and marked with pink spots. A moment later, the men might have been known as shadows, if it were not for the involuntary utterance of oaths that came from them in whispers.

A beautiful description like this will win your readers' trust and respect. They will keep reading because, through vivid flashes of description, they have been experiencing the action you've created; they will want to find out what happens next in this fight. We have been watching the fight without knowing the result. This concentration on painting a scene makes it possible for you to suspend the action, as if it is in slow motion, and to enhance the scene's suspense and the readers' expectations.

WORD CHOICE

For description, a writer depends on word choice as a painter does on the selection of paint. Gustave Flaubert explained the importance of word choice: "Whatever you want to say, there is only one word that will express it, one verb to make it move, one adjective to qualify it. You must seek that word, that verb, and that adjective, and never be satisfied with approximations, never resort to tricks, even clever ones, or to verbal pirouettes to escape the difficulty."

Le mot juste is the French expression he used, and, in English, this is still a common way of describing the right word, giving the concept an aura of

French finesse. But there's no need to mystify and treat as foreign the basic skill of choosing the right word.

Here are two examples of the right word choice, in one description from David Foster Wallace's story "Forever Overhead." Pay attention to how the words achieve vivid sensations:

> There is a huge exclamation point of a foam into your field of sight, then scattered claps into a great fizzing. Then the silent sound of the tank healing to new blue.

"Fizzing" evokes the sound of a pool after a splash. The tank "healing" to new blue is perfect. The hole in the water has filled; once the fizzing bubbles burst, the color returns to the water. The additional twist of the silent sound of the tank healing alerts your ear; as you visualize the white water becoming blue, you barely hear a murmur. All of these effects are accomplished through the right word choice—*fizzing, sound,* and *healing,* in synergy. Wallace certainly follows Vladimir Nabokov's maxim "to caress the detail."

The way you choose your words should give you power. Words do not act alone, so you need to evaluate them in your syntax. The word *syntax* comes from a Greek word that means "to deploy." Deploy your words strategically, so they can attack as well as defend. An army needs fit soldiers, so use fit and vigorous words. Trust nouns and verbs, and modify them with adjectives and adverbs only when you can't find the right noun and verb, or when you want to sneak in a metaphor.

Verbs

You must be skillful with verbs to be, literally, verbally expressive. Donald Hall says, in *Writing Well:* "Verbs act. Verbs move. Verbs do. Verbs strike, soothe, grin, cry, exasperate, decline, fly, hurt, and heal. Verbs make writing go, and they matter more to our language than any other part of speech." Since verbs act, use vigorous verbs, as in the following sentence from *Heart of Darkness* by Joseph Conrad:

> Going up that river was like traveling back to the earliest beginnings of the world, when vegetation rioted on the earth.

Rioted—what a lush verb!

For the sake of compactness and clarity, present verbs in the active voice whenever feasible. Instead of "He was struck by the ball," say "The ball struck him." Avoid weak connective verbs—*is* and *has* (and their variants)—because they stall action and impart a static quality to your writing. Instead of "A painting is on the wall," say "A painting hangs on the wall." Instead of "There are many people in the room, having a lot of loud fun," say "Many people in the room frolic." (Since no rules work consistently, use common sense. If trying to make verbs active makes your sentence stiff or odd, come up with another variation or revert to the passive and static constructions.)

But don't overdo the vigor of your verbs, because your writing will sound cruel and sadistic. "I glued the stamp" should not become "I shoved the stamp onto the envelope." You can yank a plank of wood out of a fence, but yank thread out of a needle and you will not gain vigor, but stupidity.

Even skillful and famous writers occasionally fail to measure the power of verbs. That's only natural—even top tennis players double-fault, trying to over-power the opponent; top basketball players miss dunks. It's impossible to avoid occasional slips in your writing, as in the following example from a novel by a famous novelist. I have italicized the words that I think are overly strong:

> January *knifed* through the heated Jaguar; a child sneezed as it *battled its way to freedom*, and Mrs. Dancey, *erecting* her fur coat-collar and sinking so far as might be down into it, *declared*: "I think I'll stay where I am." Eva did not reply: she had walked away. The children set off in the *reverse* direction—their mother, *impaled* on draughts, sent a whinny after them.

Knifed is too strong for air getting into a car. *Battled its way to freedom* is a little too much for a child getting out of the car; moreover, the expression is a cli-ché. *Erecting* may be all right, though its sexual implication may be too much. *Said* would have accomplished the job of *declared* without the stately formality, which may be ironic, but not enough to warrant the overblown vocabulary. *Reverse* of what? Eva's direction? This adjective is plainly vague. *Impaled* literally means to be executed by having a stick stuck through your anus, through your entrails, and into your head. The metaphor in the image may go in the right direction, but way too far.

Use strong verbs, but beware of this potential to exaggerate to the point of absurdity. Rather than go for the "kill" verb (unless you have a kill going on), go for the effective word, as does Larry Woiwode in "Silent Passengers": "The boy stared out the windshield with an intensity Steiner couldn't translate ...." *Translate* is the right word. It implies that the boy's staring was a language different from Steiner's; that Steiner tries to understand but fails. Notice that the word is not pretty—it's a relatively long word with a foreign origin (a Latin root, so it could sound academic rather than direct), not a simple Anglo-Saxon one, yet since it's well chosen, it works. Many writers rightly seek, whenever they can, to use simple, short, Anglo-Saxon words, for a punchy rhythm and a sensation of directness—like *crack, jump, do, shout*—rather than long Latin and Greek ones, like *accelerate, juxtapose, equivocate, obfuscate, metamorphose.* But these academic-sounding words with Latin or Greek origins do occasionally work best—for example, "With complex explanations, you obfuscate the basic problem." *Obfuscate*—to deliberately muddy an issue—works better than *muddy,* which evokes a clear image. In the spirit of the loss of clarity, that word, as an oblique one, is the most effective.

Of course, it's good to place a simple word effectively: "A religious man, in the grips of dying, directed his gaze to the ceiling." This will become stronger if you write: "While air wheezed out of him, he looked up with such longing that his eyes seemed to scratch the ceiling." Instead of a cliché, *grips of dying*—air wheezing out gives us a more concrete and active picture of death. Instead of *directed his gaze, scratch* accomplishes everything: frustration, futility, beastly impotence. Though *scratch* is a common word, the way it's used here is uncommon. Use words unusually for effect. Inexperienced writers often use "unusual" words fashionably—that is, usually. For example, *awesome, vivacious, hellacious, serendipitous*—avoid such trendy words and nurture your odd words. Read a dictionary and copy words that intrigue you, the simpler the better, and use them accurately, even—and especially—if you have never heard them used that way.

Sometimes you can make a verb out of a noun to create action: "Loud clashes of iron *dominoed* the coaches as our train pulled wheel by wheel onto the broad Soviet tracks from the narrow Hungarian rails." Besides setting things in motion, the metaphor of train coaches as domino pieces is packed in the verb *dominoed.*

Mary Gaitskill uses this noun-as-verb technique in "The Girl on the Plane":

There she stood with a hatchet, about to brain him.

Since we have an image of violence here, to *brain* him is the right verb, derived from a noun.

Leslie Silko, in "Yellow Woman," also uses this technique:

He shook his head and pawed the sand.

Pawed is effective; the simple word creates an image of a hand as a paw in the sand. This could have been said in a longer way: "He shook his head, and his hand, like a paw, passed through sand." Here's an example, from Gary Soto's writing, of making a picture and metaphor from a noun used as a verb:

I scissored my cigarette between fingers, very European.

To give your prose density, now and then you might pack your metaphors into image-oriented verbs.

Nouns and Concrete Description

Rely on concrete nouns—that is, names for things—because in fiction, you must give us the illusion of a world. Notice how Russell Banks gives us a world through concrete nouns in "Sarah Cole: A Type of Love Story":

> The package of shirts on the table behind her, the newspapers scattered over the couch and floor, the sound of windblown rain washing the sides of the building outside, and the silence of the room, as we stood across from one another and watched ....

Notice that there is only one adjective here (properly speaking, a noun-verb combination functioning as an adjective), *windblown*. The rest are nouns and verbs. The concrete nouns evoke the room and its atmosphere better than a string of adjectives and generalizations could. To describe, you need concrete nouns more than adjectives, which are peripheral unless deftly used. Just listing things patiently may work. The reader will contribute colors and shapes from her imagination.

Be concrete rather than abstract whenever possible, unless you write philosophy. What an ugly-sounding word *concrete* is, especially if taken concretely: Cement with iron rods rusting in it. However, its Latin origin, *crescere*, means "to grow." Growth, like a crescent moon, enchants. You can't readily make a picture from abstract words—even the ones that people find important, like *emotion*. Become a little more specific—*loneliness* and *expectation*—and you still don't see much. If you can't accomplish the task with several words, create a scene to show, to concretize, the abstract.

Tim O'Brien gives us an excellent model of concreteness in *The Things They Carried*:

> Until he was shot, Ted Lavender carried six or seven ounces of premium dope, which for him was a necessity. Mitchell Sanders, the RTO, carried condoms. Norman Bowker carried a diary. Pat Kiley carried comic books. Kiowa, a devout Baptist, carried an illustrated New Testament that had been presented to him by his father, who taught Sunday school in Oklahoma City, Oklahoma.
>
> ... [W]hen Ted Lavender was shot, they used his poncho to wrap him up, then to carry him across the paddy, then to lift him into the chopper that took him away.

Here, each person is briefly characterized by what he carries; the items say much more than summaries, interpretations, thoughts, and adjectives could express. O'Brien's orderly emphasis also offers an impression of military life.

He also uses this example to develop the story's theme. We see life's cheapness during war, where even death is handled with cheap things—ponchos. The story demonstrates the power of concreteness.

Adverbs and Adjectives

These modifiers often diminish the effect of your verbs and nouns. For example, "He ran extremely fast" does not accomplish anything more than "He sprinted." Actually, less, because it takes too long to read and therefore slows you down; the syntax of the sentence is not faithful to its meaning. To run fast means to sprint. What is extremely fast? The maximum speed of a hundred-meter dash is thirty-six kilometers (twenty-three miles) per hour; what's the point of emphasizing the extreme when humans are fairly slow creatures compared to, say, cheetahs? If we *really* want—and "to really want" means nothing more than "to want"—to emphasize the speed, we could say "He dashed."

"He ran very slowly" also wastes words. (The piled adverbs slow us down and thus the syntax reflects the meaning of the sentence, but that's a minor compensation for the awkwardness.) What's the difference between *very slowly* and *slowly*? Many writers have pointed out that *very* is the least "very" word in the language. You may be better off with "He jogged."

Some purists conduct campaigns against adjectives and adverbs. Mark Twain advocated that, after finishing a piece of writing, an author should cross out all the adjectives and adverbs and take a second look, and then bring back the ones that are absolutely necessary. He guaranteed that this strategy would improve the prose. I don't think you need to be so strict about using modifiers, but do examine them. You might accomplish more by choosing verbs and nouns precisely.

Sometimes adjectives and adverbs add a good touch to your prose. It's like using paprika wisely. Paprika, though not strong by its nature, adds taste. (Strong verbs are like hot pepper. They sting.) Here are examples of well-chosen modifiers. First, from "The Demon Lover" by Elizabeth Bowen:

> The *passé* air of the staircase was disturbed by a draught that travelled up to her face. It emanated from the basement ....

Passé surprises here. You would not expect to see a French word for something that should basically mean stale, but this makes it sound staler than stale. *Passé*, in the sense of "outdated, no longer in fashion," is *le mot juste*.

Here's an example of a perfectly descriptive adjective from "Four Meetings" by Henry James:

> I saw her but in diminished profile.

Diminished—how visually true! When you look at a person's face at an angle from behind, you may see just a bit of the nose, a shortened mouth, certainly a smaller version of the profile; this word choice accomplishes all that.

Adverbs can convey a picture, too, as in an example from "The Girl on the Plane" by Mary Gaitskill:

> He sat down, grunting territorially ....

Gaitskill describes a man taking up a seat on the plane. *Territorially* conveys an attitude, a behavior, in a picture and a sound. In the three above examples, the modifiers are precise.

You can use adjectives and adverbs to express an image; you can even compress metaphors and likenesses into these seemingly peripheral words. Lorrie Moore does this with an adverb in her story "Community Life":

> She wished to start over again, to be someone living coltishly in the world ....

Instead of saying "living like a colt," which would be a likeness, Moore compresses the likeness into a quiet metaphor conveyed in a single adverb, *coltishly*. Who says adverbs are weak? I did, didn't I? Well, let me retract it! Rules have exceptions, so be free, be coltish, when you write.

Peter Taylor strikes a metaphor with an adjective in this sentence from "The Old Forest":

> I found myself wondering for the first time if all this might actually lead to my beautiful, willowy Caroline Braxley's breaking off our engagement.

Two adjectives characterize Caroline. *Beautiful* alone would be useless, and it's not strong anyway. *Willowy* accomplishes a metaphoric compression, a picture of a woman as a willow tree—an expressionistic image of a mood. I imagine Caroline: She lets her elongated hands hang loose, effortlessly bent in the wrists; her hair, skirts, motions, all are a melancholy yet graceful assembly of hanging. *Willowy* strikes me—it's not precise, but it's right.

Metaphors and Similes

Aristotle said, "The greatest thing in style is to have a command of metaphor." In Greek, *metaphor* means "transport." (A Greek trucking company is called *Metaphora*.) You carry over a meaning from one realm to another—a human being becomes a willow tree or a horse—and thus expand your view. You borrow a strong impression from wherever you like and bring it into your picture, enriching and complicating, creating a dual reality, with a possible stereo effect, a sharper and deeper sound. Perhaps there's some kind of metaphysical assumption in using metaphors, that many things share one essential nature. A metaphor can make us see something in a way we never have before; it can make us wonder, break out of our habitual ways.

Metaphors make this shift directly, as in *heart of gold*. Similes make the shift indirectly—*as busy as a bee*, and *working like a madman*. (*As* and *like* announce the comparison; *of* doesn't.)

Metaphors and similes are stylistic devices. If your metaphors explicitly draw attention to themselves, your prose will appear labored and mannered. That's why it's particularly effective to sneak your metaphors quietly into adverbs and adjectives, as in the above examples. Sometimes, of course, when you come up with an effective metaphor, you may wish to give it center stage and express it in verbs and nouns, as does Louise Erdrich in *Love Medicine*:

> She threw the oak pole singing over my head, through my braincloud.

The pole *singing* is one metaphor expressed in a verb. It's a metaphor because it transposes the activity of a living creature to an inanimate object. *Braincloud* is another metaphor. It transposes sky and cloud to your head. It's not only a metaphor, it's an image. Who would mind reading a string of metaphors like this? The metaphors are seamlessly interwoven into the sentence. If Erdrich had said, "She threw the oak pole, which seemed to be singing over my head, as though through a cloud around my brain," she would have acknowledged importing the images from elsewhere—*as*, *like*, *seemed*, and other announcements draw attention to the comparison as an artifice.

Use metaphors bravely. But when you have many of them, squeeze some into modifiers, so your metaphors will have the humility of a footnote rather than the loudness of center stage. Even quiet bees make honey—often better than loud bees do.

Avoiding Clichés and Wrong Word Choices

Examine your words to make sure they achieve the effect you want. When they fall short of your goal, cross them out, and find the words that work. Mark Twain said, "The difference between the right word and the almost right word is the difference between the lightning and the lightning bug."

In metaphors, it is essential that the transposition of one set of elements into a new context be fresh—that you see it for the first time like that. If you have seen a metaphor or a likeness many times elsewhere, don't use it.

Otherwise, your metaphor will be a cliché, such as *busy as a bee*. No doubt, once upon a time, that used to be a fresh image, but no more. Other passé metaphors and likenesses:

> heart of gold
>
> pearly white teeth
>
> steel will
>
> strong as a bull
>
> brilliant light
>
> seamlessly interwoven (from my writing above)
>
> pretty as a picture
>
> drunk as a sailor
>
> meek as a lamb
>
> faithful like a dog
>
> postcard pretty
>
> illegible handwriting, like a doctor's
>
> like zombies
>
> chiseled features
>
> clean as a bone
>
> window of opportunity
>
> broken heart
>
> he is sweet
>
> like an idiot
>
> piercing eyes
>
> she blossomed (it's good that the image is packed in a verb, but it's been done a zillion times, to use another cliché)

There are many other clichéd metaphors. Continue the list for fun, if you like.

Strive to create fresh metaphors—though *fresh* is not fresh in this context (would *crisp* be better?)—as Lorrie Moore does in "Community Life":

> The electric fan was blowing on him; his hair was moving gently, like
> weeds in water.

This example creates a picture I hadn't seen before reading her sentence. So she has shown me something, and I am tempted to say *Thank you!* Okay, I did.

You can make something new and striking without belaboring it. See how Japanese fiction writer Mon Yoko creates an original image in "Spring Storm":

> "You were trembling like a drenched cat."

Simple, nicely done, and true to life. No doubt you have seen a drenched cat trembling. It's good to observe and jot down your observations, because sooner or later you might use them in your fiction. It's amazing how often we fail to notice things around us. There are many images like drenched cats trembling around us, but we fail to pay attention because our eyes are tired. This is one skill many poets possess—finding images that, once expressed, seem obvious. Read poetry (or, even better, write it) to sharpen the art of making images and choosing words.

Not all images need to strive for quiet simplicity. However, if in a sentence you can't come up with anything better than *chiseled features* use *chiseled features* and move on. Your main goal is to tell your story, and now and then to throw an image as refreshing as a snowball at your reader. Otherwise, keep moving. If you strive to be an original metaphorist in each sentence, you may either induce writer's block or write precious prose, which will take ten years to become a novel. Fear of clichés may be an even greater fault than using clichés, if you quit thinking of your conflicts and characters for the sake of beauty. As in most things, find the right measure.

Symbols

Many writers think that, to deepen and embellish their writing, they must use symbols. But don't worry about symbols. You've got better things to do: write, paint, play. The origin of the word is *symbolein*, which in Greek means "to throw (*bolein*) together (*sym*)." As you throw words together, you will *symbolein*, make symbols, meaningful connections between the concrete and the abstract; but the less you control how that happens, the better, because the connections will come from your subconsciousness or semi-consciousness, from the spring of words and images, spontaneous, free. *Throwing together* suggests, to me, a certain looseness.

I may be wrong in analyzing the etymology of *symbol*, but probably not in analyzing the usefulness of planning symbols in writing. I respect deliberately using and studying symbols in psychoanalysis, anthropology, religion, and literature, but in writing fiction, it's good to be spontaneous. A Ph.D. friend of mine can't mention fish without worrying about its symbolic relationship to Christianity, which he, as an academic neopagan, finds troubling. He can't mention a banana in a story without worrying that he has mentioned his penis. Consequently, he's got a huge writer's block and a small writing libido. So don't go around psychoanalyzing symbols in writing—yours or others'. Arranging symbols neatly will either inhibit you or will make your prose artificial. I don't know of any other single topic that succeeds more in obfuscating and making the craft of writing appear more complicated than it needs to. But, who knows, if they interest you, symbols may work for you. (After all, see what's happened to the gospel against adverbs in this chapter.)

EXERCISES

1. One page. Choose a fantasy figure—Dracula, Narcissus, Santa Claus, or one of your making—and convince us of his physical reality by using mundane details.

Objective: To learn how to "prove" the existence of fantastic characters. Regardless of whether you believe in Christ, it's tempting to believe in a god who sweats and bleeds. The details of his story stay with you because the spirit has become flesh, through the word.

Check: Have you mentioned enough real, daily stuff—dandruff, toothpaste, a hole in a sock, bad temper, a toothache, a mosquito bite, bronchitis, whatever? If not, go back and do it.

2. One page. Pretend that you are an architect and make up a factory or a gym. Draw it first, if that helps you imagine it, and then write a description of it.

Objective: To practice visualizing something you haven't seen, and to bring it out in a description. You may benefit from a painterly and architectonic imagination.

Check: Have you described the building so that it seems real? Cover the tracks of your artifice so that the impression will be that you have actually gone out in the streets and sketched this building by looking at it. For realism, perhaps you need cracks in the mortar, pigeon stripes on the walls, some intrusions of rude reality.

3. Three paragraphs. Describe a horse, a dog, and a cat. Don't mention the animal you portray, and avoid anthropocentric ascriptions of thoughts and emotions. Try to engage all of our senses; let us pet the beast with you. If you have animals around you, observe them, and describe them in detail. Otherwise, rely on pictures.

Objective: To practice accurate description from direct observation. Don't worry whether your writing is pretty, but whether it's precise, as though you were writing a nature textbook.

Check: Give what you've written to your brother, spouse, or whomever happens to be around, and see whether that person can identify your animals. (For the test, avoid words that would identify your animal, such as *whiskers*.) If not, go back and try again.

4. Three to four paragraphs. Describe a flower shop, a bakery, a shoe-repair shop, and any other little store you come across. Concentrate on smells and sounds.

Objective: To work from auricular and olfactory imagination. If you have to resort to metaphors, so be it.

Check: Come back to the exercise a day or two after doing it. After reading, close your eyes, contemplate the words you used, not reading into them extra meaning, and see whether what you describe comes across.

5. One page. Describe the sounds you hear from your room at midnight. Don't strain; simply list the sounds and their probable sources. Then, rewrite the list of sounds and make ghosts, lovers, thieves, and so on out of them. Exaggerate, dramatize, metaphorize. If you aren't naturally inclined to exaggerate, write from the POV of a highly paranoid and sensitive person, someone different from you.

Objective: To learn how to control usage of sounds, first for basic realistic description, then for making much out of little. No other sense can excite the creativity of imagination as much as hearing. This turning ants into elephants, the proclivity of the ear in the dark, can be particularly useful in psychological suspense.

Check: For the first half of the exercise: Have you mentioned enough sounds without making too much of them, or too little? For the second half: Have you moved beyond the banal into fantasy?

6. Write a sentence and use a simple word in an odd way—as, for example, in the following sentence, *scratch* is used: "The dying man's eyes seemed to scratch the ceiling." Write a dozen such sentences and save the three or four that work best; revise them until you think they are perfect.

Objective: To learn how to put words together in new ways. Think of what your verbs can do, even if you've never seen them do it before. Experiment. When you describe something, run through a list of verbs, until something sounds interesting.

Check: Read slowly a day later, when you are fresh. Analyze the sentences and see whether at least one of your word usages surprises you.

7. Make a verb out of a noun in a sentence. (For example, "She *brained* him with a hatchet," "I *scissored* a cigarette between fingers," "She *hatcheted* him," "Her dog *treed* my cat.") You can make verbs even out of numbers—for example, "She *360ed* and fell."

Objective: To concentrate on the activity and the words in your sentences. Merge the noun and the verb into one word, giving it both the concrete power of a thing-oriented noun, and the energy of an action-oriented verb.

Check: Does your sentence achieve the concreteness and the energy of a thing in motion? Does it create an image? It should. Does it sound good? It should. (Some nouns used as verbs would sound ridiculous—for example, "I villaged for an afternoon"; "She chemistried all day.") Use your judgment and taste, as you should, ultimately, in all matters of writing.

8. Whenever you read, be on the alert for a well-placed word, *le mot juste*. Note these in your journals, or wherever, and analyze them.

Objective: To think of words. They reveal or evoke or create images. If you want to create, know your materials.

Check: Have you collected at least a dozen gems by the end of the week of your reading? If you haven't, keep hunting for them.

9. Three to five pages. Imitate Tim O'Brien's *The Things They Carried*. Create a dramatic plot using a group of soldiers, mountain-climbers, lovers, hunters, basketball players, or some other group. Portray the drama through the items the group members carry.

Objective: To learn how to express yourself through concrete nouns. Objects placed together speak of the people who put them together. The advantage of arranging objects to speak is that the reader may infer the characteristics of the people who possess them; you need not be judgmental, let the reader be. You can always say, "You said it." (Another peripheral objective: To get in the habit of writing stories as a variation on a theme. Yours will be a variation on a theme by O'Brien.)

Check: Have you mentioned for each character one or two distinct objects, and for each group several shared objects (such as ponchos for soldiers)?

10. Write variations on Exercise 9, each one a brief paragraph: the things they wore, the things they threw into a garbage can, the things they ate. Make these items portray the characters who use them.

Objective: Same as in Exercise 9.

Check: Same as in Exercise 9.

11. One to two pages. Create images for abstractions: laziness, loneliness, envy, jealousy, joy, pleasure, lust, love, boredom, impatience. For example, for laziness,

describe the room of a lazy student, and don't mention laziness. Try to render each feeling in a concrete sentence, which may be nothing more than a list.

Objective: To concentrate on the basics, things, what the world is made of.

Check: Does your list work like symptoms of a disease or evidence of a crime, *corpus delicti*, or like an airport basket into which you empty your pockets? Why not?

12. One page. Choose an abstract word from Exercise 11—envy, jealousy, lust, joy, loneliness—and construct a scene that would express and concretize the word's nature. Don't mention the word.

Objective: To practice concretizing abstractions through a long and rich description. This is a potential source of fiction—from the mood, you jump into a scene, and if there's enough tension in the scene, you can keep going until you have a story.

Check: Has the mood expressed itself naturally, giving shape to your sequence of sentences? The mood should be like a monkey in the jungle—the description should be the mood's natural habitat. (A single sentence may trap the mood like a cage.) Let the important moods live out their natures. Read what you've written. It should read like a fine part of a story. If it doesn't, rewrite, reshape, craft!

13. Twelve sentences. Write three sentences with similes. Rewrite them so that the likenesses become metaphors. Then rewrite so that the verbs express the metaphors. Then rewrite the metaphors into adverbs. For example: (1) Joan lived like a colt. (2) Joan was a colt. (3) Joan colted around. (4) Joan lived coltishly. (If the initial likenesses cannot make the whole metaphoric journey, create new metaphors, so that you end up with three of each form.)

Objective: To learn how to control your likenesses and metaphors. Learn how to juggle them, so you can attain a flexibility with metaphors. No need to appear stiff and pompous when you can be nonchalant. This could be your method of finding the optimal placement of your metaphors. Let them find their syntactical level.

Check: Do your sentences work? If not, find new metaphors that do. Choose your three most effective sentences, one per metaphor. Some metaphors may be in the adverbial state, others in the verb state, whatever strikes you as best.

14. Six sentences. Write two sentences with likenesses. Rewrite the sentences, compressing likenesses into noun metaphors. Rewrite, squeezing the metaphors into adjectives.

Objective: Same as in Exercise 13.

Check: Same as in Exercise 13.

15. We are enchained in our chains, Wal-Mart, and so on. So while we usually hunt for authentic places, such as an old bar or an old church or old this and that, why not acknowledge our current world such as it is? Go into your neighborhood Wal-Mart or Target or T.J. Maxx and take a stroll or shop, then describe this in detail: the sights, sounds, smells, tactile sensations, snatches of overheard conversation, and perhaps your conversations along the way. This is basic reportage, but it could provide you with a few useful paragraphs for a story or a novel. Perhaps you could read John Updike's overly anthologized "A & P" to see a good paradigm, how a chain setting can still be enlivened and individualized. Maybe you can write a parody of something in the chains. Brian Evenson wrote a brilliant parody of Wal-Mart—with a chapel, religion for sale. But leave the parody for another exercise. For now, try to describe as accurately as possible what you see, without seeing it from above as something inferior and stupid—without, in other words, having a prejudice, a predictable attitude. Later, do with it whatever you will, but some accurate observation will go a long way to establish your credibility and to get us there.

Objective: To work from the world around us; no doubt we have a lot to say about it.

Check: Do you give a sensation of being in the chain store? Perhaps some strange detail, an unexpected one, might give freshness to your description? Maybe a bat is flying around Wal-Mart, and the male customers are screaming?

9

VOICE

St. Jerome figured out, centuries ago, that he could read without moving his lips. We don't need to move our lips while reading, but most of us still have a reading sound barrier. We hear some kind of voice, touching our tongue, slowing our eyes. I do, and that's why, when I tried to learn speed-reading, I always relapsed into the slow mode, listening to the words as though they were read aloud. In good pieces of writing, I wouldn't want to have it any other way; where the voice takes over, fiction engages me most.

Many critics have made *voice* a mysterious term. Since it's a metaphor, I can't—at least not right away—give a definition of what it is. However, its being a metaphor does not mean that we must treat the phenomenon as a transcendental mystery, like God lurking in the burning bush, although many people treat voice in this religious way. Novice writers go around looking for their voices just as people used to go around looking for themselves. At least the search has become more specific.

I see no reason to beat around the voice bush. The metaphor, taken directly, compares the written text with the spoken word. This is a good guideline: Write as you speak. Even better: Write as you'd speak at your best. In public readings, some writers show that they are better speakers than writers. When they interrupt the reading and improvise, they become more interesting. I wish that they had written with the same freedom with which they improvised. And some good writers are dull talkers; they come to life only on the page. This should be your goal—to make your text sound more natural and more engaging than you sound otherwise, no matter how much work and artifice this requires.

As a writer, you must be in command of at least one voice: yours. If you write in the first person, nonautobiographically, constructing personae, you must be able to create different voices, like an actor. For each persona, you might develop a different voice. But when you write in the third person, most likely you'll need only one narrative voice. In dialogue, of course, you must create many voices. But the most important voice will be yours, something that will carry the narrative in a confident and confiding manner.

Of course, you may have a literary voice, different from your daily conversational voice, but unless you are driven by some kind of theory or ideology (minimalist, maximalist, or whatever), I don't see much reason for creating a dichotomy between what goes to your tongue and what goes to your fingers. Some writers do stiffen when writing, as though they were at a formal party or a job interview.

Since metaphors can be interpreted in several ways, I'll give you one more: Voice is a metaphor for a writer's vigor. To make sure that it's you speaking, take out all the tapes surrounding you. No dubbing. The tapes in your mind, things that sound like somebody else, are mostly clichés. Get rid of them. There's nothing new that you need to discover about your voice. *Discover* means to uncover something that exists. Simply take the dirt and the lid off, and you'll see the precious earthenware. Get rid of the static in your writing, which hides your voice. Static: excessive use of adjectives, adverbs, and passives; imprecise word choice; clichés. (Later, you might like to muffle your voice and achieve a smoky sound with choice modifiers, but first make sure you can be loud and clear.)

Voice should not be confused with posturing, with trying to sound "different," with a cool attitude. When you take up a fashionable voice, you might sound like a "real cool dude," but we've heard enough "real cool dudes"—there's usually something smug and shallow about them. If you have something to say, there's no reason to *pretend* you have something to say. Write it! Yet, if you seemingly have nothing to say, don't be discouraged. Perhaps you will have a lot to say once you start a story, once you deal with a place and its people.

You don't have to be a prophet—that is, a savior of a people—to speak. Of course, being an Alexandr Solzhenitsyn or an Elie Wiesel might help your voice, but it won't necessarily improve your prose. It might worsen it, since you might be tempted to write tracts. Still, I marvel at the power of Solzhenitsyn's and Wiesel's voices. As soon as they open their fountain pens, you feel they have had to stand up to huge forces. If you want a strong voice, face the crowd of your opponents and outshout them even if they stone you and jail you. (There's an exercise for you!) That's the surest recipe, which, if you have the courage and beliefs, you might consider. This may not be silly advice. Evelyn Waugh, author of *Brideshead Revisited*, said: "An artist must be a reactionary. He has to stand out against the tenor of the age and not go flopping along; he must offer some little opposition. Even the great Victorian artists were all anti-Victorian, despite the pressure to conform." So be combative, at least a little. In anger, people's voices naturally become stronger and louder. This is true of writing voices, too.

If your passions are strong and you are a fighter, the question of voice is a superficial one. You are eager to speak; you only need the podium. That is, you need the writing technique. But don't worry about voice. If you make sure that you say what you mean, you'll have a strong voice. However, saying what you mean means being graceful and clear, which may take a lot of labor. Being yourself when you write means to edit, go back, sharpen, to say precisely what you want to say.

EXAMPLES OF PERSONA VOICES

By creating a persona voice, the writer strives to create the illusion of someone speaking to the reader, in the first person. In autobiographical fiction in the first person, the writer uses her own voice. For nonautobiographical fiction in the first person, the writer creates a voice, usually different from the writer's. Like an actor, the writer has taken up a mask and a voice, a persona, who seemingly tells the story. The persona writes as though speaking to a listener. As you read, you listen.

See how much J.D. Salinger's persona in *The Catcher in the Rye* sounds like someone talking to us:

> I don't want you to get the idea she was a goddam *icicle* or something, just because we never necked or horsed around much. She wasn't. I held hands with her all the time, for instance. That doesn't sound like much, I realize, but she was terrific to hold hands with. Most girls if you hold hands with them, their goddam hand *dies* on you, or else they think they have to keep moving their hand all the time, as if they were afraid they'd bore you or something. Jane was different. We'd get into a goddam movie or something, and right away, we'd start holding hands, and we wouldn't quit till the movie was over. And without changing the position or making a big deal out of it. You never even worried, with Jane, whether your hand was sweaty or not. All you knew was, you were happy. You really were.

In this passage, we hear a clear voice. As a reader, I am directly addressed in the phrase "I don't want you to get the idea ...." The word choice is conversational (*goddam, big deal*); and so is the syntax: Sentences end with *or something*. Some sentences are fragments: "And without changing the position or making a big deal out of it." "Jane was different" would be a fragment in standard English grammar; after *different*, the comparison should continue. But in spoken language, *different* has a different meaning, and the sentence is complete. This adolescent voice seemingly reproduces daily speech, but Salinger worked to achieve it. If you tape-recorded a kid (anybody) and transcribed the speech word for word, the text would be slow, much more fragmented, perhaps barely intelligible. As in dialogue, the "natural" sound is designed to be read. And as it is read, the syntax and word choice evokes the illusion of the spoken sound.

Mark Twain was among the first in American literature to create the illusion of the spoken word. He juggled different first-person voices, one framing another, in "The Celebrated Jumping Frog of Calaveras County":

> [The frame narrator:] In compliance with the request of a friend of mine, who wrote me from the East, I called on good-natured, garrulous old Simon Wheeler, and inquired after my friend's friend Leonidas W. Smiley, as requested to do, and I hereunto append the result.

Later, the narrator relays Simon Wheeler's speech, who talks about Smiley:

> So he set there a good while thinking and thinking to hisself, and then he got the frog out and prized his mouth open and took a teaspoon and filled him full of quail shot—filled him pretty near up to his chin—and set him on the floor. Smiley he went to the swamp and slopped around in the mud for a long time, and finally he ketched a frog, and fetched him in, and give him to this feller, and says:
>
> "Now, if you're ready, set him alongside of Dan'l, with his forepaws just even with Dan'l, and I'll give the word." Then he says, "One-two-three-jump!" and him and the feller touched up the frogs from behind, and the new frog hopped off, but Dan'l give a heave, and hysted up his shoulders—so—like a Frenchman, but it wa'n't no use—couldn't budge; he was planted as solid as an anvil, and he couldn't no more stir than if he was anchored out ....

The frame narrator sounds like a formal lawyer, Wheeler like a good colloquial talker, and Smiley like a folksy farmer. The result of these three voices working together in a polyphony is a yarn-like humor, with an ironic sound. It's interesting that to do a yarn, Twain resorts to this polyphony of speakers, three different personae.

Here is another example of a persona voice, achieved through syntax and word choice, so that it sounds more like a diary than a speech. This is from Elizabeth Dewberry Vaughn's novel *Many Things Have Happened Since He Died*:

The Lord hates fornicators. I am not one I hate them too. I don't believe in it before marriage I really don't I don't know what happened. I had never before I was saving myself.

And later on in the same novel:

But in a way it is His fault because He should have protected me more and I couldn't handle all that Daddy dying and no money and him pressuring me all the time and not knowing what to do and Mama practically having a nervous breakdown not able to help me when I needed it most when I always heard He won't give you anything you can't handle well He did. It was too much. And that is not my fault. It was just too much and I couldn't handle it I am not Superman sometimes I need help and nobody was there.

Vaughn has written exclusively in the first person in all her fiction. She works with grammar to give immediacy and urgency to her persona's voice: run-on sentences, commas and periods omitted. This resembles the writing of someone in a remedial English class—so we get a sense of a young person talking to us, a person rather than a writer, which is an advantage. By taking the liberties of someone who doesn't care about grammar, she is able to give us a mind's voice amid turmoil, doubt, passion, fear. This kind of voice is partly a matter of technique, though of course the writer makes it sound natural, not technical. If you want to write in the voice of someone who is not well educated, this may be a good model. Not having to worry about some aspects of grammar might free you to bang thoughts and impressions onto the page.

In *Normance*, Louis-Ferdinand Céline achieves a similar effect to the one above—a rush of thoughts and images—but a much faster one, through overusing punctuation, particularly his signature: "! ..." Generally, a voice can't carry over well in translation, but since his depends so much on punctuation, some of it does carry over from the French, enough to give us an idea of what punctuation can do:

Look, the windmill's tipping! and so are we! our whole house! ... a first rate eddy of air! ... the one up there pitches toward the handrail, I think he's going to go right over ... no! he stumbles against it, and chucks up on the other side! ... before he was thirsty, our gondolier, but this might be just a little bit worse! he can't have a tongue left! ... we may find ourselves cooking from the heat right here in our own rooms! ... the eyes above all! the eyes! the lids won't shut any more! ... a hundred shellholes, sending sprays up into the sky!

The rush of fragments fits the subject matter, the Allies bombing Paris. However, the roughshod appearance of this writing does not mean that little work has gone into it. Céline claimed that for some of his novels he'd write a draft of millions of words, which he'd edit down to a hundred thousand.

A constructed voice of a persona need not aim at the apparent simplicity of the spoken language. The voice in some pieces of writing may aim at an intense complexity. Here's an example, from Anthony Burgess's novel *A Clockwork Orange*. Burgess's narrator, a young English gangster, uses Russian vocabulary as a cryptic gang jargon, which, at the height of the Cold War, exploits the fear that many people in the West had of anything Russian. At the end of the novel, Burgess gives translations of the words—britva = razor; litso = face; nozh = knife; vred = hurt; etc.—so unless you know some Russian, reading this novel takes additional work:

> It was stinking fatty Billyboy I wanted now, and there I was dancing about with my britva like I might be a barber on board a ship on a very rough sea, trying to get in at him with a few fair slashes on his unclean oily litso. Billyboy had a nozh, a long flick-type, but he was a malenky bit too slow and heavy in his movements to vred anyone really bad. And, my brothers, it was real satisfaction to me to waltz—left two three, right two three—and carve left cheeky and right cheeky, so that like two curtains of blood seemed to pour out at the same time, one on either side of his fat filthy oily snout in the winter starlight.

The mixture of the foreign vocabulary (liable to rouse xenophobia), familiar gang expressions (*brothers*), piled-up adjectives (*fat filthy oily*), and poetic images (*winter starlight*) creates a unique and cultured sadistic voice. Although nobody I know talks like the narrator in *A Clockwork Orange*, the voice is convincing, because the words are put together vigorously, in constant high contrasts. This is the type of writing that many critics like to call a *tour de force*. It works against the odds through the author's vigor, skill, labor.

Similar mixing of languages, in striving for the effect not of cruelty but gentility, particularly with French, has been done too many times. So if you suffer from the finesses of Francophilia, be careful. Unless writing a satire of manners in which French is used for putting on airs, or dealing with French-speaking peoples or the culinary arts, it's best to abstain. *Cool* will most often do for *nonchalant*.

Frequently, bilingual writers, particularly Spanish-English writers, use many Spanish words, which add flavor and accent to their writing in English and enrich their voices. Since we all probably know some Spanish, this does not burden our reading, and may add color without pretentiousness.

THIRD-PERSON NARRATIVE VOICES

Some people construct their third-person narrative voices, others don't set out to do anything like that but may end up doing it anyway. Here, too, as with first-person narrative voices, you can play with syntax to achieve whatever texture you want. Whether T. Coraghessan Boyle crafted or spontaneously arrived at the following voice, from the novel *World's End*, is unclear; regardless, it exhibits a syntactical pattern:

> When they released him, when van den Post sauntered up to throw back the bars that pinioned him, he didn't fall into grandfather van der Meulen's arms or run home to where his mother sat stricken over a mount of flax and grandfather Cats anxiously paced the *stoep*—no, he took off like a sprinter, like a dog with a pair of sticks tied to its tail, streaking across the field and through the standing corn, hightailing it for the gap in the trees where his cousin had disappeared in the shock of dawn.

Boyle's voice depends largely on his maximalist syntax. Note that he doubles dependent and comparative clauses—"When they released him, when ..." and "took off like a sprinter, like a dog." He doubles his main clause with *or*: "he didn't fall ... or run home ...." He gives you both the negative (what didn't, though could have, happened) and the positive (what did happen). Though this type of syntax runs the risk of turning cumbersome, the rich images and many strong, clipped words—"shock of dawn"—sustain a quick pace and make the novel dynamic.

James Joyce's voice evolved from a direct, economical one in his early short stories to an exuberant, playful, and constant verbal high in *Ulysses*. Let's look at the economy in a passage from his relatively early work, *A Portrait of the Artist as a Young Man*:

> On a certain Tuesday the course of his triumphs was rudely broken. Mr Tate, the English master, pointed his finger at him and said bluntly:
>
> —This fellow has heresy in his essay.
>
> A hush fell on the class. Mr Tate did not break it but dug with his hands between his crossed thighs while his heavily starched linen creaked about his neck and wrists. Stephen did not look up. It was a raw spring morning and his eyes were still smarting and weak. He was conscious of failure and of detection, of the squalor of his own mind and home, and felt against his neck the raw edge of his turned and jagged collar.

The writing moves energetically, perhaps because of good sentence variety. The varied number of words in the sentences of the last paragraph—six, twenty-six, five, fourteen, thirty-one—augment a sensation of unpredictability and tension, as do alterations between declarative and negative statements. Though he uses mostly direct sentences, Joyce does not avoid adverbs and adjectives—*rudely, bluntly, heavily, raw*—and I think it's his adverbs that give tenor to his voice.

Later, in *Ulysses*, Joyce writes in larger strokes, in long giddy sentences, but his fondness for adverbs and adjectives has remained sufficiently for us to hear a similar voice after all:

> They passed the main entrance of the Great Northern railway station, the starting point for Belfast, where of course all traffic was suspended at that late hour, and, passing the back door of the morgue (a not very enticing locality, not to say gruesome to a degree, more especially at night), ultimately gained the Dock Tavern and in due course turned into Store street, famous for its C division police station. ...
>
> You frittered away your time, he very sensibly maintained, and health and also character besides which the squandermania of the thing, fast women of the *demimonde* ran away with a lot of £.s.d. into the bargain and the greatest danger of all was who you got drunk with though, touching the much vexed question of stimulants, he relished a glass of choice old wine in season as both nourishing and bloodmaking and possessing aperient virtues (notably a good burgundy which he was a staunch believer in) still never beyond a certain point where he invariably drew the line as it simply led to trouble all round to say nothing of your being at the tender mercy of others practically.

Joyce depends heavily on the peculiar diction, which at any moment may include new coinages (*squandermania*), rare words (*aperient*), foreign words, and, in other passages, old Anglo-Saxon words. His words keep coming, modifying each other, in a long breath, without a desire to stop. Joyce manages to get in touch with the basic joy of words, relishing each turn of syntax. *Ulysses* deals with many voices (in first and third person; in monologue and stream of consciousness), and they all can be recognized as Joyce's, through their exuberance.

Joyce's complex voice evolved through his obsession with language. Although the voice may sound artificial, I think it flowed out of Joyce's hyperverbal lifestyle.

SUBJECT MATTER AND VOICE

Your fictional voice in each piece should depend on who and what you write about. In the above examples, the subject matter invariably influences the writer's voice. Salinger's choice to write about adolescence certainly helped him shape the adolescent persona voice. Vaughn's writing about a confused person influenced her in choosing the diary-like, ungrammatical voice. Choosing war and madness as subject matter, Céline appropriately constructs a disjointed voice. Burgess, writing about hooligans, constructs a fitting voice, filled with a gang jargon. In *Ulysses*, Joyce's complex voices fit his project of investigating how consciousness and verbal flux shape each other. Twain finds several voices to fit the subject matter of how yarns are created and disseminated.

In this chapter, we have moved from the simple, relatively straightforward persona voices, like Salinger's, to complex ones, like Boyle's and Joyce's. I still think it's best to strive for simplicity and clarity, but if you must bring in various voice constructs—for the sake of realism, polyphony, experimentation, or complex subject matter—go ahead. However, it's probably best to find your direct way of putting sentences together, as did Joyce in the beginning, before experimenting. In the words of Oscar Wilde (a man who followed his own advice the least), "To reveal art and conceal the artist is the art's aim." Translated to voice, I think this means: Find a way of telling the story without drawing attention to how loud, varied, and complex in construction your voice can be—unless, of course, you need to construct a voice to fit the tale. But never do it the other way round.

Simplicity may scare you because of its potential blandness. Here's an example of a simple syntax with an exciting and quick voice, from Kate Braverman's "Tall Tales From the Mekong Delta":

> He fell in step with her. He was short, fat, pale. He had bad teeth. His hair was dirty. [After the man addresses her, the narrative continues like this:] She didn't say anything. He was wearing blue jeans, a black leather jacket zipped to his throat, a long red wool scarf around his neck, and a Dodgers baseball cap. It was too hot a day for the leather jacket and scarf. She didn't find that detail significant. It caught her attention, she caught it briefly and then let it go. She looked but did not see. They were standing on a curb. The meeting was in a community room across the boulevard. She was not afraid yet.

The succession of short sentences creates a hurried pace and a matter-of-fact voice. All the sentences start directly, without conjunctions (*and*, *but*), without introducing auxiliary clauses (*with*, *although*, *when*, *if*); there are no auxiliary clauses anywhere. For example, most of us would connect the sentence ending with *baseball cap* with the following one, using *although*. "He was short, fat, pale." Usually, one would be tempted to put an *and* before *pale*, but omitting them accelerates the line. In terms of voice, we could say that this is writing with a short breath, as though the narrator were running uphill. And this shortness of breath fits the subject matter—threat.

The voice that suits you may vary from one piece of fiction to another, depending on the personae and the subject matters you choose. Experiment. Write in many modes, read out loud, see what your breathing tells you. Your breath, literally, can show you the beat, the tempo, for your sentences.

Most writers find one voice, closest to themselves, which they use in most third-person POV narratives and some first-person narratives. The way you think—whether hitting things directly or obviously—should, together with the way you breathe, reveal your "natural" syntax. And that is your voice: your home in fiction. Sometimes you'll have to leave home and assume different personae, like an exile, and live in different skins, but that is the way you'll cover the most ground.

VOICE AND HUMOR

Humor in fiction, like spice in cooking, must be used in the right quantity, in the right places, and at the right time. You might think that the more humor the better, but beware. A friend of mine with a great sense of humor wrote four novels and couldn't publish any of them, he claimed, because his writing was too funny. A television audience may want humor, insatiably, but editors of novels may be a particularly humorless lot. There's another explanation, probably more accurate. A humorous novel is tough to sell because humor is largely subjective. Since first novels are risky for publishers anyway, a humorous first novel may be even riskier. Humor, despite its innocent appearance, is a double-edged sword. If you jest at a key dramatic moment, you may lose the drama, especially if the humor in any way turns on the plot. If you don't take the plot seriously, why should the reader? Your tone sets an example for how to read.

On the other hand, if you have nothing playful, no humor, anywhere in your novel—how dreary! It's like a feast without wine. Joke as much as you can, especially in a comedy (not too much in a tragedy), and later, in revision, notice whether a joke is timed poorly, in which case, place it elsewhere. In transitional moments, jokes can maintain your reader's attention, and they can provide a new mood. If the emotional tone of your novel is grim, it's good to offer a break, because unrelieved grimness can grow monotonous. Using humor as a contrast will then deepen the tragic impact of your story.

Humor often stems from a writer's voice and attitude toward his subject matter. Think of Woody Allen. Sometimes when he gets in the groove of his voice, almost anything he says is funny. I noticed the impact of voice on humor when I was a kid. When called on by a teacher, I'd use a peasant dialect in a goofy way, and though most often I said nothing funny, my classmates and sometimes the teachers laughed at the voice.

We've seen how Mark Twain uses different voices humorously. Here's a simple example of a single humorous voice from *Huckleberry Finn*:

> The widow she cried over me, and called me a poor lost lamb, and she called me a lot of other names, too, but she never meant no harm by it. She put me in them new clothes again, and I couldn't do nothing but sweat and sweat, and feel all cramped up. Well, then, the old thing commenced again. The widow rung a bell for supper, and you had to come to time. When you got to the table you couldn't go right to eating, but you had to wait for the widow to tuck down her head and grumble a little over the victuals, though there warn't anything the matter with them ....

If you rewrote this passage to get rid of the dialect and the voice with its funny diction, you would lose some of the humor. It would still be funny, no doubt, because of Huck's way of seeing things, his logic, but the voice provides a crucial element.

Although I say the voice is simple and direct, it displays irony. Huck imitates Miss Watson—"called me a poor lost lamb." Here his voice uses touches of another voice. I think that's an important aspect of humor: ironic touches imported from someone talked about, and adapted into the narrative voice.

Methods of Humor

Many people claim that humor cannot be taught or learned, that it's a natural character trait. Much humor takes place spontaneously, without being premeditated, but analyzing humor often reveals a method. You can learn how to apply various methods to create humor.

Absurdist Humor

This excerpt from Samuel Beckett's novel *Molloy* is a description of lovemaking. This may strike you as too nihilistic to be humorous, but this is humor of a kind—absurdist humor. Beckett's humor, like Twain's, depends on the voice and a peculiar logic working together. While, in Twain, voice is perhaps more important than the logic, here, logic is more important than the voice:

> And all I could see was her taut yellow nape which every now and then I set my teeth in, forgetting I had none, such is the power of instinct. ... Anyway it was she who started it, in the rubbish dump, when she laid her hand upon my fly. More precisely, I was bent double over a heap

of muck, in the hope of finding something to disgust me for ever with eating, when she, undertaking me from behind, thrust her stick between my legs and began to titillate my privates. She gave me money after each session, to me who would have consented to know love, and probe it to the bottom, without charge. But she was an idealist. I would have preferred it seems to me an orifice less arid and roomy, that would have given me a higher opinion of love it seems to me. ... The other thing that bothers me, in this connexion, is the indifference with which I learnt of her death, when one black night I was crawling towards her, an indifference softened indeed by the pain of losing a source of revenue. ... What I do know for certain is that I never sought to repeat the experience, having I suppose the intuition that it had been unique and perfect, of its kind. ... Don't talk to me about the chambermaid, I should never have mentioned her, she was long before, I was sick, perhaps there was no chambermaid, ever, in my life. Molloy, or life without a chambermaid.

The narrative voice undermines whatever it touches with indifference. Beckett treats the first love and knowledge of love—traditionally topics of much sentiment—in a reductive manner, placing them in the context of a garbage dump. That reduction, in technique, may be the same as cynicism, since it portrays a higher level of human life in animal, dog, terms. And it is cynicism. People often resort to cynicism in the hope of being humorous, for the two share much. Twain's humorous description of prayer—"to tuck down her head and grumble a little over the victuals, though there warn't anything the matter with them"— is a downshifting maneuver, bringing something in high regard—prayer—to something basic—grumbling. (Twain's humor sounds less cynical than Beckett's because of Huck's disarmingly charming voice.)

To make cynicism come to life as humor requires wit, cleverness. Molloy's trying to get rid of his hunger by finding something disgusting in a dump of discarded foods is a clever twist. That the narrator calls the woman an idealist because she pays him for lovemaking is another twist. Paying strikes us as materialistic, but you can find some logic in this—paying for a service is an idea that she sticks to even though he'd do it for free. That he gets carried away and sinks his teeth in her neck forgetting he has none—this surprises you with its logical impossibility, and evokes a potentially funny picture of naked gums biting. In the statement "perhaps there was no chambermaid," the narrator's doubt continues where we don't expect it. Perhaps there was no narrator? No life without a chambermaid? The paradoxes and sometimes logical impossibilities laid out one after another create an effect.

Sundry Humor: Slapstick, Caricature, Exaggeration, Stereotypes

Nikolai Gogol, a versatile humorist, used all kinds of humor. Though much of his humor is lost or diminished in translation from Russian, some does come through.

In describing a giant in *Dead Souls*, Gogol jokes: "He was seven feet tall, in other words, a born dentist." This is a jab at Russian dentistry, where strength to pull out teeth was the basic skill. The joke works through exaggeration and the stereotyping of a profession. Once when I visited a dental clinic in Novi Sad (Northern Serbia), three muscular dentists tied me to a chair and flexed their muscles on my jaws. I was reminded of the joke, but did not laugh.

Gogol uses stereotypes for a humorous effect. Earlier I wrote against the use of stereotypes, but sometimes they can work, if the humor is not malicious. Gogol also uses similes in an astoundingly simple way. The freshness of these metaphors works, for me, as humor. Speaking of a healthy man, Gogol says: "A lump of iron would sooner catch cold and start coughing than that wonderfully constituted landowner."

Here's another kind of humor Gogol uses. When Chichikov, the hero of *Dead Souls*, runs into an acquaintance, a landowner, their meeting goes as follows: "They immediately embraced each other and remained clasped in each other's arms for about five minutes. The kisses they exchanged were so powerful that their front teeth ached for the rest of the day. Manilov was so overjoyed that only his nose and his lips remained on his face, his eyes having completely disappeared."

This is perhaps the most common type of humor—slapstick. It depends on exaggerating and overdoing a simple social exchange. A hug with a greeting kiss becomes a major enterprise. Note Gogol's caricaturist skill: "Only his nose and his lips remained on his face, his eyes having completely disappeared." This wonderfully reductive image enhances the scene.

Gogol mostly uses typology, caricature, and exaggeration in his humor. It's not simple to reduce it to a formula, at least not as simple as in the following case study: Oscar Wilde's humor.

Substituting Opposites as Humor

Oscar Wilde's humor is like math. He creates it through substitution of values: "The old-fashioned respect for the young is fast dying out." "Divorces are made in heaven."

The technique is transparent, yet effective. Wilde substitutes one element in a cliché for its opposite, and the cliché becomes something new, surprising, certainly funny. You put in *young* for *old*, *divorces* for *marriages*.

In "The Decay of Lying," Wilde writes: "The ancient historians gave us delightful fiction in the form of fact; the modern novelist presents us with dull facts under the guise of fiction." Here, we have a role reversal. Historians, who should give us facts, give us fiction. Novelists, who should give us fiction, give us facts.

You can apply this technique not only in one-liners, but in two (or more) sentences, as does Wilde in this case from *The Importance of Being Earnest*: "I hope you have not been leading a double life, pretending to be wicked and being really good all the time. That would be hypocrisy."

As though he's put a negative sign before a parenthesis, Wilde here switches things around: good/wicked. Everything else stays the same.

In the following example from "The Decay of Lying," Wilde creates a string of reversals of what's commonly expected by the mechanics of custom:

> Many a young man starts in his life with a natural gift for exaggeration which, if nurtured in congenial and sympathetic surroundings, or by imitation of the best models, might grow into something really great and wonderful. But, as a rule, he comes to nothing. He either falls into careless habits of accuracy, or takes to frequenting the society of the aged and the well-informed. ... In a short time he develops a morbid and unhealthy faculty of truth-telling, begins to verify all statements made in his presence, has no hesitation in contradicting people who are much younger than himself, and often ends by writing novels which are so life-like that no one can possibly believe in their probability.

"Careless habit of accuracy"—usually *accuracy* strikes us as something careful, and we accept the coupling of the two words quite mechanically. Wilde breaks the couplet, as he does with contradicting people much younger. Now, this is not all formula. Part of Wilde's humor is his voice, the stylishly and ironically high-brow way of putting words together. "Frequenting the society of the aged and the well-informed," for example, strikes a tone of leisure, of the English upper-class, so Wilde's is a comedy of manners, besides being a humor of inversion.

Wilde's humor method is not unique. Much of Beckett's humor conforms to this "formula." (I put formula in quotation marks because nothing guarantees that all you write according to it will be funny. But some things will be.) Beckett's (Molloy's) softening indifference with the thought of losing revenue is a reversed phrase—we soften pain, in a cliché. He softens its near opposite, indifference.

George Bernard Shaw uses the same technique: "A drama critic is a man who leaves no turn unstoned."

Situational Humor

Much situational humor depends on timing and confusion. Here's an example from Bernard Malamud's novel *The Fixer*. In it, Yakov, on the way to Kiev, must abandon his horse in order to cross a river:

> The boatman untied the boat, dipped both oars into the water and
> they were off.
> The nag, tethered to a paling, watched from the moonlit shore.
> Like an old Jew he looks, thought the fixer.
> The horse whinnied, and when that proved useless, farted loudly.
> "I don't recognize the accent you speak," said the boatman, pull-
> ing the oars. "It's Russian but from what province?"
> "I've lived in Latvia as well as other places," the fixer muttered.

The scene taking place is sad. Thus, the contrast, the fart in the solemn moment, "cracks" the solemnity, and it cracks up the readers.

Now take this phrase—"The horse whinnied, and when that proved useless, farted loudly"—and place it one line up or down, and you'll see that the joke won't work so well, or will be lost altogether.

Timing, however, is not everything. Something high is brought low, human speech to a nag's fart. This downgrading results in humor. I don't think there's an absolute recipe for humor, but if you practice this downshifting and timing so that one thing could be taken for another, you might create humor.

Notice one more point in Malamud's example. The protagonists don't laugh. They continue being serious, they don't notice the humor; to them, the nag's fart has nothing to do with what they are doing. This increases the humor. You may take this as a paradigm: If a protagonist in your story cracks a joke, don't have him and others roll on the floor holding their sides; otherwise, your reader will get the impression that you are congratulating yourself. That's a bit like prerecorded laughter in a sitcom. Deadpan humor is the best. If it's funny, your reader will laugh. If not, all right, there was no promise of humor anyway. But if your reader encounters an orgy of laughter after a flat joke, she may resent not laughing. (Of course, when it's important that a character laugh at a joke, let him laugh.)

You can learn how to make humorous passages from what I've told you so far, or from your own analysis. Analyze writings you find funny. If you persevere, in some of them you'll find an applicable method.

EXERCISES

1. One page. Construct the voice of an uneducated person (or someone who never paid any attention to writing classes) through playing with syntax. Rarely

use a comma, but sometimes put one in the wrong place, and sometimes in the right place. Skip periods for long stretches, and here and there use sentence fragments. Take a look at Vaughn's example on page 174, but do it more extremely—misspell (not too much though, keep it readable), use possessives and contractions incorrectly. Combine this with repetitive expressions (end sentences with *or something*, like Salinger in *The Catcher in the Rye*; overuse *like*, and so on). Add to it some regional expressions. Let the character talk about her "date from hell."

Objective: To arrive at a voice through the basic syntactical technique. Can you begin to hear someone sounding like this? What's this person like? What does she wear, eat, drink? If grammar puts a strain on you, perhaps freedom from grammar will free you.

Check: Did you get a sense of character? You should. Voice without character is pale and impersonal; character without voice can hardly be alive.

2. One page. Construct the first-person voice of an immigrant from a language you are familiar with—Spanish, German, Italian—all right, even French. In every second sentence or so, use one foreign word. Don't double or triple *r*s (*verrry*) in English to give us the accent with rolled *r*s, but now and then—rarely—make a change in spelling. Let the person talk about her getting married to an American for a green card. Describe the fake wedding in detail, with many asides. (If you're not familiar with a foreign language, use a regional dialect, and make the wedding a marriage of convenience.)

Objective: In our multicultural society, languages mix, interpenetrate. This is a vast reservoir of voices. Tap it.

Check: Do the foreign words make sense in their context? If you didn't know what they meant, could you guess from their placement and tone? (Ask a colleague whether the foreign words sound convincing.) Do these words add color to the voice? If you don't have the sound of an immigrant, you might play with the consonants. For example, many Germans pronounce what should be "v" as "f" (hence, for example, the title of the story "Mademoiselle Fifi"; the officer was saying *oui oui* as *fi fi*). And many Spaniards pronounce "v" as "b," so *video* sounds like *bideo*. You don't have to distort every word.

3. Two pages. Write a polyphonous story, after the example of Twain's "The Celebrated Jumping Frog of Calaveras County." Frame the story in the voice of an overeducated persona who imitates an uneducated narrator, and let the narrator introduce a folksy character with her regional speech, in a yarn-like style. Don't worry if your narrators don't sound authentic in terms of regions and dialects. Invent your own regions and dialects, if you like.

Objective: To create an orgy of voices. If you can play different voices against each other, or with each other, you might attain a wonderful liveliness in your story.

Check: On the most basic level, do the voices sound different? Let them not use the same syntax, length of sentences, level of diction, fillers. Is each voice consistent? For example, a sales type of abbreviation (*as is* for *as it is*) would clash with highly formal syntax ("Lest he should abdicate his primogeniture, grant him the seal"). Do all these voices sound spoken? They should.

4. Three pages. Write a rough draft of a story, with a theme of abuse. Let's say a lawyer (or a doctor) exploits an elderly widow. Don't hide your tone of outrage about the injustice, but don't preach. Give us the event only. Revise a draft of what you've written. Replace all the clichés with words that address what you mean as directly as possible. Remove passive voice whenever possible. Cut redundancies, excess adverbs, and adjectives. Make sure it's always clear where the action is: Who does what to whom? Who kicks whom? Once rid of the static, your piece should sound loud and clear. The combination of emotion (outrage) with clear writing must result in a strong voice.

Objective: Nothing sharpens a voice like a sense of injustice. See if you can drive yourself to a fever pitch by standing up for an injured person.

Check: Did you speak forcefully? In simple, direct, unmincing sentences?

5. Two pages. First, imitate Joyce's early style, which we discussed earlier in this chapter. Offer a good variety of sentences, emphasized with concrete images and energetic verbs and adverbs.

Then, imitate Joyce's style in *Ulysses*. Write two long, unrestrained sentences that have the energy to keep going, with odd words (find them in a dictionary or thesaurus)—at least half a page for each sentence.

Objective: Breathing exercises. See which carries more life for you, more thrill, without making you run out of breath.

Check: Read your exercises out loud. Which suits you better, the first or the second style? Give these sentences to a colleague of yours. Which style does he prefer? If both you and your colleague prefer one, maybe something in it might work for you. You might adapt this to your work—the adverbs, the sentence variety, the alterations between negative and positive statements, whatever.

6. Three sentences. Can you imitate T.C. Boyle's syntax of doubles? Perhaps we should call it stereo syntax. Analyze his sentence on page 176 and write three similar ones.

Objective: To experiment with sentences. Whether with Boyle or someone else, you might find a rhythm that works for you, that releases your imagination. Painters study other painters' strokes. Why deny yourself a basic learning technique?

Check: Do you have many doubles, expressed with *or*, *and*, *but*? Do you express some points in a negative and others in a declarative?

7. One paragraph. Can you imitate Kate Braverman's voice and syntax in the excerpt from her story on page 178? Make all sentences direct, and some factual. No conjunctions. Clip the sentences with commas, make many of them short, and end the paragraph with a negative statement, and yet create expectations for further paragraphs. This strategy builds a good forward momentum.

Now rewrite the exercise with many *although*s, *but*s, *and*s, and *because*s. Put in more adverbs, and add several metaphors.

Objective: To find which way of writing suits you better. Some artists draw with many long, fuzzy pencil strokes, others with a few sharp, short ones.

Check: Which syntax suits you better? Read both exercises out loud, and feel the rhythm in each. Which moves better? Ask a colleague for her opinion.

8. One to two pages. Imitate Beckett's account of Molloy's first love on pages 180–181. Write in the first person. Possible themes: trying transcendental meditation, getting a college degree, publishing your first short story, eating caviar, listening to *Ode to Joy* at a glamorous concert hall, attending the funeral of someone who should be beloved. Treat each "high" with indifference. Over-analyze the experience into total banality.

Objective: To practice cynicism with a twist as a source of humor.

Check: Have you concentrated on the physical details? With transcendental meditation, you might talk about twisting your knee, incense, etc. With the college degree, you might analyze the poor quality of the paper, sunstroke, sweat, hunger. (Of course, you can do better than this.)

9. One page. Take a list of proverbs, clichés, and truisms, and insert the opposites for each subject. ("Marriages are ...")

Objective: To learn the basic technique of Wilde's humor. Don't worry whether the reversals you create are funny. If you write enough of them, some will be. Even a computer could do this.

Check: Read the ones you think are funny to someone who laughs pretty easily. If you don't spark any laughter, find someone else. If nothing happens, choose another set of truisms, twist them, and check them with your hired laughers.

10. One page. Give a twist to familiar expressions. For example, "One more drink and I'll be under the table" becomes "One more drink and I'll be under the host" (as a comedian has paraphrased this in a cartoon).

Objective: Similar to the purpose of Exercise 9, but here you don't have to substitute opposites. *Host* and *table* are not opposites, but the substitution works perfectly. Look for something that would make sense in the situation.

Check: Same as in Exercise 9.

11. Three half-page paragraphs. Imitate Wilde's quote about the decay of the art of lying on pages 182–183. Can you write something similar on the decay of the art of jealousy, stealing, flirting, drinking, smoking, chocolate-eating, procrastinating? Take three of them, and tell us something against the grain of the common wisdom.

Objective: To create humor by upgrading an apparent vice to a virtue.

Check: Are you convincing enough? Wilde's arguments make sense. Constructing lies takes imagination, and it probably develops imagination, so it should be a useful skill for a fiction writer. Make sure that your arguments are sensible, at least at some level.

12. One page. In the proverbs and clichés from Exercises 9 and 10, reverse key adjectives and see what happens. Something is bound to turn out funny. Or at least twisted.

Objective: To learn that humor can take place at almost every turn of a sentence. If you examine many possible permutations, something will work. We call witty people quick because they can quickly think of enough permutations to light upon something interesting. This is a technique, and no matter how spontaneously a witty person applies it, he still does it.

Check: Have you made enough switches?

13. One page. Make up a dialogue in which momentary confusion occurs, at least in the reading, as in Malamud's examples. Take a heartbreaking departure, or a solemn rite of passage, and make a joke; let something from the "bodily substratum" (Mikhail Bakhtin's phrase) intrude on the solemnity.

Objective: To practice situational comedy. Learn how to place and time your intrusions. Create and exploit confusions. Your characters should not laugh.

Check: Have your buddies read this. Are they laughing? Or smiling? If not, shift your intrusive line up or down. Again, check with someone around you. Humor is in the ear of the reader, not in the eye of the writer.

14. Three pages. Choose three social conventions, such as a handshake, keeping the door open for the next passerby, and holding hands. Construct three slapstick scenes, exaggerating whatever can happen, so that it becomes funny. Pattern this after Gogol's example of friends embracing and kissing each other on page 182. You might augment your humor with dialogue and with caricatures of the handshakers' faces.

Objective: To practice basic slapstick as comedy of manners.

Check: Do you make the conventions appear ridiculous? Vivid? Your readers should get the sensation of doing all these things as though participating in the scenes. Have you managed to squeeze in a good caricature? And, most important, is this funny?

15. Write in the voice of a child. You can read Frank O'Connor's story "My Oedipus Complex" (in the back of this book) for an example. Part of the voice is the way of thinking. If you have kids around, listen to how they talk. I know, the kid slang changes from year to year. I was surprised to hear my son calling things "sweet." *Sweet* became *cool*. Or you can work from memory and remember your earlier voices.

Objective: To exercise the path between your ears and fingers, and to play with voices. Sometimes, a wide shift in making a new voice that is very different from yours will liberate you to make things up, to make fiction.

Check: Read it out loud, or even better, have a kid read your passages. Does the voice you came up with fit a kid?

10

REVISION

In the revision stage, you strive to make your writing coherent, clear, and effective. Out of chaos, a fully developed story gradually emerges. Clumsy sentences become graceful; clichés become wit; muddled action becomes drama. If you wonder how to sound original, the answer is: revise and revise. Even if you think your stories don't work, you can make them work—if you revise well.

It's amazing how easy it is to lack courage as a writer. The anxiety of a concert pianist is understandable. She can't go back and improve the passages where she blundered. That you can return to your story and cut the weak parts and expand the strong ones should encourage you as you write your first draft. Therefore, don't look back until you are finished.

As you revise, don't fear changing your text radically in search of its best possible shape. And certainly don't hesitate to get rid of whatever does not work. This is how Isaac Bashevis Singer put it: "The wastepaper basket is the writer's best friend."

On the other hand, don't rush to throw things away. Give yourself time, and if in a week you still think that something you've written doesn't work and can't be made useful, get rid of it. Sometimes, what appears weak one day may appear fine the next. This is what Conrad Aiken said about his experience: "I would find a crumpled yellow ball of paper in the wastebasket in the morning, and open it to see what the hell I'd been up to; and occasionally it was something that needed only a very slight change to be brought off, which I'd missed the day before."

So that you don't have to fumble in the garbage among banana peels and cockroaches (although cockroaches come from a noble literary lineage), save an early draft. If you cut too much, you can restore. That knowledge should help you freely look at your text. See it again. Look at what fits and what doesn't. If something is pretty but does not connect to the rest of the text, cut it. Samuel Johnson advised, "Read over your compositions and, when you meet a passage that you think is particularly fine, strike it out." He has a point—if something stands out of the text, maybe it does not belong in it.

Revision used to be painful before word processors. You had to cut out pages, glue them, white out sections, so that most often you'd simply give up on changing here and there, and you'd rewrite the whole piece. (Of course, some good came out of being forced to rewrite thoroughly.) Now, with computers, you don't need to rewrite. We could say, "The delete key is the writer's best friend." You can rearrange passages, compress—revise.

Yes, there's a difference between a revision and a complete rewrite: In revision, you rearrange passages, condense sentences, add here and there, and so on, but you probably leave chunks of the text close to the original. Before word processors, Hemingway did more than thirty drafts of a story. And we got anecdotes like this one, from Isaac Babel's friend Konstantin Paustovsky: Babel showed Paustovsky a manuscript two hundred pages long. When Paustovsky asked him whether it was a novel, Babel answered that it was his short story "Lyubka the Cossack" in twenty-two versions.

In a rewrite, you take a look at what you did in the initial draft and tackle it differently, or write from scratch, not even necessarily looking at the draft again.

THE FIRST REWRITE

These days, when people tell you that they have rewritten something ten times, they probably mean that they have played around with the original text several times. Since the advent of computer-assisted word processing, for better or worse (certainly, for easier), hardly anybody does complete rewrites anymore. But many people arrange and rearrange their passages—tinker with the original draft. As a consequence, I think it has become easier to write clean sentences and paragraphs, but perhaps harder to get rid of the larger structural problems because it's simpler to remain within the initial faulty structure of a draft.

Rather than say that with computers we have gained something and lost something, we can enjoy the best of both the high-tech and low-tech worlds—if we're willing to do the extra work. Write your first draft longhand or on a typewriter. (If you work solely on the computer, you can simulate the typewriter if you don't go back too much. Print out your draft and delete the original from the computer.) Now read your draft and think what you need to do differently. Rewrite it from scratch on the computer. (Or do another longhand draft, and then type it into the system.) Save your rewrite, and treat it as your starting point for revision.

Through this method, you will make sure that you get at least one rewrite, as opposed to a series of tinkerings. Not that there's anything wrong with tinkering—on the contrary, you get to play around and have fun with the story—but it should not start too early.

Carefully read your first draft before undertaking a rewrite. Identify your major conflict, scene, plot. Outline the plot, in a basic way.

In the first rewrite, you want to see the story taking shape out of the first-draft mass of words. Cut through the words and find the story. Let it emerge. In every draft, there is a story desperately trying to get out. Cut the chains and give the keys to the prisoner.

Find the story's big moments. By knowing where they occur, you save yourself a lot of work; you will be able to build your narration on a strong foundation. Mark your main characters and main scenes. Are there too many characters? Compress two or three characters into one. Are there too many big scenes? Can you compress them into fewer?

Once you decide on your major scenes, begin your rewrite. Expand the scenes. Let the characters act, speak, move in a setting. You don't need to accomplish everything right now, since you'll have time to revise. Complete a rough rewrite—even several of them. Don't yet worry about your spelling, diction, clichés, or other minute matters.

After you finish these rough rewrites of the major moments in your story, provide the transitions and background between the big scenes. Make sense of what happens in the scenes. Put the background you cannot fit into the scenes into your narrative paragraphs, where you can simply tell us what we need to know to follow the upcoming scenes.

Read your rewrite, proofing it against the plot outline. (If you change the plot in the first rewrite, outline the new plot and proof the rewrite against it.) Whatever seems useless, cut. If something in no way contributes to your understanding of the central characters, the conflict, and the key event, cut it. Your story must make sense. Here, you may spend a lot of time thinking, analyzing.

Some writers do scene-oriented story buildup intuitively, and others arrive at the basic structure after dozens of revisions. If you don't belong in the former camp, you still might be able to avoid belonging in the latter by identifying the foundation of your story in the first rewrite stage, so that you won't need to keep restructuring. With practice, you might become so adept at this that it will appear that you work intuitively. Intuition is often simply an internalized technique that frees you from having to deliberate over what to do; a net player in tennis, who through diligence acquires good habits, can react to a passing shot without thinking about what the textbook says about footwork.

But even if you become a highly intuitive writer, you will still most likely need a lot of revision: first, rough revision (macrorevision), making sure that all the parts of the story fit together; then, fine revision (microrevision), making sure that each word is in its place.

When you finish your rewrite, save it. I always do. The knowledge that I can return to the second draft enables me to take a distant look at my story, without particular attachments to this or that passage, so I keep only what I need and revise freely. I often think I will return to that saved second draft, but I hardly ever do. And when I do, I notice that though I cut, I have lost nothing.

Be open to any change that suggests itself as important during your revising. And have fun! Most writers prefer revising to the original drafting—some write the original draft so they'll have something to play with.

MACROREVISION

There are different styles of revision, depending on how you write your initial draft. According to F. Scott Fitzgerald, writers are either putter-inners or taker-outers.

Those who work from a sketchy draft must add words to give life to a story skeleton. In revision, they pause where they need to add dialogue and description. (Some writers are extreme putter-inners, so when they revise even previously unedited torrents of words, they are more eager to add than to cut.)

Those who write in torrents of unedited words—hoping that the accumulation will contain a story—must eventually cut quite a bit to find the story. I don't need to quote anybody in support of the putter-inner aesthetics; Shakespeare, Dostoyevski, and Balzac were putter-inners.

Elie Wiesel gives us the best description of the taker-outer aesthetics: "Writing is ... like a sculpture where you remove, you eliminate in order to make the work visible. Even those pages you remove somehow remain. There is a difference between a book of two hundred pages from the very beginning, and a book of two hundred pages which is the result of an original eight hundred pages. The six hundred pages are there. Only you don't see them."

Many people are both putter-inners and taker-outers. If you are not, consider becoming both. You could rush through some parts, knowing that you can fill in later. And you can spend much time on other parts—adding line upon line, getting as much juice out of a scene as your imagination and free associations will give you—without fearing that you'll be boring, since you can clean up later.

As you look over your story, first check it against the "First Rewrite" guidelines above to find your major scenes, your story. Then leaf through this book, chapter by chapter. Each chapter raises questions about the elements of fiction. Check your setting, plot, POV, and so on. But to give you a concentrated checklist, I will offer many questions here. (Whenever you have a story, you can use these guidelines. If you have one already, get it out and examine it against the checklists to follow.) If you must rethink an element of your fiction, go to the chapters that address your concerns.

Revision Checklist

All the parts of your story must work before it can fly. Make sure that each part is the best it can be, as though you were an inspector in a Boeing factory. Keep in mind that, although a good proportion of stories could be held accountable to the rules and principles on this list, many stories set their own rules. For example, a slice-of-life story needn't be structured around a conflict. Just make sure that you don't say that your story follows its own rules merely as an excuse. And if you come up with idiosyncratic rules, hold your story accountable to them.

Plot

Does enough *happen* in your story? Something must. The event need not be huge, but it must be dramatic and significant.

Is the story structured around a conflict? Can you state the conflict in a sentence or two? What is the struggle about? This is your theme. The theme should not be separate from the conflict.

Do you introduce the conflict soon enough—preferably as a crisis in the first couple of pages? Do you sustain the conflict as a tension long enough, through most of your story?

Is the conflict carried to its logical conclusion? Does the ending make sense in light of the beginning?

Can you identify the key event and its climax? This should be the turning point. You've reached the peak and now things will inevitably slide, faster and faster, to a conclusion. Hitherto, there were options; but now the protagonist's choice has become clear.

Does the story give us enough information on the causes of the main event? Although the advice remains "show, don't tell," whenever you *can't* show us enough, tell us, summarize, fill us in. After all, you are a storyteller. Whatever happens in the story must make sense.

Do you present us with the right sequence of events (scenes and summaries) so that the story has the cogency of a good argument?

Do you avoid the stock plot? (Steer clear of plots too often encountered in pop novels—for example, the detective investigating a murder is the murderer.)

Is your plot easy to follow? Even if it's a mystery, what happens during the investigation should be easy to follow. John Gardner advised, "Don't play pointlessly subtle games in which storytelling is confused with puzzle-making."

Character

Who are the protagonists? Antagonists? In general, you should have at least two characters, engaged in some kind of action or tension. One character reminiscing and laughing out loud at his thoughts or smiling at ashtrays doesn't offer enough dialectical potential for a story.

Are the main characters well developed (round)? If not, give them sufficient complexity—desires, obstacles, weaknesses, strengths.

Are there flat characters? Perhaps they don't need to be round, but on the other hand, don't let them become stereotypes.

Can you see the basic motivation—desires and fears—of the main characters?

Do the characters encounter obstacles? Are the obstacles sufficiently tough?

Does your main character change or come to some crucial insight in the course of the story?

Setting

Is the setting appropriate? Authentic? If it's Cleveland, make sure there's no subway. If it's Venus, make sure there are no people living in forests.

Does your setting work in synergy with characters and plot? The setting should deepen your characterization and ground your plot. Realistically drawn landscapes and cityscapes increase believability, even in fantasy stories.

Have you given us the setting gradually, together with the characters and the action? Or have you dumped it all in a long chunk in the beginning or middle?

Have you used the setting for special effects (foreshadowing, mood expression, beautiful images, change of pace)?

POV

From whose POV is the story told? Would it be better from another character's POV?

Is the POV consistent? If it shifts, is there a good reason for it to do so?

Does your POV shift in midsentence? Midparagraph? Even in the omniscient POV, you might do better to sort out POVs by paragraphs.

In the omniscient POV, do you enter too many heads? Generally, limit yourself to the main characters. The minor ones can remain external.

Do you use interior monologues to your advantage? If there's a crisis point in which your POV carrier is alone, waiting, you might deliver an interior monologue to heighten suspense and clarify motives.

Do you use stream of consciousness where you can? If there's a crisis point in which your POV carrier is injured or disoriented, you might switch to stream of consciousness to reflect the crisis and to change the narrative pace.

Whom does the narrator of your story address? Is there an ostensible audience, like "Gentle reader," "Dear President," "Mimi"? Is the audience used consistently?

Who are you, as the author, addressing? An imaginary person, or a friend, or nobody? Who do you think will read your story? Children, adults, punks, U.S. Marines, Connecticut tax-evaders?

Are there authorial intrusions? Are they warranted? In the omniscient POV, they are fair game; in other POVs, they may be distracting.

Voice, Attitude, and Humor

What voices do you hear in the story? Naturally, each speaker should have a distinct voice, different from the author's in most cases, unless the narrative is a piece of overt autobiography. In the narrative part, is the voice clear enough?

Do you joke at inappropriate moments—for example, at the peak of a tragic action? Some characters may joke under stress; it's all right to reproduce that, but make sure the authorial humor does not undermine the tension.

Are your jokes in poor taste? Offensive to women or minorities?

Do you strain too hard for sentimental effects? Any *rivers of tears*? Above all, especially in the third-person POV narrative, don't tell that what happened was *devastatingly sad*, unless you parody sentimental writing.

Timing

Does the story start at the right moment? Or does it start too early, before the main action—or too late? Identify your first crisis moment, and open with it. A swimmer jumps far into the pool rather than swim from the very edge of it. The better you write, the further into the story you'll be able to jump.

Does the story end at the right moment? Find the point when things have begun to fall into place, and cut the action; ending here implies that they will continue to do so.

Do you cover enough time in the story? Or too much? (In a short story, usually you'll cover several days, and generally you shouldn't cover more than a couple of years; in a novel, you can.)

Is the chronology—and the grammar that indicates it—clear? If you frequently backtrack in time, try using the present tense for your *now* action, so you can use the simple past tense, rather than past perfect, for your *then* action.

Check your tenses. Within a chapter, unless there is a flashback or a fast-forward, the tense should remain the same. The tense should not switch in a sentence.

Keep the sequence of motions chronological, from first to last. A sentence should not ordinarily read like this: "After he lies on a sofa, upon walking in the room, he breathes out his anxiety." Readers strain to straighten out the sequence of actions here. The same holds true of paragraphs. Keep going forward, except when you have memories and flashbacks. But even then, once you switch into the past to explain what had happened, lay it out as chronologically as possible.

If you've used flashbacks or memories, did you need to? Could you tell the story from the first event to the last without backtracking and without losing the cogency of the story as an argument? This is a difficult choice. Sometimes you must go with the shape of the argument rather than with the linearity of time. It's best if you can accomplish both.

Has the story been paced well? Don't bore the reader, yet don't run out of plot too fast. Make sure that you've done enough showing to give body to any telling you may have done.

Dialogue and Scene

Is the dialogue natural? Do the characters sound like real people rather than technical books?

Do the characters sound different from the general narrative and from each other? Go through the dialogue, line by line, and give signature expressions to a character, making sure that the other characters don't use the same ones, except when being sarcastic to each other.

Is your dialogue complex enough? Combine small scenes into big ones so that they portray characters, advance the plot, and raise tension.

Do you have enough dialogue in proportion to the narrative? There's no set rule, but at least some parts of your story should be written in dialogue, unless you are doing Man Against Nature or some other type of story in which dialogue might not appear. And despite the current fashion in favor of dialogue, your fiction should include description, summary, and other sorts of narrative—for the change of pace, transitions, and quick information.

Is the story told mostly as a non-scenic narrative? If so, your story will sound like an essay. Decide where the action is, and stage it.

Are the scenes compounded ("Mondays she would pray") or are they specific ("One Monday she prayed")? Compounded scenes work well to introduce the main event, but the main event must take place as a fully developed, specific scene. Your story or novel should contain a larger proportion of specific scenes than of compounded scenes and background exposition.

Are the right scenes dramatized and the right ones summarized? Usually, your key event should be fully dramatized (though you should skip greetings and other dull exchanges, unless they can show something important). Some supporting scenes can be summarized, others dramatized. Transitions between various events are usually summarized.

Do you have too many similar scenes? Are there ten quarrels? Maybe two will do; make each unique. If you write three similar scenes to show a pattern, distill them to one, and tell us during it that the dramatic action is part of a pattern.

Are your dramatic scenes long enough? If not, expand them.

Are the dramatic scenes suspenseful enough? Though they must be fairly long, they also must be quickly paced. Achieving this balance can be difficult. Raise the tension of the conflict, and point toward the resolution, which should make sense of it all.

Description and Diction

Do you show enough? The most important story moments must be shown in scenes.

Do you describe characters in a fresh way? (No chiseled features, sky-blue eyes, pearly white teeth.)

Do you genuinely describe settings? (No ominous train stations, squalid quarters, posh offices.)

Do you have enough dynamic descriptions incorporated into the action?

Do you tell enough? You need not show absolutely everything. Sometimes it's all right to tell, for the sake of pacing the narrative. Some crucial points can be both told and shown; if you tell them, show them also.

Are there enough metaphors? Too many? Do they work? Do they create a parallel text? Is the parallel text something you want? For example, if all your metaphors concern various beasts devouring each other, are you sure you want this Hobbesian dimension in your story—and is this killing and feeding frenzy what your story is about? If you have a tame romance with such metaphors, you have a choice: Either get rid of bestial metaphors and resort to botany (although flowers have been overused in this context), or listen to your metaphors. They may suggest a major plot change. The romance might turn into a struggle and become all the more interesting. In other words, metaphors may bring out the full potential of a story. If you listen to them, your story might grow into a larger one.

Do the descriptions drag or jump?

Are the descriptions effective? Do they engage our senses? Or are some senses atrophied? Why? In most cases, if your sentences do not make us see (hear, touch, smell, taste), cross them out. Leave what you can perceive.

MICROREVISION

When you've successfully answered all of the questions above and made all the necessary changes, you are still not quite finished; you've got to polish. You must cleanse the narrative of any superfluous words. Polishing can turn out to be a lot of work. As James Baldwin put it, "Most of the rewrite is cleaning."

Polishing the manuscript may be similar for everybody—putter-inners and taker-outers alike.

Here, you want each sentence to be sharp, each word to count. Jerzy Kosinski said, "Every word is there for a reason, and if not, I cross it out. I rarely allow myself to use English in an unchecked, spontaneous way. I always have a sense of trembling—but so does a compass, after all. I cut adjectives, adverbs, and every word which is there just to make an effect."

Some cleanup is mechanical. Check your spelling. If you don't have spell-check on your computer, use a dictionary. Now and then, I encounter a student who scoffs at spelling. I haven't, however, met a violinist who doesn't care whether his pitch is perfect.

Check your paragraphs. Are they fully developed? Journalistic practices aside, your paragraphs should contain more than one sentence, except in dialogue or when you're conferring special emphasis.

Punctuate conventionally. Write in complete sentences, not comma splices or sentence fragments, except now and then for special effect. Unless you're experimenting, use conventional grammar. The less attention it attracts to itself, the more attention will remain for your story.

Make sure your sentences are not monotonous. Vary sentence length and structure. Don't start every sentence with *I* or *he*. Don't, on the other hand, start each sentence with *although*, *considering*, or other dependent clause conjunctions. It's good to alternate simple and complex sentences, to establish a pleasing rhythm and avoid choppiness and monotony.

Don't let each sentence travel like a runaway train. Some people—even some famous writers—do that, but they are hard to read. In long sentences, it's easy to lose track of the subject and the object. It must be clear who is doing what to whom. Who's kicking whom. Be sure that each pronoun has a clear precedent. Consider this sentence: "Above my garage the snow has fallen over a layer of ice, but the frozen sparrow has not moved, and now that the sun is out it's melting." What is melting—snow, sparrow, sun, or ice?

Make sure you are clear. Sometimes you must weed out the passive voice and abstract vocabulary to achieve clarity.

Is the language weak? Too many adjectives and adverbs? Passives? Clichés? On the other hand, can you find strikingly fresh usages, *le mot juste*?

Make sure your sentences are direct. Scrutinize your use of prepositional phrases—especially *of* and *in* constructions. "The paint on the table in the kitchen" could profitably become "the kitchen table's paint." You use four rather than eight words—cut the lard factor by 50 percent—and speed up the prose. Don't use double prepositions uselessly: "get off of my case" when "get off my case" would do.

Avoid official language and technical jargon unless you need it for comedy or parody. *Hereunto, aforementioned*, and the like belong in legal documents.

Get rid of repetitions. Some repetitions are not immediately visible; they are redundant and superfluous expressions, such as "She came to a complete stop." *Complete* is superfluous. If the stop is incomplete, it's not a stop. Or, "He lived his life." *Life* is redundant, since it's included in *lived*. "He blinked his eyes." "He blinked" will do, because the verb implies eyes.

If in a ten-line paragraph you use *love* or *response* (or any other words, other than articles and helping verbs) more than thrice, scrutinize each use, and eliminate it unless it's essential. Find synonyms. For *response*, perhaps *reaction* could do. Of course, some essential grammatical device words—such as *a, the, have*, and *like*—will recur, and you shouldn't worry about them, within reasonable limits.

Delete all unnecessary modifiers in dialogue tags. For example: "'Will you please please go home?' he said beseechingly." *Beseechingly* wastes time; it's clear from the sentence that a plea is going on. Moreover, *beseechingly* is an awkward adverb—to the verb we add the gerund (*-ing*) suffix, and then we add *-ly* to make an adverb. Thus, the word is twice removed from its original verb. The more removals a word undergoes from its origin, the paler it becomes. "He beseeched" might be an improvement, in that light, but since "he said" does not commit redundancy, you should prefer it.

Omit all unnecessary indications of who's speaking. On the other hand, is it always clear who is speaking? Whenever in doubt, indicate the speaker and use *said*.

Do you misspell for any kind of effect—stuttering, dialect, shouting? Keep your misspellings to a minimum. You can indicate outside the dialogue that something is said in a Southern drawl, or even better, you can rely on syntax and word choice to give us the flavor of the voice.

Don't use clichés. Cut whatever you've heard too many times (like *window of opportunity*), unless you need to show that this is how somebody talks. If you are making fun of clichés—why? To educate others? If so, do you strike a pose of being above your reader, or one in which you and your reader are both above most of humanity?

WHEN TO QUIT REVISING

Is there such a thing as too much revision? Yes. Sooner or later you must decide that the story is finished. Further revision might actually damage it. John Dos

Passos described this decision: "I usually write to a point where the work is getting worse rather than better. That's the point to stop and the time to publish."

Tolstoy too described how much rewriting may damage the text: "Often in rewriting, I omit things, substitute others, not because the new idea is better, but because I get tired of the old. Often I strike out what is vivid and replace it with something dull."

Another distinct danger in revising over and over is that you might lose a realistic perception of your story. The lines begin to sound not only familiar but inevitable. The more you listen to a piece of music, the more you may find it gratifying because you can predict the sequences. This resonance effect through too much repetition will make your work appear fabulously chiseled and meaningful. If this happens, beware. It happens to me after too much revision. What do I do then? I lay the work aside for half a year or so, forget most of it, and when I come back, I'm amazed at how rough it is. I need to revise it at least a couple of times more. The fact is that I did not revise the story too much, from the structural standpoint of the story, but I did from the psychological standpoint. Yes, after too many spins, I get crazy, filled with delusions of grand writing. Perhaps this is some kind of psychological reaction against getting stuck in the revision mode.

Avoid getting stuck in the revision mode beyond the point of diminishing returns. Find that point. Here, you need good critical abilities about your work in progress, which you can develop only with a lot of practice. And don't go much beyond that point. The problem is that the story will begin to lose your individual flavor and voice with further and further refinements. If some rough edges preserve the story's sense of life, keep them in.

The Final Test

After all the revisions, there are still two useful questions:

First, what can you still cut without damaging the story? If the word is pretty but only for its own sake, and not for the sake of the story, press your best friend, the delete key.

Second, is your story easy to follow? Give it to two or three readers. If none understands what's going on, you might have to do a lot of revising yet! Straighten out whatever is confusing—if the chronology is twisted, lay it out simply from A to Z; if the motives are not clear, spell them out simply, in summary, if need be. Writing is communication—and the burden of communication is on you. Now and then, I run into a student who, during the class critique of his story, smiles superciliously, and at the end of it, says, "None of you got it! What happens is this ...."

Invariably the writer constructed the story as a puzzle without revealing what happens. I am not saying that you should not write complex stories, but there's a difference between complex and complicated. Something simple can become complicated through unclear presentation. Above all, make sure that you are clear and that you show what happens in the story. The story should reveal, not obfuscate, an event.

To do this test, find somebody willing to read your work. Anybody who likes to read stories can do it; you don't need professional writers and editors for this. (In fact, sometimes they make the worst readers because many of them are jaded—everything may strike them as old simply because they have read too many manuscripts.) Of course, if your friends read your story, they'll probably tell you that they like it. Don't listen to this. Instead, ask them questions. What happens in the story? You need to know whether you've communicated it. Are the characters lifelike? Do they sound real when they talk? Does it make sense that they would do what they did in your story? (But don't ask for what the story means in a philosophical sense. You want a reading, not a scholarly interpretation.)

This is where a group workshop is immensely useful. You can see what comes across to the readers. You need some feedback. Your intentions about how the story should be read may be one thing, the story's reception another.

If you haven't communicated your story, go back and make it clear once again. Tell it. Maybe you've tried to show and imply too much? If the showing doesn't do it, leave the showing and add the telling. I know, this going back may drive you crazy. But the first several times you attempt a story, the hardest part is looking not only for the story, but for the *pattern for writing stories*. This is also the most important part.

Be patient and keep working. Perhaps on all matters of writing fiction, that is the best advice I can give you.

EXERCISES

1. Ten pages minimum. To do the following exercises, write a first draft of a new story. Writing the draft is your exercise. You need not spend days on it. One or two will do. Consider Raymond Carver's advice: "It doesn't take that long to do the first draft of the story, that usually happens in one sitting, but it does take a while to do the various versions of the story. I've done as many as twenty or thirty drafts of a story. Never less than ten or twelve drafts." Knowing that you can return to the story and fix it should move you forward. Find an interesting conflict, give it to engaging characters, in a setting you know enough about, and keep going for at least ten pages.

Objective: To learn how to do the initial draft, relying on the follow-up revision. You don't need to polish anything here; free your imagination, don't censor yourself, follow even the strangest impulses. Surprise yourself. Say what you don't think a person like you would say.

Check: Do the rest of the exercises. I will not supply checks at the end of the exercises, because each assignment is a form of check on your story. You will constantly go back to your story and check and recheck—that's what revision is about.

2. Print your draft, because you can survey the story more easily on paper than on the screen. You get a better sense of proportion, of distances between events, and so on if you hold the story in your hands than if you stare at it on the screen. Take out a pencil and carefully read your draft. What is your major conflict, scene, plot? Write a basic outline of the plot on a new sheet of paper.

Proofread the draft against the plot outline. Mark your main characters and main scenes. Are there too many characters? Compress them into fewer. Are there too many key scenes? Can you compress them into fewer? This is basically a thinking stage. Mark and outline your major two or three scenes.

Objective: To find the story in your draft.

3. Work from your paper draft and your plot outline rather than from your saved first draft (delete the draft!). This will force you to rewrite your story at least once rather than just add, subtract, and reshuffle elements in the draft. The advantage is that you will work from your strengths in the draft rather than from the weaknesses. You don't even have to delete what doesn't seem to contribute to the understanding of the main events. Simply type the parts that do and, as you type, change them. Now rewrite your big scene. Expand it. Don't worry about any background information at this stage. You can fill us in later.

Objective: To further clarify your characters and what you want them to do—or rather, what they want to do—and to let them do it. Basic scenes must be dynamic, dramatic, engaging.

4. Print what you have, sit down with this draft and with a pencil, and connect your major scenes. Do you need minor scenes to show the buildup of the conflict? To portray your major characters? Mark the places where you can do this. Where can you describe the setting? Can you do this as you introduce your characters? During dialogue pauses? In transitions between the scenes? Go to the computer and do what you need to do. Shorten your summaries, and let your minor scenes combine summary and drama. When you are finished, save your draft twice: once for backup, and once for a working copy. Probably you won't need the backup, but let it be your insurance policy.

Objective: To give the readers—and yourself—all they need to know. Most successful stories work as revelations. Reveal and show what happens—who did it, how, where, when, why?

5. From writer-teacher John Cussen: Tell your story to someone. (While it may dissipate your energies in the drafting stage to tell your story aloud, once you've done a draft and the first rewrite, retelling the story will concentrate your energies.) After you retell the story, you'll know which parts you need, which you don't. Go back to your story, and make it conform to this new understanding. Rewrite again if necessary. You want to write a story that works.

Objective: To find out if your story works as a basic story. When you have to keep your listener's interest, you are not likely to make lengthy digressions. You'll probably find that you gear all your information toward the climax and resolution. You'll probably also find that something must happen in the story. Who will listen to a story in which nothing takes place?

6. Print out your newest version of the story. Now read your story all the way through again. Annie Dillard uses a conference table for this purpose—she lays out dozens of pages and looks at them to see how they relate. This perspective is impossible on the screen, which works like a peephole. The peephole has its advantage of concentration, and this will be useful to you when you do microrevision. (If you are more comfortable working on the screen, you will need to survey much of the story in your head from short-term memory.)

Indicate places that don't convince you. Scrutinize them. What is missing? Details? Dialogue? Revise. Now look again. If you still aren't convinced, perhaps the problem stems from something more essential—plausible motives? Make each character's behavior sufficiently motivated (with either fear or desire). To show motivation, you might expand auxiliary scenes and narrative passages. Perhaps this leads to another big scene. Maybe you need to restructure the story. Don't be afraid to do it. Go back to Exercise 2 and change the plot outline. Hopefully, next time you come to Exercise 6, you'll be satisfied enough to move to microrevision—working with details—rather than macrorevision (plot and character).

Objective: To make the story convincing; to give verisimilitude to everything that takes place.

7. Examine the metaphors in your story. Can you group them according to a theme? Is this theme congruent with your ostensible theme? If not, try incorporating the theme into your plot. Give your story another shake-up!

Objective: To bring out your intuitive understanding of the story. Metaphors may express your deep feelings, your subconscious grasp of the story. Synergize all the levels of your understanding. If your metaphors seem in opposition to your direct understanding of the story, fine—bring the dichotomy into the main conflict. After all, the stronger the conflict, the greater its chance of becoming exciting.

8. From Mark Twain: Cross out all the adjectives and adverbs in your story. Read it and see whether you've lost anything. Restore the adjectives you absolutely need.

Objective: To become more aware of adjectives and adverbs. I suggest that you leave some restored adjectives as they are and that you flesh out others in concrete details. Select one or two to expand into mini-scenes.

9. From Exercise 8, wherever you've described something in adjectives ("ominously somber cellar"), add another sentence with details that'll flesh out the intention you expressed in the adjective.

Objective: The details must appear true; the readers should see for themselves that something looks the way you say it does.

10. Find words that mention feelings; flesh them out in concrete images, and for a couple of them, construct minor scenes. If she felt angry, let her do something to convince us of her anger.

Objective: To help you make the characters and their motives more convincing.

11. Go through the microrevision checklist in this chapter and proofread your story against it. Then apply the two "Final Test" questions from the text. Could you cut something without damaging the story? Do it. Is the story easy to follow? Let somebody read the story, and quiz him about what came across. If you haven't communicated the basic story, simplify and tell more explicitly whatever did not come across.

Objective: To keep in touch with the basics: the story shouldn't have unnecessary parts, and it should be readable.

12. If you have the time to do this one, do it, sooner or later, at least with one of your stories. Write five to six ten-page variations of a story centered around one event. You may write it in the third person, then in the first person. Write it first as an explanation of an event, backtracking as you need to illuminate the motives; let the story work as a cogent argument. Then write it out chronologically from first event to last. Then write it backward, from last event to first. Then take an interesting but minor character and write it from her point of view. Make her the central character. Then change the ending—let the story go in a completely different direction, one that you toyed with previously, but discarded. Or invent a new possibility. Brainstorm for the story's other options. Unless you

do each draft seriously, as though it were the final story, you will not know all the story's potential.

Run each variation through the macrorevision questions in the chapter, concentrating on the elements that are most essential to your story.

At the end, choose your most successful variant, and burn the rest.

Just kidding. Keep all the variants that seem successful; it's possible that more than one will.

Objective: To explore the possibilities of your story. Let it be all it can be. This should prove immensely useful to your insight as to storytelling possibilities when you write other stories. I think every writer should do complete rewrites with at least one story. This may seem to require too much time from you and to be outside of the scope of this book. Good! After all, now you are on your own, and what better way to start out than with a big project! A semester-long writing workshop could be profitably based on this variation-on-a-theme exercise.

FATHER SERGIUS
by Leo Tolstoy

I

In Petersburg in the eighteen-forties a surprising event occurred. An officer of the Cuirassier Life Guards, a handsome prince who everyone predicted would become aide-de-camp to the Emperor Nicholas I and have a brilliant career, left the service, broke off his engagement to a beautiful maid of honor, a favorite of the Empress's, gave his small estate to his sister, and retired to a monastery to become a monk.

This event appeared extraordinary and inexplicable to those who did not know his inner motives, but for Prince Stepan Kasatsky himself it all occurred so naturally that he could not imagine how he could have acted otherwise.

His father, a retired colonel of the Guards, had died when Stepan was twelve, and sorry as his mother was to part from her son, she entered him at the Military College as her deceased husband had intended.

The widow herself, with her daughter, Varvara, moved to Petersburg to be near her son and have him with her for the holidays.

The boy was distinguished both by his brilliant ability and by his immense self-esteem. He was first both in his studies—especially in mathematics, of which he was particularly fond—and also in drill and in riding. Though of more than average height, he was handsome and agile, and he would have been an altogether exemplary cadet had it not been for his quick temper. He was remarkably truthful, and was neither dissipated nor addicted to drink. The only faults that marred his conduct were fits of fury to which he was subject and during which he lost control of himself and became like a wild animal. He once nearly threw out of the window another cadet who had begun to tease him about his collection of minerals. On another occasion he came almost completely to grief by flinging a whole dish of cutlets at an officer who was acting as steward, attacking him and, it was said, striking him for having broken his word and told a barefaced lie. He would certainly have been reduced to the ranks had not the Director of the College hushed up the whole matter and dismissed the steward.

By the time he was eighteen he had finished his College course and received a commission as lieutenant in an aristocratic regiment of the Guards.

The Emperor Nicholas Pavlovich (Nicholas I) had noticed him while he was still at the College, and continued to take notice of him in the regiment, and it was on this account that people predicted for him an appointment as aide-de-camp to the Emperor. Kasatsky himself strongly desired it, not from ambition only but chiefly because since his cadet days he had been passionately devoted to Nicholas Pavlovich. The Emperor had often visited the Military College and every time Kasatsky saw that tall erect figure, with breast expanded in its military overcoat, entering with brisk step, saw the cropped side-whiskers, the moustache, the aquiline nose, and heard the sonorous voice exchanging greetings with the cadets, he was seized by the same rapture that he experienced later on when he met the woman he loved. Indeed, his passionate adoration of the Emperor was even stronger: he wished to sacrifice something—everything, even himself—to prove his complete devotion.

And the Emperor Nicholas was conscious of evoking this rapture and deliberately aroused it. He played with the cadets, surrounded himself with them, treating them sometimes with childish simplicity, sometimes as a friend, and then again with majestic solemnity. After that affair with the officer, Nicholas Pavlovich said nothing to Kasatsky, but when the latter approached he waved him away theatrically, frowned, shook his finger at him, and afterwards when leaving, said: "Remember that I know everything. There are some things I would rather not know, but they remain here," and he pointed to his heart.

When on leaving College the cadets were received by the Emperor, he did not again refer to Kasatsky's offense, but told them all, as was his custom, that they should serve him and the fatherland loyally, that he would always be their best friend, and that when necessary they might approach him direct. All the cadets were as usual greatly moved, and Kasatsky even shed tears, remembering the past, and vowed that he would serve his beloved Tsar with all his soul.

When Kasatsky took up his commission his mother moved with her daughter first to Moscow and then to their country estate. Kasatsky gave half his property to his sister and kept only enough to maintain himself in the expensive regiment he had joined.

To all appearance he was just an ordinary, brilliant young officer of the Guards making a career for himself; but intense and complex strivings went on within him. From early childhood his efforts had seemed to be very varied, but essentially they were all one and the same. He tried in everything he took up to attain such success and perfection as would evoke praise and surprise. Whether it was his studies or his military exercises, he took them up and worked at them till he was praised and held up as an example to others. Mastering one subject he took up another, and obtained first place in his studies. For example, while still at College he noticed in himself an awkwardness in French conversation, and contrived to master French till he spoke it as well as Russian, and then he took up chess and became an excellent player.

Apart from his main vocation, which was the service of his Tsar and the fatherland, he always set himself some particular aim, and however unimportant it was, devoted himself completely to it and lived for it until it was accomplished. And as soon as it was attained another aim would immediately present itself, replacing its predecessor. This passion for distinguishing himself, or for accomplishing something in order to distinguish himself, filled his life. On taking up his commission he set himself to acquire the utmost perfection in knowledge of the service, and very soon became a model officer, though still with the same fault of ungovernable irascibility, which here in the service again led him to commit actions inimical to his success. Then he took to reading, having once in conversation in society felt himself deficient in general education—and again achieved his purpose. Then, wishing to secure a brilliant position in high society, he learnt to dance excellently and very soon was invited to all the balls in the best circles, and to some of their evening gatherings. But this did not satisfy him: he was accustomed to being first, and in this society was far from being so.

The highest society then consisted, and I think always consists, of four sorts of people: rich people who are received at Court, people not wealthy but born and brought up in Court circles, rich people who ingratiate themselves into the Court set, and people neither rich nor belonging to the Court but who ingratiate themselves into the first and second sets.

Kasatsky did not belong to the first two sets, but was readily welcomed in the others. On entering society he determined to have relations with some society lady, and to his own surprise quickly accomplished this purpose. He soon realized, however, that the circles in which he moved were not the highest, and that though he was received in the highest spheres he did not belong to them. They were polite to him, but showed by their whole manner that they had their own set and that he was not of it. And Kasatsky wished to belong to that inner circle. To attain that end it would be necessary to be an aide-de-camp to the Emperor—which he expected to become—or to marry into that exclusive set, which he resolved to do. And his choice fell on a beauty belonging to the Court, who not merely belonged to the circle into which he wished to be accepted, but whose friendship was coveted by the very highest people and those most firmly established in that highest circle. This was Countess Korotkova. Kasatsky began to pay court to her, and not merely for the sake of his career. She was extremely attractive and he soon fell in love with her. At first she was noticeably cool towards him, but then suddenly changed and became gracious, and her mother gave him pressing invitations to visit them. Kasatsky proposed and was accepted. He was surprised at the facility with which he attained such happiness. But though he noticed something strange and unusual in the behavior towards him of both mother and daughter, he was blinded by being so deeply in love, and did not realize what almost the whole town knew—namely, that his fiancée had been the Emperor Nicholas's mistress the previous year.

Two weeks before the day arranged for the wedding, Kasatsky was at Tsarskoe Selo at his fiancée's country place. It was a hot day in May. He and his betrothed had walked about the garden and were sitting on a bench in a shady linden alley. Mary's white muslin dress suited her particularly well, and she seemed the personification of innocence and love as she sat, now bending her head, now gazing up at the very tall and handsome man who was speaking to her with particular tenderness and self-restraint, as if he feared by word or gesture to offend or sully her angelic purity.

Kasatsky belonged to those men of the eighteen-forties (they are now no longer to be found) who while deliberately and without any conscientious scruples condoning impurity in themselves, required ideal and angelic purity in their women, regarded all unmarried women of their circle as possessed of such purity, and treated them accordingly. There was much that was false and harmful in this outlook, as concerning the laxity the men permitted themselves, but in regard to the women that old-fashioned view (sharply differing from that held by young people today who see in every girl merely a female seeking a mate) was, I think, of value. The girls, perceiving such adoration, endeavored with more or less success to be goddesses.

Such was the view Kasatsky held of women, and that was how he regarded his fiancée. He was particularly in love that day, but did not experience any sensual desire for her. On the contrary he regarded her with tender adoration as something unattainable.

He rose to his full height, standing before her with both hands on his sabre.

"I have only now realized what happiness a man can experience! And it is you, my darling, who have given me this happiness," he said with a timid smile.

Endearments had not yet become usual between them, and feeling himself morally inferior he felt terrified at this stage to use them to such an angel.

"It is thanks to you that I have come to know myself. I have learnt that I am better than I thought."

"I have known that for a long time. That was why I began to love you."

Nightingales trilled nearby and the fresh leafage rustled, moved by a passing breeze.

He took her hand and kissed it, and tears came into his eyes.

She understood that he was thanking her for having said she loved him. He silently took a few steps up and down, and then approached her again and sat down.

"You know ... I have to tell you ... I was not disinterested when I began to make love to you. I wanted to get into society; but later ... how unimportant that became in comparison with you—when I got to know you. You are not angry with me for that?"

She did not reply but merely touched his hand. He understood that this meant: "No, I am not angry."

"You said ..." He hesitated. It seemed too bold to say. "You said that you began to love me. I believe it—but there is something that troubles you and checks your feeling. What is it?"

"Yes—now or never!" thought she. "He is bound to know of it anyway. But now he will not forsake me. Ah, if he should, it would be terrible!" And she threw a loving glance at his tall, noble, powerful figure. She loved him now more than she had loved the Tsar, and apart from the Imperial dignity would not have preferred the Emperor to him.

"Listen! I cannot deceive you. I have to tell you. You ask what it is? It is that I have loved before."

She again laid her hand on his with an imploring gesture. He was silent.

"You want to know who it was? It was—the Emperor."

"We all love him. I can imagine you, a schoolgirl at the Institute ..."

"No, it was later. I was infatuated, but it passed ... I must tell you ..."

"Well, what of it?"

"No, it was not simply—" She covered her face with her hands.

"What? You gave yourself to him?"

She was silent.

"His mistress?"

She did not answer.

He sprang up and stood before her with trembling jaws, pale as death. He now remembered how the Emperor, meeting him on the Nevsky, had amiably congratulated him.

"O God, what have I done! Stiva!"

"Don't touch me! Don't touch me! Oh, how it pains!"

He turned away and went to the house. There he met her mother.

"What is the matter, Prince? I ..." She became silent on seeing his face. The blood had suddenly rushed to his head.

"You knew it, and used me to shield them! If you weren't a woman ... !" he cried, lifting his enormous fist, and turning aside he ran away.

Had his fiancée's lover been a private person he would have killed him, but it was his beloved Tsar.

Next day he applied both for furlough and his discharge, and professing to be ill, so as to see no one, he went away to the country.

He spent the summer at his village arranging his affairs. When summer was over he did not return to Petersburg, but entered a monastery and there became a monk.

His mother wrote to try to dissuade him from this decisive step, but he replied that he felt God's call which transcended all other considerations. Only his sister, who was as proud and ambitious as he, understood him.

She understood that he had become a monk in order to be above those who considered themselves his superiors. And she understood him correctly. By becoming a monk he showed contempt for all that seemed most important to others and had seemed so to him while he was in the service, and he now ascended a height from which he could look down on those he had formerly envied. ... But it was not this alone, as his sister Varvara supposed, that influenced him. There was also in him something else—a sincere religious feeling which Varvara did not know, which intertwined itself with the feeling of pride and the desire for preeminence, and guided him. His disillusionment with Mary, whom he had thought of angelic purity, and his sense of injury, were so strong that they brought him to despair, and the despair led him—to what? To God, to his childhood's faith which had never been destroyed in him.

II

Kasatsky entered the monastery on the feast of the Intercession of the Blessed Virgin. The Abbot of that monastery was a gentleman by birth, a learned writer and a starets, that is, he belonged to that succession of monks originating in Walachia who each choose a director and teacher whom they implicitly obey. This Superior had been a disciple of the starets Ambrose, who was a disciple of Makarius, who was a disciple of the starets Leonid, who was a disciple of Paussy Velichkovsky.

To this Abbot Kasatsky submitted himself as to his chosen director. Here in the monastery, besides the feeling of ascendancy over others that such a life gave him, he felt much as he had done in the world: he found satisfaction in attaining the greatest possible perfection outwardly as well as inwardly. As in the regiment he had been not merely an irreproachable officer but had even exceeded his duties and widened the borders of perfection, so also as a monk he tried to be perfect, and was always industrious, abstemious, submissive, and meek, as well as pure both in deed and in thought, and obedient. This last quality in particular made life far easier for him. If many of the demands of life in the monastery, which was near the capital and much frequented, did not please him and were temptations to him, they were all nullified by obedience: "It is not for me to reason; my business is to do the task set me, whether it be standing beside the relics, singing in the choir, or making up accounts in the monastery guest-house." All possibility of doubt about anything was silenced by obedience to the starets. Had it not been for this, he would have been oppressed by the length and monotony of the church services, the bustle of the many visitors, and the bad qualities of the other monks. As it was, he not only bore it all joyfully but found in it solace and support. "I don't know why it is necessary to hear the same prayers several times a day, but I know that it is necessary; and knowing this I find joy in them." His director told him that as material food is necessary for the maintenance of the life of the body, so spiritual food—the church prayers—is necessary for the maintenance of the spiritual life. He believed this, and though the church services, for which he had to get up early in the morning, were a difficulty, they certainly calmed him and gave him joy. This was the result of his consciousness of humility, and the certainty that whatever he had to do, being fixed by the starets, was right.

The interest of his life consisted not only in an ever greater and greater subjugation of his will, but in the attainment of all the Christian virtues, which at first seemed to him easily attainable. He had given his whole estate to his sister and did not regret it, he had no personal claims, humility towards his inferiors was not merely easy for him but afforded him pleasure. Even victory over the sins of the flesh, greed and lust, was easily attained. His director had specially warned him against the latter sin, but Kasatsky felt free from it and was glad.

One thing only tormented him—the remembrance of his fiancée; and not merely the remembrance but the vivid image of what might have been. Involuntarily he recalled a lady he knew who had been a favorite of the Emperor's, but had afterwards married and become an admirable wife and mother. The husband had a high position, influence and honor, and a good and penitent wife.

In his better hours Kasatsky was not disturbed by such thoughts, and when he recalled them at such times he was merely glad to feel that the temptation was past. But there were moments when all that made up his present life suddenly grew dim before him, moments when, if he did not cease to believe in the aims he had set himself, he ceased to see them and could evoke no confidence in them but was seized by a remembrance of, and—terrible to say—a regret for, the change of life he had made.

The only thing that saved him in that state of mind was obedience and work, and the fact that the whole day was occupied by prayer. He went through the usual forms of prayer, he bowed in prayer, he even prayed more than usual, but it was lip-service only and his soul was not in it. This condition would continue for a day, or sometimes for two days, and would then pass of itself. But those days were dreadful. Kasatsky felt that he was neither in his own hands nor in God's, but was subject to something else. All he could do then was to obey the starets, to restrain himself, to undertake nothing, and simply to wait. In general all this time he lived not by his own will but by that of the starets, and in this obedience he found a special tranquility.

So he lived in his first monastery for seven years. At the end of the third year he received the tonsure and was ordained to the priesthood by the name of Sergius. The profession was an important event in his inner life. He had previously experienced a great consolation and spiritual exaltation when receiving communion, and now when he himself officiated, the performance of the preparation filled him with ecstatic and deep emotion. But subsequently that feeling became more and more deadened, and once when he was officiating in a depressed state of mind he felt that the influence produced on him by the service would not endure. And it did in fact weaken till only the habit remained.

In general in the seventh year of his life in the monastery Sergius grew weary. He had learnt all there was to learn and had attained all there was to attain, there was nothing more to do and his spiritual drowsiness increased. During this time he heard of his mother's death and his sister Varvara's marriage, but both events were matters of indifference to him. His whole attention and his whole interest were concentrated on his inner life.

In the fourth year of his priesthood, during which the Bishop had been particularly kind to him, the starets told him that he ought not to decline it if he were offered an appointment to higher duties. Then monastic ambition, the very thing he had found so repulsive in other monks, arose within him. He was assigned to a monastery near the metropolis. He wished to refuse but the starets ordered him to accept the appointment. He did so, and took leave of the starets and moved to the other monastery.

The exchange into the metropolitan monastery was an important event in Sergius's life. There he encountered many temptations, and his whole will-power was concentrated on meeting them.

In the first monastery, women had not been a temptation to him, but here that temptation arose with terrible strength and even took definite shape. There was a lady known for her frivolous behavior who began to seek his favor. She talked to him and asked him to visit her. Sergius sternly declined, but was horrified by the definiteness of his desire. He was so alarmed that he wrote about it to the starets. And in addition, to keep himself in hand, he spoke to a young novice and, conquering his sense of shame, confessed his weakness to him, asking him to keep watch on him and not let him go anywhere except to service and to fulfill his duties.

Besides this, a great pitfall for Sergius lay in the fact of his extreme antipathy to his new Abbot, a cunning worldly man who was making a career for himself in the Church. Struggle with himself as he might, he could not master that feeling. He was submissive to the Abbot, but in the depths of his soul he never ceased to condemn him. And in the second year of his residence at the new monastery that ill-feeling broke out.

The Vigil service was being performed in the large church on the eve of the feast of the Intercession of the Blessed Virgin, and there were many visitors. The Abbot himself was conducting the service. Father Sergius was standing in his usual place and praying: that is, he was in that condition of struggle which always occupied him during the service, especially in the large church when he was not himself conducting the service. This conflict was occasioned by his irritation at the presence of fine folk, especially ladies. He tried not to see them or to notice all that went on: how a soldier conducted them, pushing the common people aside, how the ladies pointed out the monks to one another—especially himself and a monk noted for his good looks. He tried as it were to keep his mind in blinkers, to see nothing but the light of the candles on the altar-screen, the icons, and those conducting the service. He tried to hear nothing but the prayers that were being chanted or read, to feel nothing but self-oblivion in consciousness of the fulfillment of duty—a feeling he always experienced when hearing or reciting in advance the prayers he had so often heard.

So he stood, crossing and prostrating himself when necessary, and struggled with himself, now giving way to cold condemnation and now to a consciously evoked obliteration of thought and feeling. Then the sacristan, Father Nicodemus—also a great stumbling-block to Sergius who involuntarily reproached him for flattering and fawning on the Abbot—approached him and, bowing low, requested his presence behind the holy gates. Father Sergius straightened his mantle, put on his biretta, and went circumspectly through the crowd.

"Lise, regarde a droite, c'est lui!" he heard a woman's voice say.

"Ou, ou? Il n'est pas tellement beau."

He knew that they were speaking of him. He heard them and, as always at moments of temptation, he repeated the words, "Lead us not into temptation," and bowing his head and lowering his eyes went past the ambo and in by the north door, avoiding the canons in their cassocks who were just then passing the altar-screen. On entering the sanctuary he bowed, crossing himself as usual and bending double before the icons. Then, raising his head but without turning, he glanced out of the corner of his eye at the Abbot, whom he saw standing beside another glittering figure.

The Abbot was standing by the wall in his vestments. Having freed his short plump hands from beneath his chasuble he had folded them over his fat body and protruding stomach, and fingering the cords of his vestments was smilingly saying something to a military man in the uniform of a general of the Imperial suite, with its insignia and shoulder-knots which Father Sergius's experienced eye at once recognized. This general had been the commander of the regiment in which Sergius had served. He now evidently occupied an important position, and Father Sergius at once noticed that the Abbot was aware of this and that his red face and bald head beamed with satisfaction and pleasure. This vexed and disgusted Father Sergius, the more so when he heard that the Abbot had only sent for him to satisfy the general's curiosity to see a man who had formerly served with him, as he expressed it.

"Very pleased to see you in your angelic guise," said the general, holding out his hand. "I hope you have not forgotten an old comrade."

The whole thing—the Abbot's red, smiling face amid its fringe of grey, the general's words, his well-cared-for face with its self-satisfied smile and the smell of wine from his breath and of cigars from his whiskers—revolted Father Sergius. He bowed again to the Abbot and said:

"Your reverence deigned to send for me?"—and stopped, the whole expression of his face and eyes asking why.

"Yes, to meet the General," replied the Abbot.

"Your reverence, I left the world to save myself from temptation," said Father Sergius, turning pale and with quivering lips. "Why do you expose me to it during prayers and in God's house?"

"You may go! Go!" said the Abbot, flaring up and frowning.

Next day Father Sergius asked pardon of the Abbot and of the brethren for his pride, but at the same time, after a night spent in prayer, he decided that he must leave this monastery, and he wrote to the starets begging permission to return to him. He wrote that he felt his weakness and incapacity to struggle against temptation without his help and penitently confessed his sin of pride. By return of post came a letter from the starets, who wrote that Sergius's pride was the cause of all that had happened. The old man pointed out that his fits of anger were due to the fact that in refusing all clerical honors he humiliated himself not for the sake of God but for the sake of his pride. "There now, am I not a splendid man not to want anything?" That was why he could not tolerate the Abbot's action. "I have renounced everything for the glory of God, and here I am exhibited like a wild beast!" "Had you renounced vanity for God's sake you would have borne it. Worldly pride is not yet dead in you. I have thought about you, Sergius my son, and prayed also, and this is what God has suggested to me. At the Tambov hermitage the anchorite Hilary, a man of saintly life, has died. He had lived there eighteen years. The Tambov Abbot is asking whether there is not a brother who would take his place. And here comes your letter. Go to

Father Paissy of the Tambov Monastery. I will write to him about you, and you must ask for Hilary's cell. Not that you can replace Hilary, but you need solitude to quell your pride. May God bless you!"

Sergius obeyed the starets, showed his letter to the Abbot, and having obtained his permission, gave up his cell, handed all his possessions over to the monastery, and set out for the Tambov hermitage.

There the Abbot, an excellent manager of merchant origin, received Sergius simply and quietly and placed him in Hilary's cell, at first assigning to him a lay brother but afterwards leaving him alone, at Sergius's own request. The cell was a dual cave, dug into the hillside, and in it Hilary had been buried. In the back part was Hilary's grave, while in the front was a niche for sleeping, with a straw mattress, a small table, and a shelf with icons and books. Outside the outer door, which fastened with a hook, was another shelf on which, once a day, a monk placed food from the monastery.

And so Sergius became a hermit.

III

At Carnival time, in the sixth year of Sergius's life at the hermitage, a merry company of rich people, men and women from a neighboring town, made up a troyka-party, after a meal of carnival-pancakes and wine. The company consisted of two lawyers, a wealthy landowner, an officer, and four ladies. One lady was the officer's wife, another the wife of the landowner, the third his sister—a young girl—and the fourth a divorcée, beautiful, rich, and eccentric, who amazed and shocked the town by her escapades.

The weather was excellent and the snow-covered road smooth as a floor. They drove some seven miles out of town, and then stopped and consulted as to whether they should turn back or drive farther.

"But where does this road lead to?" asked Makovkina, the beautiful divorcée.

"To Tambov, eight miles from here," replied one of the lawyers, who was having a flirtation with her.

"And then where?"

"Then on to L——, past the Monastery."

"Where that Father Sergius lives?"

"Yes."

"Kasatsky, the handsome hermit?"

"Yes."

"Mesdames et messieurs, let us drive on and see Kasatsky! We can stop at Tambov and have something to eat."

"But we shouldn't get home to-night!"

"Never mind, we will stay at Kasatsky's."

"Well, there is a very good hostelry at the Monastery. I stayed there when I was defending Makhin."

"No, I shall spend the night at Kasatsky's!"

"Impossible! Even your omnipotence could not accomplish that!"

"Impossible? Will you bet?"

"All right! If you spend the night with him, the stake shall be whatever you like."

"A discretion!"

"But on your side too!"

"Yes, of course. Let us drive on."

Vodka was handed to the drivers, and the party got out a box of pies, wine, and sweets for themselves. The ladies wrapped up in their white dogskins. The drivers disputed as to whose troyka should go ahead, and the youngest, seating himself sideways with a dashing air, swung his long knout and shouted to the horses. The troyka-bells tinkled and the sledge-runners squeaked over the snow.

The sledge swayed hardly at all. The shaft-horse, with his tightly bound tail under his decorated breechband, galloped smoothly and briskly; the smooth road seemed to run rapidly backwards, while the driver dashingly shook the reins. One of the lawyers and the officer sitting opposite talked nonsense to Makovkina's neighbor, but Makovkina herself sat motionless and in thought, tightly wrapped in her fur. "Always the same and always nasty! The same red shiny faces smelling of wine and cigars! The same talk, the same thoughts, and always about the same things! And they are all satisfied and confident that it should be so, and will go on living like that till they die. But I can't. It bores me. I want something that would upset it all and turn it upside down. Suppose it happened to us as to those people—at Saratov was it?—who kept on driving and froze to death. ... What would our people do? How would they behave? Basely, for certain. Each for himself. And I too should act badly. But I at any rate have beauty. They all know it. And how about that monk? Is it possible that he has become indifferent to it? No! That is the one thing they all care for—like that cadet last autumn. What a fool he was!"

"Ivan Nikolaevich!" she said aloud.

"What are your commands?"

"How old is he?"

"Who?"

"Kasatsky."

"Over forty, I should think."

"And does he receive all visitors?"

"Yes, everybody, but not always."

"Cover up my feet. Not like that—how clumsy you are! No! More, more—like that! But you need not squeeze them!"

So they came to the forest where the cell was.

Makovkina got out of the sledge, and told them to drive on. They tried to dissuade her, but she grew irritable and ordered them to go on.

When the sledges had gone she went up the path in her white dogskin coat. The lawyer got out and stopped to watch her.

It was Father Sergius's sixth year as a recluse, and he was now forty-nine. His life in solitude was hard—not on account of the fasts and the prayers (they were no hardship to him) but on account of an inner conflict he had not at all anticipated. The sources of that conflict were two: doubts, and the lust of the flesh. And these two enemies always appeared together. It seemed to him that they were two foes, but in reality they were one and the same. As soon as doubt was gone so was the lustful desire. But thinking them to be two different fiends he fought them separately.

"O my God, my God!" thought he. "Why dost thou not grant me faith? There is lust, of course: even the saints had to fight that—Saint Anthony and others. But they had faith, while I have moments, hours, and days, when it is absent. Why does the whole world, with all its delights, exist if it is sinful and must be renounced? Why hast Thou created this temptation? Temptation? Is it not rather a temptation that I wish to abandon all the joys of earth and prepare something for myself there where perhaps there is nothing?" And he became horrified and filled with disgust at himself. "Vile creature! And it is you who wish to become a saint!" he upbraided himself, and he began to pray. But as soon as he started to pray he saw himself vividly as he had been at the Monastery, in a majestic post in biretta and mantle, and he shook his head. "No, that is not right. It is deception. I may deceive others, but not myself or God. I am not a majestic man, but a pitiable and ridiculous one!" And he threw back the folds of his cassock and smiled as he looked at his thin legs in their underclothing.

Then he dropped the folds of the cassock again and began reading the prayers, making the sign of the cross and prostrating himself. "Can it be that this couch will be my bier?" he read. And it seemed as if a devil whispered to him: "A solitary couch is itself a bier. Falsehood!" And in imagination he saw the shoulders of a widow with whom he had lived. He shook himself, and went on reading. Having read the precepts he took up the Gospels, opened the book, and happened on a passage he often repeated and knew by heart: "Lord, I believe. Help thou my unbelief!"—and he put away all the doubts that had arisen. As one replaces an object of insecure equilibrium, so he carefully replaced his belief on its shaky pedestal and carefully stepped back from it so as not to shake or upset it. The blinkers were adjusted again and he felt tranquillized, and repeating his childhood's prayer: "Lord, receive me, receive me!" he felt not merely at ease, but thrilled and joyful. He crossed himself and lay down on the bedding on his narrow bench, tucking his summer cassock under his head. He fell asleep at once, and in his light slumber he seemed to hear the tinkling of sledge bells. He did not know whether he was dreaming or awake, but a knock at the door aroused him. He sat up, distrusting his senses, but the knock was repeated. Yes, it was a knock close at hand, at his door, and with it the sound of a woman's voice.

"My God! Can it be true, as I have read in the Lives of the Saints, that the devil takes on the form of a woman? Yes—it is a woman's voice. And a tender, timid, pleasant voice. Phui!" And he spat to exorcise the devil. "No, it was only my imagination," he assured himself, and he went to the corner where his lectern stood, falling on his knees in the regular and habitual manner which of itself gave him consolation and satisfaction. He sank down, his hair hanging over his face, and pressed his head, already going bald in front, to the cold damp strip of drugget on the draughty floor. He read the psalm old Father Pimon had told him warded off temptation. He easily raised his light and emaciated body on his strong sinewy legs and tried to continue saying his prayers, but instead of doing so he involuntarily strained his hearing. He wished to hear more. All was quiet. From the corner of the roof regular drops continued to fall into the tub below. Outside was a mist and fog eating into the snow that lay on the ground. It was still, very still. And suddenly there was a rustling at the window and a voice—that same tender, timid voice, which could only belong to an attractive woman—said:

"Let me in, for Christ's sake!"

It seemed as though his blood had all rushed to his heart and settled there. He could hardly breathe. "Let God arise and let his enemies be scattered ..."

"But I am not a devil!" It was obvious that the lips that uttered this were smiling. "I am not a devil, but only a sinful woman who has lost her way, not figuratively but literally!" She laughed. "I am frozen and beg for shelter."

He pressed his face to the window, but the little icon-lamp was reflected by it and shone on the whole pane. He put his hands to both sides of his face and peered between them. Fog, mist, a tree, and—just opposite him—she herself. Yes, there, a few inches from him, was the sweet, kindly frightened face of a woman in a cap and a coat of long white fur, leaning towards him. Their eyes met with instant recognition: not that they had ever known one another, they had never met before, but by the look they exchanged they—and he particularly—felt that they knew and understood one another. After that glance to imagine her to be a devil and not a simple, kindly, sweet, timid woman, was impossible.

"Who are you? Why have you come?" he asked.

"Do please open the door!" she replied, with capricious authority. "I am frozen. I tell you I have lost my way."

"But I am a monk—a hermit."

"Oh, do please open the door—or do you wish me to freeze under your window while you say your prayers?"

"But how have you ..."

"I shan't eat you. For God's sake let me in! I am quite frozen."

She really did feel afraid, and said this in an almost tearful voice.

He stepped back from the window and looked at an icon of the Savior in His crown of thorns. "Lord, help me! Lord, help me!" he exclaimed, crossing himself and bowing low. Then he went to the door, and opening it into the tiny porch, felt for the hook that fastened the outer door and began to lift it. He heard steps outside. She was coming from the window to the door. "Ah!" she suddenly exclaimed, and he understood that she had stepped into the puddle that the dripping from the roof had formed at the threshold. His hands trembled, and he could not raise the hook of the tightly closed door.

"Oh, what are you doing? Let me in! I am all wet. I am frozen! You are thinking about saving your soul and are letting me freeze to death ..."

He jerked the door towards him, raised the hook, and without considering what he was doing, pushed it open with such force that it struck her.

"Oh—pardon!" he suddenly exclaimed, reverting completely to his old manner with ladies.

She smiled on hearing that pardon. "He is not quite so terrible, after all," she thought. "It's all right. It is you who must pardon me," she said, stepping past him. "I should never have ventured, but such an extraordinary circumstance ..."

"If you please!" he uttered, and stood aside to let her pass him. A strong smell of fine scent, which he had long not encountered, struck him. She went through the little porch into the cell where he lived. He closed the outer door without fastening the hook, and stepped in after her.

"Lord Jesus Christ, Son of God, have mercy on me a sinner! Lord, have mercy on me a sinner!" he prayed unceasingly, not merely to himself but involuntarily moving his lips. "If you please!" he said to her again. She stood in the middle of the room, moisture dripping from her to the floor as she looked him over. Her eyes were laughing.

"Forgive me for having disturbed your solitude. But you see what a position I am in. It all came about from our starting from town for a sledge-drive, and my making a bet that I would walk back by myself from the Vorobevka to the town. But then I lost my way, and if I had not happened to come upon your cell ..." She began lying, but his face confused her so that she could not continue, but became silent. She had not expected him to be at all such as he was. He was not as handsome as she had imagined, but was nevertheless beautiful in her eyes: his greyish hair and beard, slightly curling, his fine, regular nose, and his eyes like glowing coal when he looked at her, made a strong impression on her.

He saw that she was lying.

"Yes ... so," said he, looking at her and again lowering his eyes. "I will go in there, and this place is at your disposal."

And taking down the little lamp, he lit a candle, and bowing low to her went into the small cell beyond the partition, and she heard him begin to move something about there. "Probably he is barricading himself in from me!" she thought with a smile, and throwing off her white dogskin cloak she tried to take off her cap, which had become entangled in her hair and in the woven kerchief she was wearing under it. She had not got at all wet when standing under the window, and had said so only as a pretext to get him to let her in. But she really had stepped into the puddle at the door, and her left foot was wet up to the ankle and her overshoe full of water. She sat down on his bed—a bench only covered by a bit of carpet—and began to take off her boots. The little cell seemed to her charming. The narrow little room, some seven feet by nine, was as clean as glass. There was nothing in it but the bench on which she was sitting, the book-shelf above it, and a lectern in the corner. A sheepskin coat and a cassock hung on nails by the door. Above the lectern was the little lamp and an icon of Christ in His crown of thorns. The room smelt strangely of perspiration and of earth. It all pleased her—even that smell. Her wet feet, especially one of them, were uncomfortable, and she quickly began to take off her boots and stockings without ceasing to smile, pleased not so much at having achieved her object as because she perceived that she had abashed that charming, strange, striking, and attractive man. "He did not respond, but what of that?" she said to herself.

"Father Sergius! Father Sergius! Or how does one call you?"

"What do you want?" replied a quiet voice.

"Please forgive me for disturbing your solitude, but really I could not help it. I should simply have fallen ill. And I don't know that I shan't now. I am all wet and my feet are like ice."

"Pardon me," replied the quiet voice. "I cannot be of any assistance to you."

"I would not have disturbed you if I could have helped it. I am only here till daybreak."

He did not reply and she heard him muttering something, probably his prayers.

"You will not be coming in here?" she asked, smiling. "For I must undress to dry myself."

He did not reply, but continued to read his prayers.

"Yes, that is a man!" thought she, getting her dripping boot off with difficulty. She tugged at it, but could not get it off. The absurdity of it struck her and she began to laugh almost inaudibly. But knowing that he would hear her laughter and would be moved by it just as she wished him to be, she laughed louder, and her laughter—gay, natural, and kindly—really acted on him just in the way she wished.

"Yes, I could love a man like that—such eyes and such a simple noble face, and passionate too despite all the prayers he mutters!" thought she. "You can't deceive a woman in these things. As soon as he put his face to the window and saw me, he understood and knew. The glimmer of it was in his eyes and remained there. He began to love me and desired me. Yes—desired!" said she, getting her overshoe and her boot off at last and starting to take off her stockings. To remove those long stockings fastened with elastic it was necessary to raise her skirts. She felt embarrassed and said:

"Don't come in!"

But there was no reply from the other side of the wall. The steady muttering continued and also a sound of moving.

"He is prostrating himself to the ground, no doubt," thought she. "But he won't bow himself out of it. He is thinking of me just as I am thinking of him. He is thinking of these feet of mine with the same feeling that I have!" And she pulled off her wet stockings and put her feet up on the bench, pressing them under her. She sat a while like that with her arms round her knees and looking pensively before her. "But it is a desert, here in this silence. No one would ever know. ..."

She rose, took her stockings over to the stove, and hung them on the damper. It was a queer damper, and she turned it about, and then, stepping lightly on her bare feet, returned to the bench and sat down there again with her feet up.

There was complete silence on the other side of the partition. She looked at the tiny watch that hung round her neck. It was two o'clock. "Our party should return about three!" She had not more than an hour before her. "Well, am I to sit like this all alone? What nonsense! I don't want to. I will call him at once."

"Father Sergius, Father Sergius! Sergey Dmitrich! Prince Kasatsky!"

Beyond the partition all was silent.

"Listen! This is cruel. I would not call you if it were not necessary. I am ill. I don't know what is the matter with me!" she exclaimed in a tone of suffering. "Oh! Oh!" she groaned, falling back on the bench. And strange to say she really felt that her strength was failing, that she was becoming faint, that everything in her ached, and that she was shivering with fever.

"Listen! Help me! I don't know what is the matter with me. Oh! Oh!" She unfastened her dress, exposing her breast, and lifted her arms, bare to the elbow. "Oh! Oh!"

All this time he stood on the other side of the partition and prayed. Having finished all the evening prayers, he now stood motionless, his eyes looking at the end of his nose, and mentally repeated with all his soul: "Lord Jesus Christ, Son of God, have mercy upon me!"

But he had heard everything. He had heard how the silk rustled when she took off her dress, how she stepped with bare feet on the floor, and had heard how she rubbed her feet with her hand. He felt his own weakness, and that he might be lost at any moment. That was why he prayed unceasingly. He felt rather as the hero in the fairy-tale must have felt when he had to go on and on without looking round. So Sergius heard and felt that danger and destruction were there, hovering above and around him, and that he could only save himself by not looking in that direction for an instant. But suddenly the desire to look seized him. At the same instant she said:

"This is inhuman. I may die. ..."

"Yes, I will go to her, but like the Saint who laid one hand on the adulteress and thrust his other into the brazier. But there is no brazier here." He looked round. The lamp! He put his finger over the flame and frowned, preparing himself to suffer. And for a rather long time, as it seemed to him, there was no sensation, but suddenly—he had not yet decided whether it was painful enough—he writhed all over, jerked his hand away, and waved it in the air. "No, I can't stand that!"

"For God's sake come to me! I am dying! Oh!"

"Well—shall I perish? No, not so!"

"I will come to you directly," he said, and having opened his door, he went without looking at her through the cell into the porch where he used to chop wood. There he felt for the block and for an axe which leant against the wall.

"Immediately!" he said, and taking up the axe with his right hand he laid the forefinger of his left hand on the block, swung the axe, and struck with it below the second joint. The finger flew off more lightly than a stick of similar thickness, and bounding up, turned over on the edge of the block and then fell to the floor.

He heard it fall before he felt any pain, but before he had time to be surprised he felt a burning pain and the warmth of flowing blood. He hastily wrapped the stump in the skirt of his cassock, and pressing it to his hip went back into the room, and standing in front of the woman, lowered his eyes and asked in a low voice: "What do you want?"

She looked at his pale face and his quivering left cheek, and suddenly felt ashamed. She jumped up, seized her fur cloak, and throwing it round her shoulders, wrapped herself up in it.

"I was in pain ... I have caught cold ... I ... Father Sergius ... I ..."

He let his eyes, shining with a quiet light of joy, rest upon her, and said:

"Dear sister, why did you wish to ruin your immortal soul? Temptations must come into the world, but woe to him by whom temptation comes. Pray that God may forgive us!"

She listened and looked at him. Suddenly she heard the sound of something dripping. She looked down and saw that blood was flowing from his hand and down his cassock.

"What have you done to your hand?" She remembered the sound she had heard, and seizing the little lamp ran out into the porch. There on the floor she saw the bloody finger. She returned with her face paler than his and was about to speak to him, but he silently passed into the back cell and fastened the door.

"Forgive me!" she said. "How can I atone for my sin?"

"Go away."

"Let me tie up your hand."

"Go away from here."

She dressed hurriedly and silently, and when ready sat waiting in her furs. The sledge-bells were heard outside.

"Father Sergius, forgive me!"

"Go away. God will forgive."

"Father Sergius! I will change my life. Do not forsake me!"

"Go away."

"Forgive me—and give me your blessing!"

"In the name of the Father and of the Son and of the Holy Ghost!"—she heard his voice from behind the partition. "Go!"

She burst into sobs and left the cell. The lawyer came forward to meet her.

"Well, I see I have lost the bet. It can't be helped. Where will you sit?"

"It is all the same to me."

She took a seat in the sledge, and did not utter a word all the way home.

A year later she entered a convent as a novice, and lived a strict life under the direction of the hermit Arseny, who wrote letters to her at long intervals.

IV

Father Sergius lived as a recluse for another seven years.

At first he accepted much of what people brought him—tea, sugar, white bread, milk, clothing, and fire-wood. But as time went on he led a more and more austere life, refusing everything superfluous, and finally he accepted nothing but rye bread once a week. Everything else that was brought to him he gave to the poor who came to him. He spent his entire time in his cell, in prayer or in conversation with callers, who became more and more numerous as time went on. Only three times a year did he go out to church, and when necessary he went out to fetch water and wood.

The episode with Makovkina had occurred after five years of his hermit life. That occurrence soon became generally known—her nocturnal visit, the change she underwent, and her entry into a convent. From that time Father Sergius's fame increased. More and more visitors came to see him, other monks settled down near his cell, and a church was erected there and also a hostelry. His fame, as usual exaggerating his feats, spread ever more and more widely. People began to come to him from a distance, and began bringing invalids to him whom they declared he cured.

His first cure occurred in the eighth year of his life as a hermit. It was the healing of a fourteen-year-old boy, whose mother brought him to Father Sergius insisting that he should lay his hand on the child's head. It had never occurred to Father Sergius that he could cure the sick. He would have regarded such a thought as a great sin of pride; but the mother who brought the boy implored him insistently, falling at his feet and saying: "Why do you, who heal others, refuse to help my son?" She besought him in Christ's name. When Father Sergius assured her that only God could heal the sick, she replied that she only wanted him to lay his hands on the boy and pray for him. Father Sergius refused and returned to his cell. But next day (it was in autumn and the nights were already cold) on going out for water he saw the same mother with her son, a pale boy of fourteen, and was met by the same petition.

He remembered the parable of the unjust judge, and though he had previously felt sure that he ought to refuse, he now began to hesitate and, having hesitated, took to prayer and prayed until a decision formed itself in his soul. This decision was, that he ought to accede to the woman's request and that her faith might save her son. As for himself, he would in this case be but an insignificant instrument chosen by God.

And going out to the mother he did what she asked—laid his hand on the boy's head and prayed.

The mother left with her son, and a month later the boy recovered, and the fame of the holy healing power of the starets Sergius (as they now called him) spread throughout the whole district. After that, not a week passed without sick people coming, riding or on foot, to Father Sergius; and having acceded to one petition he could not refuse others, and he laid his hands on many and prayed. Many recovered, and his fame spread more and more.

So seven years passed in the Monastery and thirteen in his hermit's cell. He now had the appearance of an old man: his beard was long and grey, but his hair, though thin, was still black and curly.

V

For some weeks Father Sergius had been living with one persistent thought: whether he was right in accepting the position in which he had not so much placed himself as been placed by the Archimandrite and the Abbot. That position had begun after the recovery of the fourteen-year-old boy. From that time, with each month, week, and day that passed, Sergius felt his own inner life wasting away and being replaced by external life. It was as if he had been turned inside out.

Sergius saw that he was a means of attracting visitors and contributions to the monastery, and that therefore the authorities arranged matters in such a way as to make as much use of him as possible. For instance, they rendered it impossible for him to do any manual work. He was supplied with everything he could want, and they only demanded of him that he should not refuse his blessing to those who came to seek it. For his convenience they appointed days when he would receive. They arranged a reception-room for men, and a place was railed in so that he should not be pushed over by the crowds of women visitors, and so that he could conveniently bless those who came.

They told him that people needed him, and that fulfilling Christ's law of love he could not refuse their demand to see him, and that to avoid them would be cruel. He could not but agree with this, but the more he gave himself up to such a life the more he felt that what was internal became external, and that the fount of living water within him dried up, and that what he did now was done more and more for men and less and less for God.

Whether he admonished people, or simply blessed them, or prayed for the sick, or advised people about their lives, or listened to expressions of gratitude from those he had helped by precepts, or alms, or healing (as they assured him)—he could not help being pleased at it, and could not be indifferent to the results of his activity and to the influence he exerted. He thought himself a shining light, and the more he felt this the more was he conscious of a weakening, a dying down of the divine light of truth that shone within him.

"In how far is what I do for God and in how far is it for men?" That was the question that insistently tormented him and to which he was not so much unable to give himself an answer as unable to face the answer.

In the depth of his soul he felt that the devil had substituted an activity for men in place of his former activity for God. He felt this because, just as it had formerly been hard for him to be torn from his solitude, so now that solitude itself was hard for him. He was oppressed and wearied by visitors, but at the bottom of his heart he was glad of their presence and glad of the praise they heaped upon him.

There was a time when he decided to go away and hide. He even planned all that was necessary for that purpose. He prepared for himself a peasant's shirt, trousers, coat, and cap. He explained that he wanted these to give to those who asked. And he kept these clothes in his cell, planning how he would put them on, cut his hair short, and go away. First he would go some three hundred versts by train, then he would leave the train and walk from village to village. He asked an old man who had been a soldier how he tramped: what people gave him, and what shelter they allowed him. The soldier told him where people were most charitable, and where they would take a wanderer in for the night, and Father Sergius intended to avail himself of this information. He even put on those clothes one night in his desire to go, but he could not decide what was best—to remain or to escape. At first he was in doubt, but afterwards this indecision passed. He submitted to custom and yielded to the devil, and only the peasant garb reminded him of the thought and feeling he had had.

Every day more and more people flocked to him and less and less time was left him for prayer and for renewing his spiritual strength. Sometimes in lucid moments he thought he was like a place where there had once been a spring. "There used to be a feeble spring of living water which flowed quietly from me and through me. That was true life, the time when she tempted me!" (He always thought with ecstasy of that night and of her who was now Mother Agnes.) She had tasted of that pure water, but since then there had not been time for it to collect before thirsty people came crowding in and pushing one another aside. And they had trampled everything down and nothing was left but mud.

So he thought in rare moments of lucidity, but his usual state of mind was one of weariness and a tender pity for himself because of that weariness.

It was in spring, on the eve of the mid-Pentecostal feast. Father Sergius was officiating at the Vigil Service in his hermitage church, where the congregation was as large as the little church could hold—about twenty people. They were all well-to-do proprietors or merchants. Father Sergius admitted anyone, but a selection was made by the monk in attendance and by an assistant who was sent to the hermitage every day from the monastery. A crowd of some eighty people—pilgrims and peasants, and especially peasant-women—stood outside waiting for Father Sergius to come out and bless them. Meanwhile he conducted the service, but at the point at which he went out to the tomb of his predecessor, he staggered and would have fallen had he not been caught by a merchant standing behind him and by the monk acting as deacon.

"What is the matter, Father Sergius? Dear man! O Lord!" exclaimed the women. "He is as white as a sheet!"

But Father Sergius recovered immediately, and though very pale, he waved the merchant and the deacon aside and continued to chant the service.

Father Seraphim, the deacon, the acolytes, and Sofya Ivanovna, a lady who always lived near the hermitage and tended Father Sergius, begged him to bring the service to an end.

"No, there's nothing the matter," said Father Sergius, slightly smiling from beneath his moustache and continuing the service. "Yes, that is the way the Saints behave!" thought he.

"A holy man—an angel of God!" he heard just then the voice of Sofya Ivanovna behind him, and also of the merchant who had supported him. He did not heed their entreaties, but went on with the service. Again crowding together they all made their way by the narrow passages back into the little church, and there, though abbreviating it slightly, Father Sergius completed vespers.

Immediately after the service, Father Sergius, having pronounced the benediction on those present, went over to the bench under the elm tree at the entrance to the cave. He wished to rest and breathe the fresh air—he felt in need of it. But as soon as he left the church the crowd of people rushed to him soliciting his blessing, his advice, and his help. There were pilgrims who constantly tramped from one holy place to another and from one starets to another, and were always entranced by every shrine and every starets. Father Sergius knew this common, cold, conventional, and most irreligious type. There were pilgrims, for the most part discharged soldiers, unaccustomed to a settled life, poverty-stricken, and many of them drunken old men, who tramped from monastery to monastery merely to be fed. And there were rough peasants and peasant-women who had come with their selfish requirements, seeking cures or to have doubts about quite practical affairs solved for them: about marrying off a daughter, or hiring a shop, or buying a bit of land, or how to atone for having overlaid a child or having an illegitimate one.

All this was an old story and not in the least interesting to him. He knew he would hear nothing new from these folk, that they would arouse no religious emotion in him; but he liked to see the crowd to which his blessing and advice was necessary and precious, so while that crowd oppressed him it also pleased him. Father Seraphim began to drive them away, saying that Father Sergius was tired.

But Father Sergius, remembering the words of the Gospel: "Forbid them" (children) "not to come unto me," and feeling tenderly towards himself at this recollection, said they should be allowed to approach.

He rose, went to the railing beyond which the crowd had gathered, and began blessing them and answering their questions, but in a voice so weak that he was touched with pity for himself. Yet despite his wish to receive them all he could not do it. Things again grew dark before his eyes, and he staggered and grasped the railings. He felt a rush of blood to his head and first went pale and then suddenly flushed.

"I must leave the rest till tomorrow. I cannot do more today," and, pronouncing a general benediction, he returned to the bench. The merchant again supported him, and leading him by the arm helped him to be seated.

"Father!" came voices from the crowd. "Dear Father! Do not forsake us. Without you we are lost!"

The merchant, having seated Father Sergius on the bench under the elm, took on himself police duties and drove the people off very resolutely. It is true that he spoke in a low voice so that Father Sergius might not hear him, but his words were incisive and angry.

"Be off, be off! He has blessed you, and what more do you want? Get along with you, or I'll wring your necks! Move on there! Get along, you old woman with your dirty leg-bands! Go, go! Where are you shoving to? You've been told that it is finished. Tomorrow will be as God wills, but for today he has finished!"

"Father! Only let my eyes have a glimpse of his dear face!" said an old woman.

"I'll glimpse you! Where are you shoving to?"

Father Sergius noticed that the merchant seemed to be acting roughly, and in a feeble voice told the attendant that the people should not be driven away. He knew that they would be driven away all the same, and he much desired to be left alone and to rest, but he sent the attendant with that message to produce an impression.

"All right, all right! I am not driving them away. I am only remonstrating with them," replied the merchant. "You know they wouldn't hesitate to drive a man to death. They have no pity, they only consider themselves. ... You've been told you cannot see him. Go away! Tomorrow!" And he got rid of them all.

He took all these pains because he liked order and liked to domineer and drive the people away, but chiefly because he wanted to have Father Sergius to himself. He was a widower with an only daughter who was an invalid and unmarried, and whom he had brought fourteen hundred versts to Father Sergius to be healed. For two years past he had been taking her to different places to be cured: first to the university clinic in the chief town of the province, but that did no good; then to a peasant in the province of Samara, where she got a little better; then to a doctor in Moscow to whom he paid much money, but this did no good at all. Now he had been told that Father Sergius wrought cures, and had brought her to him. So when all the people had been driven away he approached Father Sergius, and suddenly falling on his knees loudly exclaimed:

"Holy Father! Bless my afflicted offspring that she may be healed of her malady. I venture to prostrate myself at your holy feet."

And he placed one hand on the other, cup-wise. He said and did all this as if he were doing something clearly and firmly appointed by law and usage—as if one must and should ask for a daughter to be cured in just this way and no other. He did it with such conviction that it seemed even to Father Sergius that it should be said and done in just that way, but nevertheless he bade him rise and tell him what the trouble was. The merchant said that his daughter, a girl of twenty-two, had fallen ill two years ago, after her mother's sudden death. She had moaned (as he expressed it) and since then had not been herself. And now he had brought her fourteen hundred versts and she was waiting in the hostelry till Father Sergius should give orders to bring her. She did not go out during the day, being afraid of the light, and could only come after sunset.

"Is she very weak?" asked Father Sergius.

"No, she has no particular weakness. She is quite plump, and is only 'nerastenic' the doctors say. If you will only let me bring her this evening, Father Sergius, I'll fly like a spirit to fetch her. Holy Father! Revive a parent's heart, restore his line, save his afflicted daughter by your prayers!" And the merchant again threw himself on his knees and bending sideways, with his head resting on his clenched fists, remained stock still. Father Sergius again told him to get up, and thinking how heavy his activities were and how he went through with them patiently notwithstanding, he sighed heavily and after a few seconds of silence, said: "Well, bring her this evening. I will pray for her, but now I am tired. ...." and he closed his eyes. "I will send for you."

The merchant went away, stepping on tiptoe, which only made his boots creak the louder, and Father Sergius remained alone.

His whole life was filled by Church services and by people who came to see him, but today had been a particularly difficult one. In the morning an important official had arrived and had had a long conversation with him; after that a lady had come with her son. This son was a skeptical young professor whom the mother, an ardent believer and devoted to Father Sergius, had brought that he might talk to him. The conversation had been very trying. The young man, evidently not wishing to have a controversy with a monk, had agreed with him in everything as with someone who was mentally inferior. Father Sergius saw that the young man did not believe but yet was satisfied, tranquil, and at ease, and the memory of that conversation now disquieted him.

"Have something to eat, Father," said the attendant.

"All right, bring me something."

The attendant went to a hut that had been arranged some ten paces from the cave, and Father Sergius remained alone.

The time was long past when he had lived alone doing everything for himself and eating only rye bread, or rolls prepared for the Church. He had been advised long since that he had no right to neglect his health, and he was given wholesome, though Lenten, food. He ate sparingly, though much more than he had done, and often he ate with much pleasure, and not as formerly with aversion and a sense of guilt. So it was now. He had some gruel, drank a cup of tea, and ate half a white roll.

The attendant went away, and Father Sergius remained alone under the elm tree.

It was a wonderful May evening, when the birches, aspens, elms, wild cherries, and oaks had just burst into foliage.

The bush of wild cherries behind the elm tree was in full bloom and had not yet begun to shed its blossoms, and the nightingales—one quite near at hand and two or three others in the bushes down by the river—burst into full song after some preliminary twitters. From the river came the far-off songs of peasants returning, no doubt, from their work. The sun was setting behind the forest, its last rays glowing through the leaves. All that side was brilliant green, the other side with the elm tree was dark. The cockchafers flew clumsily about, falling to the ground when they collided with anything.

After supper Father Sergius began to repeat a silent prayer: "O Lord Jesus Christ, Son of God, have mercy upon us!" and then he read a psalm, and suddenly in the middle of the psalm a sparrow flew out from the bush, alighted on the ground, and hopped towards him chirping as it came, but then it took fright at something and flew away. He said a prayer which referred to his abandonment of the world, and hastened to finish it in order to send for the merchant with the sick daughter. She interested him in that she presented a distraction, and because both she and her father considered him a saint whose prayers were efficacious. Outwardly he disavowed that idea, but in the depths of his soul he considered it to be true.

He was often amazed that this had happened, that he, Stepan Kasatsky, had come to be such an extraordinary saint and even a worker of miracles, but of the fact that he was such there could not be the least doubt. He could not fail to believe in the miracles he himself witnessed, beginning with the sick boy and ending with the old woman who had recovered her sight when he had prayed for her.

Strange as it might be, it was so. Accordingly the merchant's daughter interested him as a new individual who had faith in him, and also as a fresh opportunity to confirm his healing powers and enhance his fame. "They bring people a thousand versts and write about it in the papers. The Emperor knows of it, and they know of it in Europe, in unbelieving Europe—thought he. And suddenly he felt ashamed of his vanity and again began to pray. "Lord, King of Heaven, Comforter, Soul of Truth! Come and enter into me and cleanse me from all sin and save and bless my soul. Cleanse me from the sin of worldly vanity that troubles me!" he repeated, and he remembered how often he had prayed about this and how vain till now his prayers had been in that respect.

His prayers worked miracles for others, but in his own case God had not granted him liberation from this petty passion.

He remembered his prayers at the commencement of his life at the hermitage, when he prayed for purity, humility, and love, and how it seemed to him then that God heard his prayers. He had retained his purity and had chopped off his finger. And he lifted the shriveled stump of that finger to his lips and kissed it. It seemed to him now that he had been humble then when he had always seemed loathsome to himself on account of his sinfulness; and when he remembered the tender feelings with which he had then met an old man who was bringing a drunken soldier to him to ask alms; and how he had received her, it seemed to him that he had then possessed love also. But now? And he asked himself whether he loved anyone, whether he loved Sofya Ivanovna, or Father Seraphim, whether he had any feeling of love for all who had come to him that day—for that learned young man with whom he had had that instructive discussion in which he was concerned only to show off his own intelligence and that he had not lagged behind the times in knowledge. He wanted and needed their love, but felt none towards them. He now had neither love nor humility nor purity.

He was pleased to know that the merchant's daughter was twenty-two, and he wondered whether she was good-looking. When he inquired whether she was weak, he really wanted to know if she had feminine charm.

"Can I have fallen so low?" he thought. "Lord, help me! Restore me, my Lord and God!" And he clasped his hands and began to pray.

The nightingales burst into song, a cockchafer knocked against him and crept up the back of his neck. He brushed it off. "But does He exist? What if I am knocking at a door fastened from outside? The bar is on the door for all to see. Nature—the nightingales and the cockchafers—is that bar. Perhaps the young man was right." And he began to pray aloud. He prayed for a long time till these thoughts vanished and he again felt calm and confident. He rang the bell and told the attendant to say that the merchant might bring his daughter to him now.

The merchant came, leading his daughter by the arm. He led her into the cell and immediately left her.

She was a very fair girl, plump and very short, with a pale, frightened, childish face and a much developed feminine figure. Father Sergius remained seated on the bench at the entrance and when she was passing and stopped beside him for his blessing he was aghast at himself for the way he looked at her figure. As she passed by him he was acutely conscious of her femininity, though he saw by her face that she was sensual and feeble-minded. He rose and went into the cell. She was sitting on a stool waiting for him, and when he entered she rose.

"I want to go back to Papa," she said.

"Don't be afraid," he replied. "What are you suffering from?"

"I am in pain all over," she said, and suddenly her face lit up with a smile.

"You will be well," said he. "Pray!"

"What is the use of praying? I have prayed and it does no good"—and she continued to smile. "I want you to pray for me and lay your hands on me. I saw you in a dream."

"How did you see me?"

"I saw you put your hands on my breast like that." She took his hand and pressed it to her breast. "Just here."

He yielded his right hand to her.

"What is your name?" he asked, trembling all over and feeling that he was overcome and that his desire had already passed beyond control.

"Marie. Why?"

She took his hand and kissed it, and then put her arm round his waist and pressed him to herself.

"What are you doing?" he said. "Marie, you are a devil!"

"Oh, perhaps. What does it matter?"

And embracing him she sat down with him on the bed.

At dawn he went out into the porch.

"Can this all have happened? Her father will come and she will tell him everything. She is a devil! What am I to do? Here is the axe with which I chopped off my finger." He snatched up the axe and moved back towards the cell.

The attendant came up.

"Do you want some wood chopped? Let me have the axe."

Sergius yielded up the axe and entered the cell. She was lying there asleep. He looked at her with horror, and passed on beyond the partition, where he took down the peasant clothes and put them on. Then he seized a pair of scissors, cut off his long hair, and went out along the path down the hill to the river, where he had not been for more than three years.

A road ran beside the river and he went along it and walked till noon. Then he went into a field of rye and lay down there. Towards evening he approached a village, but without entering it went towards the cliff that overhung the river. There he again lay down to rest.

It was early morning, half an hour before sunrise. All was damp and gloomy and a cold early wind was blowing from the west. "Yes, I must end it all. There is no God. But how am I to end it? Throw myself into the river? I can swim and should not drown. Hang myself? Yes, just throw this sash over a branch." This seemed so feasible and so easy that he felt horrified. As usual at moments of despair he felt the need of prayer. But there was no one to pray to. There was no God. He lay down resting on his arm, and suddenly such a longing for sleep overcame him that he could no longer support his head on his hand, but stretched out his arm, laid his head upon it, and fell asleep. But that sleep lasted only for a moment. He woke up immediately and began not to dream but to remember.

He saw himself as a child in his mother's home in the country. A carriage drives up, and out of it steps Uncle Nicholas Sergeevich, with his long, spade-shaped, black beard, and with him Pashenka, a thin little girl with large mild eyes and a timid pathetic face. And into their company of boys Pashenka is brought and they have to play with her, but it is dull. She is silly, and it ends by their making fun of her and forcing her to show how she can swim. She lies down on the floor and shows them, and they all laugh and make a fool of her. She sees this and blushes red in patches and becomes more pitiable than before, so pitiable that he feels ashamed and can never forget that crooked, kindly, submissive smile. And Sergius remembered having seen her since then. Long after, just before he became a monk, she had married a landowner who squandered all her fortune and was in the habit of beating her. She had had two children, a son and a daughter, but the son had died while still young. And Sergius remembered having seen her very wretched. Then again he had seen her in the monastery when she was a widow. She had been still the same, not exactly stupid, but insipid, insignificant, and pitiable. She had come with her daughter and her daughter's fiancé. They were already poor at that time and later on he had heard that she was living in a small provincial town and was very poor.

"Why am I thinking about her?" he asked himself, but he could not cease doing so. "Where is she? How is she getting on? Is she still as unhappy as she was then when she had to show us how to swim on the floor? But why should I think about her? What am I doing? I must put an end to myself."

And again he felt afraid, and again, to escape from that thought, he went on thinking about Pashenka.

So he lay for a long time, thinking now of his unavoidable end and now of Pashenka. She presented herself to him as a means of salvation. At last he fell asleep, and in his sleep he saw an angel who came to him and said: "Go to Pashenka and learn from her what you have to do, what your sin is, and wherein lies your salvation."

He awoke, and having decided that this was a vision sent by God, he felt glad, and resolved to do what had been told him in the vision. He knew the town where she lived. It was some three hundred versts (two hundred miles) away, and he set out to walk there.

VI

Pashenka had already long ceased to be Pashenka and had become old, withered, wrinkled Praskovya Mikhaylovna, mother-in-law of that failure, the drunken official Mavrikyev. She was living in the country town where he had had his last appointment, and there she was supporting the family: her daughter, her ailing neurasthenic son-in-law, and her five grandchildren. She did this by giving music lessons to tradesmen's daughters, giving four and sometimes five lessons a day of an hour each, and earning in this way some sixty rubles [six pounds] a month. So they lived for the present, in expectation of another appointment. She had sent letters to all her relations and acquaintances asking them to obtain a post for her son-in-law, and among the rest she had written to Sergius, but that letter had not reached him.

It was a Saturday, and Praskovya Mikhaylovna was herself mixing dough for currant bread such as the serf-cook on her father's estate used to make so well. She wished to give her grandchildren a treat on the Sunday.

Masha, her daughter, was nursing her youngest child, the eldest boy and girl were at school, and her son-in-law was asleep, not having slept during the night. Praskovya Mikhaylovna had remained awake too for a great part of the night, trying to soften her daughter's anger against her husband.

She saw that it was impossible for her son-in-law, a weak creature, to be other than he was, and realized that his wife's reproaches could do no good—so she used all her efforts to soften those reproaches and to avoid recrimination and anger. Unkindly relations between people caused her actual physical suffering. It was so clear to her that bitter feelings do not make anything better, but only make everything worse. She did not in fact think about this: she simply suffered at the sight of anger as she would from a bad smell, a harsh noise, or from blows on her body.

She had—with a feeling of self-satisfaction—just taught Lukerya how to mix the dough, when her six-year-old grandson Misha, wearing an apron and with darned stockings on his crooked little legs, ran into the kitchen with a frightened face.

"Grandma, a dreadful old man wants to see you."

Lukerya looked out at the door.

"There is a pilgrim of some kind, a man ..."

Praskovya Mikhaylovna rubbed her thin elbows against one another, wiped her hands on her apron and went upstairs to get a five-kopek piece [about a penny] out of her purse for him, but remembering that she had nothing less than a ten-kopek piece she decided to give him some bread instead. She returned to the cupboard, but suddenly blushed at the thought of having grudged the ten-kopek piece, and telling Lukerya to cut a slice of bread, went upstairs again to fetch it. "It serves you right," she said to herself. "You must now give twice over."

She gave both the bread and the money to the pilgrim, and when doing so— far from being proud of her generosity—she excused herself for giving so little. The man had such an imposing appearance.

Though he had tramped two hundred versts as a beggar, though he was tattered and had grown thin and weatherbeaten, though he had cropped his long hair and was wearing a peasant's cap and boots, and though he bowed very humbly, Sergius still had the impressive appearance that made him so attractive. But Praskovya Mikhaylovna did not recognize him. She could hardly do so, not having seen him for almost twenty years.

"Don't think ill of me, Father. Perhaps you want something to eat?"

He took the bread and the money, and Praskovya Mikhaylovna was surprised that he did not go, but stood looking at her.

"Pashenka, I have come to you! Take me in ..."

His beautiful black eyes, shining with the tears that started in them, were fixed on her with imploring insistence. And under his greyish moustache his lips quivered piteously.

Praskovya Mikhaylovna pressed her hands to her withered breast, opened her mouth, and stood petrified, staring at the pilgrim with dilated eyes.

"It can't be! Stepa! Sergey! Father Sergius!"

"Yes, it is I," said Sergius in a low voice. "Only not Sergius, or Father Sergius, but a great sinner, Stepan Kasatsky—a great and lost sinner. Take me in and help me!"

"It's impossible! How have you so humbled yourself? But come in."

She reached out her hand, but he did not take it and only followed her in.

But where was she to take him? The lodging was a small one. Formerly she had had a tiny room, almost a closet, for herself, but later she had given it up to her daughter, and Masha was now sitting there rocking the baby.

"Sit here for the present," she said to Sergius, pointing to a bench in the kitchen.

He sat down at once, and with an evidently accustomed movement slipped the straps of his wallet first off one shoulder and then off the other.

"My God, my God! How you have humbled yourself, Father! Such great fame, and now like this ..."

Sergius did not reply, but only smiled meekly, placing his wallet under the bench on which he sat.

"Masha, do you know who this is?"—And in a whisper Praskovya Mikhaylovna told her daughter who he was, and together they then carried the bed and the cradle out of the tiny room and cleared it for Sergius.

Praskovya Mikhaylovna led him into it.

"Here you can rest. Don't take offense ... but I must go out."

"Where to?"

"I have to go to a lesson. I am ashamed to tell you, but I teach music!"

"Music? But that is good. Only just one thing, Praskovya Mikhaylovna, I have come to you with a definite object. When can I have a talk with you?"

"I shall be very glad. Will this evening do?"

"Yes. But one thing more. Don't speak about me, or say who I am. I have revealed myself only to you. No one knows where I have gone to. It must be so."

"Oh, but I have told my daughter."

"Well, ask her not to mention it."

And Sergius took off his boots, lay down, and at once fell asleep after a sleepless night and a walk of nearly thirty miles.

When Praskovya Mikhaylovna returned, Sergius was sitting in the little room waiting for her. He did not come out for dinner, but had some soup and gruel which Lukerya brought him.

"How is it that you have come back earlier than you said?" asked Sergius. "Can I speak to you now?"

"How is it that I have the happiness to receive such a guest? I have missed one of my lessons. That can wait ... I had always been planning to go to see you. I wrote to you, and now this good fortune has come."

"Pashenka, please listen to what I am going to tell you as to a confession made to God at my last hour. Pashenka, I am not a holy man, I am not even as good as a simple ordinary man; I am a loathsome, vile, and proud sinner who has gone astray, and who, if not worse than everyone else, is at least worse than most very bad people."

Pashenka looked at him at first with staring eyes. But she believed what he said, and when she had quite grasped it she touched his hand, smiling pityingly, and said:

"Perhaps you exaggerate, Stiva?"

"No, Pashenka. I am an adulterer, a murderer, a blasphemer, and a deceiver."

"My God! How is that?" exclaimed Praskovya Mikhaylovna.

"But I must go on living. And I, who thought I knew everything, who taught others how to live—I know nothing and ask you to teach me."

"What are you saying, Stiva? You are laughing at me. Why do you always make fun of me?"

"Well, if you think I am jesting you must have it as you please. But tell me all the same how you live, and how you have lived your life."

"I? I have lived a very nasty, horrible life, and now God is punishing me as I deserve. I live so wretchedly, so wretchedly ..."

"How was it with your marriage? How did you live with your husband?"

"It was all bad. I married because I fell in love in the nastiest way. Papa did not approve. But I would not listen to anything and just got married. Then instead of helping my husband I tormented him by my jealousy, which I could not restrain."

"I heard that he drank ..."

"Yes, but I did not give him any peace. I always reproached him, though you know it is a disease! He could not refrain from it. I now remember how I tried to prevent his having it, and the frightful scenes we had!"

And she looked at Kasatsky with beautiful eyes, suffering from the remembrance.

Kasatsky remembered how he had been told that Pashenka's husband used to beat her, and now, looking at her thin withered neck with prominent veins behind her ears, and her scanty coil of hair, half grey, half auburn, he seemed to see just how it had occurred.

"Then I was left with two children and no means at all."

"But you had an estate!"

"Oh, we sold that while Vasya was still alive, and the money was all spent. We had to live, and like all our young ladies I did not know how to earn anything. I was particularly useless and helpless. So we spent all we had. I taught the children and improved my own education a little. And then Mitya fell ill when he was already in the fourth form, and God took him. Masha fell in love with Vanya, my son-in-law. And—well, he is well-meaning but unfortunate. He is ill."

"Mamma!"—her daughter's voice interrupted her—"Take Mitya! I can't be in two places at once."

Praskovya Mikhaylovna shuddered, but rose and went out of the room, stepping quickly in her patched shoes. She soon came back with a boy of two in her arms, who threw himself backwards and grabbed at her shawl with his little hands.

"Where was I? Oh yes, he had a good appointment here, and his chief was a kind man too. But Vanya could not go on, and had to give up his position."

"What is the matter with him?"

"Neurasthenia—it is a dreadful complaint. We consulted a doctor, who told us he ought to go away, but we had no means. ... I always hope it will pass of itself. He has no particular pain, but ..."

"Lukerya!" cried an angry and feeble voice. "She is always sent away when I want her. Mamma ..."

"I'm coming!" Praskovya Mikhaylovna again interrupted herself. "He has not had his dinner yet. He can't eat with us."

She went out and arranged something, and came back wiping her thin dark hands.

"So that is how I live. I always complain and am always dissatisfied, but thank God the grandchildren are all nice and healthy, and we can still live. But why talk about me?"

"But what do you live on?"

"Well, I earn a little. How I used to dislike music, but how useful it is to me now!" Her small hand lay on the chest of drawers beside which she was sitting, and she drummed an exercise with her thin fingers.

"How much do you get for a lesson?"

"Sometimes a ruble, sometimes fifty kopeks, or sometimes thirty. They are all so kind to me."

"And do your pupils get on well?" asked Kasatsky with a slight smile.

Praskovya Mikhaylovna did not at first believe that he was asking seriously, and looked inquiringly into his eyes.

"Some of them do. One of them is a splendid girl—the butcher's daughter—such a good, kind girl! If I were a clever woman I ought, of course, with the connections Papa had, to be able to get an appointment for my son-in-law. But as it is I have not been able to do anything, and have brought them all to this—as you see."

"Yes, yes," said Kasatsky, lowering his head. "And how is it, Pashenka—do you take part in Church life?"

"Oh, don't speak of it. I am so bad that way, and have neglected it so! I keep the fasts with the children and sometimes go to church, and then again sometimes I don't go for months. I only send the children."

"But why don't you go yourself?"

"To tell the truth," (she blushed) "I am ashamed, for my daughter's sake and the children's, to go there in tattered clothes, and I haven't anything else. Besides, I am just lazy."

"And do you pray at home?"

"I do. But what sort of prayer is it? Only mechanical. I know it should not be like that, but I lack real religious feeling. The only thing is that I know how bad I am ..."

"Yes, yes, that's right!" said Kasatsky, as if approvingly.

"I'm coming! I'm coming!" she replied to a call from her son-in-law, and tidying her scanty plait she left the room.

But this time it was long before she returned. When she came back, Kasatsky was sitting in the same position, his elbows resting on his knees and his head bowed. But his wallet was strapped on his back.

When she came in, carrying a small tin lamp without a shade, he raised his fine weary eyes and sighed very deeply.

"I did not tell them who you are," she began timidly. "I only said that you are a pilgrim, a nobleman, and that I used to know you. Come into the dining-room for tea."

"No ..."

"Well then, I'll bring some to you here."

"No, I don't want anything. God bless you, Pashenka! I am going now. If you pity me, don't tell anyone that you have seen me. For the love of God don't tell anyone. Thank you. I would bow to your feet but I know it would make you feel awkward. Thank you, and forgive me for Christ's sake!"

"Give me your blessing."

"God bless you! Forgive me for Christ's sake!"

He rose, but she would not let him go until she had given him bread and butter and rusks. He took it all and went away.

It was dark, and before he had passed the second house he was lost to sight. She only knew he was there because the dog at the priest's house was barking.

"So that is what my dream meant! Pashenka is what I ought to have been but failed to be. I lived for men on the pretext of living for God, while she lived for God imagining that she lives for men. Yes, one good deed—a cup of water given without thought of reward—is worth more than any benefit I imagined I was bestowing on people. But after all was there not some share of sincere desire to serve God?" he asked himself, and the answer was: "Yes, there was, but it was all soiled and overgrown by desire for human praise. Yes, there is no God for the man who lives, as I did, for human praise. I will now seek Him!"

And he walked from village to village as he had done on his way to Pashenka, meeting and parting from other pilgrims, men and women, and asking for bread and a night's rest in Christ's name. Occasionally some angry housewife scolded him, or a drunken peasant reviled him, but for the most part he was given food and drink and even something to take with him. His noble bearing disposed some people in his favor, while others on the contrary seemed pleased at the sight of a gentleman who had come to beggary.

But his gentleness prevailed with everyone.

Often, finding a copy of the Gospels in a hut he would read it aloud, and when they heard him the people were always touched and surprised, as at something new yet familiar.

When he succeeded in helping people, either by advice, or by his knowledge of reading and writing, or by settling some quarrel, he did not wait to see their gratitude but went away directly afterwards. And little by little God began to reveal Himself within him.

Once he was walking along with two old women and a soldier. They were stopped by a party consisting of a lady and gentleman in a gig and another lady and gentleman on horseback. The husband was on horseback with his daughter, while in the gig his wife was driving with a Frenchman, evidently a traveler.

The party stopped to let the Frenchman see the pilgrims who, in accord with a popular Russian superstition, tramped about from place to place instead of working.

They spoke French, thinking that the others would not understand them.

"Demandez-leur," said the Frenchman, "s'ils sont bien sur de ce que leur pelerinage est agreable a Dieu."

The question was asked, and one old woman replied:

"As God takes it. Our feet have reached the holy places, but our hearts may not have done so."

They asked the soldier. He said that he was alone in the world and had nowhere else to go.

They asked Kasatsky who he was.

"A servant of God."

"Qu'est-ce qu'il dit? Il ne répond pas."

"Il dit qu'il est un serviteur de Dieu. Cela doit être un fils de preetre. Il a de la race. Avez-vous de la petite monnaie?"

The Frenchman found some small change and gave twenty kopeks to each of the pilgrims.

"Mais dites-leur que ce n'est pas pour les cierges que je leur donne, mais pour qu'ils se regalent de the. Chay, chay pour vous, mon vieux!" he said with a smile. And he patted Kasatsky on the shoulder with his gloved hand.

"May Christ bless you," replied Kasatsky without replacing his cap and bowing his bald head.

He rejoiced particularly at this meeting, because he had disregarded the opinion of men and had done the simplest, easiest thing—humbly accepted twenty kopeks and given them to his comrade, a blind beggar. The less importance he attached to the opinion of men the more did he feel the presence of God within him.

For eight months Kasatsky tramped on in this manner, and in the ninth month he was arrested for not having a passport. This happened at a night-refuge in a provincial town where he had passed the night with some pilgrims. He was taken to the police-station, and when asked who he was and where was his passport, he replied that he had no passport and that he was a servant of God. He was classed as a tramp, sentenced, and sent to live in Siberia.

In Siberia he has settled down as the hired man of a well-to-do peasant, in which capacity he works in the kitchen-garden, teaches children, and attends to the sick.

Comments

"Father Sergius" falls in the strange zone between a short story and novella. You can call it a long story or a novelette. These days, editors frown upon this kind of length, but why worry about editors when you have so many other worries while telling a story? You needn't necessarily tame the materials, cut them, and curtail them. Sure, you might give your story a crew cut, make it sharp, etc., but there's pleasure in letting your hair grow, to let it express itself and you. Long hair can show waves and curls that short hair can't.

This story is highly instructive. It grows out of a strong and strongly principled character. We always know what he wants and what he desires. His motives are clear. He wants to be the best—first in social status, then in purity of marriage, then in purity of spiritual dedication.

Moreover, one thing leads to another in a clear logical and chronological succession. There are brief flashbacks, which are absolutely necessary to illuminate the current actions, and none are superfluous. There's hardly anything superfluous in the story. Of course, we might say that the first sentence is superfluous. Each story should be about a surprising event, that's a given, and was a given even in the time of Tolstoy, but there he is, stating the obvious story requirement straight away, taking a sweep. He doesn't merely show, but he tells with a tremendous and winning authority that sounds like wisdom—and, after all, it is wisdom.

How else to explain that, for example, one of the most intelligent men ever to have lived, philosopher and logician Ludwig Wittgenstein, became an avid follower of Tolstoy's (upon reading *The Gospel in Brief* and "Father Sergius" and for years, although of Jewish (half Jewish, half Catholic) background, was an enthusiastic Christian mystic. In the Austrian army during World War I, he was laughed at as a preacher of gospel, Tolstoy's gospel. That a strict man, who was evolving logical positivism and atomism, would find attractive Tolstoy's exposition is not surprising. The story seems to have a crystalline singularity of focus and purpose, and it is structured as an argument. One thing leads to another, but not at all accidentally, but necessarily, out of the character and his ambition to be the best, which is his undoing. And the story has an astonishing simplicity in terms of chronology and development, driven to its logical conclusion.

The story is structured as a biography, and in that sense, resembles a novel. If there were many digressions, and if each thing that is told were to be fully shown in scenes, and the lives and perspectives of the other characters given plenty of playtime, it would be a novel. But this way, it moves more cogently, without any flourishes, fitting Tolstoy's ideology at the time of modesty. In *The Gospel in Brief*, Tolstoy enunciates the idea "Only one thing is needed." And this is the kind of story, a prototype, in which only one thing is needed: a man with a strong motive.

The POV is interesting here as well. While the story focuses on Father Sergius and is told mostly from his POV, we have departures into other points of view, when it is the most effective way to portray other characters. And occasionally, Tolstoy takes up, literally, the omniscient POV, explaining exactly what is going on in Sergius's soul, and even preaching to the reader. While this kind of writing, preachy, is ridiculed and out of fashion, you might take the story as a fine example of a good preachy story. If you have an urgent thing to tell us, perhaps nothing should prevent you from telling it to us. It's risky (you might alienate the reader) but if you earn it by a clear and logical demonstration, the way Tolstoy does, in the story, nobody should object. I've been in workshops where preachy was taken as a judgment and dismissive label (akin to, let's say, Nazi or chauvinist, something obviously and unquestionably bad, after which the person so labeled completely loses credibility). Fashions change, and while a hundred years ago people looked for a message, an ideology, or wisdom in fiction, now we have reached the opposite end of the spectrum, where a message is an anathema. When I am asked what the message of my stories is—as I was, for example, about my story collection, on TV in Zagreb—I shudder. What, you want message? I don't have a message, I only have stories. It's almost a current literary axiom that fiction should not be concerned with message-giving. While I agree with the sensibility and share in it, that preaching in general is irksome, there are exceptions to the rule. And if it seems to be a rule, it's a target to attack.

I think the story should be quite inspiring to many writers—a life story is worth telling. It could be an obituary, a summary of a life.

The ending of the story has a bit of fairy-tale quality to it—Father Sergius moves to Siberia, where he still lives humbly and modestly. For Tolstoy at the time, that was the same as happily ever after, minding things eternal. The fact that there's an echo of a fairy tale to the story at the very end offers a possibility of various interpretations—and a note of skepticism, perhaps that a real spiritual life is well nigh impossible. But it's not up to me in the craft analysis to interpret the meanings in the story definitely, but to point out that in the sheer simplicity of the structure there's still a provocative multiplicity of possible interpretations.

Suggestion for a Writing Experiment

Conceive a character who converts to some kind of religion or politics, and becomes a zealot. Preferably, choose something you believe in and play it out in the fictional setting, in a character who is not you, but who struggles with the same issues. Become as preachy as you like, but make sure that you earn the sermon—show the struggles in scenes, display the moral dilemmas and choices, in the thoughts of your protagonist. In terms of POV, have full access to the character's mind, and give us his reasoning and experience.

MADEMOISELLE FIFI
by Guy de Maupassant

The Major Graf von Farlsberg, the Prussian commandant, was reading his newspaper, lying back in a great armchair, with his booted feet on the beautiful marble fireplace, where his spurs had made two holes, which grew deeper every day, during the three months that he had been in the chateau of Urville.

A cup of coffee was smoking on a small inlaid table, which was stained with liquors, burnt by cigars, notched by the penknife of the victorious officer, who occasionally would stop while sharpening a pencil, to jot down figures, or to make a drawing on it, just as it took his fancy.

When he had read his letters and the German newspapers, which his baggage-master had brought him, he got up, and after throwing three or four enormous pieces of green wood on to the fire—for these gentlemen were gradually cutting down the park in order to keep themselves warm—he went to the window. The rain was descending in torrents, a regular Normandy rain, which looked as if it were being poured out by some furious hand, a slanting rain, which was as thick as a curtain, and which formed a kind of wall with oblique stripes, and which deluged everything, a regular rain, such as one frequently experiences in the neighborhood of Rouen, which is the watering-pot of France.

For a long time the officer looked at the sodden turf, and at the swollen Andelle beyond it, which was overflowing its banks, and he was drumming a waltz from the Rhine on the window-panes, with his fingers, when a noise made him turn round; it was his second in command, Captain Baron von Kelweinstein.

The major was a giant, with broad shoulders, and a long, fair beard, which hung like a cloth on to his chest. His whole, solemn person suggested the idea of a military peacock, a peacock who was carrying his tail spread out on to his breast. He had cold, gentle, blue eyes, and the scar from a sword-cut, which he had received in the war with Austria; he was said to be an honorable man, as well as a brave officer.

The captain, a short, red-faced man, who was tightly girthed in at the waist, had his red hair cropped quite close to his head, and in certain lights almost looked as if he had been rubbed over with phosphorus. He had lost two front teeth one night, though he could not quite remember how. This defect made him speak so that he could not always be understood, and he had a bald patch on the top of his head, which made him look rather like a monk, with a fringe of curly, bright, golden hair round the circle of bare skin.

The commandant shook hands with him, and drank his cup of coffee (the sixth that morning) in one gulp, while he listened to his subordinate's report of what had occurred; and then they both went to the window, and declared that it was a very unpleasant outlook. The major, who was a quiet man, with a wife at home, could accommodate himself to everything; but the captain, who was rather fast, being in the habit of frequenting low resorts, and much given to women, was mad at having been shut up for three months in the compulsory chastity of that wretched hole.

There was a knock at the door, and when the commandant said, "Come in," one of their automatic soldiers appeared, and by his mere presence announced that breakfast was ready. In the dining-room, they met three other officers of lower rank: a lieutenant, Otto von Grossling, and two sub-lieutenants, Fritz Scheunebarg, and Count von Eyrick, a very short, fair-haired man, who was proud and brutal toward men, harsh toward prisoners, and very violent.

Since he had been in France, his comrades had called him nothing but "Mademoiselle Fifi." They had given him that nickname on account of his dandified style and small waist, which looked as if he wore stays, from his pale face, on which his budding mustache scarcely showed, and on account of the habit he had acquired of employing the French expression, *fi, fi donc*, which he pronounced with a slight whistle, when he wished to express his sovereign contempt for persons or things.

The dining-room of the chateau was a magnificent long room, whose fine old mirrors, now cracked by pistol bullets, and Flemish tapestry, now cut to ribbons and hanging in rags in places, from sword-cuts, told too well what Mademoiselle Fifi's occupation was during his spare time.

There were three family portraits on the walls; a steel-clad knight, a cardinal, and a judge, who were all smoking long porcelain pipes, which had been inserted into holes in the canvas, while a lady in a long, pointed waist proudly exhibited an enormous pair of mustaches, drawn with a piece of charcoal.

The officers ate their breakfast almost in silence in that mutilated room, which looked dull in the rain, and melancholy under its vanquished appearance, although its old, oak floor had become as solid as the stone floor of a public-house.

When they had finished eating, and were smoking and drinking, they began, as usual, to talk about the dull life they were leading. The bottles of brandy and of liquors passed from hand to hand, and all sat back in their chairs, taking repeated sips from their glasses, and scarcely removing the long, bent stems, which terminated in china bowls painted in a manner to delight a Hottentot, from their mouths.

As soon as their glasses were empty, they filled them again, with a gesture of resigned weariness, but Mademoiselle Fifi emptied his every minute, and a soldier immediately gave him another. They were enveloped in a cloud of strong tobacco smoke; they seemed to be sunk in a state of drowsy, stupid intoxication, in that dull state of drunkenness of men who have nothing to do, when suddenly, the baron sat up, and said: "By heavens! This cannot go on; we must think of something to do." And on hearing this, Lieutenant Otto and Sub-lieutenant Fritz, who pre-eminently possessed the grave, heavy German countenance, said: "What, Captain?"

He thought for a few moments, and then replied, "What? Well, we must get up some entertainment; if the commandant will allow us."

"What sort of an entertainment, captain?" the major asked, taking his pipe out of his mouth.

"I will arrange all that, commandant," the baron said. "I will send Le Devoir to Rouen, who will bring us some ladies. I know where they can be found. We will have supper here, as all the materials are at hand, and, at least, we shall have a jolly evening."

Graf von Farlsberg shrugged his shoulders with a smile: "You must surely be mad, my friend."

But all the other officers got up, surrounded their chief, and said: "Let the captain have his own way, commandant; it is terribly dull here."

And the major ended by yielding. "Very well," he replied, and the baron immediately sent for Le Devoir.

The latter was an old corporal who had never been seen to smile, but who carried out all the orders of his superiors to the letter, no matter what they might be. He stood there, with an impassive face, while he received the baron's instructions, and then went out; five minutes later a large wagon belonging to the military train, covered with a miller's tilt, galloped off as fast as four horses could take it, under the pouring rain, and the officers all seemed to awaken from their lethargy, their looks brightened, and they began to talk.

Although it was raining as hard as ever, the major declared that it was not so dull, and Lieutenant von Grossling said with conviction that the sky was clearing up, while Mademoiselle Fifi did not seem to be able to keep in his place. He got up, and sat down again, and his bright eyes seemed to be looking for something to destroy. Suddenly, looking at the lady with the mustaches, the young fellow pulled out his revolver, and said: "You shall not see it." And without leaving his seat he aimed, and with two successive bullets cut out both the eyes of the portrait.

"Let us make a mine!" he then exclaimed, and the conversation was suddenly interrupted, as if they had found some fresh and powerful subject of interest. The mine was his invention, his method of destruction, and his favorite amusement.

When he left the chateau, the lawful owner, Count Fernand d'Amoys d'Urville, had not had time to carry away or to hide anything, except the plate, which had been stowed away in a hole made in one of the walls, so that, as he was very rich and had good taste, the large drawing-room, which opened into the dining-room, had looked like the gallery in a museum, before his precipitate flight.

Expensive oil-paintings, water-colors, and drawings hung upon the walls, while on the tables, on the hanging shelves, and in elegant glass cupboards, there were a thousand knickknacks: small vases, statuettes, groups in Dresden china, grotesque Chinese figures, old ivory, and Venetian glass, which filled the large room with their precious and fantastical array.

Scarcely anything was left now; not that the things had been stolen, for the major would not have allowed that, but Mademoiselle Fifi would have a mine, and on that occasion all the officers thoroughly enjoyed themselves for five minutes. The little marquis went into the drawing-room to get what he wanted, and he brought back a small, delicate china teapot, which he filled with gunpowder, and carefully introduced a piece of German tinder into it, through the spout. Then he lighted it, and took this infernal machine into the next room; but he came back immediately and shut the door. The Germans all stood expectantly, their faces full of childish, smiling curiosity, and as soon as the explosion had shaken the chateau, they all rushed in at once.

Mademoiselle Fifi, who got in first, clapped his hands in delight at the sight of a terra-cotta Venus, whose head had been blown off, and each picked up pieces of porcelain, and wondered at the strange shape of the fragments, while the major was looking with a paternal eye at the large drawing-room which had been wrecked in such a Neronic fashion, and which was strewn with the fragments of works of art. He went out first, and said, with a smile: "He managed that very well!"

But there was such a cloud of smoke in the dining-room, mingled with the tobacco smoke, that they could not breathe, so the commandant opened the window, and all the officers, who had gone into the room for a glass of cognac, went up to it.

The moist air blew into the room, and brought a sort of spray with it, which powdered their beards. They looked at the tall trees which were dripping with the rain, at the broad valley which was covered with mist, and at the church spire in the distance, which rose up like a gray point in the beating rain.

The bells had not rung since their arrival. That was the only resistance which the invaders had met with in the neighborhood. The parish priest had not refused to take in and to feed the Prussian soldiers; he had several times even drunk a bottle of beer or claret with the hostile commandant, who often employed him as a benevolent intermediary; but it was no use to ask him for a single stroke of the bells; he would sooner have allowed himself to be shot. That was his way of protesting against the invasion, a peaceful and silent protest, the only one, he said, which was suitable to a priest, who was a man of mildness, and not of blood; and everyone, for twenty-five miles round, praised Abbé Chantavoine's firmness and heroism, in venturing to proclaim the public mourning by the obstinate silence of his church bells.

The whole village grew enthusiastic over his resistance, and was ready to back up their pastor and to risk anything, as they looked upon that silent protest as the safeguard of the national honor. It seemed to the peasants that thus they had deserved better of their country than Belfort and Strassburg, that they had set an equally valuable example, and that the name of their little village would become immortalized by that; but with that exception, they refused their Prussian conquerors nothing.

The commandant and his officers laughed among themselves at that inoffensive courage, and as the people in the whole country round showed themselves obliging and compliant toward them, they willingly tolerated their silent patriotism. Only little Count Wilhelm would have liked to have forced them to ring the bells. He was very angry at his superior's politic compliance with the priest's scruples, and every day he begged the commandant to allow him to sound "ding-dong, ding-dong," just once, only just once, just by way of a joke. And he asked it like a wheedling woman, in the tender voice of some mistress who wishes to obtain something, but the commandant would not yield, and to console herself, Mademoiselle Fifi made a mine in the chateau.

The five men stood there together for some minutes, inhaling the moist air, and at last, Lieutenant Fritz said, with a laugh: "The ladies will certainly not have fine weather for their drive." Then they separated, each to his own duties, while the captain had plenty to do in seeing about the dinner.

When they met again, as it was growing dark, they began to laugh at seeing each other as dandified and smart as on the day of a grand review. The commandant's hair did not look as gray as it did in the morning, and the captain had shaved—had only kept his mustache on, which made him look as if he had a streak of fire under his nose.

In spite of the rain, they left the window open, and one of them went to listen from time to time. At a quarter past six the baron said he heard a rumbling in the distance. They all rushed down, and soon the wagon drove up at a gallop with its four horses, splashed up to their backs, steaming and panting. Five women got out at the bottom of the steps, five handsome girls whom a comrade of the captain, to whom Le Dervoir had taken his card, had selected with care.

They had not required much pressing, as they were sure of being well treated, for they had got to know the Prussians in the three months during which they had had to do with them. So they resigned themselves to the men as they did to the state of affairs. "It is part of our business, so it must be done," they said as they drove along; no doubt to allay some slight, secret scruples of conscience.

They went into the dining-room immediately, which looked still more dismal in its dilapidated state, when it was lighted up; while the table covered with choice dishes, the beautiful china and glass, and the plate, which had been found in the hole in the wall where its owner had hidden it, gave to the place the look of a bandits' resort, where they were supping after committing a robbery. The captain was radiant; he took hold of the women as if he were familiar with them; appraising them, kissing them, valuing them for what they were worth as ladies of pleasure; and when the three young men wanted to appropriate one each, he opposed them authoritatively, reserving to himself the right to apportion them justly, according to their several ranks, so as not to wound the hierarchy. Therefore, so as to avoid all discussion, jarring, and suspicion of partiality, he placed them all in a line according to height, and addressing the tallest, he said in a voice of command:

"What is your name?"

"Pamela," she replied, raising her voice.

Then he said: "Number One, called Pamela, is adjudged to the commandant."

Then, having kissed Blondina, the second, as a sign of proprietorship, he proffered stout Amanda to Lieutenant Otto, Eva, "the Tomato," to Sub-lieutenant Fritz, and Rachel, the shortest of them all, a very young, dark girl, with eyes as black as ink, a Jewess, whose snub nose confirmed by exception the rule which allots hooked noses to all her race, to the youngest officer, frail Count Wilhelm von Eyrick.

They were all pretty and plump, without any distinctive features, and all were very much alike in look and person, from their daily dissipation, and the life common to houses of public accommodation.

The three younger men wished to carry off their women immediately, under the pretext of finding them brushes and soap; but the captain wisely opposed this, for he said they were quite fit to sit down to dinner, and that those who went up would wish for a change when they came down, and so would disturb the other couples, and his experience in such matters carried the day. There were only many kisses; expectant kisses.

Suddenly Rachel choked, and began to cough until the tears came into her eyes, while smoke came through her nostrils. Under pretense of kissing her, the count had blown a whiff of tobacco into her mouth. She did not fly into a rage, and did not say a word, but she looked at her possessor with latent hatred in her dark eyes.

They sat down to dinner. The commandant seemed delighted; he made Pamela sit on his right, and Blondina on his left, and said, as he unfolded his table napkin: "That was a delightful idea of yours, captain."

Lieutenants Otto and Fritz, who were as polite as if they had been with fashionable ladies, rather intimidated their neighbors, but Baron von Kelweinstein gave the reins to all his vicious propensities, beamed, made doubtful remarks, and seemed on fire with his crown of red hair. He paid them compliments in French from the other side of the Rhine, and sputtered out gallant remarks, only fit for a low pot-house, from between his two broken teeth.

They did not understand him, however, and their intelligence did not seem to be awakened until he uttered nasty words and broad expressions, which were mangled by his accent. Then all began to laugh at once, like mad women, and fell against each other, repeating the words, which the baron then began to say all wrong, in order that he might have the pleasure of hearing them say doubtful things. They gave him as much of that stuff as he wanted, for they were drunk after the first bottle of wine, and, becoming themselves once more, and opening the door to their usual habits, they kissed the mustaches on the right and left of them, pinched their arms, uttered furious cries, drank out of every glass, and sang French couplets, and bits of German songs, which they had picked up in their daily intercourse with the enemy.

Soon the men themselves, intoxicated by that which was displayed to their sight and touch, grew very amorous, shouted and broke the plates and dishes, while the soldiers behind them waited on them stolidly. The commandant was the only one who put any restraint upon himself.

Mademoiselle Fifi had taken Rachel on to his knees, and, getting excited, at one moment kissed the little black curls on her neck, inhaling the pleasant warmth of her body, and all the savor of her person, through the slight space there was between her dress and her skin, and at another pinched her furiously through the material, and made her scream, for he was seized with a species of ferocity, and tormented by his desire to hurt her. He often held her close to him, as if to make her part of himself, and put his lips in a long kiss on the Jewess's rosy mouth, until she lost her breath; and at last he bit her until a stream of blood ran down her chin and onto her bodice.

For the second time, she looked him full in the face, and as she bathed the wound, she said: "You will have to pay for that!"

But he merely laughed a hard laugh, and said: "I will pay."

At dessert, champagne was served, and the commandant rose, and in the same voice in which he would have drunk to the health of the Empress Augusta, he drank: "To our ladies!" Then a series of toasts began, toasts worthy of the lowest soldiers and of drunkards, mingled with filthy jokes, which were made still more brutal by their ignorance of the language. They got up, one after the other, trying to say something witty, forcing themselves to be funny, and the women, who were so drunk that they almost fell off their chairs, with vacant looks and clammy tongues, applauded madly each time.

The captain, who no doubt wished to impart an appearance of gallantry to the orgy, raised his glass again, and said: "To our victories over hearts!" Thereupon Lieutenant Otto, who was a species of bear from the Black Forest, jumped up, inflamed and saturated with drink, and seized by an access of alcoholic patriotism, cried: "To our victories over France!"

Drunk as they were, the women were silent, and Rachel turned round with a shudder, and said: "Look here, I know some Frenchmen, in whose presence you would not dare to say that." But the little count, still holding her on his knees, began to laugh, for the wine had made him very merry, and said: "Ha! ha! ha! I have never met any of them, myself. As soon as we show ourselves, they run away!"

The girl, who was in a terrible rage, shouted into his face: "You are lying, you dirty scoundrel!"

For a moment, he looked at her steadily, with his bright eyes upon her, as he had looked at the portrait before he destroyed it with revolver bullets, and then he began to laugh: "Ah! yes, talk about them, my dear! Should we be here now, if they were brave?" Then getting excited, he exclaimed: "We are the masters! France belongs to us!" She jumped off his knees with a bound, and threw herself into her chair, while he rose, held out his glass over the table, and repeated: "France and the French, the woods, the fields, and the houses of France belong to us!"

The others, who were quite drunk, and who were suddenly seized by military enthusiasm, the enthusiasm of brutes, seized their glasses, and shouting, "Long live Prussia!" emptied them in one gulp.

The girls did not protest, for they were reduced to silence, and were afraid. Even Rachel did not say a word, as she had no reply to make, and then the little count put his champagne glass, which had just been refilled, on to the head of the Jewess, and exclaimed: "All the women in France belong to us, also!"

At that she got up so quickly that the glass upset, spilling the amber colored wine on to her black hair as if to baptize her, and broke into a hundred fragments as it fell on to the floor. With trembling lips, she defied the looks of the officer, who was still laughing, and she stammered out, in a voice choked with rage: "That—that—that—is not true,—for you shall certainly not have any French women."

He sat down again, so as to laugh at his ease, and trying ineffectually to speak in the Parisian accent, he said: "That is good, very good! Then what did you come here for, my dear?"

She was thunderstruck, and made no reply for a moment, for in her agitation she did not understand him at first; but as soon as she grasped his meaning, she said to him indignantly and vehemently: "I! I! I am not a woman; I am only a strumpet, and that is all that Prussians want."

Almost before she had finished, he slapped her full in her face; but as he was raising his hand again as if he would strike her, she, almost mad with passion, took up a small dessert knife from the table, and stabbed him right in the neck, just above the breastbone. Something that he was going to say was cut short in his throat, and he sat there, with his mouth half open, and a terrible look in his eyes.

All the officers shouted in horror, and leaped up tumultuously; but throwing her chair between Lieutenant Otto's legs, who fell down at full length, she ran to the window, opened it before they could seize her, and jumped out into the night and pouring rain.

In two minutes, Mademoiselle Fifi was dead. Fritz and Otto drew their swords and wanted to kill the women, who threw themselves at their feet and clung to their knees. With some difficulty the major stopped the slaughter, and had the four terrified girls locked up in a room under the care of two soldiers. Then he organized the pursuit of the fugitive, as carefully as if he were about to engage in a skirmish, feeling quite sure that she would be caught.

Fifty men were severely warned to search the park thoroughly. Two hundred other soldiers were tasked to search the woods and all the houses in the valley.

The table, which had been cleared immediately, now served as a bed on which to lay Fifi out, and the four officers made for the window, rigid and sobered, with the stern faces of soldiers on duty, and tried to pierce through the darkness of the night, amid the steady torrent of rain. Suddenly, a shot was heard, and then another, a long way off; and for four hours they heard, from time to time, near or distant reports and rallying cries, strange words uttered as a call, in guttural voices.

In the morning they all returned. Two soldiers had been killed and three others wounded by their comrades in the ardor of that chase, and in the confusion of such a nocturnal pursuit, but they had not caught Rachel.

Then the inhabitants of the district were terrorized, the houses were turned topsy-turvy, the country was scoured and beaten up, over and over again, but the Jewess did not seem to have left a single trace of her passage behind her.

When the general was told of it, he gave orders to hush up the affair, so as not to set a bad example to the army, but he severely censured the commandant, who in turn punished his inferiors. The general had said: "One does not go to war in order to amuse oneself, and to caress prostitutes." And Graf von Farlsberg, in his exasperation, made up his mind to have his revenge on the district, but as he required a pretext for showing severity, he sent for the priest and ordered him to have the bell tolled at the funeral of Count von Eyrick.

Contrary to all expectation, the priest showed himself humble and most respectful, and when Mademoiselle Fifi's body left the Chateau d'Urville on its way to the cemetery, carried by soldiers, preceded, surrounded, and followed by soldiers, who marched with loaded rifles, for the first time the bell sounded its funereal knell in a lively manner, as if a friendly hand were caressing it. At night it sounded again, and the next day, and every day; it rang as much as anyone could desire. Sometimes even, it would start at night, and sound gently through the darkness, seized by strange joy, awakened, one could not tell why. All the peasants in the neighborhood declared that it was bewitched, and nobody, except the priest and the sacristan, would now go near the church tower, and they went because a poor girl was living there in grief and solitude, secretly nourished by those two men.

She remained there until the German troops departed, and then one evening the priest borrowed the baker's cart, and himself drove his prisoner to Rouen. When they got there, he embraced her, and she quickly went back on foot to the establishment from which she had come, where the proprietress, who thought that she was dead, was very glad to see her.

A short time afterward, a patriot who had no prejudices, who liked her because of her bold deed, and who afterward loved her for herself, married her, and made a lady of her.

Comments

Perhaps the most famous and most universally admired writer of short stories is Guy de Maupassant. When I visited his grave in Paris, it was surrounded by a large group of Polish tourists. He is not exactly neglected in the States but does deserve plenty of readings. His stories are nearly always full of surprises and twists, and they are entertaining. Overall, far more people have learned the craft of story writing from him than from Chekhov, and I must admit that I still don't understand the Chekhovian craze—so many writers who seem to have nothing in common with Chekhov claim to be influenced by him, and so many critics call writers who basically don't have much happening in their stories Chekhovian. I am sure Chekhov would be surprised and not altogether pleased. Anyway, in de Maupassant a lot happens, not only psychologically and subtly, but outwardly. This is a murder story. The Prussian army occupying France exhibits basic hubris. The giant officer who oversteps the limits and taunts a prostitute is killed by her in a flash. The underdog wins. In sports, it's frequently quite dramatic when the underdog manages to defeat the super-dog. To me, that is more surprising and rewarding than getting the expected, and I am a chronic underdog rooter. While Rachel's murdering the officer is a surprise, it doesn't come out of the blue. The officer taunts her and provokes her for a couple of pages. The POV alternates in focus between being third-person limited, quite focused on a character, and being quite wide and omniscient, historical in perspective.

Suggestion for a Writing Experiment

Write a scene in a war setting. Choose any war you like. Bring together the officers of your army and the local population and have them interact and see what happens. The drama in "Mademoiselle Fifi" proceeds from the clash of characters—we are told early on that Fifi has an abusive and somewhat sadistic temperament, and that Rachel is proud. The conflict is there in the making simply from the character differential. So no matter how historically inclusive your story is, how wide your canvas, once you get to the characters, get into their psychology, and create some personality clash or conflict. America seems to be covering quite a bit of ground in a variety of wars, and it shouldn't be too difficult to imagine a story with a culture clash with some native populations.

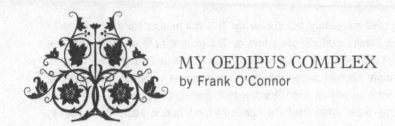

MY OEDIPUS COMPLEX
by Frank O'Connor

Father was in the army all through the war—the first war, I mean—so, up to the age of five, I never saw much of him, and what I saw did not worry me. Sometimes I woke and there was a big figure in khaki peering down at me in the candlelight. Sometimes in the early morning I heard the slamming of the front door and the clatter of nailed boots down the cobbles of the lane. These were Father's exits and entrances. Like Santa Claus he came and went mysteriously.

In fact, I rather liked his visits, though it was an uncomfortable squeeze between Mother and him when I got into the big bed in the early morning. He smoked, which gave him a pleasant musty smell, and shaved, an operation of astounding interest. Each time he left a trail of souvenirs—model tanks and Gurkha knives with handles made of bullet cases, and German helmets and cap badges and buttonsticks, and all sorts of military equipment—carefully stored away in a long box on top of the wardrobe, in case they ever came in handy. There was a bit of the magpie about Father; he expected everything to come in handy. When his back was turned, Mother let me get a chair and rummage through his treasures. She didn't seem to think so highly of them as he did.

The war was the most peaceful period of my life. The window of my attic faced southeast. My mother had curtained it, but that had small effect. I always woke with the first light and, with all the responsibilities of the previous day melted, feeling myself rather like the sun, ready to illuminate and rejoice. Life never seemed so simple and clear and full of possibilities as then. I put my feet out from under the clothes—I called them Mrs. Left and Mrs. Right—and invented dramatic situations for them in which they discussed the problems of the day. At least Mrs. Right did; she was very demonstrative, but I had not the same control of Mrs. Left, so she mostly contented herself with nodding agreement.

They discussed what Mother and I should do during the day, what Santa Claus should give a fellow for Christmas, and what steps should be taken to brighten the home. There was that little matter of the baby, for instance. Mother and I could never agree about that. Ours was the only house in the terrace without a new baby, and Mother said we couldn't afford one till Father came back from the war because they cost seventeen and six. That showed how simple she was. The Geneys up the road had a baby, and everyone knew they couldn't afford seventeen and six. It was probably a cheap baby, and Mother wanted something really good, but I felt she was too exclusive. The Geneys' baby would have done us fine.

Having settled my plans for the day, I got up, put a chair under the attic window, and lifted the frame high enough to stick out my head. The window overlooked the front gardens of the terrace behind ours, and beyond these it looked over a deep valley to the tall, red-brick houses terraced up the opposite hillside, which were all still in shadow, while those at our side of the valley were all lit up, though with long strange shadows that made them seem unfamiliar; rigid and painted.

After that I went into Mother's room and climbed into the big bed. She woke and I began to tell her of my schemes. By this time, though I never seem to have noticed it, I was petrified in my nightshirt, and I thawed as I talked until, the last frost melted, I fell asleep beside her and woke again only when I heard her below in the kitchen, making the breakfast.

After breakfast we went into town; heard Mass at St. Augustine's and said a prayer for Father, and did the shopping. If the afternoon is fine we either went for a walk in the country or a visit to Mother's great friend in the convent, Mother St. Dominic. Mother had them all praying for Father, and every night, going to bed, I asked God to send him back safe from the war to us. Little, indeed, did I know what I was praying for!

One morning, I got into the big bed, and there, sure enough, was Father in his usual Santa Claus manner, but later, instead of uniform, he put on his best blue suit, and Mother was as pleased as anything. I saw nothing to be pleased about, because, out of uniform, Father was altogether less interesting, but she only beamed, and explained that our prayers had been answered, and off we went to Mass to thank God for having brought Father safely home.

The irony of it! That very day when he came in to dinner he took off his boots and put on his slippers, donned the dirty old cap he wore about the house to save him from colds, crossed his legs, and began to talk gravely to Mother, who looked anxious. Naturally, I disliked her looking anxious, because it destroyed her good looks, so I interrupted him.

"Just a moment, Larry!" she said gently.

This was only what she said when we had boring visitors, so I attached no importance to it and went on talking.

"Do be quiet, Larry!" she said impatiently. "Don't you hear me talking to Daddy?"

This was the first time I had heard those ominous words, "talking to Daddy," and I couldn't help feeling that if this was how God answers prayers, he couldn't listen to them very attentively.

"Why are you talking to Daddy?" I asked with as great show of indifference as I could muster.

"Because Daddy and I have business to discuss. Now, don't interrupt again!"

In the afternoon, at Mother's request, Father took me for a walk. This time we went into town instead of out the country, and I thought at first, in my usual optimistic way, that it might be an improvement. It was nothing of the sort. Father and I had quite different notions of a walk in town. He had no proper interest in trams, ships, and horses, and the only thing that seemed to divert him was talking to fellows as old as himself. When I wanted to stop he simply went on, dragging me behind him by the hand; when he wanted to stop I had no alternative but to do the same. I noticed that it seemed to be a sign that he wanted to stop for a long time whenever he leaned against a wall. The second time I saw him do it I got wild. He seemed to be settling himself forever. I pulled him by the coat and trousers, but, unlike Mother who, if you were too persistent, got into a wax and said: "Larry if you don't behave yourself, I'll give you a good slap," Father had an extraordinary capacity for amiable inattention. I sized him up and wondered would I cry, but he seemed to be too remote to be annoyed even by that. Really, it was like going for a walk with a mountain! He either ignored the wrenching and pummeling entirely, or else glanced down with a grin of amusement from his peak. I had never met anyone so absorbed in himself as he seemed.

At teatime, "talking to Daddy" began again, complicated this time by the fact that he had an evening paper, and every few minutes he put it down and told Mother something new out of it. I felt this was foul play.

Man for man, I was prepared to compete with him any time for Mother's attention, but when he had it all made up for him by other people it left me no chance. Several times I tried to change the subject without success.

"You must be quiet while Daddy is reading, Larry," Mother said impatiently.

It was clear that she either genuinely liked talking to Father better than talking to me, or else he had some terrible hold on her which made her afraid to admit the truth.

"Mummy," I said that night when she was tucking me up, "do you think that if I prayed hard God would send Daddy back to war?"

She seemed to think about that for a moment.

"No, dear," she said with a smile. "I don't think he would."

"Why wouldn't he, Mummy?"

"Because there isn't a war any longer, dear."

"But, Mummy, couldn't God make another war, if He liked?"

"He wouldn't like to, dear. It's not God who makes wars, but bad people."

"Oh!" I said.

I was disappointed about that. I began to think that God wasn't quite what he was cracked up to be.

Next morning I woke at my usual hour, feeling like a bottle of champagne. I put out my feet and invented a long conversation in which Mrs. Right talked of the trouble she had with her own father till she put him in the Home. I didn't quite know what the Home was but it sounded the right place for Father. Then I got my chair and stuck my head out of the attic window. Dawn was just breaking, with a guilty air that made me feel I had caught it in the act. My head bursting with stories and schemes, I stumbled in next door, and in the half-darkness scrambled into the big bed. There was no room at Mother's side so I had to get between her and Father. For the time being I had forgotten about him, and for several minutes I sat bolt upright, racking my brains to know what I could do with him. He was taking up more than his fair share of the bed, and I couldn't get comfortable, so I gave him several kicks that made him grunt and stretch. He made room all right, though. Mother waked and felt for me.

I settled back comfortably in the warmth of the bed with my thumb in my mouth.

"Mummy!" I hummed, loudly and contentedly.

"Sssh! dear," she whispered. "Don't wake Daddy!"

This was a new development, which threatened to be more serious than "talking to Daddy." Life without my early-morning conferences was unthinkable.

"Why?" I asked severely.

"Because poor Daddy is tired."

This seemed to me a quite inadequate reason, and I was sickened by the sentimentality of her "poor Daddy." I never liked that sort of gush; it always struck me as insincere.

"Oh!" I said lightly. Then in my most winning tone: "Do you know where I want to go with you today, Mummy?"

"No, dear," she sighed.

"I want to go down the Glen and fish for thornybacks with my new net, and then I want to go out to the Fox and Hounds, and—"

"Don't-wake-Daddy!" she hissed angrily, clapping her hand across my mouth.

But it was too late. He was awake, or nearly so. He grunted and reached for the matches. Then he stared incredulously at his watch.

"Like a cup of tea, dear?" asked Mother in a meek, hushed voice I had never heard her use before. It sounded almost as though she were afraid.

"Tea?" he exclaimed indignantly. "Do you know what the time is?"

"And after that I want to go up the Rathcooney Road," I said loudly, afraid I'd forget something in all those interruptions.

"Go to sleep at once, Larry!" she said sharply.

I began to snivel. I couldn't concentrate, the way that pair went on, and smothering my early-morning schemes was like burying a family from the cradle.

Father said nothing, but lit his pipe and sucked it, looking out into the shadows without minding Mother or me. I knew he was mad. Every time I made a remark Mother hushed me irritably. I was mortified. I felt it wasn't fair; there was even something sinister in it. Every time I had pointed out to her the waste of making up two beds when we could both sleep in one, she had told me it was healthier like that, and now here was this man, this stranger, sleeping with her without the least regard for her health! He got up early and made tea, but though he brought Mother a cup he brought none for me.

"Mummy," I shouted, "I want a cup of tea, too."

"Yes, dear," she said patiently. "You can drink from Mummy's saucer."

That settled it. Either Father or I would have to leave the house. I didn't want to drink from Mother's saucer; I wanted to be treated as an equal in my own home, so, just to spite her, I drank it all and left none for her. She took that quietly, too.

But that night while she was putting me to bed she said gently:

"Larry, I want you to promise me something."

"What is it?" I asked.

"Not to come in and disturb poor Daddy in the morning. Promise?"

"Poor Daddy" again! I was becoming suspicious of everything involving that quite impossible man.

"Why?" I asked.

"Because poor Daddy is worried and tired and he doesn't sleep well."

"Why doesn't he, Mummy?"

"Well, you know, don't you, that while he was at the war Mummy got the pennies from the Post Office?"

"From Miss MacCarthy?"

"That's right. But now, you see, Miss MacCarthy hasn't anymore pennies, so Daddy must go out and find us some. You know what would happen if he couldn't?"

"No," I said, "tell us."

"Well, I think we might have to go out and beg for them like the poor old woman on Fridays. We wouldn't like that, would we?"

"No," I agreed. "We wouldn't."

"So you'll promise not to come in and wake him?"

"Promise."

Mind you, I meant that. I knew pennies were a serious matter, and I was all against having to go out and beg like the old woman on Fridays. Mother laid out all my toys in a complete ring round the bed so that, whatever way I got out, I was bound to fall over one of them.

When I woke I remembered my promise all right. I got up and sat on the floor and played—for hours, it seemed to me. Then I got my chair and looked out the attic window for more hours. I wished it was time for Father to wake; I wished someone would make me a cup of tea. I didn't feel in the least like the sun; instead, I was bored and so very, very cold! I simply longed for the warmth and depth of the big featherbed.

At last I could stand it no longer. I went into the next room. As there was still no room at Mother's side I climbed over her and she woke with a start.

"Larry," she whispered, gripping my arms very tightly, "what did you promise?"

"But I did, Mummy," I wailed, caught in the very act. "I was quiet for ever so long."

"Oh, dear, and you're perished!" she said sadly, feeling me all over. "Now if I let you stay will you promise not to talk?"

"But I want to talk, Mummy," I wailed.

"That has nothing to do with it," she said with a firmness that was new to me. "Daddy wants to sleep. Now, do you understand that?"

I understood it only too well. I wanted to talk, he wanted to sleep—whose house was it, anyway?

"Mummy," I said with equal firmness, "I think it would be healthier for Daddy to sleep in his own bed."

That seemed to stagger her, because she said nothing for a while.

"Now, once for all," she went on, "you're to be perfectly quiet or go back to your own bed. Which is it to be?"

The injustice of it got me down. I had convicted her out of her own mouth of inconsistency and unreasonableness, and she hadn't even attempted to reply. Full of spite, I gave Father a kick, which she didn't notice but which made him grunt and open his eyes in alarm.

"What time is it?" he asked in a panic-stricken voice, not looking at Mother but at the door, as if he saw someone there.

"It's early yet," she replied soothingly. "It's only the child. Go to sleep again. ... Now, Larry," she added, getting out of bed, "you've wakened Daddy and you must go back."

This time, for all her quiet air, I knew she meant it, and knew that my principal rights and privileges were as good as lost unless I asserted them at once. As she lifted me, I gave a screech, enough to wake the dead, not to mind Father. He groaned.

"That damn child! Doesn't he ever sleep?"

"It's only a habit, dear," she said quietly, though I could see she was vexed.

"Well, it's time he got out of it," shouted Father, beginning to heave in the bed. He suddenly gathered all the bedclothes about him, turned to the wall, and then looked back over his shoulder with nothing showing only two small, spiteful, dark eyes. The man looked very wicked.

To open the bedroom door, Mother had to let me down, and I broke free and dashed for the farthest corner, screeching. Father sat bolt upright in bed.

"Shut up, you little puppy!" he said in a choking voice.

I was so astonished that I stopped screeching. Never, never had anyone spoken to me in that tone before. I looked at him incredulously and saw his face convulsed with rage. It was only then that I fully realized how God had codded me, listening to my prayers for the safe return of this monster.

"Shut up, you!" I bawled, beside myself.

"What's that you said?" shouted Father, making a wild leap out of the bed.

"Mick, Mick!" cried Mother. "Don't you see the child isn't used to you?"

"I see he's better fed than taught," snarled Father, waving his arms wildly. "He wants his bottom smacked."

All his previous shouting was as nothing to these obscene words referring to my person. They really made my blood boil.

"Smack your own!" I screamed hysterically. "Smack your own! Shut up! Shut up!"

At this he lost his patience and let fly at me. He did it with the lack of conviction you'd expect of a man under Mother's horrified eyes, and it ended up as a mere tap, but the sheer indignity of being struck at all by a stranger, a total stranger who had cajoled his way back from the war into our big bed as a result of my innocent intercession, made me completely dotty. I shrieked and shrieked, and danced in my bare feet, and Father, looking awkward and hairy in nothing but a short gray army shirt, glared down at me like a mountain out for murder. I think it must have been then that I realized he was jealous too. And there stood Mother in her nightdress, looking as if her heart was broken between us. I hoped she felt as she looked. It seemed to me that she deserved it all.

From that morning out my life was a hell. Father and I were enemies, open and avowed. We conducted a series of skirmishes against one another, he trying to steal my time with Mother and I his. When she was sitting on my bed, telling me a story, he took to looking for some pair of old boots which he alleged he had left behind him at the beginning of the war. While he talked to Mother I played loudly with my toys to show my total lack of concern. He created a terrible scene one evening when he came in from work and found me at his box, playing with his regimental badges, Gurkha knives, and button-sticks. Mother got up and took the box from me.

"You mustn't play with Daddy's toys unless he lets you, Larry," she said severely. "Daddy doesn't play with yours."

For some reason Father looked at her as if she had struck him and then turned away with a scowl.

"Those are not toys," he growled, taking down the box again to see had I lifted anything. "Some of those curios are very rare and valuable."

But as time went on I saw more and more how he managed to alienate Mother and me. What made it worse was that I couldn't grasp his method or see what attraction he had for Mother. In every possible way he was less winning than I. He had a common accent and made noises at his tea. I thought for a while that it might be the newspapers she was interested in, so I made up bits of news of my own to read to her. Then I thought it might be the smoking, which I personally thought attractive, and took his pipes and went round the house dribbling into them till he caught me. I even made noises at my tea, but Mother only told me I was disgusting. It all seemed to hinge round that unhealthy habit of sleeping together, so I made a point of dropping into their bedroom and nosing around, talking to myself, so that they wouldn't know I was watching them, but they were never up to anything that I could see. In the end it beat me. It seemed to depend on being grown-up and giving people rings, and I realized I'd have to wait.

But at the same time I wanted him to see that I was only waiting, not giving up the fight. One evening when he was being particularly obnoxious, chattering away well above my head, I let him have it.

"Mummy," I said, "do you know what I'm going to do when I grow up?"

"No, dear," she replied. "What?"

"I'm going to marry you," I said quietly.

Father gave a great guffaw out of him, but he didn't take me in. I knew it must be only pretense. And Mother, in spite of everything, was pleased. I felt she was probably relieved to know that one day Father's hold on her would be broken.

"Won't that be nice?" she said with a smile.

"It'll be very nice," I said confidently. "Because we're going to have lots and lots of babies."

"That's right, dear," she said placidly. "I think we'll have one soon, and then you'll have plenty of company."

I was no end pleased about that because it showed that in spite of the way she gave in to Father she still considered my wishes. Besides, it would put the Geneys in their place.

It didn't turn out like that, though. To begin with, she was very preoccupied—I supposed about where she would get the seventeen and six—and though Father took to staying out late in the evenings it did me no particular good. She stopped taking me for walks, became as touchy as blazes, and smacked me for nothing at all. Sometimes I wished I'd never mentioned the confounded baby—I seemed to have a genius for bringing calamity on myself.

And calamity it was! Sonny arrived in the most appalling hullabaloo—even that much he couldn't do without a fuss—and from the first moment I disliked him. He was a difficult child—so far as I was concerned he was always difficult—and demanded far too much attention. Mother was simply silly about him, and couldn't see when he was only showing off. As company he was worse than useless. He slept all day, and I had to go round the house on tiptoe to avoid waking him. It wasn't any longer a question of not waking Father. The slogan now was "Don't-wake-Sonny!" I couldn't understand why the child wouldn't sleep at the proper time, so whenever Mother's back was turned I woke him. Sometimes to keep him awake I pinched him as well. Mother caught me at it one day and gave me a most unmerciful flaking.

One evening, when Father was coming in from work, I was playing trains in the front garden. I let on not to notice him; instead I pretended to be talking to myself, and said in a loud voice: "If another bloody baby comes into this house, I'm going out."

Father stopped dead and looked at me over his shoulder.

"What's that you said?" he asked sternly.

"I was only talking to myself," I replied, trying to conceal my panic. "It's private."

He turned and went in without a word. Mind you, I intended it as a solemn warning, but its effect was quite different. Father started being quite nice to me. I could understand that, of course. Mother was quite sickening about Sonny. Even at mealtimes she'd get up and gawk at him in the cradle with an idiotic smile, and tell Father to do the same. He was always polite about it, but he looked so puzzled you could see he didn't know what she was talking about. He complained of the way Sonny cried at night, but she only got cross and said that Sonny never cried except when there was something up with him—which was a flaming lie, because Sonny never had anything up with him, and only cried for attention. It was really painful to see how simple-minded she was. Father wasn't attractive, but he had a fine intelligence. He saw through Sonny, and now he knew that I saw through him as well.

One night I woke with a start. There was someone beside me in bed. For one wild moment I felt sure it must be Mother, having come to her senses and left Father for good, but then I heard Sonny in convulsions in the next room, and Mother saying: "There! There! There!" and I knew it wasn't she. It was Father. He was lying beside me, wide awake, breathing hard and apparently as mad as hell.

After a while it came to me what he was mad about. It was his turn now. After turning me out of the big bed, he had been turned out himself. Mother had no consideration now for anyone but that poisonous pup, Sonny. I couldn't help feeling sorry for Father. I had been through it all myself, and even at that age I was magnanimous. I began to stroke him down and say: "There! There!" He wasn't exactly responsive.

"Aren't you asleep either?" he snarled.

"Ah, come on and put your arm around us, can't you?" I said, and he did, in a sort of way. Gingerly, I suppose, is how you'd describe it. He was very bony but better than nothing.

At Christmas he went out of his way to buy me a really nice model railway.

Comments

This humorous short story, about fifteen pages in manuscript form, accomplishes quite a bit in small space. O'Connor manages to bring us into the mind of a young boy, and to display a family through his perspective, while at the same time, obviously writing from an adult perspective in a memoiristic fashion. The title indicates an adult perspective, too, but when we are in the scenes, especially in the dialogue, the kid sounds very childlike. O'Connor worked primarily from auditory impressions; he was excellent with voices, and here, as you read the story, you can easily hear the voice of the Irish boy narrator.

An ordinary home situation wouldn't generate a story, but creating a clear conflict between the father and the boy—competition for mother's love—makes the scenes relatively easy to organize for the author.

There's a lot of wit here. "The war was the most peaceful period of my life." Maybe that's too neat, the paradox obvious and loud, but I enjoyed reading the line. And in the context of the story, it does make perfect sense: the father's return brings upheaval to the household:

> "Mummy," I said that night when she was tucking me up, "do you
> think that if I prayed hard God would send Daddy back to war?"

Although the story is simple and charming, it is plotted classically. The conflict leads to skirmishes, a war of sorts, between the son and the father. The son gets both of his wishes—a new baby brother, and the father kicked out of the big bed—but the unpredictable (from the narrator's perspective) occurs: the baby now takes over, and two defeated guys, father and son, sleep together, comforting each other. The enemies become friends. The boy no longer hates his father.

At the same time, the story does playfully work out a psychological scenario, straight out of Freud, simplified but nevertheless insightful.

Suggestion for a Writing Experiment

Write a childhood story, in the shape of a memoir (whether it comes from your experience or an imaginary one). Can you contrast a child's perspective and the adults' world? The way children misunderstand what adults are doing can often be humorous and illuminate what actually is going on.

A COMPOSER AND HIS PARAKEETS
by Ha Jin

Before departing for Thailand with her film crew, Supriya left in Fanlin's care the parakeet she had inherited from a friend. Fanlin had never asked his girlfriend from whom exactly, but was sure that Bori, the bird, used to belong to a man. Supriya must have had a number of boyfriends prior to himself. A pretty Indian actress, she always got admiring stares. Whenever she was away from New York, Fanlin couldn't help but fear she might hit it off with another man.

He had hinted several times that he might propose to her, but she'd either dodge the subject or say her career would end before she was thirty-four, and she must seize the five years left to make more movies. In fact, she had never gotten a leading part, always taking a supporting role. If only she hadn't been able to get any part at all, then she might have accepted the role of a wife and prospective mother.

Fanlin wasn't very familiar with Bori, a small pinkish parakeet with a white tail, and he had never let the bird enter his music studio. Supriya used to leave Bori at Animal Haven when she was away; and if a trip lasted just two or three days, she'd simply lock him in the cage with enough food and water. But this time she'd stay abroad for three months, so she asked Fanlin to take care of the bird.

Unlike some other parrots, Bori couldn't talk; he was so quiet Fanlin often wondered if he were dumb. At night the bird slept near the window, in a cage held by a stand like a colossal floor lamp. During the day he sat on the windowsill or on top of the cage, basking in the sunlight, which seemed to have blanched his feathers.

Fanlin knew Bori liked millet; having no idea where a pet store was in Flushing, he went to Hong Kong Supermarket down the street and bought a bag. At times he'd give the parakeet what he himself ate: boiled rice, bread, apples, watermelon, grapes. He found Bori enjoyed this food. Whenever he placed his own meal on the dining table, the bird would hover beside him, waiting for a bite. With his Supriya away, Fanlin could eat more Chinese food—the only advantage of her absence.

"You want Cheerios too?" Fanlin asked Bori one morning as he was eating breakfast.

The bird gazed at him with a white-ringed eye. Fanlin picked a saucer, put a fingerful of the cereal in it, and placed it before Bori. He added, "Your mother has dumped you, and you're stuck with me." Bori pecked at the Cheerios, his eyelids flapping. Somehow Fanlin felt for the bird that day, so he found a tiny wine cup and poured a bit of milk for Bori too.

After breakfast, he let Bori into his studio for the first time. Fanlin composed on a synthesizer, having no room for a piano. The bird sat still on the edge of his desk, watching him, as if able to understand the musical notes he was inscribing. Then, as Fanlin tested a tune on the keyboard, Bori began fluttering his wings and swaying his head. "You like my work?" Fanlin asked Bori.

The bird didn't respond.

As Fanlin revised some notes, Bori alighted on the keys and stomped out a few feeble notes, which encouraged him to play more. "Get lost!" Fanlin said. "Don't be in my way."

The bird flew back to the desk, again motionlessly watching the man making little black squiggles on paper.

Around eleven o'clock, as Fanlin stretched up his arms and leaned back on his chair, he noticed two whitish spots beside Bori, one bigger than the other. "Damn you, don't poop on my desk!" he screamed.

At those words the parakeet darted out of the room. His escape calmed Fanlin a little. He told himself he ought to be patient with Bori, who must be like an incontinent baby. He got up and wiped off the mess with a paper towel.

***

Three times a week he gave music lessons to a group of five students. The tuition they paid was his regular income. They would come to his apartment on 37th Avenue in the evening and stay two hours. One of the students, Wona Kernan, an angular woman of twenty-two, became quite fond of Bori and often held out her index finger to him, saying, "Come here, come here." The parakeet never responded to her coaxing, instead sitting on Fanlin's lap as if also attending the class. Wona once scooped up the bird and put him on her head, but Bori returned to Fanlin immediately. She muttered, "Stupid budgie, only know how to suck up to your boss."

Fanlin was also collaborating with a local theater group on an opera based on the legendary folk musician Ah Bing. In his early years, Ah Bing, like his father, was a monk; then he lost his eyesight and was forced to leave his temple. He began to compose music, which he played on the streets to eke out a living.

Fanlin didn't like the libretto, which emphasized the chance nature of artistic creation. The hero of the opera, Ah Bing, was to claim, "Greatness in art is merely an accident." To Fanlin, that kind of logic did not explain the great symphonies of Beethoven or Tchaikovsky, which could not have existed without artistic theory, vision, or purpose. No art should be accidental.

Nevertheless, Fanlin worked hard on the music for *The Blind Musician*. According to the contract he had signed, he'd get a six-thousand-dollar advance, to be paid in two installments, and twelve percent of the opera's earnings. These days he was so occupied with the composition that he seldom cooked. He'd compose from 7 A.M. to 2 P.M., then go out for lunch, often taking Bori along. The bird perched on his shoulder, and Fanlin would feel Bori's claws scratching his skin as he walked.

One afternoon at the Taipan Café on Roosevelt Avenue, after paying at the counter for lunch, Fanlin returned to his seat to finish his tea. He put a dollar tip on the table, which Bori picked up and dropped back in Fanlin's hand.

"Wow, he knows money!" a bulging-eyed waitress cried. "Don't steal my money, little thief!"

That night on the phone, Fanlin told Supriya about Bori's feat. She replied, "I never thought you'd like him. He wouldn't get money for me, that's for sure."

"I'm just his caretaker," Fanlin said. "He's yours." He had expected she'd be more enthusiastic, but her voice sounded as usual, mezzo soprano and a little sleepy. He refrained from telling her that he missed her, often touching her clothes in the closet.

***

It was a rainy morning. Outside the drizzle swayed in the wind like endless tangled threads; traffic rumbled in the west. Lying in bed with a sheet crumpled over his belly, Fanlin was thinking of Supriya. She always dreamed of having children, and her parents in Calcutta had urged her to marry. Still, Fanlin felt he might be just her safety net—a fallback in case she couldn't find a more suitable man. He tried not to think too many negative thoughts and recalled those passionate nights that had thrilled and exhausted both of them. He missed her, a lot, but he knew that love was like another person's favor one might fall out of anytime.

Suddenly a high note broke from his studio—Bori on the synthesizer. "Stop it!" Fanlin shouted to the bird. But the note kept tinkling. He got out of bed and made for the studio.

Passing through the living room, its window somehow open and its floor scattered with sheets of paper fluttering in a draft, he heard another noise, then caught sight of a shadow slipping into the kitchen. He hurried in pursuit and saw a teenage boy crawling out the window. Fanlin, not fast enough to catch him, leaned over the sill and yelled at the burglar bolting down the fire escape, "If you come again, I'll have you arrested. Damn you!"

The boy jumped to the pavement below, his legs buckling, but he picked himself up. The seat of his jeans was dark-wet. In a flash he veered into the street and disappeared.

When Fanlin returned to the living room, Bori whizzed over and landed on his chest. The bird looked frightened, his wings quivering. With both hands Fanlin held the parakeet up and kissed him. "Thank you," he whispered. "Are you scared?"

***

Bori usually relieved himself in the cage, the door of which remained open day and night. Every two or three days Fanlin would change the newspaper on the bottom to keep the tiny aviary clean. In fact, the whole apartment had become an aviary of sorts, since Bori was allowed to go anywhere, including the studio. When he wasn't sleeping, the bird seldom stayed in the cage, inside which stretched a plastic perch. Even at night he avoided the perch, sleeping with his claws clutching the side of the cage, his body suspended in the air. Isn't it tiring to sleep like that? Fanlin thought. No wonder Bori often looks torpid in the daytime.

One afternoon as the parakeet nestled on his elbow, Fanlin noticed one of Bori's feet was thicker than the other. He turned the bird over. To his surprise, he saw a blister on Bori's left foot in the shape of half a soybean. He wondered if the plastic perch were too slippery for the parakeet to hold, and if the wire cage the bird gripped instead while sleeping had blistered his foot. Maybe he should get a new cage for Bori. He flipped through the yellow pages to locate a pet store.

That evening as he was strolling in Queens Botanical Garden, he ran into Elbert Chang, the director of the opera project for which Fanlin had been composing. Elbert had been jogging, and as he stopped to chat with Fanlin, Bori took off for an immense cypress tree, flitting in its straggly crown before landing on a branch.

"Come down," Fanlin called, but the bird wouldn't budge, just clasping the declining branch and looking at the men.

"That little parrot is so homely," observed Elbert. He blew his nose, brushed his sweatpants with his fingers, and jogged away, the flesh on his nape trembling a little. Beyond him a young couple walked a dachshund on a long leash.

Fanlin turned as if he were leaving, and Bori swooped down and alighted on his head. Fanlin settled the bird on his arm. "Afraid I'm going to leave you behind, eh?" he asked. "If you don't listen to me, I won't take you out again, understood?" He patted Bori's head.

The parakeet just blinked at him.

Fanlin realized that Bori must like the feel of the wooden perch. He looked around and found a branch under a tall oak and brought it home. He dismantled the plastic bar, whittled a new perch out of the branch, cut a groove on either end, and fixed it in the cage. From then on, Bori slept on the branch every night.

Proudly Fanlin told Supriya about the new perch, but she was too occupied to get excited. She sounded tired and merely said, "I'm glad I left him with you." She didn't even thank him. He had planned to ask her about the progress of the filming, but refrained.

***

The composition for the opera was going well. When Fanlin handed in the first half of the music score—132 pages altogether—Elbert Chang was elated, saying he had worried whether Fanlin had embarked on the project. Now Elbert could relax—everything was coming together. Several singers had signed up. It looked like they could stage the opera the next summer.

Puffing on a cigar in his office, Elbert gave a nervous grin and told Fanlin, "I'm afraid I cannot pay you the first half of the advance now."

"Why not? Our contract states that you must."

"I know, but we just don't have the cash on hand. I'll pay you early next month when we get the money."

Fanlin's face fell, his mothy eyebrows tilting upward. He was too deep in the project to back out, yet he feared he might have more difficulty getting paid in the future. He had never worked for Elbert Chang before.

"The bird looks uglier today," Elbert said, pointing his cigar at Bori, who was standing on the desk, between Fanlin's hands.

At those words, the parakeet whooshed up and landed on Elbert's shoulder. "Hey, hey, he likes me!" cried the man. He took Bori down, and the bird fled back to Fanlin in a panic.

Fanlin noticed a greenish splotch on Elbert's jacket, on the shoulder. He stifled the laughter rising in his throat.

"Don't worry about the payment," Elbert assured him, his fingers drumming the desktop. "You have a contract and can sue me if I don't pay you. This time is just an exception. The money is already committed by the donors. I promise this won't happen again."

Feeling better, Fanlin shook hands with the man and stepped out of the office.

Upon signing the contract for *The Blind Musician* three months earlier, the librettist, an exiled poet living on Staten Island, had insisted that the composer mustn't change a single word of the libretto. The writer, Benyong, didn't understand that unlike poetry, opera is a public form of art and depends on collaborative efforts. Elbert Chang liked the libretto so much he conceded to the terms the author demanded. This, however, posed a problem for Fanlin, who had in mind a music structure that didn't always agree with the verbal text. Furthermore, some words were unsingable, such as *smoothest* and *feudalism*. He had to replace them, ideally with words ending with open vowels.

One morning Fanlin set out for Staten Island to see Benyong intending to get permission to change some words. He didn't intend to take Bori along, but the second he stepped out of his apartment, he heard the bird bump against the door repeatedly, scratching the wood. He unlocked the door and said, "Want to come with me?" The parakeet leapt to his chest, clutching his T-shirt and uttering tinny chirps. Fanlin caressed Bori and together they headed for the train station.

It was a fine summer day, the sky washed clean by a shower the previous night. On the ferryboat Fanlin stayed on the deck all the way, watching seabirds wheel around. Some strutted or scurried on the bow, where two small girls were tossing bits of bread at them. Bori joined the other birds, picking up food but not eating any. Fanlin knew the parakeet was doing that just for fun, yet no matter how he called, the bird wouldn't come back to him. So he stood by, watching Bori walking excitedly among gulls, terns, petrels. He was amazed that Bori wasn't afraid of the bigger birds and wondered if the parakeet were lonely at home.

Benyong received Fanlin warmly, as if they were friends. In fact, they'd met only twice, both occasions for business. Fanlin liked this man, who, already forty-three, hadn't lost the child in him and often threw his head back and laughed aloud.

Sitting on a sofa in the living room, Fanlin sang some lines to demonstrate the cumbersomeness of the original words. He had an ordinary voice, a bit hoarse; yet whenever he sang his own compositions, he was confident and expressive with a vivid face and vigorous gestures, as if he were oblivious of anyone else's presence.

While he was singing, Bori frolicked on the coffee table, flapping his wings and wagging his head, his hooked bill opening and closing and emitting happy but unintelligible cries. Then the bird paused to tap his feet as if beating time, which delighted the poet.

"Can he talk?" Benyong asked Fanlin.

"No, he can't, but he's smart and even knows money."

"You should teach him how to talk. Come here, little fellow." Benyong beckoned to the bird, who ignored his outstretched hand.

Without difficulty Fanlin got the librettist's agreement, on the condition that they talk before Fanlin made any wording changes. For lunch they went to a small restaurant nearby and each had a pan-fried pizza. Dabbing his mouth with a red napkin, Benyong said, "I love this place and have lunch here five days a week. Sometimes I work on my poems in here. Cheers." He lifted his beer and clinked it with Fanlin's water.

Fanlin was amazed by what the poet said. Benyong didn't hold a regular job and could hardly have made any money from his writing; few people in his situation would dine out five times a week. In addition, he enjoyed movies and popular music; two tall shelves in his apartment were loaded with CDs, more with DVDs. Evidently the writer was well kept by his wife, a nurse. Fanlin was touched by the woman's generosity.

After lunch they strolled along the beach of white sand, carrying their shoes and walking barefoot. The air smelled fishy, tinged with the stink of seaweeds washed ashore. Bori liked the ocean and kept flying away, skipping along the brink of the surf, pecking at the sand.

"Ah, this sea breeze is so invigorating," Benyong said as he watched Bori. "Whenever I walk here, the view of the ocean makes me think a lot. Before this immense body of water, even life and death become unimportant, irrelevant."

"What's important to you, then?"

"Art, only art is immortal."

"That's why you've been writing full-time all along?"

"Yes, I want only to be a free artist."

Fanlin said no more, unable to suppress the image of Benyong's self-sacrificing wife. A photo in their study showed her to be quite pretty, with a wide but handsome face. The wind increased, and dark clouds were gathering on the sea in the distance.

***

As the ferryboat cast off, rain clouds were billowing over Brooklyn, soundless lightning zigzagging across the sky. On deck, a man, skinny and gray-bearded, was ranting about the evildoing of big corporations. Eyes shut, he cried, "Brothers and sisters, think about who gets all the money that's yours, think about who puts all the drugs on streets to kill our kids. I know them, I see them sinning against our Lord every day. What this country needs is a revolution, so we can put every crook behind bars or ship them all to Cuba—" Fanlin was fascinated by the way words were pouring out of the man's mouth, as if the fellow were possessed by a demon, his eyes radiating a steely light. Few other passengers paid him any mind.

While Fanlin focused his attention on the man, Bori left Fanlin's shoulder and fluttered away toward the waves. "Come back, come back," Fanlin called, but the bird went on flying alongside the boat.

Suddenly a gust of wind caught Bori and swept him into the tumbling water. "Bori! Bori!" Fanlin cried, rushing toward the stern, his eyes fastened on the bird bobbing in the tumult.

He kicked off his sandals, plunged into the water, and swam toward Bori, still calling his name. A wave crashed into Fanlin's face and filled his mouth with seawater. He coughed and lost sight of the bird. "Bori, Bori, where are you?" he called, looking around frantically. Then he saw the parakeet lying supine on the slope of a swell about thirty yards away. With all his might he plunged toward the bird.

Behind him, the boat slowed and a crowd gathered on the deck. A man shouted through a bullhorn, "Don't panic! We're coming to help you!"

At last Fanlin grabbed hold of Bori, who was already motionless, his bill ajar. Tears gushed out of Fanlin's salt-stung eyes as he held the parakeet and looked into his face, turning him upside down to drain water out of his crop. Meanwhile, the boat circled back, chugging toward Fanlin.

A ladder dropped from the boat. Holding Bori between his teeth, Fanlin hauled himself out of the water. When he reached the deck, the grey-bearded man stepped over and handed Fanlin his sandals without a word. People massed around as Fanlin laid the bird on the steel deck and gently pressed Bori's chest with two fingers to pump water from his lifeless body.

Thunder rumbled in the distance and lightning cracked the city's skyline, but patches of sunlight still fell on the ocean. As the boat picked up speed heading north, the bird's knotted feet opened, then clawed the air. "He's come to," a man exclaimed.

Sluggishly Bori opened his eyes. Cheerful cries broke out on the deck while Fanlin sobbed gratefully. A middle-aged woman took two photos of Fanlin and the parakeet, saying, "This is extraordinary."

***

Two days later, a short article appeared in the Metro section of the *New York Times*, reporting on the rescue of the bird. It described how Fanlin had plunged into the ocean without a second thought and patiently resuscitated Bori. The piece was brief, under two hundred words, but it created some buzz in the local community. Within a week a small Chinese-language newspaper, the *North American Tribune*, printed a long article on Fanlin and his parakeet, with a photo of them together.

Elbert Chang came one afternoon to deliver the half of the advance he'd promised. He had read about the rescue and said to Fanlin, "This little parrot is really something. He doesn't look smart but is full of tricks." He held out his hand to Bori, his fingers wiggling. "Come here," he coaxed. "You forgot crapping on me?"

Fanlin laughed. Bori still didn't stir, his eyes half shut as if he were sleepy.

Elbert then asked about the progress of the composition, to which Fanlin hadn't attended since the bird's accident. The director reassured him that the opera would be performed as planned. Fanlin promised to return to his work with redoubled effort.

***

Despite the attention Bori continued to wither. He didn't eat much or move around. During the day he sat on the windowsill, hiccupping frequently. Fanlin wondered if Bori had a cold or was simply getting old. He asked Supriya about his age. She had no idea but said, "He must already be senile."

"What do you mean? Like in his seventies or eighties?"

"I'm not sure."

"Can you ask his former owner?"

"How can I do that in Thailand?"

He didn't press her further, unhappy about her lack of interest in Bori. Maybe she really wasn't in contact with the bird's former owner, yet Fanlin suspected that was unlikely.

One morning Fanlin looked into Bori's cage, and to his horror, found the parakeet lying still. He picked Bori up, the lifeless body still warm. Fanlin couldn't hold back his tears while stroking the bird's feathers; he had failed to save his friend.

He laid the tiny corpse on the dining table and observed it for a long time. The parakeet looked peaceful and must have passed in sleep. Fanlin consoled himself with the thought that Bori hadn't suffered a miserable old age.

He buried the bird under a ginkgo in the backyard. The whole day he couldn't do anything and but sit absentmindedly in his studio. His students arrived that evening, but he didn't do much teaching. After they left, he phoned Supriya, who sounded harried. With a sob in his throat he told her, "Bori died early this morning."

"Gosh, you sound like you just lost a sibling."

"I feel terrible."

"I'm sorry, but don't be silly, and don't be too hard on yourself. If you really miss the budgie, you can buy another one at a pet shop."

"He was your bird."

"I know. I don't blame you. I can't talk anymore now, sweetie, I need to go."

Fanlin didn't sleep until the wee hours that night. He reviewed his conversation with Supriya, reproaching her as if she were responsible for Bori's death. What rankled him was her casual attitude. She must have put the bird out of her mind long ago. He wondered if he should volunteer to break up with her upon her return the following month, since it would be just a matter of time before they parted.

For days Fanlin cancelled his class and worked intensely on the opera. The music flowed from his pen with ease, the melodies so fluent and fresh that he paused to wonder whether he had unconsciously copied them from master composers. No, every note he had put down was original.

His negligence of teaching worried his students. One afternoon they came with a small cage containing a bright yellow parakeet. "We got this for you," Wona told Fanlin.

While certain no bird could replace Bori, Fanlin appreciated the gesture and allowed them to put the new parakeet in Bori's cage. He told them to return for class that evening.

The parakeet already had a name, Devin. Every day Fanlin left him alone, saying nothing to him, though the bird let out all kinds of words, including obscenities. At mealtimes Fanlin would put a bit of whatever he ate in Bori's saucer for Devin, yet he often kept the transom open in hopes that the bird would fly away.

***

The second half of the music for the opera was complete. When Elbert Chang read the score, he phoned Fanlin and asked to see him. Fanlin went to Elbert's office the next morning, unsure what the director wanted to discuss.

The moment Fanlin sat down, Elbert shook his head and smiled. "I'm puzzled, this half is so different from the first."

"You mean better or worse?"

"That I can't say, but the second half seems to have more feelings. Sing a couple passages. Let's see what it sounds like."

Fanlin sang one passage after another, with grief as if the music were gushing from the depths of his belly. He felt the blind musician, the hero of the opera, lamenting through him the loss of his beloved, a local beauty forced by her parents to marry a general, to be his concubine. Fanlin's voice trembled, which had never happened before in his demonstrations.

"Ah, it's so sad," said Elbert's assistant. "It makes me want to cry."

Somehow the woman's words cooled Fanlin. Then he sang a few passages from the first half of the score, which sounded elegant and lighthearted, especially the beautiful refrain that would recur five times in the opera.

Elbert said, "I'm pretty sure the second half is emotionally right. It has more soul—sorrow without anger, affectionate but not soft. I'm impressed."

"That's true," the woman chimed in.

"What should I do?" sighed Fanlin.

"Make the whole piece more consistent," Elbert suggested.

"That will take a few weeks."

"We have time."

Fanlin set about revising the score; in fact, he overhauled the first half. He worked so hard that after a week he collapsed and had to stay in bed. Even with his eyes closed, he could not suppress the music ringing in his head. The next day he resumed his writing. Despite the fatigue, he was happy, even rapturous in this composing frenzy. He ignored Devin entirely except to feed him. The parakeet came to his side from time to time, but Fanlin was too busy to pay him any mind.

One afternoon, after working for hours, he was lying in bed to rest. Devin landed beside him. The bird tossed his long blue-tipped tail, then jumped on Fanlin's chest, fixing a beady eye on him. "Ha wa ya?" the parakeet squawked. At first Fanlin didn't understand the sharp-edged words, pronounced as if Devin were short of breath. "Ha wa ya?" the bird repeated.

"Fine, I'm all right." Fanlin smiled, his eyes filling.

Devin flew away and alighted on the half open window. The white curtain swayed in the breeze, as if about to dance; outside sycamore leaves were rustling. "Come back," Fanlin called.

Comments

Here, the story of an artist, a composer, by itself might not be emotionally stirring, but combined with the story of a parakeet, it achieves emotional resonance. The parakeet is instrumental in achieving the dimension, the echoing, of the emotional life of the composer.

It's in general pretty tricky to write stories about artists (whether writers or painters or composers) because the story can become easily too effete and solipsistic, art commenting on itself, but nevertheless, if it appears to be a rule of sorts, it's there to be broken, and to serve as a challenge. So can you write a story about an artist? You might choose an art form you are particularly familiar with, perhaps even writing.

Picasso said (I am paraphrasing as I am working from my corrupt memory) that there are essentially only four themes for art: Love, Death, War, and Art. This story is about at least two, perhaps three, of these basic themes: art and death, and love.

Suggestion for a Writing Experiment

Import an animal into the arena of your fiction. You might find out that a pet is indeed your fiction's best friend. I have found it quite helpful to mirror drama in several of my stories in the lives of cats, dogs, and in one, a hawk. See whether you can create a parallel action and emotional mirror in a story by bringing in an animal, such as a horse, or even a mouse, whatever animal you respond to. Maybe you have a story that is almost done, but it lacks some passion and charm. How about putting in an animal—give your character this mirror of blood and fur, and see what happens. A parallel action might give dimension to whatever is happening, might be a catalyst for releasing or creating some passion.

REPLY ALL
by Robin Hemley

To: Poetry Association of the Western Suburbs listserv
From: Lisa Drago-Harse
Subject: Next Meeting
Date: July 17th

Hi all,

I wanted to confirm that our next meeting will be held in the Sir Francis Drake Room at the Bensonville Hampton Inn on August 3rd. Minutes from our last meeting and an agenda for the next meeting will follow shortly.

Peace and Poetry,
Lisa Drago-Harse
Secretary/PAWS

To: Poetry Association of the Western Suburbs listserv
From: Michael Stroud
Re: Re: Next Meeting
Date: July 17th

Dearest Lisa,

First of all, I LOVE your mole and don't find it unsightly in the least! There is absolutely no reason for you to be ashamed of it (though it might be a good idea to have it checked out). But please don't remove it! Heaven forbid, my darling! As I recall, I gave you considerable pleasure when I sucked and licked it like a nipple. A nipple it is in size and shape, if not placement. That no one else knows your mole's position on your body (other than your benighted husband, poor limp Richard, that Son[net] of a Bitch as you call him) is more the pity (if Marvell had known such a mole, he undoubtedly would have added an extra stanza to his poem). But my coy mistress is not SO terribly coy as all that, if I remember correctly (and how could I forget!). You were not at all what I had expected in bed—not that I had any expectations at all. When you started massaging my crotch with your foot underneath the table in the Sir Francis Drake Room, I was at first shocked. For a moment, I thought perhaps the unseen massager was none other than our esteemed president, the redoubtable Darcy McFee (makeup and wardrobe courtesy of Yoda). Is that terrible of me? I have nothing personal against her, really, except for her execrable taste in poetry, and the fact that you should be president, not she. And her breath. And that habit of pulling her nose when she speaks and that absolutely horrific expression of hers, Twee. As in, "I find his poetry just so twee." What does twee mean and why does she keep inflicting it upon us! So imagine my horror when I felt this foot in my crotch and I stared across the table at the two of you—she twitching like a slug that's had salt poured on it and you immobile except for your Mont Blanc pen taking down the minutes. Ah, to think that the taking down of minutes could be such an erotic activity, but in your capable hands, it is. To think that mere hours later, it would be my Mont Blanc you'd grasp so firmly, guiding me into the lyrical book of your body. But initially, I thought the worst, that it was Darcy, not you. My only consolation was the idea that at least I had her on a sexual harassment suit, her being my boss after all at Roosevelt. Another reason I thought it was her and not you was because I know you're married and she isn't and I knew that Richard is a member of our esteemed organization, too (and he was in the room, seated beside you no less!). It was only that sly smile in your eyes that tipped me off. I, too, love the danger that illicit public sex brings, as long as it's kept under the table, so to speak. And yes, maybe someday we can make love on that very same table in the Sir Francis Drake Room, my darling. But I must ask you, sweetheart, where did you learn that amazing trick. I have seen people wiggle their ears before, but never that! What amazing talent and such a pity that this is not something you bring out at parties or poetry readings to awe the dumb masses! Would Darcy find that too twee? I think not! Thinking of you now makes me so hot. I want to nibble you. I want to live in your panties. I want to write a series of odes to you equal in number to every lucky taste bud on my tongue, every nerve ending (no, not endings but beginnings!) on my body that lives in rapture of your every pore. No, not poor, but rich. I am rich. I make metaphors of your muscles, of your thighs, of the fecund wetness bursting with your being and effulgence. I must swallow now. I must breathe. I must take my leave, my darling, and go now to relieve myself of my private thoughts of you and you alone.

With undying love and erotic daydreams,
Mikey

P.S. Do you think you could get away for an evening next week? Could you be called away from Richard for an emergency meeting of the Public Relations Committee?

To: PAWS listserv
From: Darcy McFee
Re: Re: Re: Next Meeting
Date: July 17th

I am traveling now and will not be answering e-mails until I return on July 21st. Thanks!

Darcy

To: PAWS listserv
From: Sam Fulgram, Jr.
Re: Re: Re: Re: Next Meeting
Date: July 17th

Whoa boy! Do you realize you just sent out your love note to the entire Poetry Association of the Western Suburbs listserv?

Cheers,
Sam

P.S.—That mole? You've got my imagination running wild. As long as the entire organization knows about it now, would you mind divulging its location? I'd sleep better at night knowing it.

To: PAWS listserv
From: Betsy Midchester
Re: Re: Re: Re: Re: Next Meeting
Date: July 17th

Hi all,

Well! That last message from "Mikey" Stroud certainly made my day. I thought at first the message was addressed to me. As I had no memory of placing my foot in Mike's crotch, I naturally assumed that I needed an adjustment of my medication so that I wouldn't forget such episodes in the future. Now I see it's simply Michael ("Down Boy") Stroud and our esteemed Secretary of the Galloping Mont Blaaaaanc who need the medication adjustments. Thanks, in any case, for a much needed lift in an otherwise humdrum day.

Betsy Midchester
Treasurer/PAWS

To: PAWS listserv
From: Lisa Drago-Harse
Re: Re: Re: Re: Re: Re: Next Meeting
Date: July 17th

This is a nightmare. I'm not quite sure what to say except that life is unpredictable and often irreversible. While I do not wish to go into details or make excuses for the above e-mail from Michael Stroud, I would like to clarify one thing: that was not my foot in your crotch Michael. But your belief that it was my foot in your crotch explains a few things concerning your subsequent behavior towards me that were up until this moment a mystery.

LDH

To: PAWS listserv
From: Michael Stroud
Re: Re: Re: Re: Re: Re: Re: Next Meeting
Date: July 17th

I'm

To: PAWS listserv
From: Michael Stroud
Re: Re: Re: Re: Re: Re: Re: Next Meeting
Date: July 17th

I hit the send button by mistake before I was ready. This isn't my day, to say the least! I'm sorry!!!! I'd like to apologize to the entire PAWS community, and also to Lisa's husband Richard and to Darcy. And to you, Lisa. I don't mean to make excuses for myself, but I would like to say that I've been under a tremendous amount of pressure of late, at school, at home, and I am nothing if not vulnerable and flawed. All I can say is that in poetry I find some solace for the petty actions of others and the sometimes monstrous actions of which I'm all too capable. As déclassé as Truth and Beauty are these days, it is in such expressions as those of Matthew Arnold, Keats, Byron, and Shelley to whom I look for my meager draught of the Divine. And sometimes, I must admit, I seek in the affection of my fellow poetry lovers, the divinity which I myself lack. I ask you all to blame me, not Lisa, for what has happened.

But if not your foot, Lisa, then whose?

Michael Stroud

To PAWS listserv
From: Greg Rudolfsky
Re: Re: Re: Re: Re: Re: Re: Re: Re: RESPECT
Date: July 17th

Just a little bit, Just a little bit.

Sock it to me, sock it to me, sock it to me, sock it to me, sock it to me, sock it to me, sock it to me, sock it to me, RESPECT, Just a little bit, just a little bit ....

To PAWS listserv
From: Samantha M. Poulsen, RN
Subject: Fecund Poets
Date: July 17th

I do not care whose foot is in whose crotch, but I think it's insulting and idiotic that so-called educated people would use such phrases as, "the fecund wetness bursting with your being and effulgence." And officers of the PAWS at that!

To: PAWS listserv
From: Richard Harse
Re: Fecund Poets
Date: July 17th

I would like to tender my resignation in the Poets of the Western Suburbs, as I will be tendering my resignation in several other areas of my life. I only be-longed to PAWS in any case because of my wife's interest in poetry. I wanted to share her interests, but clearly not all of them.

To PAWS listserv
From: Darcy McFee
Re: Fecund Poets
Date: July 22nd

Well, it seems that our little organization has been busy in my absence. I have over 300 new messages in my e-mail account, all, it seems from my fellow po-etry lovers! I haven't yet had a chance to read your exchanges, but I will soon. In the meantime, I wanted to convey some exciting news. This weekend, while attending a workshop at Wright State in Dayton, I ran into the former Poet Laureate, Billy Collins, who has agreed to be our special guest at our annual Poetry Bash in Oak Park. He said he's heard quite a lot about our organization in recent days and that our board had achieved near legendary status in the poetry community. I knew this would make you as proud as it makes me.

To: PAWS listerv
From: Darcy McFee
Subject: Twee
Date: July 24th

So this is how it is. Upon reading the 300 e-mails that collected in my inbox over the weekend, my mind is a riot of emotions. I have not slept for nearly 48 hours. Never before have I been so insulted. Yet, I also know that I am, at least in part, to blame. Had I not stuck my foot in Michael Stroud's crotch, none of this would have happened. Twitching like a slug that's had salt poured on it? That hurts, Michael. It really does. I didn't realize you were so shallow. But in reading your collective e-mails, I see that at least half our membership has a decidedly sadistic bent. In any case, it was not your crotch, I aimed for, Michael, but the crotch of our Vice-President, Amir Bathshiri, with whom I have long been intimately acquainted, both of us having lost our spouses several years ago. If the seating arrangements in the Sir Francis Drake Room were any less cramped, none of these misunderstandings would have occurred. Of course, I never would have tried to fondle you, Michael. In the first place, you are the most boring, tedious person I have met in my life, and believe me, as Chair of the English Dept. at Roosevelt, I have met my share of boring, tedious people. You recite poetry with all the grace of a highway sign that cautions one to beware of falling rocks. In fact, I would rather make love to a falling rock. But enough! I know that it is my errant foot to blame. Amir and I have talked this over and have decided to withdraw from PAWS as well as from academia. Early retirement calls, Michael and Lisa, and I will give neither of you a thought as I walk along the beach hand in hand with Amir in the months and years to come, listening to the mermaids singing each to each.

Yes, Michael, I find you and your crotch and your paramour the very essence of Twee.

To: PAWS listserv
From: Betsy Midchester/Treasurer
Subject: New Elections
Date: July 30th

Please note that the agenda for our next meeting has changed. We will spend most of the meeting on new elections to be held for the positions of President,

Vice-President and Secretary of our organization. Note, too, that we will no longer be meeting in the Sir Francis Drake Room of the Bensonville Hampton Inn. Instead, we will be meeting in the cafeteria of Enchanted Gardens Residence for Seniors in Glen Ellyn. The change in venue was planned well in advance of recent events, so members should not read anything into this (though if any organization's members are skilled at reading between the lines, it should be ours). Please think about whom you would like to nominate for these important positions in our organization. And in the meantime, please remember to always be conscious and considerate of your audience.

Peace and Poetry,
Betsy Midchester
Treasurer and Acting President/PAWS

Comments

"Reply All" is a fine example of how new technology can give rise to new shapes of fiction. The story basically has the shape of a series of e-mails. A lot of drama these days takes place in the form of e-mails, and it's great to use the new form of our communication as a form of fiction. Hemley deftly uses bits of e-mail languages, such as *Re: Re: Re:*, so we are always aware that this whole communication takes place as an electronic correspondence, but he doesn't overdo it. It would be possible to do e-mails in different fonts and different colors as people these days do, but it's not necessary for the verisimilitude of the story.

Out of a common occurrence, hitting the Reply-All button, in virtual reality, of course a lot of confusion and embarrassment has happened in "real life" and Hemley uses that common experience and merges it with academic stuffiness and touchiness, and he has a comic story. The basic aspect of comedy, a misunderstanding, works quite well here.

Most of us have communicated quite a bit via e-mail, so why not shape a story in the form of e-mails? Perhaps some such stories wouldn't have to be in the form of e-mail correspondence, but this one hinges upon the technology, the Reply-All option, which one can mistakenly press.

Suggestion for a Writing Experiment

See whether you have an interesting e-mail story in your computer system, or whether you can make one up.

There have been stories written as a series of cell-phone text messages. That's an obvious challenge. Can you do one like that?

And of course, blogs. Some blogs are written in order to be stories and to be published, and the paradox is that they are being published as they are being written. There are so many blogs now that it is impossible to keep track of a mere fraction of them, but never mind. Perhaps you can be posting your blogs and thus evolve a story. However, once you are done with a spurt of blogging, perhaps it's best to go back to the blogs and cut out a lot, revise some, add some, and form a story, which could still look like a blog.

THE BLUE HOTEL
by Stephen Crane

I

The Palace Hotel at Fort Romper was painted a light blue, a shade that is on the legs of a kind of heron, causing the bird to declare its position against any background. The Palace Hotel, then, was always screaming and howling in a way that made the dazzling winter landscape of Nebraska seem only a gray swampish hush. It stood alone on the prairie, and when the snow was falling the town two hundred yards away was not visible. But when the traveler alighted at the railway station he was obliged to pass the Palace Hotel before he could come upon the company of low clap-board houses which composed Fort Romper, and it was not to be thought that any traveler could pass the Palace Hotel without looking at it. Pat Scully, the proprietor, had proved himself a master of strategy when he chose his paints. It is true that on clear days, when the great trans-continental expresses, long lines of swaying Pullmans, swept through Fort Romper, passengers were overcome at the sight, and the cult that knows the brown-reds and the subdivisions of the dark greens of the East expressed shame, pity, horror, in a laugh. But to the citizens of this prairie town, and to the people who would naturally stop there, Pat Scully had performed a feat. With this opulence and splendor, these creeds, classes, egotisms, that streamed through Romper on the rails day after day, they had no color in common.

As if the displayed delights of such a blue hotel were not sufficiently enticing, it was Scully's habit to go every morning and evening to meet the leisurely trains that stopped at Romper and work his seductions upon any man that he might see wavering, gripsack in hand.

One morning, when a snow-crusted engine dragged its long string of freight cars and its one passenger coach to the station, Scully performed the marvel of catching three men. One was a shaky and quick-eyed Swede, with a great shining cheap valise; one was a tall bronzed cowboy, who was on his way to a ranch near the Dakota line; one was a little silent man from the East, who didn't look it, and didn't announce it. Scully practically made them prisoners. He was so nimble and merry and kindly that each probably felt it would be the height of brutality to try to escape. They trudged off over the creaking board sidewalks in the wake of the eager little Irishman. He wore a heavy fur cap squeezed tightly down on his head. It caused his two red ears to stick out stiffly, as if they were made of tin.

At last Scully, elaborately, with boisterous hospitality, conducted them through the portals of the blue hotel. The room which they entered was small. It seemed to be merely a proper temple for an enormous stove, which, in the center, was humming with godlike violence. At various points on its surface the iron had become luminous and glowed yellow from the heat. Beside the stove Scully's son Johnnie was playing High-Five with an old farmer who had whiskers both gray and sandy. They were quarreling. Frequently the old farmer turned his face toward a box of sawdust—colored brown from tobacco juice—that was behind the stove, and spat with an air of great impatience and irritation. With a loud flourish of words Scully destroyed the game of cards, and bustled his son upstairs with part of the baggage of the new guests. He himself conducted them to three basins of the coldest water in the world. The cowboy and the Easterner burnished themselves fiery red with this water, until it seemed to be some kind of a metal polish. The Swede, however, merely dipped his fingers gingerly and with trepidation. It was notable that throughout this series of small ceremonies the three travelers were made to feel that Scully was very benevolent. He was conferring great favors upon them. He handed the towel from one to the other with an air of philanthropic impulse.

Afterward they went to the first room, and, sitting about the stove, listened to Scully's officious clamor at his daughters, who were preparing the midday meal. They reflected in the silence of experienced men who tread carefully amid new people. Nevertheless, the old farmer, stationary, invincible in his chair near the warmest part of the stove, turned his face from the sawdust box frequently and addressed a glowing commonplace to the strangers. Usually he was answered in short but adequate sentences by either the cowboy or the Easterner. The Swede said nothing. He seemed to be occupied in making furtive estimates of each man in the room. One might have thought that he had the sense of silly suspicion which comes to guilt. He resembled a badly frightened man.

Later, at dinner, he spoke a little, addressing his conversation entirely to Scully. He volunteered that he had come from New York, where for ten years he had worked as a tailor. These facts seemed to strike Scully as fascinating, and afterward he volunteered that he had lived at Romper for fourteen years. The Swede asked about the crops and the price of labor. He seemed barely to listen to Scully's extended replies. His eyes continued to rove from man to man.

Finally, with a laugh and a wink, he said that some of these Western communities were very dangerous; and after his statement he straightened his legs under the table, tilted his head, and laughed again, loudly. It was plain that the demonstration had no meaning to the others. They looked at him wondering and in silence.

II

As the men trooped heavily back into the front room, the two little windows presented views of a turmoiling sea of snow. The huge arms of the wind were making attempts—mighty, circular, futile—to embrace the flakes as they sped. A gate-post like a still man with a blanched face stood aghast amid this profligate fury. In a hearty voice Scully announced the presence of a blizzard. The guests of the blue hotel, lighting their pipes, assented with grunts of lazy masculine contentment. No island of the sea could be exempt in the degree of this little room with its humming stove. Johnnie, son of Scully, in a tone which defined his opinion of his ability as a card-player, challenged the old farmer of both gray and sandy whiskers to a game of High-Five. The farmer agreed with a contemptuous and bitter scoff. They sat close to the stove, and squared their knees under a wide board. The cowboy and the Easterner watched the game with interest. The Swede remained near the window, aloof, but with a countenance that showed signs of an inexplicable excitement.

The play of Johnnie and the gray-beard was suddenly ended by another quarrel. The old man arose while casting a look of heated scorn at his adversary. He slowly buttoned his coat, and then stalked with fabulous dignity from the room. In the discreet silence of all other men the Swede laughed. His laughter rang somehow childish. Men by this time had begun to look at him askance, as if they wished to inquire what ailed him.

A new game was formed jocosely. The cowboy volunteered to become the partner of Johnnie, and they all then turned to ask the Swede to throw in his lot with the little Easterner. He asked some questions about the game, and learning that it wore many names, and that he had played it when it was under an alias, he accepted the invitation. He strode toward the men nervously, as if he expected to be assaulted. Finally, seated, he gazed from face to face and laughed shrilly. This laugh was so strange that the Easterner looked up quickly, the cowboy sat intent and with his mouth open, and Johnnie paused, holding the cards with still fingers.

Afterward there was a short silence. Then Johnnie said: "Well, let's get at it. Come on now!" They pulled their chairs forward until their knees were bunched under the board. They began to play, and their interest in the game caused the others to forget the manner of the Swede.

The cowboy was a board-whacker. Each time that he held superior cards he whanged them, one by one, with exceeding force, down upon the improvised table, and took the tricks with a glowing air of prowess and pride that sent thrills of indignation into the hearts of his opponents. A game with a board-whacker in it is sure to become intense. The countenances of the Easterner and the Swede were miserable whenever the cowboy thundered down his aces and kings, while Johnnie, his eyes gleaming with joy, chuckled and chuckled.

Because of the absorbing play none considered the strange ways of the Swede. They paid strict heed to the game. Finally, during a lull caused by a new deal, the Swede suddenly addressed Johnnie: "I suppose there have been a good many men killed in this room." The jaws of the others dropped and they looked at him.

"What in hell are you talking about?" said Johnnie.

The Swede laughed again his blatant laugh, full of a kind of false courage and defiance. "Oh, you know what I mean all right," he answered.

"I'm a liar if I do!" Johnnie protested. The card was halted, and the men stared at the Swede. Johnnie evidently felt that as the son of the proprietor he should make a direct inquiry. "Now, what might you be drivin' at, mister?" he asked. The Swede winked at him. It was a wink full of cunning. His fingers shook on the edge of the board. "Oh, maybe you think I have been to nowheres. Maybe you think I'm a tenderfoot?"

"I don't know nothin' about you," answered Johnnie, "and I don't give a damn where you've been. All I got to say is that I don't know what you're driving at. There hain't never been nobody killed in this room."

The cowboy, who had been steadily gazing at the Swede, then spoke. "What's wrong with you, mister?"

Apparently it seemed to the Swede that he was formidably menaced. He shivered and turned white near the corners of his mouth. He sent an appealing glance in the direction of the little Easterner. During these moments he did not forget to wear his air of advanced pot-valor. "They say they don't know what I mean," he remarked mockingly to the Easterner.

The latter answered after prolonged and cautious reflection. "I don't understand you," he said, impassively.

The Swede made a movement then which announced that he thought he had encountered treachery from the only quarter where he had expected sympathy if not help. "Oh, I see you are all against me. I see—"

The cowboy was in a state of deep stupefaction. "Say," he cried, as he tumbled the deck violently down upon the board. "Say, what are you gittin' at, hey?"

The Swede sprang up with the celerity of a man escaping from a snake on the floor. "I don't want to fight!" he shouted. "I don't want to fight!"

The cowboy stretched his long legs indolently and deliberately. His hands were in his pockets. He spat into the sawdust box. "Well, who the hell thought you did?" he inquired.

The Swede backed rapidly toward a corner of the room. His hands were out protectingly in front of his chest, but he was making an obvious struggle to control his fright. "Gentlemen," he quavered, "I suppose I am going to be killed before I can leave this house! I suppose I am going to be killed before I can leave this house." In his eyes was the dying swan look. Through the windows could be seen the snow turning blue in the shadow of dusk. The wind tore at the house and some loose thing beat regularly against the clap-boards like a spirit tapping.

A door opened, and Scully himself entered. He paused in surprise as he noted the tragic attitude of the Swede. Then he said: "What's the matter here?"

The Swede answered him swiftly and eagerly: "These men are going to kill me."

"Kill you!" ejaculated Scully. "Kill you! What are you talkin'?"

The Swede made the gesture of a martyr.

Scully wheeled sternly upon his son. "What is this, Johnnie?"

The lad had grown sullen. "Damned if I know," he answered. "I can't make no sense to it." He began to shuffle the cards, fluttering them together with an angry snap. "He says a good many men have been killed in this room, or something like that. And he says he's goin' to be killed here too. I don't know what ails him. He's crazy, I shouldn't wonder."

Scully then looked for explanation to the cowboy, but the cowboy simply shrugged his shoulders.

"Kill you?" said Scully again to the Swede. "Kill you? Man, you're off your nut."

"Oh, I know," burst out the Swede. "I know what will happen. Yes, I'm crazy—yes. Yes, of course, I'm crazy—yes. But I know one thing—" There was a sort of sweat of misery and terror upon his face. "I know I won't get out of here alive."

The Swede held a huge fist in front of Johnnie's face.

The cowboy drew a deep breath, as if his mind was passing into the last stages of dissolution. "Well, I'm dog-goned," he whispered to himself.

Scully wheeled suddenly and faced his son. "You've been troublin' this man!"

Johnnie's voice was loud with its burden of grievance. "Why, good Gawd, I ain't done nothin' to 'im."

The Swede broke in. "Gentlemen, do not disturb yourselves. I will leave this house. I will go 'way because—" He accused them dramatically with his glance. "Because I do not want to be killed."

Scully was furious with his son. "Will you tell me what is the matter, you young divil? What's the matter, anyhow? Speak out!"

"Blame it," cried Johnnie in despair, "don't I tell you I don't know. He—he says we want to kill him, and that's all I know. I can't tell what ails him."

The Swede continued to repeat: "Never mind, Mr. Scully, never mind. I will leave this house. I will go away, because I do not wish to be killed. Yes, of course, I am crazy—yes. But I know one thing! I will go away. I will leave this house. Never mind, Mr. Scully, never mind. I will go away."

"You will not go 'way," said Scully. "You will not go 'way until I hear the reason of this business. If anybody has troubled you I will take care of him. This is my house. You are under my roof, and I will not allow any peaceable man to be troubled here. He cast a terrible eye upon Johnnie, the cowboy, and the Easterner.

"Never mind, Mr. Scully; never mind. I will go 'way. I do not wish to be killed." The Swede moved toward the door, which opened upon the stairs. It was evidently his intention to go at once for his baggage.

"No, no," shouted Scully peremptorily; but the white-faced man slid by him and disappeared. "Now," said Scully severely, "what does this mane?"

Johnnie and the cowboy cried together: "Why, we didn't do nothin' to 'im!"

Scully's eyes were cold. "No," he said, "you didn't?"

Johnnie swore a deep oath. "Why, this is the wildest loon I ever see. We didn't do nothin' at all. We were jest sittin' here playin' cards and he—"

The father suddenly spoke to the Easterner. "Mr. Blanc," he asked, "what has these boys been doin'?"

The Easterner reflected again. "I didn't see anything wrong at all," he said at last slowly.

Scully began to howl. "But what does it mane?" He stared ferociously at his son. "I have a mind to lather you for this, me boy."

Johnnie was frantic. "Well, what have I done?" he bawled at his father.

III

"I think you are tongue-tied," said Scully finally to his son, the cowboy and the Easterner, and at the end of this scornful sentence he left the room.

Upstairs the Swede was swiftly fastening the straps of his great valise. Once his back happened to be half-turned toward the door, and hearing a noise there, he wheeled and sprang up, uttering a loud cry. Scully's wrinkled visage showed

grimly in the light of the small lamp he carried. This yellow effulgence, streaming upward, colored only his prominent features, and left his eyes, for instance,
in mysterious shadow. He resembled a murderer.

"Man, man!" he exclaimed, "have you gone daffy?"

"Oh, no! Oh, no!" rejoined the other. "There are people in this world who
know pretty nearly as much as you do—understand?"

For a moment they stood gazing at each other. Upon the Swede's deathly
pale cheeks were two spots brightly crimson and sharply edged, as if they had
been carefully painted. Scully placed the light on the table and sat himself on
the edge of the bed. He spoke ruminatively. "By cracky, I never heard of such a
thing in my life. It's a complete muddle. I can't for the soul of me think how you
ever got this idea into your head." Presently he lifted his eyes and asked: "And
did you sure think they were going to kill you?"

The Swede scanned the old man as if he wished to see into his mind. "I did,"
he said at last. He obviously suspected that this answer might precipitate an
outbreak. As he pulled on a strap his whole arm shook, the elbow wavering like
a bit of paper.

Scully banged his hand impressively on the foot-board of the bed. "Why,
man, we're goin' to have a line of ilictric street-cars in this town next spring."

"'A line of electric street-cars,'" repeated the Swede stupidly.

"And," said Scully, "there's a new railroad goin' to be built down from Broken Arm to here. Not to mintion the four churches and the smashin' big brick
school-house. Then there's the big factory, too. Why, in two years Romper'll be
a met-tro-pol-is."

Having finished the preparation of his baggage, the Swede straightened
himself. "Mr. Scully," he said with sudden hardihood, "how much do I owe you?"

"You don't owe me anythin'," said the old man angrily.

"Yes, I do," retorted the Swede. He took seventy-five cents from his pocket
and tendered it to Scully; but the latter snapped his fingers in disdainful refusal. However, it happened that they both stood gazing in a strange fashion at
three silver pieces on the Swede's open palm.

"I'll not take your money," said Scully at last. "Not after what's been goin' on
here." Then a plan seemed to strike him. "Here," he cried, picking up his lamp
and moving toward the door. "Here! Come with me a minute."

"No," said the Swede in overwhelming alarm.

"Yes," urged the old man. "Come on! I want you to come and see a picter—just
across the hall—in my room."

The Swede must have concluded that his hour was come. His jaw dropped
and his teeth showed like a dead man's. He ultimately followed Scully across
the corridor, but he had the step of one hung in chains.

Scully flashed the light high on the wall of his own chamber. There was revealed a ridiculous photograph of a little girl. She was leaning against a balustrade of gorgeous decoration, and the formidable bang to her hair was prominent. The figure was as graceful as an upright sled-stake, and, withal, it was of the hue of lead. "There," said Scully tenderly. "That's the picter of my little girl that died. Her name was Carrie. She had the purtiest hair you ever saw! I was that fond of her, she—"

Turning then he saw that the Swede was not contemplating the picture at all, but, instead, was keeping keen watch on the gloom in the rear.

"Look, man!" shouted Scully heartily. "That's the picter of my little gal that died. Her name was Carrie. And then here's the picter of my oldest boy, Michael. He's a lawyer in Lincoln an' doin' well. I gave that boy a grand eddycation, and I'm glad for it now. He's a fine boy. Look at 'im now. Ain't he bold as blazes, him there in Lincoln, an honored an' respicted gintleman. An honored an' respicted gintleman," concluded Scully with a flourish. And so saying, he smote the Swede jovially on the back.

The Swede faintly smiled.

"Now," said the old man, "there's only one more thing." He dropped suddenly to the floor and thrust his head beneath the bed. The Swede could hear his muffled voice. "I'd keep it under me piller if it wasn't for that boy Johnnie. Then there's the old woman—Where is it now? I never put it twice in the same place. Ah, now come out with you!"

Presently he backed clumsily from under the bed, dragging with him an old coat rolled into a bundle. "I've fetched him," he muttered. Kneeling on the floor he unrolled the coat and extracted from its heart a large yellow-brown whisky bottle.

His first maneuver was to hold the bottle up to the light. Reassured, apparently, that nobody had been tampering with it, he thrust it with a generous movement toward the Swede.

The weak-kneed Swede was about to eagerly clutch this element of strength, but he suddenly jerked his hand away and cast a look of horror upon Scully.

"Drink," said the old man affectionately. He had arisen to his feet, and now stood facing the Swede.

There was a silence. Then again Scully said: "Drink!"

The Swede laughed wildly. He grabbed the bottle, put it to his mouth, and as his lips curled absurdly around the opening and his throat worked, he kept his glance burning with hatred upon the old man's face.

IV

After the departure of Scully the three men, with the card-board still upon their knees, preserved for a long time an astounded silence. Then Johnnie said: "That's the dod-dangest Swede I ever see."

"He ain't no Swede," said the cowboy scornfully.

"Well, what is he then?" cried Johnnie. "What is he then?"

"It's my opinion," replied the cowboy deliberately, "he's some kind of a Dutchman." It was a venerable custom of the country to entitle as Swedes all light-haired men who spoke with a heavy tongue. In consequence the idea of the cowboy was not without its daring. "Yes, sir," he repeated. "It's my opinion this feller is some kind of a Dutchman."

"Well, he says he's a Swede, anyhow," muttered Johnnie sulkily. He turned to the Easterner. "What do you think, Mr. Blanc?"

"Oh, I don't know," replied the Easterner.

"Well, what do you think makes him act that way?" asked the cowboy.

"Why, he's frightened!" The Easterner knocked his pipe against a rim of the stove. "He's clear frightened out of his boots."

"What at?" cried Johnnie and cowboy together.

The Easterner reflected over his answer.

"What at?" cried the others again.

"Oh, I don't know, but it seems to me this man has been reading dime-novels, and he thinks he's right out in the middle of it—the shootin' and stabbin' and all."

"But," said the cowboy, deeply scandalized, "this ain't Wyoming, ner none of them places. This is Nebrasker."

"Yes," added Johnnie, "an' why don't he wait till he gits out West?"

The traveled Easterner laughed. "It isn't different there even—not in these days. But he thinks he's right in the middle of hell."

Johnnie and the cowboy mused long.

"It's awful funny," remarked Johnnie at last.

"Yes," said the cowboy. "This is a queer game. I hope we don't git snowed in, because then we'd have to stand this here man bein' around with us all the time. That wouldn't be no good."

"I wish pop would throw him out," said Johnnie.

Presently they heard a loud stamping on the stairs, accompanied by ringing jokes in the voice of old Scully, and laughter, evidently from the Swede. The men around the stove stared vacantly at each other. "Gosh," said the cowboy. The door flew open, and old Scully, flushed and anecdotal, came into the room. He was jabbering at the Swede, who followed him, laughing bravely. It was the entry of two roysterers from a banquet hall.

"Come now," said Scully sharply to the three seated men, "move up and give us a chance at the stove." The cowboy and the Easterner obediently sidled their chairs to make room for the newcomers. Johnnie, however, simply arranged himself in a more indolent attitude, and then remained motionless.

"Come! Git over, there," said Scully.

"Plenty of room on the other side of the stove," said Johnnie.

"Do you think we want to sit in the draught?" roared the father.

But the Swede here interposed with a grandeur of confidence. "No, no. Let the boy sit where he likes," he cried in a bullying voice to the father.

"All right! All right!" said Scully deferentially. The cowboy and the Easterner exchanged glances of wonder.

The five chairs were formed in a crescent about one side of the stove. The Swede began to talk; he talked arrogantly, profanely, angrily. Johnnie, the cowboy and the Easterner maintained a morose silence, while old Scully appeared to be receptive and eager, breaking in constantly with sympathetic ejaculations.

Finally the Swede announced that he was thirsty. He moved in his chair, and said that he would go for a drink of water.

"I'll git it for you," cried Scully at once.

"No," said the Swede contemptuously. "I'll get it for myself." He arose and stalked with the air of an owner off into the executive parts of the hotel.

As soon as the Swede was out of hearing Scully sprang to his feet and whispered intensely to the others. "Upstairs he thought I was tryin' to poison 'im."

"Say," said Johnnie, "this makes me sick. Why don't you throw 'im out in the snow?"

"Why, he's all right now," declared Scully. "It was only that he was from the East and he thought this was a tough place. That's all. He's all right now."

The cowboy looked with admiration upon the Easterner. "You were straight," he said. "You were on to that there Dutchman."

"Well," said Johnnie to his father, "he may be all right now, but I don't see it. Other time he was scared, and now he's too fresh."

Scully's speech was always a combination of Irish brogue and idiom, Western twang and idiom, and scraps of curiously formal diction taken from the story-books and newspapers. He now hurled a strange mass of language at the head of his son. "What do I keep? What do I keep? What do I keep?" he demanded in a voice of thunder. He slapped his knee impressively, to indicate that he himself was going to make reply, and that all should heed. "I keep a hotel," he shouted. "A hotel, do you mind? A guest under my roof has sacred privileges. He is to be intimidated by none. Not one word shall he hear that would prijudice him in favor of goin' away. I'll not have it. There's no place in this here town where they can say they iver took in a guest of mine because he was afraid to stay here." He wheeled suddenly upon the cowboy and the Easterner. "Am I right?"

"Yes, Mr. Scully," said the cowboy, "I think you're right."

"Yes, Mr. Scully," said the Easterner, "I think you're right."

V

At six-o'clock supper, the Swede fizzed like a fire-wheel. He sometimes seemed on the point of bursting into riotous song, and in all his madness he was encouraged by old Scully. The Easterner was incased in reserve; the cowboy sat in wide-mouthed amazement, forgetting to eat, while Johnnie wrathily demolished great plates of food. The daughters of the house when they were obliged to replenish the biscuits approached as warily as Indians, and, having succeeded in their purposes, fled with ill-concealed trepidation. The Swede domineered the whole feast, and he gave it the appearance of a cruel bacchanal. He seemed to have grown suddenly taller; he gazed, brutally disdainful, into every face. His voice rang through the room. Once when he jabbed out harpoon-fashion with his fork to pinion a biscuit the weapon nearly impaled the hand of the Easterner which had been stretched quietly out for the same biscuit.

After supper, as the men filed toward the other room, the Swede smote Scully ruthlessly on the shoulder. "Well, old boy, that was a good square meal." Johnnie looked hopefully at his father; he knew that shoulder was tender from an old fall; and indeed it appeared for a moment as if Scully was going to flame out over the matter, but in the end he smiled a sickly smile and remained silent. The others understood from his manner that he was admitting his responsibility for the Swede's new viewpoint.

Johnnie, however, addressed his parent in an aside. "Why don't you license somebody to kick you downstairs?" Scully scowled darkly by way of reply.

When they were gathered about the stove, the Swede insisted on another game of High-Five. Scully gently deprecated the plan at first, but the Swede turned a wolfish glare upon him. The old man subsided, and the Swede canvassed the others. In his tone there was always a great threat. The cowboy and the Easterner both remarked indifferently that they would play. Scully said that he would presently have to go to meet the 6.58 train, and so the Swede turned menacingly upon Johnnie. For a moment their glances crossed like blades, and then Johnnie smiled and said: "Yes, I'll play."

They formed a square with the little board on their knees. The Easterner and the Swede were again partners. As the play went on, it was noticeable that the cowboy was not board-whacking as usual. Meanwhile, Scully, near the lamp, had put on his spectacles and, with an appearance curiously like an old priest, was reading a newspaper. In time he went out to meet the 6.58 train, and, despite his precautions, a gust of polar wind whirled into the room as he opened the door. Besides scattering the cards, it chilled the players to the marrow. The Swede cursed frightfully. When Scully returned, his entrance disturbed a cozy and friendly scene. The Swede again cursed. But presently they were once more intent, their heads bent forward and their hands moving swiftly. The Swede had adopted the fashion of board-whacking.

Scully took up his paper and for a long time remained immersed in matters which were extraordinarily remote from him. The lamp burned badly, and once he stopped to adjust the wick. The newspaper as he turned from page to page rustled with a slow and comfortable sound. Then suddenly he heard three terrible words: "You are cheatin'!"

Such scenes often prove that there can be little of dramatic import in environment. Any room can present a tragic front; any room can be comic. This little den was now hideous as a torture-chamber. The new faces of the men themselves had changed it upon the instant. The Swede held a huge fist in front of Johnnie's face, while the latter looked steadily over it into the blazing orbs of his accuser. The Easterner had grown pallid; the cowboy's jaw had dropped in that expression of bovine amazement which was one of his important mannerisms. After the three words, the first sound in the room was made by Scully's paper as it floated forgotten to his feet. His spectacles had also fallen from his nose, but by a clutch he had saved them in air. His hand, grasping the spectacles, now remained poised awkwardly and near his shoulder. He stared at the card-players.

Probably the silence was while a second elapsed. Then, if the floor had been suddenly twitched out from under the men they could not have moved quicker. The five had projected themselves headlong toward a common point. It happened that Johnnie in rising to hurl himself upon the Swede had stumbled slightly because of his curiously instinctive care for the cards and the board. The loss of the moment allowed time for the arrival of Scully, and also allowed the cowboy time to give the Swede a great push which sent him staggering back. The men found tongue together, and hoarse shouts of rage, appeal or fear burst from every throat. The cowboy pushed and jostled feverishly at the Swede, and the Easterner and Scully clung wildly to Johnnie; but, through the smoky air, above the swaying bodies of the peace-compellers, the eyes of the two warriors ever sought each other in glances of challenge that were at once hot and steely.

Of course the board had been overturned, and now the whole company of cards was scattered over the floor, where the boots of the men trampled the fat and painted kings and queens as they gazed with their silly eyes at the war that was waging above them.

Scully's voice was dominating the yells. "Stop now! Stop, I say! Stop, now—"

Johnnie, as he struggled to burst through the rank formed by Scully and the Easterner, was crying: "Well, he says I cheated! He says I cheated! I won't allow no man to say I cheated! If he says I cheated, he's a ——!"

The cowboy was telling the Swede: "Quit, now! Quit, d'ye hear—"

The screams of the Swede never ceased. "He did cheat! I saw him! I saw him—"

As for the Easterner, he was importuning in a voice that was not heeded. "Wait a moment, can't you? Oh, wait a moment. What's the good of a fight over a game of cards? Wait a moment—"

In this tumult no complete sentences were clear. "Cheat"—"Quit"—"He says"—These fragments pierced the uproar and rang out sharply. It was remarkable that whereas Scully undoubtedly made the most noise, he was the least heard of any of the riotous band.

Then suddenly there was a great cessation. It was as if each man had paused for breath, and although the room was still lighted with the anger of men, it could be seen that there was no danger of immediate conflict, and at once Johnnie, shouldering his way forward, almost succeeded in confronting the Swede. "What did you say I cheated for? What did you say I cheated for? I don't cheat and I won't let no man say I do!"

The Swede said: "I saw you! I saw you!"

"Well," cried Johnnie, "I'll fight any man what says I cheat!"

"No, you won't," said the cowboy. "Not here."

"Ah, be still, can't you?" said Scully, coming between them.

The quiet was sufficient to allow the Easterner's voice to be heard. He was repeating: "Oh, wait a moment, can't you? What's the good of a fight over a game of cards? Wait a moment."

Johnnie, his red face appearing above his father's shoulder, hailed the Swede again. "Did you say I cheated?"

The Swede showed his teeth. "Yes."

"Then," said Johnnie, "we must fight."

"Yes, fight," roared the Swede. He was like a demoniac. "Yes, fight! I'll show you what kind of a man I am! I'll show you who you want to fight! Maybe you think I can't fight! Maybe you think I can't! I'll show you, you skin, you card-sharp! Yes, you cheated! You cheated! You cheated!"

"Well, let's git at it, then, mister," said Johnnie coolly.

The cowboy's brow was beaded with sweat from his efforts in intercepting all sorts of raids. He turned in despair to Scully. "What are you goin' to do now?"

A change had come over the Celtic visage of the old man. He now seemed all eagerness; his eyes glowed.

"We'll let them fight," he answered stalwartly. "I can't put up with it any longer. I've stood this damned Swede till I'm sick. We'll let them fight."

<h1 style="text-align:center">VI</h1>

The men prepared to go out of doors. The Easterner was so nervous that he had great difficulty in getting his arms into the sleeves of his new leather-coat. As the cowboy drew his fur-cap down over his ears his hands trembled. In fact, Johnnie and old Scully were the only ones who displayed no agitation. These preliminaries were conducted without words.

Scully threw open the door. "Well, come on," he said. Instantly a terrific wind caused the flame of the lamp to struggle at its wick, while a puff of black smoke sprang from the chimney-top. The stove was in mid-current of the blast, and its voice swelled to equal the roar of the storm. Some of the scarred and bedabbled cards were caught up from the floor and dashed helplessly against the further wall. The men lowered their heads and plunged into the tempest as into a sea.

No snow was falling, but great whirls and clouds of flakes, swept up from the ground by the frantic winds, were streaming southward with the speed of bullets. The covered land was blue with the sheen of an unearthly satin, and there was no other hue save where at the low black railway station—which seemed incredibly distant—one light gleamed like a tiny jewel. As the men floundered into a thigh-deep drift, it was known that the Swede was bawling out something. Scully went to him, put a hand on his shoulder and projected an ear. "What's that you say?" he shouted.

"I say," bawled the Swede again, "I won't stand much show against this gang. I know you'll all pitch on me."

Scully smote him reproachfully on the arm. "Tut, man," he yelled. The wind tore the words from Scully's lips and scattered them far a-lee.

"You are all a gang of—" boomed the Swede, but the storm also seized the remainder of this sentence.

Immediately turning their backs upon the wind, the men had swung around a corner to the sheltered side of the hotel. It was the function of the little house to preserve here, amid this great devastation of snow, an irregular V-shape of heavily-incrusted grass, which crackled beneath the feet. One could imagine the great drifts piled against the windward side. When the party reached the comparative peace of this spot it was found that the Swede was still bellowing.

"Oh, I know what kind of a thing this is! I know you'll all pitch on me. I can't lick you all!"

Scully turned upon him panther-fashion. "You'll not have to whip all of us. You'll have to whip my son Johnnie. An' the man what troubles you durin' that time will have me to dale with."

The arrangements were swiftly made. The two men faced each other, obedient to the harsh commands of Scully, whose face, in the subtly luminous gloom, could be seen set in the austere impersonal lines that are pictured on the countenances of the Roman veterans. The Easterner's teeth were chattering, and he was hopping up and down like a mechanical toy. The cowboy stood rock-like.

The contestants had not stripped off any clothing. Each was in his ordinary attire. Their fists were up, and they eyed each other in a calm that had the elements of leonine cruelty in it.

During this pause, the Easterner's mind, like a film, took lasting impressions of three men—the iron-nerved master of the ceremony; the Swede, pale, motionless, terrible; and Johnnie, serene yet ferocious, brutish yet heroic. The entire prelude had in it a tragedy greater than the tragedy of action, and this aspect was accentuated by the long mellow cry of the blizzard, as it sped the tumbling and wailing flakes into the black abyss of the south.

"Now!" said Scully.

The two combatants leaped forward and crashed together like bullocks. There was heard the cushioned sound of blows, and of a curse squeezing out from between the tight teeth of one.

As for the spectators, the Easterner's pent-up breath exploded from him with a pop of relief, absolute relief from the tension of the preliminaries. The cowboy bounded into the air with a yowl. Scully was immovable as from supreme amazement and fear at the fury of the fight which he himself had permitted and arranged.

For a time the encounter in the darkness was such a perplexity of flying arms that it presented no more detail than would a swiftly-revolving wheel. Occasionally a face, as if illumined by a flash of light, would shine out, ghastly and marked with pink spots. A moment later, the men might have been known as shadows, if it were not for the involuntary utterance of oaths that came from them in whispers.

Suddenly a holocaust of warlike desire caught the cowboy, and he bolted forward with the speed of a broncho. "Go it, Johnnie; go it! Kill him! Kill him!"

Scully confronted him. "Kape back," he said; and by his glance the cowboy could tell that this man was Johnnie's father.

To the Easterner there was a monotony of unchangeable fighting that was an abomination. This confused mingling was eternal to his sense, which was concentrated in a longing for the end, the priceless end. Once the fighters lurched near him, and as he scrambled hastily backward, he heard them breathe like men on the rack.

"Kill him, Johnnie! Kill him! Kill him! Kill him!" The cowboy's face was contorted like one of those agony masks in museums.

"Keep still," said Scully icily.

Then there was a sudden loud grunt, incomplete, cut short, and Johnnie's body swung away from the Swede and fell with sickening heaviness to the grass. The cowboy was barely in time to prevent the mad Swede from flinging himself upon his prone adversary. "No, you don't," said the cowboy, interposing an arm. "Wait a second."

Scully was at his son's side. "Johnnie! Johnnie, me boy?" His voice had a quality of melancholy tenderness. "Johnnie? Can you go on with it?" He looked anxiously down into the bloody pulpy face of his son.

There was a moment of silence, and then Johnnie answered in his ordinary voice: "Yes, I—it—yes."

Assisted by his father he struggled to his feet. "Wait a bit now till you git your wind," said the old man.

A few paces away the cowboy was lecturing the Swede. "No, you don't! Wait a second!"

The Easterner was plucking at Scully's sleeve. "Oh, this is enough," he pleaded. "This is enough! Let it go as it stands. This is enough!"

"Bill," said Scully, "git out of the road." The cowboy stepped aside. "Now." The combatants were actuated by a new caution as they advanced toward collision. They glared at each other, and then the Swede aimed a lightning blow that carried with it his entire weight. Johnnie was evidently half-stupid from weakness, but he miraculously dodged, and his fist sent the over-balanced Swede sprawling.

The cowboy, Scully and the Easterner burst into a cheer that was like a chorus of triumphant soldiery, but before its conclusion the Swede had scuffled agilely to his feet and come in berserk abandon at his foe. There was another perplexity of flying arms, and Johnnie's body again swung away and fell, even as a bundle might fall from a roof. The Swede instantly staggered to a little wind-waved tree and leaned upon it, breathing like an engine, while his savage and flame-lit eyes roamed from face to face as the men bent over Johnnie. There was a splendor of isolation in his situation at this time which the Easterner felt once when, lifting his eyes from the man on the ground, he beheld that mysterious and lonely figure, waiting.

"Are you any good yet, Johnnie?" asked Scully in a broken voice.

The son gasped and opened his eyes languidly. After a moment he answered: "No—I ain't—any good—any—more." Then, from shame and bodily ill, he began to weep, the tears furrowing down through the bloodstains on his face. "He was too—too—too heavy for me."

Scully straightened and addressed the waiting figure. "Stranger," he said, evenly, "it's all up with our side." Then his voice changed into that vibrant huskiness which is commonly the tone of the most simple and deadly announcements. "Johnnie is whipped."

Without replying, the victor moved off on the route to the front door of the hotel.

The cowboy was formulating new and unspellable blasphemies. The Easterner was startled to find that they were out in a wind that seemed to come direct from the shadowed arctic floes. He heard again the wail of the snow as it was flung to its grave in the south. He knew now that all this time the cold had been sinking into him deeper and deeper, and he wondered that he had not perished. He felt indifferent to the condition of the vanquished man.

"Johnnie, can you walk?" asked Scully.

"Did I hurt—hurt him any?" asked the son.

"Can you walk, boy? Can you walk?"

Johnnie's voice was suddenly strong. There was a robust impatience in it. "I asked you whether I hurt him any!"

"Yes, yes, Johnnie," answered the cowboy consolingly; "he's hurt a good deal."

They raised him from the ground, and as soon as he was on his feet he went tottering off, rebuffing all attempts at assistance. When the party rounded the corner they were fairly blinded by the pelting of the snow. It burned their faces like fire. The cowboy carried Johnnie through the drift to the door. As they entered some cards again rose from the floor and beat against the wall.

The Easterner rushed to the stove. He was so profoundly chilled that he almost dared to embrace the glowing iron. The Swede was not in the room. Johnnie sank into a chair, and folding his arms on his knees, buried his face in them. Scully, warming one foot and then the other at a rim of the stove, muttered to himself with Celtic mournfulness. The cowboy had removed his fur-cap, and with a dazed and rueful air he was now running one hand through his tousled locks. From overhead they could hear the creaking of boards, as the Swede tramped here and there in his room.

The sad quiet was broken by the sudden flinging open of a door that led toward the kitchen. It was instantly followed by an inrush of women. They precipitated themselves upon Johnnie amid a chorus of lamentation. Before they carried their prey off to the kitchen, there to be bathed and harangued with that mixture of sympathy and abuse which is a feat of their sex, the mother straightened herself and fixed old Scully with an eye of stern reproach. "Shame be upon you, Patrick Scully!" she cried. "Your own son, too. Shame be upon you!"

"There, now! Be quiet, now!" said the old man weakly.

"Shame be upon you, Patrick Scully!" The girls rallying to this slogan, sniffed disdainfully in the direction of those trembling accomplices, the cowboy and the Easterner. Presently they bore Johnnie away, and left the three men to dismal reflection.

VII

"I'd like to fight this here Dutchman myself," said the cowboy, breaking a long silence.

Scully wagged his head sadly. "No, that wouldn't do. It wouldn't be right. It wouldn't be right."

"Well, why wouldn't it?" argued the cowboy. "I don't see no harm in it."

"No," answered Scully with mournful heroism. "It wouldn't be right. It was Johnnie's fight, and now we mustn't whip the man just because he whipped Johnnie."

"Yes, that's true enough," said the cowboy; "but—he better not get fresh with me, because I couldn't stand no more of it."

"You'll not say a word to him," commanded Scully, and even then they heard the tread of the Swede on the stairs. His entrance was made theatric. He swept the door back with a bang and swaggered to the middle of the room. No one looked at him. "Well," he cried, insolently, at Scully, "I s'pose you'll tell me now how much I owe you?"

The old man remained stolid. "You don't owe me nothin'."

"Huh!" said the Swede, "huh! Don't owe 'im nothin'."

The cowboy addressed the Swede. "Stranger, I don't see how you come to be so gay around here."

Old Scully was instantly alert. "Stop!" he shouted, holding his hand forth, fingers upward. "Bill, you shut up!"

The cowboy spat carelessly into the sawdust box. "I didn't say a word, did I?" he asked.

"Mr. Scully," called the Swede, "how much do I owe you?" It was seen that he was attired for departure, and that he had his valise in his hand.

"You don't owe me nothin'," repeated Scully in his same imperturbable way.

"Huh!" said the Swede. "I guess you're right. I guess if it was any way at all, you'd owe me somethin'. That's what I guess." He turned to the cowboy. "Kill him! Kill him! Kill him!" he mimicked, and then guffawed victoriously. "Kill him!" He was convulsed with ironical humor.

But he might have been jeering the dead. The three men were immovable and silent, staring with glassy eyes at the stove.

The Swede opened the door and passed into the storm, giving one derisive glance backward at the still group.

As soon as the door was closed, Scully and the cowboy leaped to their feet and began to curse. They trampled to and fro, waving their arms and smashing into the air with their fists. "Oh, but that was a hard minute!" wailed Scully. "That was a hard minute! Him there leerin' and scoffin'! One bang at his nose was worth forty dollars to me that minute! How did you stand it, Bill?"

"How did I stand it?" cried the cowboy in a quivering voice. "How did I stand it? Oh!"

The old man burst into sudden brogue. "I'd loike to take that Swade," he wailed, "and hould 'im down on a shtone flure and bate 'im to a jelly wid a shtick!"

The cowboy groaned in sympathy. "I'd like to git him by the neck and ha-ammer him"—he brought his hand down on a chair with a noise like a pistol-shot—"hammer that there Dutchman until he couldn't tell himself from a dead coyote!"

"I'd bate 'im until he—"

"I'd show him some things—"

And then together they raised a yearning fanatic cry. "Oh-o-oh! if we only could—"

"Yes!"

"Yes!"

"And then I'd—"

"O-o-oh!"

VIII

The Swede, tightly gripping his valise, tacked across the face of the storm as if he carried sails. He was following a line of little naked gasping trees, which he knew must mark the way of the road. His face, fresh from the pounding of Johnnie's fists, felt more pleasure than pain in the wind and the driving snow. A number of square shapes loomed upon him finally, and he knew them as the houses of the main body of the town. He found a street and made travel along it, leaning heavily upon the wind whenever, at a corner, a terrific blast caught him.

He might have been in a deserted village. We picture the world as thick with conquering and elate humanity, but here, with the bugles of the tempest pealing, it was hard to imagine a peopled earth. One viewed the existence of man then as a marvel, and conceded a glamour of wonder to these lice which were caused to cling to a whirling, fire-smote, ice-locked, disease-stricken, space-lost bulb. The conceit of man was explained by this storm to be the very engine of life. One was a coxcomb not to die in it. However, the Swede found a saloon.

In front of it an indomitable red light was burning, and the snow-flakes were made blood-colour as they flew through the circumscribed territory of the lamp's shining. The Swede pushed open the door of the saloon and entered. A sanded expanse was before him, and at the end of it four men sat about a table drinking. Down one side of the room extended a radiant bar, and its guardian was leaning upon his elbows listening to the talk of the men at the table. The Swede dropped his valise upon the floor, and, smiling fraternally upon the barkeeper, said: "Gimme some whisky, will you?" The man placed a bottle, a whisky-glass, and glass of ice-thick water upon the bar. The Swede poured himself an abnormal portion of whisky and drank it in three gulps. "Pretty bad night," remarked the bartender indifferently. He was making the pretension of blindness, which is usually a distinction of his class; but it could have been seen that he was furtively studying the half-erased blood-stains on the face of the Swede. "Bad night," he said again.

"Oh, it's good enough for me," replied the Swede, hardily, as he poured himself some more whisky. The barkeeper took his coin and maneuvered it through its reception by the highly-nickeled cash-machine. A bell rang; a card labeled "20 cts." had appeared.

"No," continued the Swede, "this isn't too bad weather. It's good enough for me."

"So?" murmured the barkeeper languidly.

The copious drams made the Swede's eyes swim, and he breathed a trifle heavier. "Yes, I like this weather. I like it. It suits me." It was apparently his design to impart a deep significance to these words.

"So?" murmured the bartender again. He turned to gaze dreamily at the scroll-like birds and bird-like scrolls which had been drawn with soap upon the mirrors back of the bar.

"Well, I guess I'll take another drink," said the Swede presently. "Have something?"

"No, thanks; I'm not drinkin'," answered the bartender. Afterward he asked: "How did you hurt your face?"

The Swede immediately began to boast loudly. "Why, in a fight. I thumped the soul out of a man down here at Scully's hotel."

The interest of the four men at the table was at last aroused.

"Who was it?" said one.

"Johnnie Scully," blustered the Swede. "Son of the man what runs it. He will be pretty near dead for some weeks, I can tell you. I made a nice thing of him, I did. He couldn't get up. They carried him in the house. Have a drink?"

Instantly the men in some subtle way incased themselves in reserve. "No, thanks," said one. The group was of curious formation. Two were prominent local business men; one was the district-attorney; and one was a professional gambler of the kind known as "square." But a scrutiny of the group would not have enabled an observer to pick the gambler from the men of more reputable pursuits. He was, in fact, a man so delicate in manner, when among people of fair class, and so judicious in his choice of victims, that in the strictly masculine part of the town's life he had come to be explicitly trusted and admired. People called him a thoroughbred. The fear and contempt with which his craft was regarded was undoubtedly the reason that his quiet dignity shone conspicuous above the quiet dignity of men who might be merely hatters, billiard markers or grocery clerks. Beyond an occasional unwary traveler, who came by rail, this gambler was supposed to prey solely upon reckless and senile farmers, who, when flush with good crops, drove into town in all the pride and confidence of an absolutely invulnerable stupidity. Hearing at times in circuitous fashion of the despoilment of such a farmer, the important men of Romper invariably laughed in contempt of the victim, and if they thought of the wolf at all, it was with a kind of pride at the knowledge that he would never dare think of attacking their wisdom and courage. Besides, it was popular that this gambler had a real wife, and two real children in a neat cottage in a suburb, where he led an exemplary home life, and when any one even suggested a discrepancy in his character, the crowd immediately vociferated descriptions of this virtuous family circle. Then men who led exemplary home lives, and men who did not lead exemplary home lives, all subsided in a bunch, remarking that there was nothing more to be said.

However, when a restriction was placed upon him—as, for instance, when a strong clique of members of the new Pollywog Club refused to permit him, even as a spectator, to appear in the rooms of the organization—the candor and gentleness with which he accepted the judgment disarmed many of his foes and made his friends more desperately partisan. He invariably distinguished between himself and a respectable Romper man so quickly and frankly that his manner actually appeared to be a continual broadcast compliment.

And one must not forget to declare the fundamental fact of his entire position in Romper. It is irrefutable that in all affairs outside of his business, in all matters that occur eternally and commonly between man and man, this thieving card-player was so generous, so just, so moral, that, in a contest, he could have put to flight the consciences of nine-tenths of the citizens of Romper.

And so it happened that he was seated in this saloon with the two prominent local merchants and the district-attorney.

The Swede continued to drink raw whisky, meanwhile babbling at the barkeeper and trying to induce him to indulge in potations. "Come on. Have a drink. Come on. What—no? Well, have a little one then. By gawd, I've whipped a man to-night, and I want to celebrate. I whipped him good, too. Gentlemen," the Swede cried to the men at the table, "have a drink?"

"Ssh!" said the barkeeper.

The group at the table, although furtively attentive, had been pretending to be deep in talk, but now a man lifted his eyes toward the Swede and said shortly: "Thanks. We don't want any more."

At this reply the Swede ruffled out his chest like a rooster. "Well," he exploded, "it seems I can't get anybody to drink with me in this town. Seems so, don't it? Well!"

"Ssh!" said the barkeeper.

"Say," snarled the Swede, "don't you try to shut me up. I won't have it. I'm a gentleman, and I want people to drink with me. And I want 'em to drink with me now. Now—do you understand?" He rapped the bar with his knuckles.

Years of experience had calloused the bartender. He merely grew sulky. "I hear you," he answered.

"Well," cried the Swede, "listen hard then. See those men over there? Well, they're going to drink with me, and don't you forget it. Now you watch."

"Hi!" yelled the barkeeper, "this won't do!"

"Why won't it?" demanded the Swede. He stalked over to the table, and by chance laid his hand upon the shoulder of the gambler. "How about this?" he asked, wrathfully. "I asked you to drink with me."

The gambler simply twisted his head and spoke over his shoulder. "My friend, I don't know you."

"Oh, hell!" answered the Swede, "come and have a drink."

"Now, my boy," advised the gambler kindly, "take your hand off my shoulder and go 'way and mind your own business." He was a little slim man, and it seemed strange to hear him use this tone of heroic patronage to the burly Swede. The other men at the table said nothing.

"What? You won't drink with me, you little dude! I'll make you then! I'll make you!" The Swede had grasped the gambler frenziedly at the throat, and was dragging him from his chair. The other men sprang up. The barkeeper dashed around the corner of his bar. There was a great tumult, and then was seen a long blade in the hand of the gambler. It shot forward, and a human body, this citadel of virtue, wisdom, power, was pierced as easily as if it had been a melon. The Swede fell with a cry of supreme astonishment.

The prominent merchants and the district-attorney must have at once tumbled out of the place backward. The bartender found himself hanging limply to the arm of a chair and gazing into the eyes of a murderer.

"Henry," said the latter, as he wiped his knife on one of the towels that hung beneath the bar-rail, "you tell 'em where to find me. I'll be home, waiting for 'em." Then he vanished. A moment afterward the barkeeper was in the street dinning through the storm for help, and, moreover, companionship.

The corpse of the Swede, alone in the saloon, had its eyes fixed upon a dreadful legend that dwelt a-top of the cash-machine. "This registers the amount of your purchase."

IX

Months later, the cowboy was frying pork over the stove of a little ranch near the Dakota line, when there was a quick thud of hoofs outside, and, presently, the Easterner entered with the letters and the papers.

"Well," said the Easterner at once, "the chap that killed the Swede has got three years. Wasn't much, was it?"

"He has? Three years?" The cowboy poised his pan of pork, while he ruminated upon the news. "Three years. That ain't much."

"No. It was a light sentence," replied the Easterner as he unbuckled his spurs. "Seems there was a good deal of sympathy for him in Romper."

"If the bartender had been any good," observed the cowboy thoughtfully, "he would have gone in and cracked that there Dutchman on the head with a bottle in the beginnin' of it and stopped all this here murderin'."

"Yes, a thousand things might have happened," said the Easterner tartly.

The cowboy returned his pan of pork to the fire, but his philosophy continued. "It's funny, ain't it? If he hadn't said Johnnie was cheatin' he'd be alive this minute. He was an awful fool. Game played for fun, too. Not for money. I believe he was crazy."

"I feel sorry for that gambler," said the Easterner.

"Oh, so do I," said the cowboy. "He don't deserve none of it for killin' who he did."

"The Swede might not have been killed if everything had been square."

"Might not have been killed?" exclaimed the cowboy. "Everythin' square? Why, when he said that Johnnie was cheatin' and acted like such a jackass? And then in the saloon he fairly walked up to git hurt?" With these arguments the cowboy browbeat the Easterner and reduced him to rage.

"You're a fool!" cried the Easterner viciously. "You're a bigger jackass than the Swede by a million majority. Now let me tell you one thing. Let me tell you something. Listen! Johnnie was cheating!"

"Johnnie," said the cowboy blankly. There was a minute of silence, and then he said robustly: "Why, no. The game was only for fun."

"Fun or not," said the Easterner, "Johnnie was cheating. I saw him. I know it. I saw him. And I refused to stand up and be a man. I let the Swede fight it out alone. And you—you were simply puffing around the place and wanting to fight. And then old Scully himself! We are all in it! This poor gambler isn't even a noun. He is kind of an adverb. Every sin is the result of a collaboration. We, five of us, have collaborated in the murder of this Swede. Usually there are from a dozen to forty women really involved in every murder, but in this case it seems to be only five men—you, I, Johnnie, old Scully, and that fool of an unfortunate gambler came merely as a culmination, the apex of a human movement, and gets all the punishment."

The cowboy, injured and rebellious, cried out blindly into this fog of mysterious theory. "Well, I didn't do anythin', did I?"

Comments

The action of "The Blue Hotel" covers a brief time segment (two days) and one location (one town, two taverns), and it is easy to visualize it as a play. Unlike "Father Sergius," it's dramatically concentrated in time and space. There are clear scenes on a limited stage. We have already analyzed the generating force of the story—motivation. Rather than desire, it is fear. The plot is a projection of a character's mind in conflict with the setting.

This story is instructive as well, and I have relied on it to illustrate scene-making, various usages of vividly drawn setting, and character clashing with the setting. It's classically well-structured, evolving out of the major elements of fiction in synergy. The setting prepares the conflict, which arises from the main character's psychology in interaction with the setting and other characters who are rooted in the setting. The conflict leads to a climactic action, which in turn leads to the resolution, in the form of another climax and revelation. The shape of the plot is that of a double-humped camel, which I think is perhaps just as common as the sinusoid plot graph, and usually more effective, as it reflects a major plot turn and surprise.

We have already discussed many aspects of this story, and therefore, it's useful to include the entire story here so you can see for yourself how it works. On rereading the story, I am struck by how well the plot proceeds from the character's mind. The character is not simply stuck in the precooked scheme of events—the danger with much genre fiction is that the players are simply used to fill in a slot. Here, even though the story is a genre story, a Western, with a strong plot and lot going on, we have also an evolved character, the whole ensemble of elements working together, no lip sync.

Suggestion for a Writing Experiment

One potential exercise, and not necessarily simply an exercise, but a serious work, is to write a genre story, a Western or war story or horror story, with well-drawn characters. The important thing is to make the motivation clear and strong, and to make the events stem from the character's struggle to realize his motives (if it's fear, to avoid what he fears). In "The Blue Hotel," the pervasive suspicion becomes fear, and fear drives the actions of the "hero" and the consequent events and plot.

THE MONKEY GARDEN
by Sandra Cisneros

The monkey doesn't live there anymore. The monkey moved—to Kentucky—and took his people with him. And I was glad because I couldn't listen anymore to his wild screaming at night, the twangy yakkety-yak of the people who owned him. The green metal cage, the porcelain table top, the family that spoke like guitars. Monkey, family, table. All gone.

And it was then we took over the garden we had been afraid to go into when the monkey screamed and showed its yellow teeth.

There were sunflowers big as flowers on Mars and thick cockscombs bleeding the deep red fringe of theater curtains. There were dizzy bees and bow-tied fruit flies turning somersaults and humming in the air. Sweet sweet peach trees. Thorn roses and thistle and pears. Weeds like so many squinty-eyed stars and brush that made your ankles itch and itch until you washed with soap and water. There were big green apples hard as knees. And everywhere the sleepy smell of rotting wood, damp earth and dusty hollyhocks thick and perfumy like the blue-blond hair of the dead.

Yellow spiders ran when we turned rocks over and pale worms blind and afraid of light rolled over in their sleep. Poke a stick in the sandy soil and a few blue-skinned beetles would appear, an avenue of ants, so many crusty lady bugs. This was a garden, a wonderful thing to look at in the spring. But bit by bit, after the monkey left, the garden began to take over itself. Flowers stopped obeying the little bricks that kept them from growing beyond their paths. Weeds mixed in. Dead cars appeared overnight like mushrooms. First one and then another and then a pale blue pickup with the front windshield missing. Before you knew it, the monkey garden became filled with sleepy cars.

Things had a way of disappearing in the garden, as if the garden itself ate them, or, as if with its old-man memory, it put them away and forgot them. Nenny found a dollar and a dead mouse between two rocks in the stone wall where the morning glories climbed, and once when we were playing hide-and-seek, Eddie Vargas laid his head beneath a hibiscus tree and fell asleep there like a Rip Van Winkle until somebody remembered he was in the game and went to look for him.

This, I supposed, was the reason why we went there. Far away from where our mothers could find us. We and a few old dogs who lived inside the empty cars. We made a clubhouse once on the back of that old blue pickup. And besides, we liked to jump from the roof of one car to another and pretend they were giant mushrooms.

Somebody started the lie that the monkey garden had been there before anything. We liked to think the garden could hide things for a thousand years. There beneath the roots of soggy flowers were the bones of murdered pirates and dinosaurs, the eye of a unicorn turned to coal.

This is where I wanted to die and where I tried one day but not even the monkey garden would have me. It was the last day I would go there.

Who was it that said I was getting too old to play the games? Who was it I didn't listen to? I only remember that when the others ran, I wanted to run too, up and down and through the monkey garden, fast as the boys, not like Sally who screamed if she got her stockings muddy.

I said, Sally, come on, but she wouldn't. She stayed by the curb talking to Tito and his friends. Play with the kids if you want, she said, I'm staying here. She could be stuck-up like that if she wanted to, so I just left.

It was her own fault too. When I got back Sally was pretending to be mad ... something about the boys having stolen her keys. Please give them back to me, she said, punching the nearest one with a soft fist. They were laughing. She was too. It was a joke I didn't get.

I wanted to go back with the other kids who were still jumping on cars, still chasing each other through the garden, but Sally had her own game.

One of the boys invented the rules. One of Tito's friends said you can't get the keys back unless you kiss us and Sally pretended to be mad at first but she said yes. It was that simple.

I don't know why, but something inside me wanted to throw a stick. Something wanted to say no when I watched Sally going into the garden with Tito's buddies all grinning. It was just a kiss, that's all. A kiss for each one. So what, she said.

Only how come I felt angry inside. Like something wasn't right. Sally went behind that old blue pickup to kiss the boys and get her keys back, and I ran up the three flights of stairs to where Tito lived. His mother was ironing shirts. She was sprinkling water on them from an empty pop bottle and smoking a cigarette.

Your son and his friends stole Sally's keys and now they won't give them back unless she kisses them and right now they're making her kiss them, I said all out of breath from the three flights of stairs.

Those kids, she said, not looking up from her ironing.

That's all?

What do you want me to do, she said, call the cops? And kept on ironing.

I looked at her a long time, but couldn't think of anything to say, and ran back down the three flights to the garden where Sally needed to be saved. I took three big sticks and a brick and figured this was enough.

But when I got there Sally said go home. Those boys said leave us alone. I felt stupid with my brick. They all looked at me as if I was the one that was crazy and made me feel ashamed.

And then I don't know why but I had to run away. I had to hide myself at the other end of the garden, in the jungle part, under a tree that wouldn't mind if I lay down and cried a long time. I closed my eyes like tight stars so that I wouldn't, but I did. My face felt hot. Everything inside hiccupped.

I read somewhere in India there are priests who can will their heart to stop beating. I wanted to will my blood to stop, my heart to quit its pumping. I wanted to be dead, to turn into the rain, my eyes melt into the ground like two black snails. I wished and wished. I closed my eyes and willed it, but when I got up my dress was green and I had a headache.

I looked at my feet in their white socks and ugly round shoes. They seemed far away. They didn't seem to be my feet anymore. And the garden that had been such a good place to play didn't seem mine either.

Comments

This is another story stemming from childhood experiences and observations. The setting is drawn with poetic care and flair. Like "We Didn't," the story crosses genres between prose-poem and short story. "There were sunflowers big as flowers on Mars and thick cockscombs bleeding the deep red fringe of theater curtains." What a description for color! "And everywhere the sleepy smell of rotting wood, damp earth and dusty hollyhocks thick and perfumy like the blue-blond hair of the dead." Our senses are provoked here—smell, touch (*damp, dusty*), sight. And there are lots of sounds, starting with the "twangy yakkety-yak" of the people who owned the monkey. With these enchantingly vivid descriptions, we are invited to live in the garden for the duration of the story.

The narrator, a girl, observes the playground with curiosity and wonder. She is too old to play childhood games and too young to play with the boys, unlike her pal Sally, and left out, she grows fearful of the adult games the boys and girls play in the junked cars and perhaps jealous, feeling left out and terrified.

The voice of the narrator is convincingly childlike. The story comes out of the collection *The House on Mango Street*, in which the main character, Esperanza, goes through a variety of experiences, and in other stories, there's a lot of Spanish, Spanglish. But not in this one, although the echoes from the other stories still somehow create that sound in the background. This is an example of how connected short stories can work almost as a novel.

There are many spectacular word choices in the story, which could provide many illustrations for *le mot juste* ideology of writing. So the assignment here is to read slowly, and to identify interesting word choices, metaphors, likenesses. Although nothing strange occurs in the story, there's a sensation of magical realism here.

Suggestion for a Writing Experiment

Describe lavishly and poetically a setting where kids play—a park, a garden, or a street—and set some kind of conflict there. It could be a little gang warfare with other kids who appear, or it could be a story about some kind of injury (whether psychological or physical) in this location, from a child's POV. You can bring some magic to the story through a sensation of a child's wonder—perceiving the details vividly, even metaphorically.

WE DIDN'T
by Stuart Dybek

We did it in front of the mirror
And in the light. We did it in darkness,
In water, and in the high grass.

—Yehuda Amichai, "We Did It"

We didn't in the light; we didn't in the darkness. We didn't in the fresh-cut summer grass or in the mounds of autumn leaves or on the snow where moonlight threw down our shadows. We didn't in your room on the canopy bed you slept in, the bed you'd slept in as a child, or in the backseat of my father's rusted Rambler, which smelled of the smoked chubs and kielbasa he delivered on weekends from my uncle Vincent's meat market. We didn't in your mother's Buick Eight, where your rosary twined the rearview mirror like a beaded, black snake with silver, cruciform fangs.

At the dead end of our lovers' lane—a side street of abandoned factories— where I perfected the pinch that springs open a bra; behind the lilac bushes in Marquette Park, where you first touched me through my jeans, and your nipples, swollen against transparent cotton, seemed the shade of lilacs; in the balcony of the now defunct Clark Theater, where I wiped popcorn salt from my palms and slid them up your thighs and you whispered, "I feel like Doris Day is watching us," we didn't.

How adept we were at fumbling, how perfectly mistimed our timing, how utterly we confused energy with ecstasy.

Remember that night becalmed by heat, and the two of us, fused by sweat, trembling as if a wind from outer space that only we could feel was gusting across Oak Street Beach? Entwined in your faded Navajo blanket, we lay soul-kissing until you wept with wanting.

We'd been kissing all day—all summer—kisses tasting of different shades of lip gloss and too many Cokes. The lake had turned hot pink, rose rapture, pear amethyst with dusk, then washed in the night black with a ruff of silver foam. Beyond a momentary horizon, silent bolts of heat lightning throbbed, perhaps setting barns on fire somewhere in Indiana. The beach that had been so crowded was deserted as if there was a curfew. Only the bodies of lovers remained, visible in lightning flashes, scattered like the fallen on a battlefield, a few of them moaning, waiting for the gulls to pick them clean.

On my fingers your slick scent mixed with the coconut musk of the suntan lotion we'd repeatedly smeared over each other's bodies. When your bikini top fell away, my hand caught your breasts, memorizing their delicate weight, my palms cupped as if bringing water to parched lips.

Along the Gold Coast, high-rises began to glow, window added to window, against the dark. In every lighted bedroom, couples home from work were stripping off their business suits, falling to the bed, and doing it. They did it before mirrors and pressed against the glass in streaming shower stalls; they did it against walls and on furniture in ways that required previously unimagined gymnastics, which they invented on the spot. They did it in honor of man and woman, in honor of beast, in honor of God. They did it because they'd been released, because they were home free, alive, and private, because they couldn't wait any longer, couldn't wait for the appointed hour, for the right time or temperature, couldn't wait for the future, for Messiahs, for peace on earth and justice for all. They did it because of the Bomb, because of pollution, because of the Four Horsemen of the Apocalypse, because extinction might be just a blink away. They did it because it was Friday night. It was Friday night and somewhere delirious music was playing—flutter-tongued flutes, muted trumpets meowing like cats in heat, feverish plucking and twanging, tom-toms, congas, and gongs all pounding the same pulsebeat.

I stripped your bikini bottom down the skinny rails of your legs, and you tugged my swimsuit past my tan. Swimsuits at our ankles, we kicked like swimmers to free our legs, almost expecting a tide to wash over us the way the tide rushes in on Burt Lancaster and Deborah Kerr in *From Here to Eternity*—a love scene so famous that although neither of us had seen the movie, our bodies assumed the exact position of movie stars on the sand and you whispered to me softly, "I'm afraid of getting pregnant," and I whispered back, "Don't worry, I have protection," then, still kissing you, felt for my discarded cutoffs and the wallet in which for the last several months I had carried a Trojan as if it was a talisman. Still kissing, I tore the flattened, dried-out wrapper, and it sprang through my fingers like a spring from a clock and dropped to the sand between our legs. My hands were shaking. In a panic, I groped for it, found it, tried to dust it off, tried as Burt Lancaster never had to, to slip it on without breaking the mood, felt the grains of sand inside it, a throb of lightning, and the Great Lake behind us became, for all practical purposes, the Pacific, and your skin tasted of salt and to the insistent question that my hips were asking your body answered yes, your thighs opened like wings from my waist as we surfaced panting from a kiss that left you pleading Oh, Christ yes, a yes gasped sharply as a cry of pain so that for a moment I thought that we were already doing it and that somehow I had missed the instant when I entered you, entered you in the bloodless way in which a young man discards his own virginity, entered you as if passing through a gateway in to the rest of my life, into a life as I wanted it to be lived yes but Oh then I realized that we were still floundering unconnected in the slick between us and there was sand in the Trojan as we slammed together still feeling for that perfect fit, still in the Here groping for an Eternity that was only a fine adjustment away, just a millimeter to the left or a fraction of an inch farther south though with all the adjusting the sandy Trojan was slipping off and then it was gone but yes you kept repeating although your head was shaking no-not-quite-almost and our hearts were going like mad and you said, Yes. Yes wait ... Stop!

"What?" I asked, still futilely thrusting as if I hadn't quite heard you.

"Oh. God!" You gasped, pushing yourself up. "What's coming?"

"Gin, what's the matter?" I asked, confused, and then the beam of a spotlight swept over us and I glanced into its blinding eye.

All around us lights were coming, speeding across the sand. Blinking blindness away, I rolled from your body to my knees, feeling utterly defenseless in the way that only nakedness can leave one feeling. Headlights bounded toward us, spotlights crisscrossing, blue dome lights revolving as squad cars converged. I could see other lovers, caught in the beams, fleeing bare-assed through the litter of garbage that daytime hordes had left behind and that the night had deceptively concealed. You were crying, clutching the Navajo blanket to your breasts with one hand and clawing for your bikini with the other, and I was trying to calm your terror with reassuring phrases such as "Holy shit! I don't fucking believe this!"

Swerving and fishtailing in the sand, police calls pouring from their radios, the squad cars were on us, and then they were by us while we struggled to pull on our clothes.

They braked at the water's edge, and cops slammed out, brandishing huge flashlights, their beams deflecting over the dark water. Beyond the darting of those beams, the far-off throbs of lightning seemed faint by comparison.

"Over there, goddamn it!" one of them hollered, and two cops sloshed out into the shallow water without even pausing to kick off their shoes, huffing aloud for breath, their leather cartridge belts creaking against their bellies.

"Grab the sonofabitch! It ain't gonna bite!" one of them yelled, then they came sloshing back to shore with a body slung between them.

It was a woman—young, naked, her body limp and bluish beneath the play of the flashlight beams. They set her on the sand just past the ring of drying, washed up alewives. Her face was almost totally concealed by her hair. Her hair was brown and tangled in a way that even wind or sleep can't tangle hair, tangled as if it had absorbed the ripples of water—thick strands, slimy-looking like dead seaweed.

"She's been in there awhile, that's for sure," a cop with a beer belly said to a younger, crew-cut cop, who had knelt beside the body and removed his hat as if he might be considering the kiss of life.

The crew-cut officer brushed the hair away from her face, and the flashlight beams settled there. Her eyes were closed. A bruise or a birthmark stained the side of one eye. Her features appeared swollen, her lower lip protruding as if she was pouting.

An ambulance siren echoed across the sand, its revolving red light rapidly approaching.

"Might as well take their sweet-ass time," the beer-bellied cop said.

We had joined the circle of police surrounding the drowned woman without realizing that we had. You were back in your bikini, robed in the Navajo blanket, and I had slipped on my cutoffs, my underwear dangling out of a back pocket.

Their flashlight beams explored her body, causing its whiteness to gleam. Her breasts were floppy; her nipples looked shriveled. Her belly appeared inflated by gallons of water. For a moment, a beam focused on her mound of pubic hair, which was overlapped by the swell of her belly, and then moved almost shyly down her legs, and the cops all glanced at us—at you, especially—above their lights, and you hugged your blanket closer as if they might confiscate it as evidence or to use as a shroud.

When the ambulance pulled up, one of the black attendants immediately put a stethoscope to the drowned woman's swollen belly and announced, "Drowned the baby, too."

Without saying anything, we turned from the group, as unconsciously as we'd joined them, and walked off across the sand, stopping only long enough at the spot where we had lain together like lovers, in order to stuff the rest of our gear into a beach bag, to gather our shoes, and for me to find my wallet and kick sand over the forlorn, deflated Trojan that you pretended not to notice. I was grateful for that.

Behind us, the police were snapping photos, flashbulbs throbbing like lightning flashes, and the lightning itself, still distant but moving closer, rumbling audibly now, driving a lake wind before it so that gusts of sand tingled against the metal sides of the ambulance.

Squinting, we walked toward the lighted windows of the Gold Coast, while the shadows of gapers attracted by the whirling emergency lights hurried past us toward the shore.

"What happened? What's going on?" they asked without waiting for an answer, and we didn't offer one, just continued walking silently in the dark.

It was only later that we talked about it, and once we began talking about the drowned woman it seemed we couldn't stop.

"She was pregnant," you said. "I mean, I don't want to sound morbid, but I can't help thinking how the whole time we were almost—you know—there was this poor, dead woman and her unborn child washing in and out behind us."

"It's not like we could have done anything for her even if we had known she was there."

"But what if we had found her? What if after we had—you know," you said, your eyes glancing away from mine and your voice tailing into a whisper, "what if after we did it, we went for a night swim and found her in the water?"

"But, Gin, we didn't," I tried to reason, though it was no more a matter of reason that anything else between us had ever been.

It began to seem as if each time we went somewhere to make out—on the back porch of your half-deaf, whiskery Italian grandmother, who sat in the front of the apartment cackling at *I Love Lucy* reruns; or in your girlfriend Tina's basement rec room when her parents were away on bowling league nights and Tina was upstairs with her current crush, Brad; or way off in the burbs, at the Giant Twin Drive-In during the weekend they called Elvis Fest—the drowned woman was with us.

We would kiss, your mouth would open, and when your tongue flicked repeatedly after mine, I would unbutton the first button of your blouse, revealing the beauty spot at the base of your throat, which matched a smaller spot I loved above the corner of your lips, and then the second button, which opened on a delicate gold cross—which I had always tried to regard as merely a fashion statement—dangling above the cleft of your breasts. The third button exposed the lacy swell of your bra, and I would slide my hand over the patterned mesh, feeling for the firmness of your nipple rising to my fingertip, but you would pull slightly away, and behind your rapid breath your kiss would grow distant, and I would kiss harder, trying to lure you back from wherever you had gone, and finally, holding as if only consoling a friend, I'd ask, "What are you thinking?" although of course I knew.

"I don't want to think about her but I can't help it. I mean, it seems like some kind of weird omen or something, you know?"

"No, I don't know," I said. "It was just a coincidence."

"Maybe if she'd been farther away down the beach, but she was so close to us. A good wave could have washed her up right beside us."

"Great, then we could have had a ménage à trois."

"Gross! I don't believe you just said that! Just because you said it in French doesn't make it less disgusting."

"You're driving me to it. Come on, Gin, I'm sorry," I said. "I was just making a dumb joke to get a little different perspective on things."

"What's so goddamn funny about a woman who drowned herself and her baby?"

"We don't even know for sure she did."

"Yeah, right, it was just an accident. Like she just happened to be going for a walk pregnant and naked, and she fell in."

"She could have been on a sailboat or something. Accidents happen; so do murders."

"Oh, like murder makes it less horrible? Don't think that hasn't occurred to me. Maybe the bastard who knocked her up killed her, huh?"

"How should I know? You're the one who says you don't want to talk about it and then gets obsessed with all kinds of theories and scenarios. Why are we arguing about a woman we don't even know, who doesn't have the slightest thing to do with us?"

"I do know about her," you said. "I dream about her."

"You dream about her?" I repeated, surprised. "Dreams you remember?"

"Sometimes they wake me up. In one I'm at my nonna's cottage in Michigan, swimming for a raft that keeps drifting farther away, until I'm too tired to turn back. Then I notice there's a naked person sunning on the raft and start yelling, 'Help!' and she looks up and offers me a hand, but I'm too tired to take it even though I'm drowning because it's her."

"God! Gin, that's creepy."

"I dreamed you and I are at the beach and you bring us a couple hot dogs but forget the mustard, so you have to go all the way back to the stand for it."

"Hot dogs, no mustard—a little too Freudian, isn't it?"

"Honest to God, I dreamed it. You go back for mustard and I'm wondering why you're gone so long, then a woman screams that a kid has drowned and everyone stampedes for the water. I'm swept in by the mob and forced under, and I think, This is it, I'm going to drown, but I'm able to hold my breath longer than I ever thought possible. It feels like a flying dream—flying under water—and then I see this baby down there flying, too, and realize it's the kid everyone thinks has drowned, but he's no more drowned than I am. He looks like Cupid or one of those baby angels that cluster around the face of God."

"Pretty weird. What do you think all the symbols mean?—hot dogs, water, drowning ..."

"It means the baby who drowned inside her that night was a love child—a boy—and his soul was released there to wander through the water."

"You don't really believe that?"

We argued about the drowned woman, about whether her death was a suicide or a murder, about whether her appearance that night was an omen or a coincidence which, you argued, is what an omen is anyway: a coincidence that means something. By the end of summer, even if we were no longer arguing about the woman, we had acquired the habit of arguing about everything else. What was better: dogs or cats, rock or jazz, Cubs or Sox, tacos or egg rolls, right or left, night or day?—we could argue about anything.

It no longer required arguing or necking to summon the drowned woman; everywhere we went she surfaced by her own volition: at Rocky's Italian Beef, at Lindo Mexico, at the House of Dong, our favorite Chinese restaurant, a place we still frequented because when we'd first started seeing each other they had let us sit and talk until late over tiny cups of jasmine tea and broken fortune cookies. We would always kid about going there. "Are you in the mood for Dong tonight?" I'd whisper conspiratorially. It was a dopey joke, meant for you to roll your eyes at its repeated dopiness. Back then, in winter, if one of us ordered garlic shrimp we would both be sure to eat them so that later our mouths tasted the same when we kissed.

Even when she wasn't mentioned, she was there with her drowned body—so dumpy next to yours—and her sad breasts, with their wrinkled nipples and sour milk—so saggy beside yours, which were still budding—with her swollen belly and her pubic bush colorless in the glare of electric light, with her tangled, slimy hair and her pouting, placid face—so lifeless beside yours—and her skin a pallid white, lightning-flash white, flashbulb white, a whiteness that couldn't be duplicated in daylight—how I'd come to hate that pallor, so cold beside the flush of your skin.

There wasn't a particular night when we finally broke up, just as there wasn't a particular night when we began going together, but it was a night in fall when I guessed that it was over. We were parked in the Rambler at the dead end of the street of factories that had been our lover's lane, listening to a drizzle of rain and dry leaves sprinkle the hood. As always, rain revitalized the smells of smoked fish and kielbasa in the upholstery. The radio was on too low to hear, the windshield wipers swished at intervals as if we were driving, and the windows were steamed as if we'd been making out. But we'd been arguing, as usual, this time about a woman poet who had committed suicide, whose work you were reading. We were sitting, no longer talking or touching, and I remember thinking that I didn't want to argue with you anymore. I didn't want to sit like this in hurt silence; I wanted to talk excitedly all night as we once had. I wanted to find some way that wasn't corny sounding to tell you how much fun I'd had in your company, how much knowing you had meant to me, and how I had suddenly realized that I'd been so intent on becoming lovers that I'd overlooked how close we'd been as friends. I wanted you to know that. I wanted you to like me again.

"It's sad," I started to say, meaning that I was sorry we had reached the point of silence, but before I could continue you challenged the statement.

"What makes you so sure it's sad?"

"What do you mean, what makes me so sure?" I asked, confused by your question.

You looked at me as if what was sad was that I would never understand. "For all either of us know," you said, "death could have been her triumph!"

Maybe when it really ended was the night I felt we had just reached the beginning, that one time on the beach in the summer when our bodies rammed so desperately together that for a moment I thought we did it, and maybe in our hearts we did, although for me, then, doing it in one's heart didn't quite count. If it did, I supposed we'd all be Casanovas.

We rode home together on the El train that night, and I felt sick and defeated in a way I was embarrassed to mention. Our mute reflections emerged like negative exposures on the dark, greasy window of the train. Lightning branched over the city, and when the train entered the subway tunnel, the lights inside flickered as if the power was disrupted, though the train continued rocketing beneath the Loop.

When the train emerged again we were on the South Side of the city and it was pouring, a deluge as if the sky had opened to drown the innocent and guilty alike. We hurried from the El station to your house, holding the Navajo blanket over our heads until, soaked, it collapsed. In the dripping doorway of your apartment building, we said good night. You were shivering. Your bikini top showed through the thin blouse plastered to your skin. I swept the wet hair away from your face and kissed you lightly on the lips, then you turned and went inside. I stepped into the rain, and you came back out, calling after me.

"What?" I asked, feeling a surge of gladness to be summoned back to the doorway with you.

"Want an umbrella?"

I didn't. The downpour was letting up. It felt better to walk back to the station feeling the rain rinse the sand out of my hair, off my legs, until the only places where I could still feel its grit were in the crotch of my cutoffs and each squish of my shoes. A block down the street, I passed a pair of jockey shorts lying in a puddle and realized they were mine, dropped from my back pocket as we ran to your house. I left them behind, wondering if you'd see them and recognize them the next day.

By the time I had climbed the stairs back to the El platform, the rain had stopped. Your scent still hadn't washed from my fingers. The station—the entire city it seemed—dripped and steamed. The summer sound of crickets and nighthawks echoed from the drenched neighborhood. Alone, I could admit how sick I felt. For you, it was a night that would haunt your dreams. For me, it was another night when I waited, swollen and aching, for what I had secretly nicknamed the Blue Ball Express.

Literally lovesick, groaning inwardly with each lurch of the train and worried that I was damaged for good, I peered out at the passing yellow-lit stations, where lonely men stood posted before giant advertisements, pictures of glamorous models defaced by graffiti—the same old scrawled insults and pleas: FUCK YOU, EAT ME. At this late hour the world seemed given over to men without women, men waiting in abject patience for something indeterminate, the way I waited for our next times. I avoided their eyes so that they wouldn't see the pity in mine, pity for them because I'd just been with you, your scent was still on my hands, and there seemed to be so much future ahead.

For me it was another night like that, and by the time I reached my stop I knew I would be feeling better, recovered enough to walk the dark street home making up poems of longing that I never wrote down. I was the D.H. Lawrence of not doing it, the voice of all the would-be lovers who ached and squirmed. From our contortions in doorways, on stairwells, and in the bucket seats of cars we could have composed a Kama Sutra of interrupted bliss. It must have been that night when I recalled all the other times of walking home after seeing you, so that it seemed as if I was falling into step behind a parade of my former selves—myself walking home on the night we first kissed, myself on the night when I unbuttoned your blouse and kissed your breasts, myself on the night when I lifted your skirt above your thighs and dropped to my knees—each succeeding self another step closer to that irrevocable moment for which our lives seemed poised.

But we didn't, not in the moonlight, or by the phosphorescent lanterns of lightning bugs in your back yard, not beneath the constellations we couldn't see, let alone decipher, or in the dark glow that replaced the real darkness of night, a darkness already stolen from us, not with the skyline rising behind us while a city gradually decayed, despite the freedom of youth and the license of first love—because of fate, karma, luck, what does it matter?—we made not doing it a wonder, and yet we didn't, we didn't, we never did.

Comments

"We Didn't" is a lyrical story in many ways. The repetition of *we didn't* leading into succeeding paragraphs and into different scenes is a poetic device. The cross-genre approach gives wonderful energy and rhythm to the story—it's a piece of music. The word choices are spun—with lots of imagery. And the voice of the narrator is fresh and local. Moreover, the POV, a mix of "we," "I," and "you," is intimate and immediate. The story reads as an address, me speaking to you (also common in poetry). In some ways this is a long narrative poem, but at the same time it is a murder mystery, and a surprising story. Dybek gives away a bit of the plot and suspense in the title. We know right away that the two protagonists didn't make love, but then we are surprised at how much else they have done.

I have had productive experiences with crossing genres, sometimes unwittingly. Once, I sent a prose poem to a magazine, *Boulevard*, and the editor misplaced my cover letter and published the story as an essay. I didn't object, but smiled at the confusion, for after all it was an essay as well. It got listed as a distinguished one in *Best American Essays*, and I think if I had had it published as a narrative poem, it wouldn't have been noticed because it wouldn't have sounded so unusual. Putting a bit of another genre in your writing, or having an approach from the other genres, can vitalize your writing and make it more interesting not only for you but also for the reader. Out of genre-crossing, now we even have a new genre, the lyrical essay. And of course, we've had the lyrical story, and some people argue that, in so far as a story is good, it is lyrical, and vice versa. Such an ideology might lead to word fetishism, but it's a healthy kind of perversion in writing. After all, what could be regarded as the first novel, a serial, *The Iliad* and *The Odyssey*, is a poem, and a story, and a novel.

Suggestion for a Writing Experiment

Enjoy the story and see whether you can play with crossing genres. Put some poetry into your prose! Or put some prose into your poetry ... whichever way. Some drama into your prose. Some prose into your drama. Be a bit promiscuous with the forms, play dirty. See what happens. Words are there to be enjoyed, admired, savored, not merely used as square bricks.

In a way, the story works almost as an exercise, which we already have in this book. "Start a story with 'My mother never....'" (exercise from teacher James Magnuson). Three Dog Night has a fine song, "Never Been to Spain." I was once denied a visa to Spain because I lived in a communist country, Yugoslavia, and Spain was still run by Franco, who hated Yugoslavia as it provided many guerrilla fighters in the civil war. For a long while, I wanted to write an imaginary travelogue set in Spain, a totally absurd one, but I didn't. Franz Kafka has never been to America, to the best of our knowledge, yet he wrote a novel, *Amerika*, as an absurdist exercise in imagining this strange land of ours. See whether this holds some appeal to you, an experience that didn't happen but could have—and it does, in your imagination.

INDEX

A

Abstraction, describing
without naming, 168
Absurdist humor, 180–181, 187
Action
beginning story with, 136
repeated, character's, 52
Adjectives
and adverbs, 160–161
paring down, 205
Adverbs
and adjectives, 160–161
in dialogue tags, 117, 124
paring down, 205
Aksenov, Vasily, 114
*All Quiet on the Western
Front*, 121
Ancestors, drawing on
stories of, 19
Anecdote, beginning story
with, 139
Animal(s)
description, 165–166
mirroring drama in,
266–277
writing about, and POV,
106–107
Anna Karenina, 65–66
Antagonist
setting as, 30–33
turning into protagonist, 107
vs. protagonist, classic
conflict plots, 66–68
Appearance, character's,
53–55
combined with other
character techniques, 57
Aristotle, 65–66

"The Art of Fiction," 9
"The Artificial Nigger," 57
Artist, story about, 266–277
The Assistant, 113
Atmosphere, mood and,
34–36
Atwood, Margaret, 97
"August 2002: Night Meet-
ing," 93
Autobiographical method, for
creating characters, 48

B

"Ball of Fat," 30–31
Banks, Russell, 97, 159
Bartheleme, Donald, 115
"Basil From Her Garden," 115
"The Beast in the Jungle," 46
Beckett, Samuel, 180–181
Beginnings, 130–140
borrowing from another
writer, 148
exercises, 147–150
matching with endings,
149–150
options for, 134–139
using ending for, 148
Bellow, Saul, 139
Bernhard, Thomas, 25
Bible stories, writing
variations of, 22–23
Bierce, Ambrose, 83, 143–144
Biographical method, for
creating characters,
48–49
Biography, creating fiction
based on, 25
Blog, writing story as, 285

"The Blue Hotel," 46, 122–124,
154–155, 286–309
Body language, 127–128
character, and dialogue,
116–117
*The Book of Laughter and
Forgetting*, 146
Books, as sources of fiction,
19–20
Bowen, Elizabeth, 160
Boyle, T. Coraghessan, 176
Bradbury, Ray, 93
Braverman, Kate, 178–179
"Bread and Blood," 153–154
"The Bride Comes to Yellow
Sky," 75–76
Brontë, Emily, 35–36
Burgess, Anthony, 175
"The Burning Shoe," 14–18,
118–119
Butler, Robert Olen, 12

C

Capote, Truman, 131
Caricature, 182
The Catcher in the Rye,
172–173
"The Celebrated Jumping Frog
of Calaveras County," 173
Céline, Louis-Ferdinand,
174–175
Character portrait
beginning story with, 137
setting as, 38–39
through setting, 43
Character(s)
animal, 266–277
appearance, 53–55

child, 105, 114, 189, 265
combining techniques for, 57–58
creating from idea, 60
depicting body language, 116–117, 127–128
and dialogue, 116–117
different from self, 61
exercises, 58–63
fantasy, describing, 165
as first-person narrator, 88
flat, 47
giving intense emotion to, 23
giving voice to, 112
indistinct, 32
introduction, 45–47
physical description, 59–60, 62
portraying, 51–58
presenting multiple ways, 62
protagonist, turning into antagonist, 107
repeated action or habit, 52
revealed through scene, 55–57
revising, 195
round, 47, 62
and scene, 118
self-portrait, 53
sources of, 48–51
and temptation, 62–63
thoughts, beginning story with, 139
Character-conflict plots, 66–68
Character summary, 51–52
Cheever, John, 120
Chekhov, Anton, 58–59, 103, 139
Child character
speech of, 114
voice of, 189
writing from POV of, 105, 265
Childhood
drawing on, 18
story stemming from, 312
"Children on Their Birthdays," 131
Circular ending, 141–142
Cisneros, Sandra, 43, 310–313
The Citadel, 55
Cliché, 158, 162–164
A Clockwork Orange, 175
Combined POVs, 97, 106
"Community Life," 161, 163–164

"A Composer and His Parakeets," 266–277
Composite scene, 124–125
Computers, revising on, 191
"Concerning Mold Upon the Skin, Etc.," 12
Conflict
character, as basis of plot, 66–68
comedic, 61
and dialogue, 126–127
exploring possibilities of, 80
and scene, 119
traditional types, 67
writing about, 21–22
Conrad, Joseph, 156
Conversation
dialogue as, 111–114
real vs. written, 126
Corriveau, Art, 74–75
"A Country Love Story," 137, 142
Cradle, robbing, for story ideas, 18
Crane, Stephen, 46, 75–76, 122–124, 133–134, 154–155, 286–309
Creation plot, 70
Cronin, A.J., 55
Cynicism, and absurdist humor, 181, 187

D
D'Ambrosio, Charles, 137
de Cervantes, Miguel, 51
de Maupassant, Guy, 30–31, 37, 46, 143, 144, 245–255
"The Dead," 37–38, 68–69
"Dead Possum," 32
Dead Souls, 31, 38–39, 182
Death, character's, 150
"The Death of Ivan Ilych," 102–103
"The Decay of Lying," 183
"The Demon Lover, 160
Description, 151–155, 165–166, 168
character's appearance, 53–55, 59–60, 62
concrete, nouns and, 159–160
emotions, 152–153
exercises, 39–44, 58–60, 62, 165–166, 168
mundane details, 165

objects, 40
places, 40–41
revising, 198
setting, 26–28
unique character, 58–59
Desire
creating fiction around, 23–24
drawing character around, 61–63
Details, mundane, 165
Determination, 6–7
Dialect, 112–114
Dialogue, 110–118
and body language, 116–117, 127–128
and character, 116–117
and conflict, 126–127
as conversation, 111–114
evasive, 128
exercises, 127–129
forms of, 114–115
and information, 117–118
revising, 197–198
and situational comedy, 188
various characters', 127
weaving setting into scenes of, 33–34
written vs. real, 126
Dialogue tags
adverbs in, 117, 124
avoiding, 128
Dickens, Charles, 37, 133, 135
Dogeaters, 135
Dog Years, 35–36
Don Quixote, 51
Dostoyevski, Fyodor, 53, 90
Draft, first, 202–203
Dream journal, 24
Dreams, earliest, 21
Dybek, Stuart, 314–323

E
The Easter Parade, 33–34, 139
"The Eighty-Yard Run," 136
Einstein's Dreams, 92
Eliot, George, 53–54, 92
Emotional experience, writing about, 22
Emotions
accessing, 22–25
describing, 152–153
fleshing out, 205
giving to character, 23

Endings, 140–146
  and beginnings, matching, 149–150
  exercises, 149–150
  matching vs. nonmatching, 142–143
  musing about, 146
  options for, 141–146
  romance novel, 149
  using for beginning, 148
The English Patient, 34
Epiphany, 69
Epistolary fiction, 89–90
  e-mail, 278–285
Erdrich, Louise, 162
Exaggeration, 182

F

Fantasy
  describing character with mundane details, 165
  in first-person POV, 106
"Father Sergius," 207–244
Fathers and Sons, 137–138
Faulkner, William, 89, 98
Fear
  character's, 61–62
  creating fiction around, 23–24
  as motivation, 309
Fiction
  blending with fact, 11–14
  creating from other sources, 20, 23, 25, 83–85
  epistolary, 89–90, 278–285
  fan, 25
  and nonfiction, 10–14
  and painting, similarities between, 27
  setting as groundwork, 28–30
  sources of, 9–14, 18–20
Final draft, plot as guide for, 77
"Firefly," 11
First-person POV, 87–91, 105, 108–109
  child vs. adult, 105
  collective observer, 98–99
  multiple, 89
  primary protagonist and observer, 103–104
  pros and cons, 90–91
  writing fantasy in, 106
Fitzgerald, F. Scott, 134–135
The Fixer, 145, 184

Flashbacks
  necessary, 243
  and scenic characterization method, 56–57
Flaubert, Gustave, 58, 101
Foreshadowing, 125–126
  setting and, 36
Forester, E.M., 100–102
"Forever Overhead," 156
"Four Meetings," 116–117, 160–161

G

Gaitskill, Mary, 69, 158, 161
Gardner, John, 6
Genre fiction
  crossing, 322–323
  "mood," 34–36
Ginzburg, Natalia, 98
"The Girl on the Plane," 69, 158, 161
"The Girls in Their Summer Dresses," 46, 115
Gissing, George, 131
God-Against-Everybody story, 67
Gogol, Nikolai, 9, 31, 38–39, 182
"A Good Man Is Hard to Find," 153
"A Good Scent From a Strange Mountain," 12
The Gospel in Brief, 243
Grass, Günter, 35–36
Grave, robbing, for story ideas, 19
"Great Barrier Reef," 69–70

H

Habit, character's
  combined with other character techniques, 57
  repeated, 52
"The Habit of Loving," 94
Hagedorn, Jessica, 135
"Hair Jewellery," 97
Hamartia, defined, 46
Hard Times, 135
Hardy, Thomas, 54
Heart of Darkness, 156
Hemingway, Ernest, 52, 95–96, 102
Hemley, Robin, 12, 278–285
"Her Real Name," 137
Herodotus, 83–84

Herzog, 139
Heynen, Jim, 32
"Hills Like White Elephants," 95–96, 102
The Histories, 83–84
History, creating fiction from, 23
Horror story, setting, 42
Huckleberry Finn, 87–88, 180
Humor, 278–285
  methods of, 180–184
  in "My Oedipus Complex," 265
  revising, 196
  scene, 61
  substituting opposites as, 182–183, 187–188
  and voice, 179–184, 187–188

I

Idea
  beginning story with, 135
  and image, ending with, 146
Image, and idea, ending with, 146
"In the Ravine," 139
Information, dialogue and, 117–118
Isherwood, Christopher, 55–56, 116

J

James, Henry, 9–10, 46, 116–117, 160–161
Janowitz, Tama, 136
Jin, Ha, 266–277
Johnson, Diane, 69–70
Jones, James, 110
Jönsson, Reidar, 138, 142
Journey
  as plot, 69–70
  story, 82–83
Joyce, James, 37–38, 68, 99, 176–177

K

Kafka, Franz, 142–143
Kingston, Maxine Hong, 19
Kundera, Milan, 95, 146

L

"Lady With the Dog," 103
Language, mixing, and voice, 175, 185

"The Last of Mr. Norris," 116
Laughter in the Dark, 79
Lessing, Doris, 94, 116
"Let the Old Dead Make Room
    for the Young Dead," 95
Lightman, Alan, 92
Little Dorrit, 133
"Little Whale, Varnisher of
    Reality," 114
London, Jack, 31
Lonesome Dove, 147
The Loser, 25
Love, writing about, 24–25
Love Medicine, 162
Love story, combining points
    of view in, 106

M

Macrorevision, 193–198
Madame Bovary, 58, 101–102
"Mademoiselle Fifi," 37, 144,
    245–255
Mahfouz, Naguib, 146
Mailer, Norman, 113
"Main Street Morning," 96
Malamud, Bernard, 113, 145, 184
Man-Against-God story, 67
Man-Against-Machine story, 67
Man-Against-Man story, 67
Man-Against-Nature story,
    31, 67
    describing setting, 41–42
Man-Against-Self story, 67
Man-Against-Society story, 67
Mansfield, Katherine, 136
*Many Things Have Happened
    Since He Died*, 173–174
Márquez, Gabriel García,
    121–122, 151
"The Marquise of O--," 132
"Marriage a la Mode," 136
Mason, Bobbie Ann, 56
The Mayor of Casterbridge, 54
McMurtry, Larry, 147
"The Metamorphosis," 142–143
Metaphor(s), 161–162, 168
    building story from, 13
    examining, 204–205
    revising, 198
    voice as, 170–171
Michael Kohlhaas, 46–47, 132
Microrevision, 198–200, 205
Midaq Alley, 146
Middlemarch, 53–54, 92

Mishima, Yukio, 54
Mixed method, for creating
    characters, 49–51
Molloy, 180–181
"The Monkey Garden," 43–44,
    310–313
Mood
    and atmosphere, 34–36
    setting through descrip-
    tion, 42–43
Moore, Lorrie, 161, 163–164
"Mother," 98
Motivation
    beginning story with sense
    of, 136
    desire, 23–24, 61
    fear, 309
    temptation, 62–63
Multiple point of view, third-
    person, 95
Murder mystery
    parodying, 81–82
    time sequence in, 72
My Life as a Dog, 138–139, 142
"My Oedipus Complex," 256–265

N

Nabokov, Vladimir, 79
The Naked and the Dead,
    113–114
Narrator
    major or minor character, 88
    reliability of, 90, 105
"The Necklace, 46, 143
New Grub Street, 131
Nonconfrontational plots,
    68–70
Nonfiction, and fiction,
    10–14
Normance, 174–175
Notes From Underground, 53, 90
Nouns
    concrete, 167
    and description, 159–160
    using verbs as, 167
Novel, plot of, vs. short-story
    plot, 77–79
Novelette
    defined, 77
    "Father Sergius," 207–244
Novella, defined, 77

O

Oates, Joyce Carol, 52

Objective POV, 95–96
    third-person, 93, 108
O'Brien, Edna, 87
O'Brien, Tim, 159–160
Obscenities, 114
Observations, describing,
    20–21
O'Connor, Flannery, 57, 153
O'Connor, Frank, 256–265
"An Occurrence at Owl Creek
    Bridge," 83, 143–144
"The Old Forest," 71, 161
Ondaatje, Michael, 34
One Hundred Years of Solitude,
    121–122
Open ending, 144–145
Oral tradition, 14–18
Our Mutual Friend, 37
Outline
    to contrast beginning and
    ending, 150
    plot, 79–80, 82, 85, 203
"Overcoat," 9
"O Youth and Beauty!" 120

P

Painting, and fiction,
    similarities between, 27
Parody, existing plots, 75–76,
    81–82
Patesch, Natalie M., 96
"Patriotism," 54
Personality type,
    portraying, 62
Perspective, and setting, 42–43
Place
    describing, 40–41
    exotic, 31–32
Plot(s)
    borrowing, 83–85
    character-conflict, 66–68
    and character's psychol-
    ogy, 309
    combination, 70–71
    exercises, 80–86
    expressing simply, 82
    as guide for final draft, 77
    how to generate, 73–77
    introduction to, 64–65
    logical and chronologi-
    cal, 243
    nonconfrontational, 68–70
    novel vs. short-story, 77–79
    origins and types, 65–71

parodying existing, 75–76, 81–82
vs. plot outline, 79–80
revising, 194
and scene, 118
and time sequence, 71–73
Plot outlines, 79–80, 82, 85
comparing with draft, 203
Plot summary, 82
Poetic device, 322–323
Point of view
combining types, 97, 106
exercises, 103–109
in "Father Sergius," 244
learning to see from others', 107
objective, 95–96, 108
omniscient, 91–93, 104
revising, 195–196
second-person, 109
shifting, 100–103
switching between, 107–108
unusual types, 96–100
virtual shift, 103
and writing about animals, 106–107
Point of view, first-person, 87–91, 105, 108–109
child vs. adult, 105
writing fantasy in, 106
Point of view, third-person, 91–96, 106
objective, subjective, and limited, 108–109
subjective, 104
A Portrait of the Artist as a Young Man, 176–177
Prediction, beginning story with, 139
Protagonist
turning antagonist into, 107
vs. antagonist, classic conflict plots, 66–68
Psychological theme, selecting details around, 61–62
Punctuation, and voice, 174–175
Pushkin, Alexander, 138

Q
"The Queen of Spades," 138
Question, beginning story with, 137–138
Questionnaire, character, 50

Quotes, using, 147–148

R
"The Real Thing," 116
The Red Badge of Courage, 133–134
Remarque, Erich Maria, 121
"Reply All," 278–285
Revelation plot, 68–69
Revision
checklist, 194–198
exercises, 202–206
introduction to, 190–191
macrorevision, 193–198
microrevision, 198–200, 205
when to stop, 200–202
Rewrite, first, 191–193
Richard, Mark, 12
Romance
ending for, 149
opening, 147
parodying, 81–82
"A Rose for Emily," 98
"Rust," 29–30, 45–46

S
Salinger, J.D., 172–173
"Sally Bowles," 55–56
"Sarah Cole: A Type of Love Story," 97, 159
Scene(s), 118–124
beginning story with, 138
big, 119–124
climax, 125–126
comic, 61
composite, 124–125
constructing, from fight, 21–22
exercises, 124–126
introducing character in, 55–57
lovemaking, 125
major and minor, connecting, 203
preparing for major, 119–121
revising, 197–198
silent, 121–122
war, 125
well-constructed, 309
writing from glimpse, 20
Scott, Joanna, 12
Second-person POV, 96–97
combined with first-person, 109

Self-portrait, 53
Sensations
building story from, 13
strong, beginning story with, 135
Senses
describing, 166
engaging, 312
insinuating and foreshadowing through, 125–126
Setting
actively leading into, 1417
as alpha and omega, 36–38
as antagonist, 30–33
beginning story with, 134–135
as character portrait, 38–39
creating mood through, 42–43
describing vividly and quickly, 26–28
exercises, 39–44
and foreshadowing, 36
as groundwork of fiction, 28–30
introduction to, 26
real or imagined, 28
revising, 195
for special effects, 33–39
Sex, beginning story with, 136
Sex scene, 125
Shaw, Irwin, 46, 115, 136
Shifting POVs, 100–103
"Shiloh," 56
Short story
exercises, 82
plot of, vs. novel plot, 77–79
Showing, vs. telling
character, 51–52
scene, 125
Silko, Leslie, 158
Similes, 161–162, 168
Simon, Claude, 9–10
"Sister Imelda," 87
Situational humor, 184, 188
Slapstick humor, 182, 188–189
Slaves of New York, 136
Slice of life, 68
Soto, Gary, 158
The Sound and the Fury, 89
Special effects, setting for, 33–39
Speech, child's, 114
"Spring Storm," 164

Stafford, Jean, 137, 142
Stereotypes, 182
Story(ies)
  autobiographical, in third-person limited POV, 106
  crisis point of, 81
  defined, 77
  finding seed of, 9–14, 18–20
  telling verbally, 204
  writing first draft, 202–203
  writing variations of, 205–206
Story ideas, exercises for generating, 20–25
Stream of consciousness, 99–100
Struggle, internal and external, 62–63
Subject matter, and voice, 177–179
Subjective POV, third-person, 93–94, 104–105, 107–109
Summary
  character, 51–52
  combined with habit and appearance, as character technique, 57
  plot, 82
Summary ending, 144
The Sun Also Rises, 52–53
Surprise ending, 143, 150
Suspense, 125–126
Symbols, 164–165
  beginning story with, 136–137
Syntax
  maximalist, 176
  playing with, 176–177, 184–185
  simple, 178, 187

T
"Tall Tales From the Mekong Delta," 178–179
Taylor, Peter, 71, 161
Temptation, character's resistance to, 62–63
Tender Is the Night, 134–135
Theme
  freedom, 74
  psychological, selecting details around, 61–62
  variations on other writers', 19–20, 22–23
  working from, 86
The Things They Carried, 159–160
Third-person narrative voices, 176–177
Third-person POV, 91–96
  limited, 93–95, 106
  limited omniscient, 93–95, 104
  multiple, 95
  objective, 108–109
  omniscient, 91–93, 104
  plural observer, 98
  subjective, 93–94, 104–105, 107–109
Thoughts, character's, beginning story with, 139
Time sequence
  plot and, 71–73
  short, 309
Timing, revising, 196–197
"To Build a Fire," 31
Tolstoy, Leo, 65–66, 102–103, 207–244
Tragedy, 65–66
Travel
  beginning story with, 138–139
  describing place through, 147–148
  showing experience of, 41
Trick, using to create plot, 74–75
Trick ending, 143–144
Turgenev, Ivan, 137–138
Twain, Mark, 87–88, 173, 180

U
Ulysses, 99, 177
Unreliable narrator, 90, 105

V
Vaughn, Elizabeth Dewberry, 173–174
Verbs, 156–158
  using as noun, 167
"A Very Old Man With Enormous Wings," 151
Virtual shift of POV, 103
Vision, quality of, setting as, 33–34
Visualization, and description, 165
Voice
  child's, 189
  creating many different, 185–186
  exercises, 184–189
  giving to each character, 112
  and humor, 179–184
  introduction to, 170–172
  meeting character through, 55–56
  persona, 172–175
  revising, 196
  and subject matter, 177–179
  third-person narrative, 176–177
von Kleist, Heinrich, 46–47, 132

W
Wallace, David Foster, 156
War scene, 125
"Ward VI," 57–58
Waugh, Evelyn, 171
Westerns
  "The Blue Hotel," 46, 122–124, 154–155, 286–309
  parodying plot, 75–76, 81
"Where Are You Going, Where Have You Been?" 52
Wilde, Oscar, 182–183
"With Mirrors," 74–75
Wolff, Tobias, 11–12
Word choice, 151–152, 155–165
  exercises, 166–168
  studying, 313
  using in new ways, 166
  wrong, 162–164
Workplace, describing, 41
World's End, 176
Writing, and myth of inspiration, 6
Wuthering Heights, 35

Y
Yates, Richard, 33–34, 139
"Yellow Woman," 158
Yoko, Mon, 164

ABOUT THE AUTHOR

Josip Novakovich is a Croatian-American writer. At the age of 20, he left Yugoslavia, continuing his education at Vassar College, Yale University, and the University of Texas. He has published a novel (*April Fool's Day*), three short story collections (*Yolk, Salvation and Other Disasters, Infidelities: Stories of War and Lust*), and two collections of narrative essays (*Apricots from Chernobyl, Plum Brandy: Croatian Journeys*). Novakovich has taught at Nebraska Indian Community College, Bard College, Moorhead State University, Antioch University in Los Angeles, the University of Cincinnati, and is now a professor in the Master's of Fine Arts program at Pennsylvania State University.

Novakovich is the recipient of the Whiting Writers' Award, a Guggenheim Fellowship, two fellowships from the National Endowment for the Arts, the Ingram Merrill Award, and an American Book Award from the Before Columbus Foundation. He has been anthologized in *Best American Poetry, Pushcart Prize*, and *O. Henry Prize Stories*.